Roe v. Wade

ALSO BY MARIAN FAUX

Childless by Choice:
Choosing Childlessness in the '80s

Roe v. Wade

The Untold Story of the Landmark Supreme Court Decision That Made Abortion Legal

Marian Faux

Macmillan Publishing Company   *New York*

Macmillan Publishing Company
866 Third Avenue, New York, N.Y. 10022
Collier Macmillan Canada, Inc.

Library of Congress Cataloging-in-Publication Data
Faux, Marian.
Roe v. Wade : the untold story of the landmark Supreme Court
decision that made abortion legal / Marian Faux.
p.   cm.
Bibliography: p.
Includes index.
ISBN 0-02-537151-7
1. Roe, Jane—Trials, litigation, etc.   2. Wade, Henry—Trials,
litigation, etc.   3. Abortion—Law and legislation—United States.
I. Title.
KF228.R59F38   1988
345.73'0285—dc19   87-34827
[347.305285]   CIP

Macmillan books are available at special discounts for bulk purchases
for sales promotions, premiums, fund-raising, or educational use.
For details, contact:

Special Sales Director
Macmillan Publishing Company
866 Third Avenue
New York, N.Y. 10022

10 9 8 7 6 5 4 3 2 1

Printed in the United States of America

FOR BILL

Contents

Preface

Sometimes the most complicated story can be told in the simplest manner. Sometimes it must be. I originally tried to write a more general book on abortion, one in which I would deal with nothing less than its ethical, moral, religious, and philosophical aspects. After several months of work I reluctantly concluded that such a book could not be written—at least not by me—and I note that no one else has attempted so broad a handling of the subject.

Abortion is too large, too amorphous a subject, to be dealt with in so broad a manner. It quickly becomes reduced to a polemic. It was only when Macmillan editor Ned Chase suggested that I try a book on a somewhat smaller scale—by dealing with the real events that surrounded the legalization of abortion—that the subject became manageable.

On the simplest level, this is a story about how two young, inexperienced women, barely out of law school, without any thought of larger glory, decided to test the constitutionality of the abortion law in Texas. Although experienced lawyers in several states were racing to get an abortion suit before the Supreme Court, *Roe* v. *Wade* became the landmark Supreme Court case that legalized abortion.

Of course, within the framework of the "simple" story, this is also a book about the larger issues—the discriminatory nature of restrictive abortion laws, the inequality women suffer when they cannot control their own bodies, the right of the state versus the federal government to regulate its citizens, and most important, one of our most precious rights, that of privacy, which a recent poll shows most people now feel ranks alongside life, liberty, and the pursuit of happiness.

The story of *Roe* v. *Wade* has never been told before, and despite the Supreme Court decision, the abortion issue has never been resolved. Every year antiabortion forces fight a more aggressive battle to undo the abortion decision. They have begun to make inroads in some states and have repeatedly brought before the Supreme Court cases designed to chip away at the abortion right. Only in the past few years have the pro-choice reformers awakened to the need to continue their struggle.

Because abortion is an issue that never seems to fade in our collective public consciousness, and because all of us must constantly rethink and reevaluate our position on abortion, I thought it might be helpful to review the relevant issues in their original context, as well as to examine them from the distance that time can provide. That is why I wrote this book.

Abortion is, I think, one of the most trying issues of our time. A great deal of pain and rage exists on both sides of the debate. After all, abortion concerns nothing less than the value we place on human life. Those who oppose abortion believe that the value must be held collectively, that one standard must apply to everyone and to all circumstances, while those who support the abortion right believe that the choice can only be made individually.

Adding to the conflict is the fact that what people believe, at least where abortion is concerned, they tend to believe fervently. This, if nothing else, makes abortion an unresolvable issue, one about which people cannot be rational.

As I interviewed people for this book, I was repeatedly asked what "side" I was on. It is a difficult question to answer. Professionally, I was committed to writing an objective book about the legalization of abortion. Personally, like most other women, I could only answer that whether or not I would have an abortion would depend upon the circumstances.

After looking at abortion from every conceivable angle, I find that I am firmer than ever in my conviction that criminalization of abortion is wrong. It solves nothing. I agree with George Devereux, author of *A Study of Abortion in Primitive Societies*, who wrote: "Were the contracting of typhoid fever defined as a crime, this would dispense society from doing something about pollution and public health. The branding of abortion as a crime also seeks to sidestep our obligation to create a world . . . into which it would be good to be born."

Am I, as I am so often asked, for abortion? That, to paraphrase Betty Friedan, is like being for mastectomy. I do support the abortion right, which means I believe each individual woman must have the right to decide for herself whether to undergo an abortion. Most Americans agree with me. In the fifteen years since the decision was issued, and despite a vociferous outcry from those who oppose abortion and almost nothing from those who worked to legalize it, slightly more than 50 percent of Americans believe the abortion decision is up to the individual woman. It is the only view, I believe, that offers any real relief to an otherwise irresoluble dilemma. Each person can make a decision based on his or her personal beliefs and conscience. No one is forced to have an abortion; no one is forced not to have one.

Marian Faux
February 1988
New York City

Acknowledgments

No book is the work of one person, and I am indebted to many who shared with me their memories and information and gave me advice, encouragement, and support. I did not always take the advice I was given, and any mistakes are entirely my own.

I am especially indebted to Virginia Whitehill, for her historian's eye and sensitivity, access to her personal archive on abortion reform in Texas, her marvelous ability to facilitate. She pointed me toward persons she thought I should interview and, in turn, prodded those who were reluctant about being interviewed into talking with me. And not least, she arranged a sizable dose of Texas hospitality for me when I visited Dallas.

I must thank Doris Middleton, who graciously opened her home to me and gave me a lovely, quiet place to do research while I was in Dallas.

Another person who was especially helpful to me was Norman Dorsen, who talked with me at length about the legal aspects of the book, but whose greater function was to make sure I stayed on course and told the story as even-handedly as possible.

One friend, Susan Mason, spent many hours serving as a sounding board in the early stages of the book when many of my ideas were beginning to take shape; I am grateful for her probing, incisive mind and thought-provoking ideas.

I am grateful to others who also gave generously of their time and shared their memories of the abortion movement and their ideas about abortion reform: Linda Coffee, Sarah Weddington, Roy Lucas,

ACKNOWLEDGMENTS

James and Carolyn Clark, Ellen and Victor Lewis, Justice Irving Goldberg, Harriet Pilpel, Lawrence Lader, Joseph Nellis, Sylvia Law, Jimmye Kimmey, Robert Flowers, John Tolle, Ron Weddington, Rhonda Copelan, Cyril Means, Louise Raggio, and Ruth McLean Bowers.

Of the many interviews I did for this book, a few involved persons who for obvious reasons wished to remain anonymous; I am no less grateful to them for their help.

Special thanks to my readers Kathryn Stechert and Barbara Bean, who saw the manuscript in its initial rough stages and offered excellent advice; Nan Bases, for reading the manuscript with special attention to the legal details; Joy Willig, who answered many legal questions for me and provided me with access to Lexis; Mark Satloff, for his legal research.

I am grateful to the institutions and the people there who helped me: the librarians at the James Madison Law Library, Library of Congress; the New York Bar Association Library; the New York Law School Library; and the New York Public Library; Kathy Arburg at the Supreme Court Public Information Office; Gilbert Ganasheau, at the Fifth Circuit Court in New Orleans.

Out of the mountain of information that must be consumed to write a book, at least one source usually proves to be especially influential or inspirational. I was fortunate in having three such books to shape my thinking: *Woman's Body, Woman's Right* by Linda Gordon; *Our Right to Choose: Toward a New Ethic of Abortion* by Beverly Wildung Harrison; and *Abortion and Woman's Choice* by Rosalind Pollack Petchesky.

I am grateful to my editors at Macmillan, Ned Chase and Dominick Anfuso, and copy editors Sona Vogel and Sharon L. Gonzalez, and to my agent, Dominick Abel, for their excellent ideas and editorial insights.

I could not conclude without thanking several friends who listened, stood by, and were invaluable sources of support: Stephen Breskin, Richard Foster, Sharon McIntosh, Shelly and Tom Martin, Marilyn Miller, Tom and Barbara Moore, Jonathan Schwartz, Lisa Sheiman, Katherine Goldring, and Joan Iaconetti.

I am, of course, most indebted to my husband, William Willig, who lent not only his emotional support, but also his keen editorial eye.

Part I

THE ABORTION CONTROVERSY

1

A Meeting

Linda Coffee and Norma McCorvey were the first to arrive at Colombo's Pizza, an unpretentious family restaurant on Mockingbird Lane in Dallas, Texas. The restaurant was chosen for its central location and hearty, cheap food. None of the three women coming to this dinner meeting had much money.

Coffee, age twenty-six and a lawyer, was still dressed in the suit she had worn to work. The December chill that passed for winter in Dallas had settled over the city, but as usual it was not enough to make a winter coat a necessity. Medium height and small-boned, Coffee was one of those women with a solid torso and birdlike limbs.

Her name was aptly descriptive: Coffee's skin was the color of richly creamed coffee, and she had dark brown eyes. She wore beiges and browns a lot, which intensified her coloring. In the late sixties, an era of heavy makeup and beehive hairdos, Coffee stood out because she wore no makeup and styled her hair simply, either down over her shoulders or in a plain twist. What people noticed first about her was her dark brown, curly, and very fine hair. Its most distinctive feature was that it looked tousled no matter how many times a day she combed it, which was not often in any event. Coffee was a woman with too many other things on her mind to be overly concerned with appearances. Despite her usually disheveled appearance, though, she managed to dress the role of the young corporate lawyer that she was.

Coffee's demeanor could best be described as diffident. She tended to wait for others to take the lead—to introduce themselves and start a conversation. That trait was misleading in that it some-

3

times caused someone meeting her for the first time to think she was not especially smart, an appraisal that vanished as soon as she began to talk about the law or any other subject she knew well. Decidedly ill at ease in most social situations, even those involving her peers, Coffee blossomed when she discussed her work. She spoke with the authority of one who not only knew the rules but also thoroughly understood how to use them. Where a lesser lawyer might mull over what color suit to wear to impress a judge or jury, Coffee would confidently count on the logic of the law to influence. She was unimposing in her knowledge, though, and her conversations were blessedly free of legal jargon. Coffee never feigned what she did not know, and what she knew, she knew cold.

Across the table from her sat Norma McCorvey, a waif in appearance and manner. A short, wiry woman with dark brown hair and small features—a stingy mouth, pug nose, and deep-set, mischievous green eyes—she also had an impish air. Her friends called her Pixie, a name that both suited and pleased her. Dressed in blue jeans and a shirt, she looked working class, and she was. At twenty-one she had been married, divorced, and was the mother of a five-year-old daughter. Her hard life already showed in her face. For someone as street-worn as Norma obviously was, she had some unusual qualities. Vulnerability spilled out of her at times, and she had a naive enthusiasm that occasionally made her a too willing party for the wrong opportunity and sometimes, as would happen tonight, for the right one.

Coffee and McCorvey were struggling with a conversation while they awaited the arrival of the third woman who was going to join them. The silences between the polite chitchat grew longer. Linda never was any good at small talk, and Norma, having grown up in a family where simple survival was a skill, had never learned any social graces. They would not have helped much with the life she led, anyway.

Norma had met with Linda twice before, once in her lawyer's office and once in Coffee's office. At each of those meetings, at Linda's urging, Norma talked more about herself—her background and her problem, which was hanging heavily over her right now. Norma had not minded telling her story to Coffee, even though Coffee was a stranger. These days Norma was talking to anyone who might be able to help her out of her predicament. At the moment, however,

4

between these two taciturn women, there seemed to be little left to say. Coffee was biding her time, waiting for her colleague to arrive so that Norma could tell her story once again. Norma was curious, anxious, eager to hear what these women could do for her.

Sarah Weddington pulled her car into a parking spot. A tall, heavy-set woman, she moved with unusual grace. Her most striking feature was her strawberry-blond hair, something she was enormously proud of and often used as a point of reference in conversation. Long, wavy, and thick (truly the kind of hair that used to be described as a woman's crowning glory), Sarah's hair framed a diamond-shaped face that was further enhanced by a flawless, pink-toned complexion, a prim mouth, and clear, blue eyes. Unlike Coffee, she wore makeup, just the right touch of it. She also wore ruffled, pastel clothes, the kind of ultrafeminine dress that many big women shy away from but which looked right on her. Her choice of clothing was neither an affectation nor wishful thinking on her part but came from a strong sense of what worked for her. She liked to project an image that was both womanly and businesslike.

Tonight, dressed in casual pants and a blouse that she had changed into after work, she looked like a teenager, much younger than her twenty-three years. Sarah lived forty miles away in Ft. Worth. She had recently taken a job as an assistant city attorney and was the first woman hired for that position, a fact of which she was inordinately proud.

She walked into the restaurant, scanned the room until she spotted Coffee, and headed toward the table where the two women sat. She had a real take-charge manner that others either appreciated or resented, depending upon what they wanted from her. On this occasion Linda felt only relief that Sarah had arrived, welcoming her presence on this night when the two of them must make an important decision.

In contrast with Coffee, Sarah Weddington emanated poise. She had the kind of social polish and softspoken, if somewhat programmed, manner of talking that one associated with beauty contestants. An intent listener, Sarah was at ease with all kinds of people, an ability she attributed to having been reared a minister's daughter.

Coffee introduced Sarah Weddington and Norma McCorvey to one another. For a few minutes the three women busied themselves discussing what kind of pizza to order. They ordered beer to drink.

Even before the pizza arrived, Weddington began talking to Norma, deftly moving from small talk about the weather, which was uneventful, and the restaurant, which was undistinguished, to the reason they were there. She questioned Norma gently and politely, as was her style, and Norma began to tell her story one more time.

Norma said she had been living with a woman friend and working as a waitress in Dallas when she first suspected that she might be pregnant. One clue was an attack of nausea, even though, as she later recalled, no one was frying eggs. The nausea persisted, and then, a few days later, the friend with whom she was staying commented that she somehow looked different. "Swollen" was the word her friend had used. Norma attributed this to having downed a couple of beers the previous night. She had eyelids that got puffy over any little change in her system. The nausea still bothered her, and she imagined it had gotten even worse.

Norma was worried that her period was late, but she could still rationalize away her symptoms. In her family such delays were attributed to "nerves," and she thought this was merely one more sign of her inability to cope with her topsy-turvy life.

She had been knocking around from place to place since returning to Dallas a few weeks earlier. First she had lived for a week or two with one woman friend, but by mutual agreement that was only a temporary agreement. Since then she had crashed wherever a friend had a spare bed or corner for the night or, if she got lucky, for a few nights. She had tried living with her father, but that had not worked out. He was mean to her when he got drunk, which was fairly often. Besides, he had just gotten his second divorce and was in no mood to have his unmarried, adult daughter living with him. Even though Norma did the housework and tried to make the arrangement work, she found the situation intolerable and soon left to live with another friend.

Her nausea worsened, so much so that she was unable to work. Gradually, over several weeks, Norma had to acknowledge what she had been denying. She felt pregnant. She was beginning to look pregnant. She felt the way she had felt when she was pregnant with her daughter. She finally went to a physician, who tested her and reported back a couple of days later that she was indeed pregnant.

Involved as she was in her own story, Norma had not failed to notice the effect her story was having on her audience. She had told the story several times over the past two weeks, each time adding certain flourishes and embellishing the drama she felt it to be. Nor was she too involved to be quietly forming impressions of the two other women. In previous meetings, Norma had found Linda Coffee to be "nice" and "quiet," a voice of calm in her otherwise tumultuous life. Norma decided she liked Linda even though she sometimes found her slightly distant.

She was discovering that she liked Sarah even more, however. From the first moment she met her, Norma sensed that Sarah had something she badly needed in her life—an ability to nurture and comfort, to offer a kind of reassurance that there might be solutions to even the most pressing of problems. Norma decided right then and there—and forever—that she liked and trusted Sarah Weddington.

Even when she was down, Norma had a natural vivaciousness that was not unlike Sarah's. As Norma told her story, she began to relish being the center of attention. Never had she had so sympathetic an audience. It encouraged her to talk even more about what had happened to her.

A few months earlier, during August 1969, Norma had been traveling throughout the South with a carnival. Her job selling tickets to an animal sideshow was not exciting, but she loved the life. It was the people who attracted her to the carnival. These people were theater. They were even better than theater, these exotic vagabonds who got paid for roaming the country and performing their various acts and tricks for delighted audiences. Norma liked this life more than anything she had ever done. For once she did not feel like an outsider, as she so often had with her family. The carnival felt like the home she had been searching for and had never found. Unlike her parents, her co-workers simply accepted her for what she was and asked few questions. She had even made a couple of special friends, two women with whom she shared a motel room.

Norma told Linda and Sarah how she was selling tickets one

sultry summer night, the last night of the carnival's gig in a small town outside Augusta, Georgia, when some minor trouble broke out. She and several of her co-workers were harassed by a group of rough-looking, tough-talking young men. Since it was the kind of disruption that often rippled through a traveling show, it was no cause for alarm. Because this was the carnival's last night in town, the atmosphere was more festive than usual, and the women treated the men with good humor, even bantering with them a little bit.

After the show closed that night, several hours' work remained to be done, taking down the big tents and packing them away so the show could leave the next morning. As a result, Norma and her roommates decided to walk back to their motel rather than wait for their usual ride. It was during the walk back to the hotel with her friends, Norma recalled, that real trouble broke out. On the way back to her room, she told Weddington and Coffee, she was raped.

Norma could remember few details of what had happened to her. She thought she had lain by the side of the road for several hours. The rest of the evening passed in a haze. When Weddington gently probed for more, Norma's story became confused and vague. She thought the rapist might have been one of the men who had disrupted the circus earlier in the evening.

What had happened to the women who were with her? Sarah asked. Norma said she did not know, she only knew that when she managed to rouse herself, she was alone. She stumbled back to her motel room, only to find it empty. Her roommates had vanished, taking her belongings with them. She did not report her rape to anyone, nor did she talk to or even see anyone in the hours immediately following the rape. She crawled into bed.

When she awakened in the motel room the next day, Norma was still alone. The circus had left town without her and, in the course of doing so, had left her with no money, no way even to pay for the motel for another night. A defeated Norma decided she would return to Dallas, where her family and friends lived. She knew no one in Augusta, Georgia, whom she could ask for help. Norma telephoned an old friend in Dallas to ask her to send enough money for the bus trip home. To her chagrin, the friend wired only the exact amount of the bus fare. Norma sold the taxi driver the radio from her motel room to pay for her fare to the bus station. The trip back seemed endless, Norma said, particularly since she had no money to buy food and thought she had changed buses several times.

Upon her return to Dallas, Norma found her way to her friend's mobile home, crawled into bed again, and slept for two days. When she awoke, feeling only slightly better, her friend helped her get a job as a waitress in a bar. That was what she was doing when she began to realize she was pregnant.

Norma told the two women about her search for an abortionist. She knew that she did not want to have this child. She did not know the father. She had no way to support a child—no home and little income. She was not even managing to rear her daughter, who was living with her mother and stepfather in Arkansas. Her life was a mess, and she had no idea when or how she would pull it together.

She asked the physician who had told her she was pregnant about an abortion. In 1969 abortion was illegal in Texas. Asking a licensed physician for help in getting one generated any number of responses. A few recoiled in horror at any patient who even suggested they perform an illegal surgery. Some lectured their patients about their lack of maternal feeling and their selfishness for not wanting a child, any child, regardless of the circumstances under which it was conceived. Most reassured their patients that once the baby was born all doubts would vanish, and the maternal instinct would take over, a line of reasoning they borrowed from the leading obstetrical texts of the day.

A few brave physicians tried to help their patients, often endangering their careers to do so. One Texas woman recalled the type of cautious help she received when she asked her family doctor about an abortion. He opened the phone book and had her run her finger down several columns of physicians' names, telling her that she was hot, then cold, then hot again, there, no, not there, but *there*, until finally her finger rested on the precious number of someone who would perform an illegal abortion on her.

If a woman were really lucky, her doctor wrote out a name on a piece of paper and handed it to her. A name that came through a doctor was considered especially valuable because the assumption could be made that the abortionist, if not a licensed physician, would at least be competent, or a physician would not be recommending him. If a woman were unlucky, her physician declined to help in any way, and she had to embark on her own search for an illegal abortionist.

Norma was not one of the lucky ones. Her physician curtly informed her that abortion was illegal in Texas and suggested that she travel to where the laws were more liberal. In 1967 abortion was legal in Colorado and California, two nearby states, as well as in Georgia, but even the new, so-called liberal laws had restrictions, such as residency and time requirements, that would have made obtaining a legal abortion difficult for Norma. Texas women frequently went to Mexico to obtain illegal abortions in the numerous clinics operated for that purpose, but Norma had heard about those—especially the cheap ones—and did not want any part of them. Besides, she barely had carfare home from the doctor's office, let alone the money to travel anywhere to get an abortion. It seemed her only alternative was an illegal abortion in Texas. She hoped she could find someone skilled to do the surgery.

Norma spent the next few weeks in a futile search for an abortionist. She talked to a few women she knew, hoping one of them would give her the name of someone who could help. She learned that a competent abortion, even an illegal one, cost a lot of money. The kind that could be bought for $50 or $100 was not, in Norma's opinion, worth risking.

Gradually, over several weeks, she began to consider the only other option she could think of, which was adoption. She returned to her physician for help. He gave her the name of a young lawyer, Henry McCloskey, who sometimes arranged private adoptions. Norma called McCloskey, and he agreed to meet with her.

McCloskey turned out to be a kind man who took time to listen to Norma and get to know her. She told him that she really wanted an abortion, but since she could not afford one she had no choice but to have her child and put it up for adoption.

Without telling her why, McCloskey asked Norma to meet another lawyer. He promised Norma she could return to him if the other lawyer was not helpful. That was how Norma met Linda Coffee and why she was sitting in a restaurant recounting her story for Coffee and Weddington.

Now it was time for Coffee and Weddington to tell McCorvey what she could do for them. They told her they were looking for a woman to be a plaintiff in an abortion suit. They asked Norma if she were aware that many people wanted to change the abortion laws. Norma was not alone in her attempts to obtain a legal abortion, nor was she alone in her failure to get one. Many women who needed abortions found themselves unable to obtain one and were forced into illegal ones. Because abortion was illegal, no one knew for sure how many women terminated their pregnancies, but one study found that the women surveyed ended between one-fifth and one-fourth of all their pregnancies.

Only eight to ten thousand legal abortions were done each year in the United States, while experts guessed that between a million and a million and a half abortions were done annually. Women who got illegal abortions took a much greater risk than those who were able to obtain legal ones. Some women got to competent illegal abortionists, Weddington said, but many more suffered at the hands of uncaring, unscrupulous, illegal practitioners.

While she was looking for someone to perform an abortion, McCorvey told the two women, she had heard many horror stories about what happened if a woman went to the wrong kind of abortionist. That was why she had not been able to go through with the surgery. No licensed doctor would agree to perform the operation, and although one abortionist had offered to do it for $500, he did not have a medical license, and she was afraid to let him touch her.

Weddington asked Norma how she had felt when she could not get an abortion. Norma replied that she was angry at being forced to have a child whom she did not want and could not care for. Sarah said that she and Coffee were angry, too, and that they wanted to help women in her plight. That was why they needed her help.

Weddington and Coffee's motivation in taking on the Texas abortion laws was, I discovered somewhat to my surprise, primarily ideological. On one of my visits to Texas, I asked the two women why they had decided to work on abortion reform, as opposed to any number of other women's issues. Neither woman had undergone an abortion nor had any firsthand experience with one. Like so many other women their age, they had known or heard of women who had undergone illegal abortions, but abortion had not touched either woman in a close, personal way. But like many women, although their interest was impersonal and somewhat abstract, they were angry. As they told Norma, they wanted to help women, and since they had legal skills—something few women could claim at that time—they thought they could use them to do something about the present restrictive laws. Each woman told me separately, in remarkably similar words, how attuned she was to the rapid changes occurring in women's lives. The idea of abortion liberalization was in the air from the mid-1960s on, and the two women thought they could do something, at least about the Texas law.

Norma knew nothing about the legal system. She had no idea what a plaintiff was and consequently was not sure what she was being asked to do. Coffee and Weddington told her they were planning to challenge the abortion law of the state of Texas. They could not do this, they explained, simply by going into court and asking a judge to overturn the law. Instead, they had to bring a suit—in this instance, obviously, a suit involving a pregnant woman—into court. The pregnant woman, not Coffee or Weddington, would actually sue the state of Texas. Because she was the person filing the formal complaint, she was considered the plaintiff. After the suit was filed, there would be a trial or a hearing, perhaps several hearings. Norma might have to be present; she might even have to testify. Sarah and Linda assured her, however, that they would do most of the talking in the courtroom.

A judge would then weigh the facts of the suit and use them to decide whether or not to permit the plaintiff to have an abortion. If a Texas judge ruled that one woman could undergo an abortion, then all the women in Texas in similar circumstances would be entitled to one. Coffee and Weddington wanted to build a broad-enough case so that any Texas women who wanted an abortion would be able to get one as a result of the ruling they hoped to obtain. They hoped their case would result in a clear-cut rejection of the Texas abortion law.

It would not be easy to build such a case, and the risks were high, they knew. Once they went into court, a judge could decide in their favor, ruling that the Texas abortion law was illegal. He could decide to strike only certain parts but not all of the law, or, worst of all from their point of view, a judge could decide that no part of the law was illegal and in effect let the law stand as it was. In that event women would not be allowed to have abortions, and it would be difficult for anyone else to challenge the Texas abortion law after a recent ruling supporting its legality.

It was this last instance—a decision that the law was acceptable as it was written—that Coffee and Weddington wanted to avoid at all costs; that would be a serious setback for the abortion-reform movement beginning to take shape all over the country. Many people favored liberalizing the strict abortion laws, but a number of institutions and persons had no intention of letting that happen. If Coffee and Weddington did not prepare their case well, and if as a result a judge ruled that the Texas abortion law was legal, it would be a victory for the antiabortion forces.

Sarah told Norma she thought this would be a very important case, not only for Texas women, but for women everywhere. It might even go to the Supreme Court. Even though Norma was still unsure what Sarah was talking about or what court she had in mind, she was impressed.

The two lawyers told Norma they thought she might make a good plaintiff for their suit. Although they would not make a decision right away, and suggested she take some time to think over what they would need her to do, they wanted to know whether she was interested. Norma was immediately enthusiastic. The two women had affected her, not least because of the way they treated her, as if she were an important person to them. Norma wanted to help Coffee and Weddington if she could, to be part of this case they were talking about. She agreed on the spot to be their plaintiff.

Pleased as they were with her offer, Coffee and Weddington felt they could not in good conscience let Norma become their plaintiff until she had been given a chance to think things over. They also wanted to talk to her some more, to make sure she knew exactly what she was getting into. As women who felt deeply for Norma's plight, Weddington and Coffee wanted nothing less than a fully informed client.

Coffee and Weddington also had to be sure that Norma was the right plaintiff for their job, and that would take some thinking and discussion on their part.

The evening ended with the women agreeing that they would each go home and think about what had been discussed. Coffee and Weddington said they would need to meet a few more times with Norma before any final decision could be reached. They promised they would be in touch with her.

2

Finding
Jane Roe

Coffee and Weddington were excited—more so than they had let on in McCorvey's presence—about her potential as a plaintiff. Still, they could not afford to let their desire to get an abortion case under way interfere with their choice of a plaintiff, especially since both women knew that this would be no run-of-the-mill lawsuit. More than anything else, this perception would guide them in their selection of a plaintiff and would ultimately lead them to the realization that their personal desire to be the lawyers who successfully challenged the Texas abortion law or their fire to find a plaintiff and get a case—any case—under way was less important than the overall goal of overturning the Texas abortion law. A case like this was not intended to benefit one person, but the hundreds of thousands and even millions of Americans whose lives would be affected by a change in the abortion laws. To the extent that it was possible to do so, they wanted to choose a plaintiff who would be helpful to them in achieving the larger goal. It was not necessarily an easy task.

For one thing, they would need to exercise more control over the plaintiff than they would in another kind of suit. They would use her, if necessary, in and out of the courtroom to build their case. If they wanted to build public sympathy for the case, for example, they might leak all or part of her story to the press. Conversely, they might want to avoid publicity. Some judges forbade participants in a lawsuit to talk to the press, and in a situation like this, when a gag order was imposed, they would have to be able to prevent their client from talking.

For another thing, if it would help, they would want their plaintiff present in the courtroom during the proceedings, an event that would almost certainly destroy any anonymity she had. Her presence might even be required by the court. Alternately, they might try to play down her role, in hopes that she would be seen as a sort of Everywoman, a symbol of the need to reform the abortion laws. Either way, their plaintiff would have to be under their control. Would McCorvey, they asked themselves, submit to their guidance in matters like these?

Yet such considerations were just theoretical possibilities that might or might not occur in the course of the lawsuit. The most pressing practical issue, Coffee would recall in our conversations, was whether they could actually help Norma get the abortion she wanted. Just possibly they could arrange for her to obtain a court-sanctioned one, but chances were far greater that they would not be able to do so. The wheels of justice did not turn rapidly. By the time the legal system was through chewing on the wisdom of whether to allow her to have an abortion, Norma would most likely have had her baby.

Norma had looked pregnant to Linda Coffee since their first meeting. It seemed to Coffee that she was pushing, if not into, her second trimester. This meant that if Norma were to undergo an abortion, she should do so right away—probably within the next two or three weeks. The only way the two lawyers could see to act quickly enough was to file a request for a restraining order.

A restraining order, always temporary in nature (and thus often referred to as a temporary restraining order or TRO), could be granted without a hearing, although one would be held later to determine what relief was appropriate. Such an order would prevent officials from enforcing the abortion law and—in theory, at least—would then leave the physicians of Texas free to perform abortions. TROs, however, were basically designed to protect the status quo, and in this case the status quo dictated that abortion was illegal. It was unlikely that any judge would order an abortion to be performed without first examining the constitutionality of the Texas abortion law.

Furthermore, although this was something they had yet to research, Weddington and Coffee thought they could take their case into a federal court, that this was the proper forum for challenging a state law. It offered the possibility of a more encompassing decision, one that could set a precedent for decisions outside Texas. But it also made their case more difficult. The federal courts, ever wary of states' rights issues, were being ultracautious, largely because of some recent rulings involving criminal cases in which they were perceived, at least by some, as having overstepped their power to rule on state laws. In fact, there was every reason to believe that a federal judge would be even more reluctant than a local or a state judge to issue a restraining order that would overturn a state criminal law.

Apart from all these considerations, even if they did find a judge willing to issue a TRO, they would still have to find a physician willing to do the abortion. That they suspected would be an impossible task as long as the law was still in limbo and the physician might risk later prosecution.

The first and most difficult decision the two lawyers made, then, was not to seek a TRO for Norma, even though that was her only chance for getting court permission in time to have a legal abortion. Since she wanted an abortion badly, this might mean she was not the best plaintiff for them after all. They needed to impress upon her exactly what this meant—namely, that she would most likely have to go ahead and have the baby if she became their plaintiff.

As the two lawyers met with Norma several times over the next few weeks and learned more about her, another potential problem emerged. Coffee and Weddington began to understand better something they had suspected from their first meeting with Norma— namely, that their potential plaintiff had a past and a present life that would not withstand much scrutiny.

Norma grew up in an unstable family. Her father was a military career man, and the family moved every two or three years. The frequent moves made school difficult for Norma, and she had never done well. Even after her father left the army when she was still in school and settled in Dallas, where he worked as an electrician, life did not become any easier for Norma or her only sibling, a younger brother. Between the two of them, Norma told one interviewer, her brother was a "punko" and she was a "freako."

Her home life was trying. Her parents' marriage was on the skids, aggravated by her father's drinking problem. From an early age, Norma was a child who had nowhere to go. She avoided home because she could not stand listening to the drunken arguments of her parents, and she avoided school because she had been labeled a troublemaker and was often in trouble with the juvenile authorities.

Norma recalled the shock of coming home from school one day to learn, out of the blue as far as she was concerned, that her parents were divorcing. Her father had moved out. Once gone, he made no attempt to stay in touch with either Norma or her younger brother. She was now left with only her mother, with whom she had never gotten along. Later, Norma would always recall her mother as a cold, domineering woman who never gave her credit for doing anything right.

With so hostile an environment at home, nothing went right at school, either, and she soon dropped out of high school in the tenth grade and went to work at the only job she could find, a carhop in a drive-in restaurant. At the drive-in she met and began dating a twenty-year-old drifter who had dreams of glory. An aspiring rock singer, he promised Norma that he could build a better life for both of them in Los Angeles. Since she was still sixteen, Norma needed her parents' consent to get married. Happy to have her out of the house, her mother agreed, and Norma married her would-be rock star and moved to Los Angeles with him.

Their new life did not go well from the beginning. Her husband could not find work, and Norma soon found herself pregnant. When she told her husband the news, he beat her. She waited until he fell asleep that night, gathered her clothes and the few dollars she had saved, and bought herself a bus ticket back to Dallas.

The period right before and after her baby was born was one of the lowest times of her life. At first Norma's mother suggested that Norma put her child up for adoption, but gradually she softened and let Norma live with her. Norma tried to go back to high school after the baby was born, but she felt too out of place, in her own words, "like a pool cue in a china cabinet, like a big idiot." She walked away from that. After her baby, a little girl, was born, she worked at a string of jobs, mostly waiting tables in bars at night.

Norma's relations with her mother, never good, worsened after the baby was born. Norma's mother constantly undermined Norma's ability to care for her new little daughter. Norma recalls having been awakened by her mother from a sound sleep and, while still groggy, being forced to sign some papers that she believed gave her mother custody of her infant daughter. Shortly after that, her mother and stepfather moved to Arkansas, taking the child with them.

Norma missed her daughter terribly but had no money to visit her and did not know what she could do to regain custody. Moreover, she could not support a child on what she earned, nor could she care for a child properly with her unsettled life.

Left alone in Dallas, Norma maintained occasional contact with her father, although she was always the one to call him. Norma remembered those years as ones in which she struggled simply to make it through each day. She suffered from severe bouts of depression and would later recall, "It seemed like there wasn't anything to live for. Everything I did or said was wrong. I just wanted to vanish."

Vanish she did, in a sense, during the summer of 1969. She had gotten together enough money to visit her mother and daughter in Arkansas. The visit was not going well. The two women fought constantly over the child, while the little girl watched and listened. Norma sensed she was losing her daughter to her mother, who had taught the child to call Norma "Mama Big Sister." After a week of quarreling, when Norma thought she could not stand much more of her mother's house but had no idea where she would go, a new acquaintance offered to drive her to a nearby town for the day. She readily accepted.

The blocks around the town's courthouse were occupied by a small carnival. Norma hung around, struck up a conversation with some of the people who worked there, and learned that there was a job available as a ticket seller. She took it and moved out with the traveling show that night. She had worked with the carnival only a few weeks when she got into the trouble that resulted in her second pregnancy.

After hearing so much about McCorvey's background, Weddington and Coffee became concerned that she might not be such a good plaintiff after all. Her life thus far—a high school dropout, married at sixteen, a daughter she did not have custody of, walking out on a visit with her daughter to join a carnival, her present hand-to-mouth existence—was a major problem.

Another problem was the rape. In our talks, both Weddington

and Coffee recalled that it was a delicate issue. Sensitive as the two women were to any woman's claim that she had been raped—a claim that was too often ignored or, worse, challenged—they were also lawyers, trained to size up a potential witness's credibility. And whatever had happened to Norma McCorvey, they did not feel that she would be a credible plaintiff in a rape case, let alone in an abortion case involving a rape.

Coffee in particular was struck by McCorvey's lack of emotion when she described the rape at their first meeting. Some rape victims are stoic, even with the people who try to counsel or otherwise help them, but McCorvey's remarkably unemotional recounting of how she had been raped made her lawyer uneasy. McCorvey was vague about the circumstances of the rape, and her story became more unclear and the details more bizarre with each retelling. She told Coffee and Weddington she had not gone to the police or filed any kind of official report. Initially, she said she had been raped by one man; she later changed her story and claimed she had been gang-raped, sometimes by several men and her female companions, sometimes by a white, black, and Hispanic man, a highly unlikely combination to have been walking together down a Georgia country road late at night in 1969.

Weddington and Coffee wondered whether McCorvey had, in fact, been raped, but regardless of the circumstances, they were concerned that the rape not become an issue in their case. Rape victims did not fare well in court. Their lives were often subjected to excessive scrutiny. In fact, much more attention was typically focused on the character of the women who were raped than on the men who raped them, and women who pressed rape charges frequently had to prove that they had not in some way "invited" the rape. Beyond that, there was the problem of blame—and punishment. However much rape (and, for that matter, abortion) laws appeared to be neutral, they were not. They were based at least in part on society's standards and expectations regarding sexual mores. Therefore, a woman who was perceived as having "invited" a rape was seen as having gotten what she deserved, and similarly, a woman who "needed" an abortion had better be prepared to prove that she deserved one.

Such thinking made many movement lawyers cautious about whom they would take on as a plaintiff. Most abortion-reform lawyers speculated that any woman who became a plaintiff in an abortion suit would be subject to the same kind of scrutiny as a rape victim—a reason, they held, to find a plaintiff whose life and character were as impeccable as possible.

McCorvey's clearly were not. Although Coffee and Weddington spent hours thrashing out the pros and cons of using her as their plaintiff, the issues were simple. On the one hand, the more they learned about her background, especially her claim that she had been raped, the more worried they became. On the other hand, in a year of looking, they had not found anyone who was better. For a start, not many women existed who were pregnant *and* wanted an abortion *and* were willing to become involved in a lawsuit to change the abortion law. Coffee and Weddington had learned from experience that finding a plaintiff was an almost impossible task, not least because, as one New York abortion reformer noted sardonically, "Short of a virgin, there is no such thing as the perfect abortion plaintiff." Eager to get on with the business of challenging the Texas law, the two young lawyers were inclined to take their chances with someone who was less than perfect.

Their problem with McCorvey's claim that she had been raped receded once they realized there were other reasons not to assign the rape any role in the case. Like any lawyer working on abortion reform, they hoped to obtain as broad a ruling on abortion as possible. They did not want a court to rule that women were entitled to an abortion when a pregnancy resulted from rape or incest—and this, they realized, was a distinct possibility, since current Texas law permitted abortion only to save a woman's life, not in cases of rape or incest. No one had ever challenged the law on these grounds, and Coffee and Weddington had no intention of being the first to do so. So narrow a ruling would be a waste of time.

As a result, they decided that if McCorvey did become their plaintiff, they would do everything possible to keep the rape from becoming an issue in the case. They reasoned this would not be hard to do since there were no police reports or witnesses or any other records to attest to the rape.

Ironically, had Norma decided to pursue an abortion in Georgia, the state in which she was living when she claimed she was raped, she would have been legally entitled to one. Georgia's reform-style law, passed in 1968, permitted abortion in cases of statutory and forcible rape (but not for incest).

Norma would have had great difficulty, however, obtaining an abortion in Georgia. Although intended to liberalize abortion, most of the reform laws were now even more complicated than they had been in the past. Under the new reform law in Georgia, for example, Norma would have had to reside in the state for a specified period of time, and she would have needed the approval of two physician-consultants and the hospital's therapeutic board, also composed of three physicians. Lawyers were already mounting a challenge to this complex reform law.

Once Coffee and Weddington decided they wanted to keep any mention of the rape out of the case, they had to figure out how best to do this. This Weddington said they accomplished by making sure that no references to the rape appeared anywhere in the court papers. They had no qualms about doing this, no sense that they were manipulating their client's story or interests.

The idea of not mentioning the rape also appealed to them on another level. Just as they did not want the case decided on narrow grounds, neither did they want the record to contain anything that might later be subject to a legal challenge. Their aim of compiling a flawless court record, one that would be acceptable to any higher court and would also stand the test of time, was well served by omitting the rape.

They did realize that some potential existed for an embarrassing and possibly damaging episode if McCorvey decided to talk to the press at some later date, or worse, if the press decided to ferret out her past. If she revealed her story, attempts would undoubtedly be made to verify the rape. While Coffee and Weddington strongly suspected that any such investigation would not pan out, they recognized that the disclosure alone could result in a damaging contradiction between the official court record and McCorvey's version of what had happened. As they discussed this potential scenario for disaster, they found yet another cause for relief in their decision not to mention the rape. Without a reference to it in the court papers, the rape would never become a legal issue.

Mostly, they hoped to be able to keep the press and their client far apart. Apart from any legal considerations, they recognized that if the case did catch the media's attention, they might also have to contend with the opponents of liberalization, who would make political hay of the fact that Norma McCorvey was not the most stable personality. Fortunately there was no crime in that, and particularly if a decision had already been rendered, her personality and life-style would not be grounds for any legal action to overturn the case.

The second time the three women met, the lawyers explained to McCorvey that in all likelihood she would have to go ahead and have her baby if she became their plaintiff. They told her there was almost no chance that a court would decide her case in time for her to get an abortion, and that possibly the law would not be overturned at all.

Coffee and Weddington offered to help Norma get an abortion if she wanted one. They felt honor-bound to do so. There was a slight chance that they could still use her as a plaintiff even if she got one. Coffee thought they could perhaps build a case around the argument that their client had been forced into a dangerous, possibly septic and illegal act, and that it was a violation of her (and by implication, other women's) civil rights to put her in this position. Both women knew, however, that they were far more likely not to use Norma as their plaintiff if she got an abortion. They would probably go looking again for a pregnant woman who would be willing to be their plaintiff.

Norma turned down their offer and agreed to go ahead and have the child. Although Weddington would recall that her motives for doing so had been largely altruistic, her decision was also undoubtedly motivated, at least in part, by the simple fact that four months into her pregnancy she was not likely to get an abortion anyway. After three months, abortion was done by a mini-Caesarean section and was considered major surgery. Rarely could a "legal" hospital abortion be arranged at that stage, and illegal abortionists never risked this kind of surgery. In another fifteen years, the technology would be developed to make late abortions safe, but in 1969 it did not yet exist.

The next thing Coffee and Weddington brought up with Norma was how long the case might take—months or even years, if it were appealed. Although the legal maneuverings would be complicated and difficult for any layperson to understand, they promised they would do their best to keep her informed throughout the case.

Finally, the three women discussed the publicity that would quite likely ensue from the case. Abortion was rapidly becoming a hot topic with the media, and hardly a week went by without another newspaper series, editorial, or nationwide poll pointing out the mounting pressure for reform. Although the subject had been taboo only two or three years ago, women's magazines now wrote regularly about abortion—usually touting reform. Weddington and Coffee suspected that a torrent of publicity would begin once the press got wind of their suit. With it, they feared, might also come some harassment of their client or, at minimum, the loss of her privacy.

The latter would be more overwhelmingly intrusive than she might imagine, they warned. They could try to protect her from it but might not be able to do so. If the court insisted that she appear or testify, they would not be able to keep the press from identifying her and delving into her background. The press would be eager to interview her. She would, they warned, become the "human interest" in an otherwise relatively dry legal case.

Norma's fears about publicity had more to do with her family than anything else. Her father was a Jehovah's Witness, and her mother was nominally a Roman Catholic; while neither parent was particularly religious, she worried that they might have strong antiabortion opinions. They had never expressed any feelings one way or the other about abortion, but then she had not told them she was trying to get one.

On the one hand, Norma was acutely aware that very little she had done in life had met with her parents' approval, especially her mother's. Her mother had shown no sympathy or inclination to help when she learned that Norma was pregnant and homeless the first time, and she was hardly likely to take a more generous view of her daughter's situation now, especially if it were reported in the local newspapers.

On the other hand, although Norma was a rebel, like most youthful renegades what she really wanted from those she railed against was acceptance. Just possibly the case might give her some of that. Certainly the fact that she knew two women like Linda Coffee and Sarah Weddington would impress her mother, and that she was a plaintiff in so important a case might also carry some weight.

Ultimately Norma decided to go ahead with the lawsuit but indicated she wanted as little publicity as possible. She specifically did not want her parents or her daughter to know of her role in the case. Nor would she tell her friends. When Coffee and Weddington suggested the use of a pseudonym, she readily agreed. It would at least offer her some protection. They quickly settled on Jane Roe.

Coffee and Weddington would prove to be quite successful at

protecting their client's privacy. Over the years, reporters would occasionally try to discover Jane Roe's identity, usually on important anniversaries of the case. Her lawyers grew so used to her refusals to grant interviews that they no longer called her with requests. For ten years, until Norma herself broke the silence, no one, not even other lawyers who would work on the case, knew who Jane Roe was.

When McCorvey broke her silence in the early 1980s, she talked only to a handful of reporters and writers before engaging the services of an entertainment lawyer in Dallas. After that, she would only agree to be interviewed if she were paid. As a result, she was never interviewed for this book.

Coffee and Weddington had only one last concern to bring up with McCorvey before settling on her as their plaintiff, and that was whether she would be able to go the whole way with them. After having come so far, they could not bear the thought of putting in months of work on the case only to have their plaintiff get cold feet and ask them to drop the suit. They talked to Norma about this, too, until both women were convinced she would stay with them.

From their first meeting with Norma, Coffee and Weddington had been impressed with her enthusiasm and spunk, as well as her desire to help other women who were in the same situation. Through all their discussions, Norma never wavered from her willingness to proceed. In our conversations, Weddington would recall that Norma seemed to have some sense of the historic proportions of the case.

The three women agreed that it was settled: Norma McCorvey would become their plaintiff. A challenge to the Texas abortion law, which had stood inviolate for over one hundred years, was under way.

3

Two Women
in Search of a Case

The forces that drew Sarah Weddington and Linda Coffee together to challenge the Texas abortion laws were not entirely the result of fate. These two young lawyers who came of age during the tumultuous sixties, eager to try out their law degrees and test their ideologies, could just as easily have thrown their energies into the civil rights movement. That was the area for someone with a finely honed social conscience, and it did not hurt that, with a little good luck and timing, careers could hastily be made.

The newly emerging women's rights movement, by contrast, was not a proven career maker, nor did it have the cachet of working in civil rights. Women's rights, however, were accessible to women, which is more than one could say for most other areas of the law. At least in part, Weddington's and Coffee's involvement in women's issues and ultimately with abortion came about because of the doors that were still closed to them in other areas.

Their interest in women's rights paralleled that of hundreds of thousands of other young, mostly college-educated women during the 1960s. Feminism was emerging as an important social issue for the second time in a hundred years.

The first organized attempt at achieving women's equality took shape after the Civil War, when a group of mostly elite, middle- and upper-class women who had worked in the abolitionist movement and had seen parallels between the plights of women and blacks began to press for greater equality for women. The women's suffrage movement eventually focused on, and in 1920 succeeded in winning, the right to vote. However, the suffragists had tied their cause to their roles as mothers. They argued that women would be better mothers, worthy of greater respect, if they could vote. It was essentially a conservative doctrine.

After the suffragists' victory, feminism entered a dormant era, undoubtedly because women believed that in winning the vote, they had gained more than they actually had. For obvious reasons, women's reproductive rights had not become an issue during the first wave of feminism, nor would it become one until the early part of the twentieth century, at which point Americans became involved in an extended public debate over birth control.

The debate arose in the first decade of the new century among Socialists and anarchists and was promoted by political radicals such as Emma Goldman and Moses Harmon. Socialists were not, however, particularly concerned with women's rights, preferring to focus debate on whether the working class would fare better or worse by limiting its size. Despite its radical origins, this debate touched a nerve throughout society, and the birth control movement (not yet named that) was spawned.

When Margaret Sanger rose from the radical ranks to ride the crest of the new movement and to convert birth control, an expression she coined, into a less radical, single-issue cause, she found herself at odds with the suffragists, who were politically conservative and feared that contraception, by any name, would destroy family life. Although much was accomplished in the birth control movement, for the second time a cause involving women's lives had failed to engender any real discussion of women's right to control their reproduction.

Even after Simone de Beauvoir wrote prophetically in 1945 that without the right to choose when they would bear children, women could never consider themselves truly free, another generation would have to come of age before women would begin to understand her message. Not until 1963, when the first magazine excerpts of Betty Friedan's *The Feminine Mystique* rocked the female consciousness, did women begin to examine the relationship between reproduction and equality.

The impact of Friedan's book on women's lives was astounding. In response to requests from women for help, Betty Friedan founded the National Organization for Women (NOW), and in a stroke of genius for the budding organization and the movement,

NOW began to encourage women to form something called consciousness-raising groups, intimate support groups in which women could meet and discuss their mutual concerns. The groups were not only attractive to the converted, they were also an excellent way of recruiting women to their own movement.

Throughout the late 1960s, following an agenda established by NOW, women began meeting in small, informal groups all over the country to discuss such topics as marriage, careers, motherhood, and sexuality. Women who participated in those groups recall that discussions about sexuality inevitably worked their way around to abortion, something rarely discussed publicly before. Until the late sixties, a woman who underwent an abortion often told no one—not her best friend, not her sister, and sometimes not even her husband—about her choice. Once an abortion was over, most women tried to put it behind them, tried never to think about it again.

Abortion was a painful, lonely, and, with its imposed secrecy, sometimes guilt-producing event in a woman's life. Now, perhaps for the first time, women began to share the pain they felt over the decision to abort—as well as the problems of being unable to control one's fertility as well as one might like. They shared their common experiences with abortion—the desperate attempts to raise money; the trip, often alone, to a nearby city; the often humiliating experience at the hands of an illegal abortionist. They talked about the abortions that went smoothly: their surprise at discovering that abortion was really minor surgery; their shock and relief at learning that their family doctor would help them, perhaps even perform the surgery himself; their surprise in finding out that an illegal abortionist ran what amounted to a storefront clinic and employed the most up-to-date surgical techniques. And they spoke, in hushed tones, about the bad parts: the fears that they might be maimed or injured and left to die in a strange place; the unsanitary conditions and the risk of infection; the degradation of undergoing an illegal operation; the condescension and insults; even the occasional rape.

For the moment, it was enough just to be able to talk about abortion after all those years of societally imposed silence. Action could come later, and it would, of course, because those meetings, with all their shared intensity, planted the seeds of reform.

Like so many other women of their generation, Coffee and Weddington were swept up into the women's movement. In law school, each woman joined a consciousness-raising group. Although they had no way of knowing it then, they would soon have more reason than most women their age to become involved in the women's movement. Weddington and Coffee were two of five women in the freshman law school class of 1965 at the University of Texas. They were the only two who were planning to practice law; the rest were married and had decided to postpone law careers to start families. It was just as well, as Coffee and Weddington would discover, since obtaining a law degree in 1969 was no guarantee that a woman would be able to practice law.

The ideas of attending law school did not dawn on either woman until both were almost through with undergraduate school. Few women planned to have any kind of career at that time, and there were many stumbling blocks even for those ambitious enough to want one.

Coffee was finishing undergraduate school at Rice when she began to weigh what she would do next. She knew only that she wanted to have a serious career. No one she knew encouraged or discouraged her when she began to look into law school. The law seemed like a good-enough choice for her because she thought she had an orderly, logical mind. Her parents supported her choice only to the extent of telling her they preferred law to teaching. Coffee's father was a research chemist, and her mother had worked off and on as a judge's secretary, so the idea of a professional daughter probably appealed to them.

Coffee was born in Houston but had moved to Dallas when she was a small child. Having rarely been outside Texas, she felt most comfortable there and decided to apply to the University of Texas. When she was accepted, she felt pleased but not surprised. Her undergraduate record was excellent.

Despite the fact that she was readily accepted, her parents proved to be less than eager to pay for her advanced education. They offered a little financial support during her first year of law school. That and a loan from an aunt guaranteed that she would be able to devote her energies to her courses. Student loans paid the way her second year. By the third year, Coffee was doing well enough to support herself while she attended school full-time.

* * *

Weddington, the daughter of a Methodist minister and a teacher, basked in the attention she received as a child from her father's congregations. She soon learned what pleased the adults—a smiling face, a willingness to help when needed, and a drive to be the best at whatever she tried.

Despite frequent moves throughout her childhood (she lived in Dallas while her father finished seminary; in Abilene, where he taught religion; in Wiley, where he tended his first congregation; and in Munday, Canyon, and Vernon), her school record was excellent, and she would always be proud of it. After skipping sixth grade and a year of high school, she went off to McMurry College, a small Methodist church school, from which she graduated at age nineteen in 1965.

In interviews, Weddington speaks more often of her mother than her father, always referring to her as an educator, never a housewife. She was proud of the fact that her mother completed a master's degree in education while she was in high school and liked to recall that her mother and a friend of her mother's encouraged her to go to law school.

Her father appears to have been a more distant figure, but it was from him that she derived much of her image of herself. Long after she had seen something of the world and accomplished many things on her own, the fact that she was a minister's daughter still provided a frame of reference for much of what she saw and did.

As a child Weddington rarely traveled outside Texas and then only to church meetings. People who knew her in her twenties recall her freshness and innocence. Her husband, Ron, whom she met in law school and married shortly after she graduated, was considered the "outgoing, social Weddington," while Sarah's "natural reserve made her the quieter, less partygoing type."

Weddington's family could not afford to send her to law school, but hard work was nothing new to Sarah, who had held various jobs since junior high school. To support herself in law school, she worked as a records librarian for a hospital, an assistant housemother, and a free-lance typist.

She began to toy with the idea of graduate school as she was finishing undergraduate school. She wanted to get some kind of advanced degree and thought for a while that she might continue in English, her undergraduate major. But while doing her student teaching, she realized that teaching held little reward for her. She did not feel that it offered as much of an opportunity to have an impact on people's lives as she wanted. More important, she disliked the fact that her success was so directly dependent upon others. She briefly considered medicine but had not taken enough science courses to get into a good medical school. She began to think about law school.

Her interest in politics undoubtedly provided an added incentive to study law. When she graduated from undergraduate school at McMurry College, her family was living in Vernon, Texas. Weddington's mother took her and her brother to see their representative in the state legislature, who as a family friend was delighted to help them both acquire jobs in the state Capitol. Her brother became a page, and she worked as a clerk-typist and legal proofer in a department of the Texas legislature.

Even though the Texas legislature only met every other year for four months, life was intensely political in Texas and especially in Austin, its capital city. Sarah took to the hustle and bustle that echoed through the halls of the elegant, brownstone-Victorian statehouse, and it was while working there that she began to seriously consider the idea of a law degree. At that time, most law schools still admitted people with a variety of undergraduate degrees, including liberal arts, and the University of Texas automatically admitted anyone above a certain grade-point average. Weddington had always been an excellent student. She decided to apply to the University of Texas Law School.

During Weddington's admissions interview, the dean of the law school tried to discourage her by emphasizing how difficult his son was finding the law school. Typically, Weddington was merely spurred on by the dean's words: "Being redheaded, I rose to the challenge and decided I was sure going to go to law school." Weddington would later recall of her decision: "I think in some ways I just never questioned that I couldn't do it. I'd always made excellent grades. . . . I can't remember worrying about whether I could make it through law school. I just figured if I wanted to, I could do it."

Do it she did. Weddington graduated from the University of Texas Law School in 1967—at the tender age of twenty-one. She had spent a record twenty-seven months in law school and had supported herself the entire time. She would later note ruefully that she was so frugal she managed to save money while paying her own way.

*　　*　　*

Neither Coffee nor Weddington found law school difficult, and that only made them even more unprepared for what awaited them upon graduation. They soon discovered that while they might be, in theory, valued commodities as lawyers, they were nowhere near as valuable as their male colleagues. Both women, ambitious for the same things as their male colleagues, told me how they had expected the major law firms to wine and dine them just as they did the men, after which several offers would be forthcoming. In the late sixties, employers in some parts of the country were actively seeking women to work for them, if only as tokens of equal opportunity. The good old boys who dominated life in Texas, however, had not caught up with the rest of the country; women were still an unwanted, mistrusted, and largely undesirable commodity in Texas boardrooms and law firms—except, of course, as secretaries.

Coffee, who was Order of the Coif and had been invited to join the law review in her senior year (although the honor came too late, and she was unable to accept it because of other time commitments), thought that working for a judge would put her in even better stead for the corporate position she eventually hoped to land. She applied for and landed a highly coveted clerk's job on the prestigious Fifth Circuit, among the most active of the federal benches.

With a bent for real estate and corporate law, she had assumed she would have no trouble joining a major Dallas firm after her year of clerking. To her surprise, her only offer came from a small firm in Dallas that specialized in bankruptcy law. Although bankruptcy's star has since ascended, in the late 1960s it was not an area of the law that bright, eager young law school graduates were burning to get into. If anything, it was looked upon as something only slightly removed from ambulance chasing. Coffee was offered the position with Palmer and Palmer, a small corporate firm, not so much because of her stellar record but because the firm needed to hire a young lawyer, and she was one of the few willing to do bankruptcy law.

Weddington was more confident than Coffee that she would be able to open the door to some important corporate firm. She rarely failed once she put her mind to something, and she took pride in her ability not only to be a team player, but also to play the game the way the coaches wanted it played. She was and has for the most part remained the consummate corporate woman, attuned to achieving her goals by working within the system. To build up her résumé, she had begun to work part-time with a law professor named John Sutton on a special project for the American Bar Association even before she graduated.

Weddington was thrilled to be the first woman in her class who was invited to fly to Dallas for an interview with a major law firm. Her hopes were shattered, however, when she realized that the firm had no intention of hiring her or any other woman. The partners, perhaps feeling some pressure to hire a woman but clearly unwilling to do so, let the interview disintegrate into a discussion of why they could not hire her.

One partner told her, in all seriousness as far as she could tell, that lawyers used foul language in conferences, language that might offend her. Worse, another lawyer commented, the only way to train a clerk was to "cuss him out occasionally," and they just would not feel comfortable doing that to someone as pretty and sweet as she apparently was. Besides, they noted, she had a husband. Wouldn't she need to be home to cook dinner for him? Lawyers, especially young lawyers, worked long hours. How could she possibly work the hours a job with their firm would require and handle her obligations at home?

The final problem with hiring her, as far as the partners were concerned, was that their wives had reservations about having them working with professional women. Secretaries were enough of a threat without adding attractive new law school graduates, women who would be colleagues. They were sure she would sympathize with their wives' thinking and perhaps even share it one day if she did not now. Before Weddington left the firm, she knew that an offer would not be forthcoming.

Without the law firm job she had hoped to obtain, Sarah continued working for John Sutton on the ABA ethics project after she graduated. The job actually worked out well, since her husband, whom she had met on a blind date her last year of law school and had married shortly after graduation, was still finishing law school. He was Sarah's age, but serving in the military had put him a year behind her. The job also gave her an opportunity to travel all over the country meeting other lawyers, some of whom would be invaluable contacts to her in her future work. It was during this period that she developed a lifelong appetite for travel. The result of her two and one half years of committee work was the *Code of Professional Responsibility*, a book that is still widely used by lawyers and state bar associations.

Spurned by the big law firms, Weddington found herself even more interested than she might otherwise have been in the women's movement. She had joined Austin's first consciousness-raising group during law school and now became active in the National Organization for Women (NOW) and Planned Parenthood. She also joined a group of Texas women who were trying to find women to run for public office.

Had she joined a law firm, Weddington's feminist side might never have developed so fully. Like most junior members of such firms, she would have had little spare time for any kind of extracurricular activity, and she would not have been encouraged to pursue anything related to the women's movement, which was viewed as a radical activity in Texas. If Sarah, a traditionalist to the core, had a radical feminist period, this was it. An acquaintance recalls her appearing at the many meetings that filled her life at that time wearing a black cape—fairly avant-garde garb in a state like Texas, where women were given to wearing pastel colors and dainty prints.

Weddington's first involvement with abortion occurred when she was still living in Austin and working for the bar association. A group of women who were loosely affiliated with the University of Texas— students and staff—approached her at a garage sale and asked if she would help them organize a problem-pregnancy counseling service. She would later recall having jumped at the chance not so much because it involved abortion as because it gave her a chance to practice law.

Pregnancy counseling services were springing up all over the country, in emulation of the first, bravely named New York group called the Clergy Consultation Service on Abortion. Formed in 1967 by the Reverend Howard Moody of the Judson Memorial Church, a longtime social activist, and twenty-one other Protestant and Jewish clergymen, CCS was a response to growing concern over the millions of women who were forced into illegal abortions every year, many at great risk to themselves.

The counseling services, which required no money or accepted only nominal fees, advised pregnant women about the choices open to them if they did not want to have a baby and referred them to sources of help—either adoption agencies or abortion services. Most of the women who sought counseling, about 95 percent of CCS cases, for example, chose abortion.

The services were a brilliant and in retrospect rather flagrant form of civil rebellion. They advertised openly, making little attempt to hide what they were doing; most practiced some circumspection, however, refusing, for example, to refer women to doctors over the telephone and insisting that the service did not provide abortions, only abortion conseling. In one or two states, a person who counseled abortion was considered an accomplice to the crime, but even where this was not the case, referral services obviously fell into an indeterminate gray area regarding their legality. Obviously one of their goals was to subvert the abortion laws. The pioneering clergy-run services were especially successful, largely because law enforcement agencies were reluctant to take on the clergy. The clergymen, in turn, lent credibility to the abortion-reform movement and made people see that abortion was an issue that could no longer be ignored.

The New York services sent women to Puerto Rico and, when abortion became legal in England in 1968, to London. Sometimes women were sent to Eastern European countries and Scandinavia, where abortion was either legal or illegal but accessible. Texas and California women were sent to Mexican clinics that had been inspected and preapproved by the people who ran the services. Even though abortion was illegal in Mexico, a Catholic country, the laws were ignored, and an abortion was easily obtained.

In addition, illegal abortionists thrived in most towns of any size across the United States, and referral services used them if they were skilled and reputable. The organization also referred women to private physicians who were brave enough to do in-office abortions.

The services were a response to the fact that a legal abortion was almost impossible to arrange. Only eight to ten thousand were done each year throughout the country, compared with the million to a million and a half illegal abortions that experts such as Planned Parenthood and the National Committee on Maternal Health estimated were obtained each year. A legal abortion could only be gotten through a physician, who could and frequently did exercise his own personal judgment about which of his patients were entitled to one; and these were done in hospitals, which were reluctant to permit them. Even large metropolitan hospitals averaged only twenty-five to thirty-five a year.

Hospital abortions were reserved primarily for women with clout—doctors' wives, the woman whose husband had donated a wing to a hospital, wives and teen-age daughters of families lucky enough to count a physician as a personal friend. To put it bluntly, to the extent that abortion was legally available, a rich, well-connected woman always had a better chance of getting one than did a poor woman with no connections. One doctor at a major Texas hospital summed up the prevailing philosophy among his colleagues: "There are only so many times you're going to go to bat against the [hospital] administration, that you like to save it for regular patients."

Poor women were another story entirely. As evidence of the discrimination against them, lawyer Harriet Pilpel, who was active in birth control and later the abortion-reform movement, testified before the New York State Assembly in 1967 (when New York activists were trying to pass a reform law) that the ratio of abortions to live births for private patients in New York State was 1 to 250, whereas for ward service it was 1 to 10,000. Most poor women lacked a network of friends and acquaintances who could direct them to the skilled local abortionist, and those who could find one frequently did not have the funds to pay for his services, which ranged from $250 to $1,000.

More often than not, poor women got the bad abortions. They became the bloody statistics, their heart-rending stories plastered across the front pages of newspapers. By 1968 abortion was a relatively safe medical procedure, but it could and did turn foul when done on a dirty kitchen table with septic instruments by an unskilled abortionist. The counseling services that sprang up across the country in the late 1960s and early 1970s were as much as anything an attempt to provide abortion services to all women and not just the fortunate few who had the right connections.

The Austin group that asked Weddington to work with them intended to run a straightforward referral and counseling service, and to this aim they hoped that legal counsel would help them avoid any clashes with the law. Although willing to skirt the law, they were not seeking to challenge it openly.

As Weddington worked with the group and learned more about abortion, she developed a desire to do even more than she was. One day she decided to get in touch with Linda Coffee, partly because she was the only other woman from her law school class who was practicing, but also because while they were in law school together they had occasionally talked to one another about women's lives and issues. She thought Coffee might be interested in helping her do something about abortion.

After her disappointment over not receiving an offer from a major law firm when she finished her clerkship, Coffee, like Weddington, had involved herself more deeply in feminist concerns. She had joined NOW and was also active in a Dallas-based feminist group called the Women's Equity Action League (WEAL), which worked for better employment opportunities for women. Unlike Weddington, Coffee was quick to call herself a feminist. She would later tell me she was the "only feminist lawyer in Dallas," that she alone went out of her way to use the label at a time when most active professional women would not touch feminism with a ten-foot pole out of fear that doing so would jeopardize their careers.

Although the two women had not been friends in college, they were now drawn together by their common interest in women's lives. They spent hours on the telephone and occasionally met in person. During this period they compared their lives, sharing stories about the doors that had been closed to them professionally and always thinking about what they could do to change things.

Their discussions invariably returned to abortion and what could be done about it. Like many women, they were finally beginning to see, as de Beauvoir had predicted, that women needed to be able to control their fertility to be free—and that abortion was one key to doing so. The idea that women could not control when and under what circumstances they would choose to reproduce struck them as unfair—the one thing that truly hindered women as they planned careers. They began to talk about what specifically might be done to change the Texas abortion law.

One possible means of change, a painstakingly slow one, was the state legislature. But that would require the cooperation of Texas state legislators, most of whom wanted nothing to do with "libbers'" causes or even, for that matter, causes of women who were not "libbers." Besides, Weddington and Coffee had no political clout with the Texas state legislature—and, in fact, they knew few Texas women who did.

A court challenge was the other possibility, one that seemed more viable. The courts, especially the federal benches and the Supreme Court under Chief Justice Earl Warren, were the scene of most battles over civil rights legislation in the reform-oriented 1960s, in large part because they had proved to be the branch of government most receptive to social change. Of course, a court challenge could drag on, too, as witnessed by the years of courtroom squabbling that had followed the Supreme Court decision ordering the desegregation of public schools. The city of Dallas had been embroiled in a suit to work out an acceptable desegregation plan for almost a decade.

Coffee had experience with the judicial system, and that would be helpful. Another advantage to a court challenge was the element of surprise it would provide. Law enforcement officials would not be expecting a court challenge, so the state might not offer much opposition. All things considered, both women thought the courts were probably the way to go, in Texas at least. They decided they would each begin looking for a potential test case to take into court.

In all their hours of planning and speculating, the one thing the two young, inexperienced lawyers never discussed or even considered was their boldness in planning to challenge a state law. This was because the idea of taking on a state government or even the federal government, for that matter, was not as unusual or difficult a task in the late 1960s as it has since become. In those heady days of civil rights activity, countless lawyers, many of them fresh out of law school and imbued with a sense of idealism, were hoping and praying to make their mark somewhere. At issue was not so much whether they would challenge a law, but which law they would challenge. Coffee and Weddington later admitted they were simply too young and inexperienced to understand fully what they were taking on. In one of her rare expansive moods, Coffee told me, "When you're young, you have high aspirations, and you just do what needs to be done."

The first order of business was to find a suitable plaintiff. Thinking that their best resources were the numerous feminist organizations that they had joined, each woman stepped up her activities, Weddington in Austin, where she was still living at that time, and Coffee in Dallas. Both women made themselves available as speakers on the subject of abortion. They gave speeches intended to educate women on the need for abortion reform, but always, as they made the rounds of various women's groups, the more traditional volunteer groups as well as the feminist ones, each was looking for a certain kind of woman, someone with the potential to become an abortion-case plaintiff.

It was also not unusual for a lawyer who was looking for a plaintiff in a test case to put out feelers among his or her colleagues to be on the lookout for someone suitable, and Coffee had done that in Dallas.

For a while, Weddington was hopeful that a plaintiff could be found among the women in the problem-pregnancy counseling group—if not among the organizers, then among the women they counseled. She met several times with the abortion-counseling group to discuss the possibility of developing a test case. She talked about what was needed to overturn the laws, how such a case would proceed, and of the demands that might be made of anyone who volunteered to become a plaintiff. Gradually, though, her hopes faded, at least for finding a plaintiff among the referral group. One problem was that most of the women who sought counseling knew they wanted an abortion. The sooner a woman underwent an abortion, the healthier it was for her, and few were willing—or could justifiably be asked—to risk the delay that even brief legal proceedings might entail.

The other possibility was to use a member of the referral group who happened to be pregnant, even a woman who did not want an abortion but was willing to claim that she did in order to press an abortion suit against the state. It certainly was not Weddington's first choice to use a kind of trumped-up defendant, but if no one else turned up, she realized that it might be her only option. That might be more humane in the long run, anyway, since she knew that any suit she filed would most likely not be decided in time for a plaintiff to undergo an abortion.

Still another thought was to file a class-action suit using the Austin referral group. The members were eager to help in any way they could, so much so that when Weddington once asked if anyone in the group happened to be pregnant, several voices chorused, "No, but that can be arranged." The problem with using the group was that at least one plaintiff had to be representative of the class. In this case, that meant pregnant and desiring an abortion.

Coffee, too, had begun to do more public speaking in Dallas in an attempt to find a plaintiff. One night, at a meeting of a feminist-oriented group, Coffee was approached by a couple who began to talk to her about her work in abortion reform. Eventually the couple got around to suggesting that they might be willing to become plaintiffs in an abortion suit. The woman told Coffee that since 1968 she had suffered from a neural-chemical condition that caused backaches and depression severe enough that her physician had suggested she not become pregnant for the time being. She had to stop using the Pill, then the most reliable form of birth control, because it blurred her vision. Four months after the onset of her physical problems, she had become pregnant. Apart from her illness, she and her husband did not feel they were ready for a child, so they decided on an abortion. Through an abortion-counseling service, the woman had made arrangements to obtain an abortion at a clinic outside the United States.

Despite using contraception, the couple were worried that the woman might become pregnant again. They could not afford another abortion if it meant traveling outside the country. In an interview they would later give to Barbara Richardson, a reporter for the *Dallas Times Herald*, they shed more light on their willingness to become plaintiffs. Both felt a "moral imperative" to help legalize abortion. The husband added: "Our personal, moral, and ethical codes were outraged by the law."

On the one hand, Coffee thought the couple would make excellent plaintiffs. They were impressive: young, married two years, both professionals with advanced degrees, churchgoing Methodists, active and involved in community life, and most important, they had an excellent reason for using abortion as a method of backup birth control.

On the other hand, there were problems with using them, not least of which would be the need to explain to the court why the woman's own physician had not done an abortion when she became pregnant. Coffee suspected that although the woman's physical condition was serious, it was not really so threatening that she could not bear a child.

The biggest drawback to using the couple as plaintiffs was that their case was weak, legally speaking. Like most other states, Texas permitted abortion to save the mother's life, and the present law could easily be interpreted as sufficient to cover their situation. Coffee believed the case would be thrown out of court on the grounds that it involved no controversy. Such an evasive action would have particular appeal, Coffee feared, to a judge who was not eager to become involved in something as controversial as abortion.

Despite several major disadvantages to using the couple, Coffee decided to go ahead and try to build a case around them anyway, largely because in several months of looking for a plaintiff, she had not found anyone else. Meanwhile, she would continue her search. The young couple were eager to protect their anonymity, so they agreed with Coffee to be known only as John and Mary Doe.

A few weeks later Coffee thought she might have found not one but several other plaintiffs in the local Unitarian Church's women's group. In Dallas Unitarians were viewed as being on the cutting edge of social reform, which meant that they were not merely liberal but active in liberal causes. Their interest in abortion had grown out of a national annual meeting at which abortion had been the topic several years earlier. One member of the group had returned to Dallas with a sense of urgency about the need to reform the abortion laws. She urged the group to study abortion, which they did. Some of the women heard Coffee speak elsewhere on the subject of abortion reform and wanted her to address their group to tell them what they might be doing to promote liberalization of abortion laws.

The night she spoke, Coffee talked at length about the case she hoped to develop with the Does as plaintiffs. She had come to the meeting with a vivacious, dark-haired young woman, whom several group members were thrilled to realize must be the Mary Doe Coffee was talking about. As soon as Coffee finished speaking, several women raised the question of whether they as a group might not become plaintiffs in a class-action suit.

Coffee was interested in class-action suits, having worked on several, and she knew they were enjoying considerable receptivity in the federal courts at that time. Although she had not been thinking in terms of a class-action suit, one might be a possibility. She soon rejected the idea, however. The Dallas women would not make good plaintiffs for the same reason the Austin referral service would not: none of the women was pregnant. To appease their disappointment, Coffee suggested that the Unitarian women might want to prepare an amicus curiae, or friend-of-the-court, brief to support her case, which they eagerly agreed to do.

Convinced she would find no other plaintiff, Coffee decided to move ahead as quickly as possible with the Does' case. Then, in early December 1969, just as she was about to file a lawsuit, luck struck in the form of a potential plaintiff who was suitable for the case, if only because she was pregnant and wanted an abortion.

Coffee learned about Norma McCorvey through a colleague, Henry McCloskey. The two women met for the first time in McCloskey's office. From the start Coffee was interested in McCorvey. Within a few days she met with her once more alone so that she could hear more about Norma's situation and background.

The next time Coffee talked to Weddington, she described Norma McCorvey to her. Weddington was enthusiastic, so much so that she asked Coffee if she might join her in the suit as co-counsel. Coffee was not surprised at the request to join forces officially, since they had in effect been working together unofficially for the better part of a year. She could see the advantages of having someone to work with. As an overworked junior partner in her law firm, she worried that she would not have as much time as she would like to work on the case. She had already rejected the idea of asking to do the case pro bono; it was too radical for that. With two people, the work could be divided. She also welcomed Weddington's thoughts and ideas about how best to approach the issues. And of course, the bottom line was that it would be fun to have someone to share the excitement with. Coffee had a feeling this case might generate a lot of that.

4

Awakening a Nation's Conscience

The public attitude toward abortion was gradually becoming more liberal throughout the 1960s, and Coffee and Weddington were right to suspect that the time was ripe for reform. Not surprisingly, since abortion was permitted in all states to save the mother's life, most people—90 percent, according to major polls—approved of abortions done for this reason. This figure changed little over the next decade.

The most surprising change in attitude was occurring among the Roman Catholic population. In 1962, 36 percent of Roman Catholic men and women generally disapproved of abortion. By 1969, that disapproval rate had dropped to 20 percent. Americans of all religious persuasions were less approving of abortions done for reasons other than to save a woman's life, but their disapproval also declined steadily throughout the decade. In 1962, for example, 29 percent of Americans disapproved of abortion for fetal deformity, and 74 percent disapproved of those done for economic reasons. By 1969 those disapproval rates had dropped to 25 and 68 percent respectively.

In effect, between 1960 and 1969 abortion had shifted from a forbidden topic—as taboo as incest—to a subject that was increasingly discussed and debated in public. Two events, however, served to catalyze public interest in abortion and set the stage for reform. The first, which occurred in the early sixties, was the story of one woman's difficulty in obtaining an abortion.

In 1962 Sherri Finkbine was a twenty-nine-year-old resident of

Phoenix, Arizona, the mother of four children, all under the age of seven, and the star of her own local children's television show when she found herself pregnant with her fifth child. She was not unhappy about the pregnancy but did experience some nervousness, which she treated herself with some tranquilizers her husband had brought home a year earlier from a business trip to England.

Twenty years and a world of sophistication later, most people would have difficulty recalling the naïveté of both laypersons and the medical community with regard to drug use during the 1950s and 1960s. Nothing was unusual about Sherri Finkbine's "prescribing" a tranquilizer for herself or using a drug that had been sitting in her medicine cabinet for twelve months. The fact that she was pregnant also would not have stopped her from using the medication, because like most people at that time, she erroneously believed that the placenta acted as a barrier between a woman and a fetus, preventing the penetration of any harmful substances. Drugs like Librium and Valium were in practically everyone's medicine chest. Why waste time with a psychotherapist when miracle pills existed that could, with one swallow, banish depression, insomnia, and nervousness?

The era of heady innocence ended abruptly in 1962 when the first of several major drug dramas unfolded in the European newspapers. First reports indicated that over five thousand babies were born severely deformed in England, West Germany, Canada, and Australia as a result of their mothers having taken a drug called thalidomide during the early weeks of pregnancy. Eventually over ten thousand deformed babies would be born in West Germany alone.

Thalidomide babies, as these infants were dubbed by the press, had a defect called phocomelia, which meant they had seallike flippers rather than fully developed arms and legs. They also suffered from serious internal deformities, and fewer than half of the infants born with thalidomide deformities survived longer than a few weeks or months.

Finkbine became aware of her problem when she read the reports of deformed babies being born in Europe. Upon reading the label of the tranquilizer she had taken, she learned that it was indeed thalidomide. Based on the reports coming from Europe, she knew the chances that her baby would be born seriously deformed were great. Sherri thought immediately of abortion. She had some reservations about it at first but within a few days had sorted out her feelings and knew she wanted one. Her husband, Robert, agreed with her.

She put in a call to her personal physician, who was sympathetic to her plight and willing to terminate her pregnancy. Strictly speaking, it was illegal for him to do so since the Arizona law, like most other state abortion laws, permitted abortion only to save the life of a mother. But in cases like this, the law was widely ignored. For example, physicians routinely did abortions on women who had been exposed to German measles (also a cause of serious fetal deformities) early in their pregnancies.

Finkbine and her physicians would have to obtain medical certification to do the abortion. This typically consisted of approval by a hospital therapeutic committee, which was usually made up of an obstetrician-gynecologist (not the one requesting permission to do the surgery), an internist, and a psychiatrist. Sherri Finkbine would have to appear personally before the committee, but she had every reason to assume that the approval would be routine. Therapeutic abortion committees were notably stingy about the number of abortions they permitted at their hospitals, but when they did approve one, it was invariably for someone like Sherri Finkbine—a respected member of the community, married, and the mother of at least two and preferably three children.

Finkbine would not, of course, tell the hospital committee that she wanted an abortion so she would not have to give birth to a severely deformed child. Instead, she would say that giving birth to such a child would be too much pressure on her, so much so that it might cause her to have a nervous breakdown or even to take her own life. Everyone would then agree that this would pose an undue hardship on her and her family.

Like the thousands of women who managed to obtain legal abortions each year, Finkbine meekly and unquestioningly acquiesced to this charade and even went into the committee hearing (as did most other women in her situation) with statements by two psychiatrists attesting to the fact that her mental health would be adversely affected were she to be forced to bear a child that was severely deformed. Finkbine fully expected to check into the hospital the day after she met with the hospital abortion committee for a dilation and evacuation (D & E), the technique then used for abortions done during the first three months of pregnancy.

At first everything appeared to go as expected. With little deliberation, the three committee physicians agreed with Finkbine's doctor that she should be aborted on grounds that the birth of a severely deformed child would be an undue hardship on a family with four other small children to care for. Finkbine's surgery was scheduled for Thursday, July 26.

The process broke down unexpectedly, however, when a routine request for approval from the Maricopa County Medical Association was delayed while their lawyers reviewed the case. Finkbine's physician, realizing immediately that the situation was out of his and the Finkbines' control, told a *New York Times* reporter: "It is now a legal decision. It is no longer a medical or a humanitarian one, I'm afraid."

Without waiting for the medical association's official response, the Finkbines hired a lawyer. The situation was growing urgent since she was almost three months pregnant. After three months, physicians could no longer do a dilation and evacuation, a relatively simple medical procedure, and instead would have to perform a Caesarean section. The Finkbines' lawyer recommended that Sherri go into court to seek a legal judgment that she was entitled to an abortion, so the Finkbines filed suit against the Maricopa County Attorney and the Arizona Attorney General on Friday, July 27. Joining her in the suit was the Good Samaritan Hospital.

Heeding the urgency of the situation, Arizona attorneys immediately began drawing up a legal response, which they filed on the same day the suit was initiated. By now the nation's attention was riveted on the Finkbines. Their dilemma was front-page news and a regular nightly story on the national television news, and public sympathy was running high on their behalf. Their situation was undeniably tragic, regardless of one's view on abortion, and thus the state's lawyers could be forgiven for not wanting to play the role of villains. If, as Finkbine was claiming, and as her lawyers and the two psychiatrists had attested in the court papers, she might take her own life if forced to bear the child, then the state of Arizona would raise no objections to an abortion. They asked for dismissal of the case on grounds that there was no legal controversy.

Sensing that things were going their way, the Finkbines' lawyer pleaded for an early decision, informing the court that if an abortion were not done within the next two weeks, his client might have to undergo the more dangerous abdominal surgery. Late Friday afternoon, Arizona Supreme Court Judge Yale McFate postponed his decision, saying that he would rule Monday on the motion by the state to dismiss the case.

The Finkbines' only concern was that they be allowed to get on with the abortion without the threat of legal prosecution hanging over their heads. They wanted the court to issue a clear-cut ruling that Sherri Finkbine had a right to obtain an abortion. Over the weekend the Finkbines' attorney, Walter Cheifetz, said he would advise her to drop the suit if the public attorneys would promise not to prosecute her for having an abortion.

Arizona officials, not unsympathetic to her plight and despite the obviously skewed "facts" of her case, did not, however, feel that they could bend the law to the extent of publicly agreeing not to prosecute Finkbine.

The matter was resolved, at least as far as the state of Arizona was concerned, on Tuesday when Judge McFate dismissed the case on grounds there was no real legal controversy. He gave the Finkbines' attorney ten days to amend the case to show controversy, that is, to build a case around the real reason that Finkbine wanted an abortion, her unwillingness to bear what would almost certainly be a seriously deformed child. If she asked for an abortion on this ground, the state would almost certainly contest her plea, since no provision existed in the Arizona law for granting an abortion on this ground. At that point the judge would be forced to rule on the case, although he might not rule—indeed most likely would not be able to rule—in the Finkbines' favor. Although the judge's personal sympathies clearly lay with the Finkbines, legally his hands were tied, as he noted when he said: "As a person, this judge is impelled to grant a hearing; as a judge, I cannot do it."

As the Finkbines mulled over their next step, the by now ravenous public turned its attention to the larger thalidomide problem. After heated debate, in a move that only increased public sympathy for more liberal abortion laws, the British Parliament voted not to change the law to permit abortions on pregnant women who had taken thalidomide. It also refused to grant any aid to thalidomide babies, even though it was clear that the British government had not required adequate testing of the drug before releasing it.

Americans, who thought they were safe from this disaster since thalidomide had not been approved for general distribution in the United States, were shocked to learn that the drug had been tested in the United States by one drug manufacturer. First reports indicated that it had only been given to several hundred persons, but within days it was revealed that thalidomide probably had been tested on several thousand people. The drug was distributed to 1,129 doctors in thirty-nine states. If each doctor had tested the drug on only three patients, that meant more than three thousand persons had taken it, and some of those would almost certainly be pregnant women, since nervousness and depression were frequent complaints of pregnancy. On July 21 in Queens, a borough of New York City, a woman gave birth to a thalidomide-deformed infant who lived only forty-one minutes; and other reports of thalidomide babies soon began to filter in.

Having hinted that they might go ahead with the abortion, the Finkbines now awaited word from the hospital that it was still willing to perform the surgery. After Judge McFate's ruling, on advice of its attorneys Good Samaritan Hospital announced that it would have to reconsider its role in this rapidly escalating controversy. On Wednesday night, July 31, hospital officials huddled to discuss the problem. Worried about repeated threats of prosecution, they declined to perform the abortion.

The door had now been slammed on the possibility that the Finkbines might obtain a legal abortion in the state of Arizona. And although abortion to save the mother's life was legal in all fifty states, and Alabama, Oregon, and Washington, D.C., allowed it to preserve a mother's health, in the glare of publicity that surrounded the Finkbines' every move, it would not be easy to find a state willing to permit the abortion. Furthermore, although the initial response had been an outpouring of sympathy, the publicity also had brought out the critics of abortion. Hate mail was arriving daily, and the Finkbines were receiving anonymous, threatening telephone calls.

They began to realize that their best course of action was to leave the country for an abortion. They could go to Denmark, Sweden, or Japan, where abortion laws were more liberal and, they hoped, public attitudes more tolerant.

By Thursday, August 2, Sherri Finkbine still had not decided where to go, although her doctors had warned her to have an abortion by Sunday in order to avoid a Caesarean section. The Finkbines had booked a flight to Sweden but canceled their reservations thirty minutes before departure. They said they were leaning toward Japan, where an abortion could be obtained with no red tape for about $50.

Their attempts to make plans were hindered by the fact that their every move, including the cancellation of the plane flight to Sweden, continued to be front-page news across the nation. In addition, on Friday a broadcast by Vatican radio, obviously referring to the Finkbine case but not using the name, denounced a "mother who desires, at any cost, to interrupt her maternity for fear that her child be born deformed." The Vatican radio report never mentioned thalidomide and its role in causing life-threatening deformities.

The New York Times, while previously respecting Finkbine's wish that her religion not be reported, revealed that she was Unitarian. Clergy across the country were invited to respond but seemed reluctant to do so, although a few, such as Reverend Howard Moody of New York City's Judson Memorial Church and a founder of CCS, and Rabbi Israel Margolies, defended Finkbine's desire to obtain an abortion.

The clergy's reluctance to speak out was undoubtedly due in part to the fact that so many Protestant denominations had no clear-cut view on abortion, although the leading, mainstream denominations, such as the Reform and Conservative branches of Judaism, accepted abortion when done to save a woman's life and often for other humane reasons as well. When Roman Catholic Bishop Thomas J. Riley of Boston condemned the Finkbines for "killing an innocent boy or girl," only the Seventh-Day Adventists replied, stating that they believed the abortion would be therapeutic.

On Saturday, August 4, Sherri and Robert Finkbine were en route to Stockholm, Sweden. Japan had been their first choice, but the Japanese government had also been reluctant to get involved in what was threatening to turn into an international incident. Officials at the Japanese consulate did not tell Finkbine outright that she could not have an abortion in their country; rather, they spoke of the long delay that would be involved in granting her a visa. She got the message.

Even in Sweden there was no assurance that an abortion would be granted. Government officials had warned that there could be an official delay and were careful to note that Sherri Finkbine would still have to prove she was mentally ill to obtain an abortion right away. Swedes and their government, though, took a more liberal view of abortion than did U.S. citizens and officials, and Finkbine had reason to believe she would be granted an abortion in Sweden.

Before leaving, the Finkbines had granted one television interview to a local station. In it Sherri Finkbine had revealed the toll that being the center of such an intense controversy was taking on her: "I've tried to keep control of myself emotionally." She said even though she had awakened at night and heard newborn babies crying, she was still determined to get an abortion because it was "right and the only thing to do." She revealed how she had "burst into a rage when a San Francisco couple offered to adopt the baby. If it were born, the last thing I would want to do would be to place the burden on someone else."

Based on these statements alone, Finkbine, who would never participate in the abortion-reform movement, must nonetheless be counted as one of its more articulate spokespersons. The honesty and ambivalence she revealed in the television interview would become rare as pro-choice reformers grew increasingly strident in their defense of the abortion right—and antiabortionists equally vehement in their view that no abortions were permissible. Yet Finkbine only revealed feelings that are present in every woman, regardless of whether or not she supports the abortion right, when she knows she must make a decision to terminate a pregnancy. The decision to undergo an abortion, except in the most insensitive of women, is not an easy one, nor is it lightly made.

By the time the Finkbines were headed to Sweden, the rumble in the United States over the safety of prescription drugs and adequate drug testing had become a roar. New reports surfaced in *The New York Times* about the increased incidence of thrombosis in women taking Enovid, a birth control pill. There had been warnings of problems associated with the Pill, but before the thalidomide scare they were never taken seriously.

When President John F. Kennedy held a press conference on August 12, thalidomide was the first topic reporters raised. The administration seemed to have found a clever way, however, to deflect attention from whether the first Roman Catholic president approved or disapproved of Finkbine's decision to get an abortion and whether he thought the abortion laws should be liberalized in light of developments surrounding thalidomide. Instead, one slightly bewildered government scientist, Dr. Frances Oldham Kelsey of the Food and Drug Administration, became an overnight heroine for her refusal to approve thalidomide for general distribution. She was invited to the White House and decorated despite her gentle protests that she was only doing her job. The press, for its part, never removed its kid gloves and asked the president how he felt about the abortion laws in light of the thalidomide controversy.

The second week of August, while Senate hearings were being conducted about the need to tighten the drug laws, Sherri Finkbine was experiencing more routine delay in Sweden. By August 6 she had not yet seen a physician. Swedish officials reiterated that she would be treated like any other woman seeking an abortion, which meant she would be subject to "penetrating investigation."

The next day she saw a physician and was scheduled to see him again on Friday. For the second time the Finkbines' hopes were raised that Sherri would be able to obtain an abortion before the week was out. On August 9 she completed the psychiatric examination. The Swedish State Medical Board met on August 17, at which time they unanimously agreed to permit her to have an abortion. She was operated on the next day. According to the physician's report, the fetus was seriously deformed.

While the Finkbines were in Sweden, a trial was being held in Belgium in which a woman, her husband, mother, sister, and physician were accused of murdering her thalidomide-deformed infant. The mother admitted she had put an overdose of a drug in the baby's milk, and the other defendants were being tried as accessories. Public pressure to acquit the group was so great that on the day the decision was handed down, hundreds of extra police were assigned to the courtroom to control the angry mob that was expected to materialize should the decision go against the defendants. All were acquitted.

The Finkbines returned to the United States a week later and tried to resume life as private citizens. Sherri felt she could not return to her job as hostess of *Romper Room*, that doing so would, in her words, place the television station in a "precarious position."

Throughout the last two weeks of August, the newspapers continued to report on the numbers of babies that were expected to be—and were—born with deformities caused by thalidomide, which was now banned everywhere. In November Sweden's Medical Board, responding to the Finkbines' case, asked the government to liberalize the country's abortion laws. Abortions should be permitted, they urged, when a fetus was likely to be born with a severe birth defect, so women like Sherri Finkbine would not have to lie to terminate a pregnancy.

Finkbine's struggle to obtain an abortion left a lasting impression on the public. It demonstrated the hypocrisy of the present laws and revealed how badly reform was needed, even though it would be another few years in coming. Most important, it personalized abortion for millions of people, few of whom could deny that they would have wanted an abortion had they been in Sherri Finkbine's shoes.

Ironically, the difficulty Finkbine encountered in trying to obtain an abortion in the United States would not have occurred only a few years earlier, even though abortion was illegal. The controversy was a sign that battle lines were being drawn between two enormous clashing factions in American life: those who approved of abortion or could at least condone it under certain humane circumstances and those who could not condone it under any circumstances.

Had unusual forces not intervened to bring the Finkbines' dilemma to the attention of legal authorities, Sherri's fate would have rested entirely with her physicians, as happened with all women who hoped to obtain a legal abortion in the United States. Physicians had played a major role in bringing about the current restrictive laws, which put abortion firmly in their control, and only through an understanding of their role in outlawing abortion can we begin to understand why they were later willing to work—however halfheartedly—to liberalize it.

The restrictive Texas abortion law had only been in existence for about a hundred years when Coffee and Weddington challenged it—in the long view of history, not very much time at all. Prior to the mid-nineteenth century, abortion was widely available. Many historians and demographers considered it to be the most frequently used method of birth control, there being little else available for most of human history.

Abortion is known to have existed for at least five thousand years and in fact was once so widespread that it is safe to say there are no societies in which it never occurred, although it characteristically met with varying shades of approval, denial, ambivalence, disapproval, and outright ostracism, as George Devereux revealed in *A Study of Abortion in Primitive Societies*. Despite its name, the book is a survey of abortion practices in twenty modern and historical societies as well as four hundred primitive ones. Abortion was known to be practiced widely in ancient Greece and Rome. Plato and Aristotle viewed abortion as an acceptable means of population control. Even Hippocrates, who gave physicians the oath on which they later based their ideological opposition to abortion, reportedly instructed a young woman musician on the best means of self-abortion. Devereux found that women typically aborted themselves, that abortion was almost exclusively a female activity, which may account for its prevalence even when it has been outlawed. In many cultures, women have formed networks among themselves to help one another, when necessary, to obtain illegal abortions.

Old German tribal law recognized that the right to terminate a pregnancy rested with the woman, and in common-law nations throughout the world, women were at liberty to obtain abortions when they needed and wanted them. Under common law, a fetus was not recognized as a legal person until birth. This did not mean it was not considered human, but rather that it could make or receive no legal claims prior to birth. Fetuses could, for example, inherit property, but the inheritance was contingent upon live birth. Similarly, fetuses could sue, but again settlement was contingent upon live birth. In the United States fetuses did not have the rights of personhood that were guaranteed in the Constitution.

No infringement of the common-law right to abortion occurred until 1803, when England enacted the Ellenborough law, which among other things outlawed abortion. The law was not so much the result of any moral or philosophical opposition to abortion as it was an attempt on the part of Lord Ellenborough, an archconservative, to do something about what he viewed as the increasingly liberal criminal laws; the new abortion statute was merely one part of an omnibus crime bill.

In theory, the Ellenborough law meant that British women went overnight from a common-law liberty to obtain abortions to a situation where they could be prosecuted and punished for aborting a pregnancy. In practice, however, the poorly written and vague law was unclear on such issues as whether a woman, as opposed to the abortionist, could actually be "convicted" of abortion.

No similar action to restrict the abortion right would be taken in the United States for almost fifty years. Throughout the colonial era, from 1664 to 1776, the United States followed the common law, which meant abortion was permitted. When the United States became a nation in 1776, most states adopted the common law, and women were still free to terminate pregnancies at will.

No one knows why abortion was not mentioned in the U.S. Constitution, but scholars tend to agree that it was not an issue at the time the Constitution was written—abortion being commonly accepted and fairly widespread. The public attitude toward abortion was one of sympathy and understanding.

Devereux has pointed out that societies' attitudes toward abortion often display great "plasticity and variability of behavior" and seem to alternate between periods of ignoring abortion and bursts of activity designed to "do something" about it. "Doing something" about abortion, however, has proven to be a nearly impossible task, since women continue to manage to obtain abortions regardless of whether they are legal or illegal or otherwise culturally restrained.

Prior to 1820 in the United States, abortion had been ignored for hundreds of years. Between 1821 and 1840, however, a wave of restrictive abortion laws were passed. The effort to change the abortion laws was almost entirely the work of the medical profession or, to be more accurate, a group of physicians known as "regulars." James C. Mohr, author of *Abortion in America*, an excellent analysis of American abortion policy, has attributed the physicians' motives in pushing for restrictive legislation in part to a desire to upgrade themselves professionally and become the exclusive providers of health care services in the United States. Physicians mounted a campaign to drive out or bring under their control the "irregular" medical practitioners, which at that time included pharmacists, surgeons, homeopaths, and midwives. Midwives and pharmacists were special targets in part because the former were the chief source of women's medical care and the latter were the chief suppliers of chemicals that caused abortion.

By 1841 restrictive laws had been passed in ten states and one federal territory. The content of these laws would seem to indicate that they were intended to limit the practice of medicine to the regulars as much as to outlaw abortion. They seemed not to have been based on any moral or philosophical opposition to abortion. For example, the new laws typically outlawed the use of abortifacients but said nothing about abortion done through surgical means, a medical procedure that was the exclusive province of the regular physicians. When New York State passed a restrictive law in 1830, it included something called the "therapeutic exception," which soon made its way into most other states' laws. The therapeutic exception permitted abortions done to save a woman's life. New York, like several other states, also mandated that abortion was a crime only when someone—either the woman or the fetus—died; unsuccessful abortions were not criminal. No state held that the woman who sought an abortion was guilty of any criminal activity; the illegal abortionist was the sole target of these restrictive laws.

A striking feature of the new laws was that they restricted abortion only after quickening, the point at which a woman first felt movement within the womb. Juries and judges were reluctant to convict an illegal abortionist or find anyone guilty of causing a miscarriage prior to quickening, and legislatures in the nineteenth century were similarly reluctant to impose any restrictions on un-quickened pregnancies. Among other legal problems with quickening was the fact that proof of its existence depended entirely on the woman's testimony.

These omissions and the overall vagueness in many of the new laws were indicative, as much as anything, of the legislators' general reluctance to place any kind of restrictions on abortion. Women continued to obtain abortions without fear of reprisal, and the public remained sympathetic and tolerant of a woman who needed one.

Throughout the 1830s physicians seemed to lose ground in their battle to professionalize themselves and, in the process, to restrict abortion. Many of the medical regulation statutes passed in the previous decade were repealed, and concern over limiting abortion receded once again.

This time, however, the lull was only temporary, and interest in regulating abortion was rekindled around 1840, largely because it had become increasingly common. Like much else in American life in that period, abortion had become a highly commercial venture.

Ladies' magazines and newspapers ran countless advertisements for potions designed to "unblock the menses," as abortion was delicately referred to. A number of illegal abortionists—among them the infamous Madame Restell of New York City—sold their potions and, when those failed, provided surgical relief at openly operated abortion clinics. Madame Restell, who catered to the rich and famous in New York, reputedly spent $60,000 annually advertising her wares and also operated clinics in Boston and Philadelphia.

Between 1840 and 1860, the states responded in patchwork fashion to the so-called abortion epidemic. Some tightened their laws; some that had not had any laws restricting abortion now passed them. By 1860, though, thirteen of the thirty-three states still had no laws on abortion, and the reluctance to restrict abortion prior to quickening was still evident from the tone of the laws written during that period.

In the late 1850s the regular physicians decided the time had come to reinstate their campaign against abortion. This time their campaign, with its decidedly moral tone, began to look like a crusade. While addressing a group of Michigan regulars in April 1867, physician E. P. Christian stated: "It is not sufficient that the medical profession should set up a standard of morality for themselves, but the people are to be educated up to it. The profession must become aggressive toward those wrongs and errors which it can only properly expose, and successfully impose." In *The Physical Life of the Woman*, a best-selling home medical treatise published in 1870, George H. Naphey, M.D., wrote that those "who take in charge public morals" would join him and other physicians in the fight to eliminate abortion, a "frequently . . . prevalent sin."

The physicians tried and failed to round up support from the clergy, but they did receive help from unexpected sources, most notably the antiobscenity crusaders, led by Anthony Comstock, who almost single-handedly aroused the nation to fever pitch about obscenity, and several newspapers, which campaigned extensively against abortion, dubbing it the "evil of the age." Splashed across the front pages of several newspapers, including *The New York Times*, throughout the 1870s, were lurid stories of women who died in the course of obtaining illegal abortions. The women were depicted not as victims, but rather as moral examples, while the illegal abortionists were painted as true villains—unsavory, uncaring, money-hungry characters.

55

The morality march culminated in 1878 when Comstock arrested Madame Restell. Her suicide on the eve of her trial in May 1878 did as much as any other single event or strain of crusading to turn the American public against abortion. Deluged with highly inflammatory and not always accurate propaganda about the evils of abortion, people were finally persuaded that something needed to be done. That something turned out to be the passage of even more restrictive laws.

Between 1860 and 1880, laws were written in forty states and territories, and twenty-one states revised laws they already had to make them stricter. Many states outlawed abortion for the first time, and by 1900, when the crusade against abortion was finally dying out, only Kentucky had no law against abortion, and even there one court had ruled it illegal.

The second wave of abortion laws was far tougher than the first. The distinction between a quickened and unquickened fetus was removed in most state laws, making abortion illegal at any stage of pregnancy. In several states, such as Indiana and New York, women, who had always been seen as the victims of illegal abortions even when they sought them, lost their immunity and for the first time could be prosecuted for obtaining an abortion or aborting themselves.

Even the courts fell under the influence of the "evil of the age." Before the mid-nineteenth century, it was difficult to find a jury that would convict an illegal abortionist, so much so that Mohr noted prosecutors did not even want to tarnish their records with abortion cases they were sure to lose. Courts followed the precedent set in *Commonwealth* v. *Bangs*, an 1812 Massachusetts decision in which a man was acquitted of charges of administering an abortifacient on grounds that the fetus had not yet quickened.

All that changed as the morality of abortion became a basis for further restriction of the laws. In a New York court in 1892, for example, when the plaintiff's attorneys pleaded that inadmissible evidence had been used to convict their plaintiff of undertaking an illegal abortion, the court upheld the conviction despite the irregularities; it was a case that would have been dismissed a few decades earlier. In an even more startling 1882 decision, *Commonwealth* v. *Taylor*, the Massachusetts Supreme Court held that prosecutors did not have to prove a woman had been pregnant to prosecute her abortionist.

The restrictive laws stayed on the books, diligently enforced at first and not so diligently enforced after a few decades, but abortion once again was not an issue that concerned anyone. Over the years some accommodation was worked out between women and their physicians, an accommodation that would ordinarily have enabled a woman such as Sherri Finkbine to obtain an abortion with relative ease.

For the next fifty years, doctors seemed remarkably united in the consensus that abortion was morally wrong and should be permitted only in those instances where it was necessary to save a woman's life. It would have been difficult for anyone outside the profession, and even for many inside it, to realize that a crisis of huge moral proportions was looming on the horizon. If the Finkbines' tragic story served to educate the public about the need to change the current state laws, another legal controversy was brewing that would, four years later, spur the medical profession into action on behalf of abortion reform.

After 1900 medicine began to make progress in reducing the numbers and kinds of situations where pregnancy was life-threatening. Anti-nausea drugs eliminated excessive vomiting, a common reason to terminate a pregnancy. Tuberculosis was no longer life-threatening, and its female victims recovered and could bear children with no ill effects to their health. Advances in the treatment of heart and kidney disease made it possible for women suffering from these conditions to have children, and women with diabetes could be carefully managed through pregnancy.

Conservative, mostly Catholic physicians who opposed abortion but accepted it when performed to save a life began to look forward to the day when no doctor would have any reason to perform an abortion because no woman's life would be at risk during pregnancy.

More liberal, mostly Protestant physicians, however, saw the situation in a different light. They began to question whether the time had not come to apply more liberal standards to abortion, which was also now a safer procedure. They asked whether an abortion might not be justified when a fetus would be born with gross deformities, or because a couple had several children and could not afford another, or even because a mother had borne too many children too close together and would have great difficulty coping with another child. Women continued to ask for abortions, and these doctors were at a loss to explain why they could not have them. Wasn't it possible that saving a mother's emotional or physical health was as important as preserving her physical life? Were there not perhaps some purely humanitarian reasons for abortion?

The threatened schism was postponed in 1945, when birth-control expert Alan Guttmacher introduced the idea of therapeutic abortion committees, special hospital boards composed of three or more physicians who would supervise abortion services. By 1950 virtually every hospital had one. Because the committees completed the trend toward moving abortions out of doctors' offices and into hospitals, thus making them more public and therefore subject to moral censure, the immediate effect of the abortion boards was to drastically decrease the number of abortions. One hospital that did eleven abortions per year before an abortion board was installed did one abortion per year afterward. But this was a typical figure for any hospital after a committee was installed. Hospitals even developed quotas, permitting so many abortions per live births.

The committees at least temporarily eased the tension between the physicians who were increasingly uncomfortable with any abortion done other than to save a woman's life and those who felt there were other reasons to abort a pregnancy. For the time being, at least, Roman Catholic doctors would not express disapproval of their colleagues who performed an occasional, committee-approved abortion for a reason that did not follow the letter of the law, so long as relatively few of these abortions were done. It went without saying that Protestant and Jewish doctors did not pressure Roman Catholics to do abortions, and that abortions would not be performed in Roman Catholic hospitals.

The tension between the two factions changed when the number of hospital-sanctioned abortions began to increase. A crisis occurred in spring 1966 in San Francisco, when the city found itself in the throes of a German measles epidemic.

Health professionals had long recognized the dangers of rubella, or German measles, to a woman in the early months of pregnancy. Fully 90 percent of women who caught the German measles while pregnant could be expected to give birth to a child with serious birth defects, which included blindness, deafness, heart defects, and other maladies.

The epidemic brought with it the usual corresponding rise in the number of abortions, but even more alarming to some was the fact that more abortion requests came from married than single women—a reversal of the usual ratio. Ironically, a perceived rise in abortions among married women had triggered the opposition to abortion in the late nineteenth century, and history would now repeat itself one hundred years later.

San Francisco physicians were not unaware that abortions done on women exposed to German measles were, strictly speaking, illegal, but they went ahead anyway, confident that public opinion was with them. A survey taken after the Finkbine case had shown that 50 percent of Americans believed she had made the right decision, that fetal deformity was a legitimate cause for seeking an abortion. Only 32 percent disagreed with her decision, and 18 percent were undecided. Reform laws permitting abortion to preserve a woman's health had recently passed in Alabama, Colorado, New Mexico, Oregon, and Washington, D.C., and there was talk of a similar law in California. It had been in this spirit of reform that the California Medical Association in March of 1966 had voted to press for reforms in the abortion law.

Not everyone wanted the law changed, however. Dr. James McNulty, a Los Angeles obstetrician, Roman Catholic, and member of the California State Board of Medical Examiners, had responded to the CMA vote by threatening action by the board. McNulty and others who shared his opposition to abortion were acutely aware of the increase in abortions as a result of the measles epidemic, and they disapproved of those, too. Hospital abortion committees, once protective of their institutions' reputations, seemed even to have colluded by approving the abortions.

The action McNulty threatened was not long in coming, and it proved to be far more severe than anyone expected. Eight weeks after the CMA vote, on a Saturday in May, local investigators entered several San Francisco hospitals and, even though they did not have a court order, secured files revealing which physicians had performed abortions because of German measles in the last year. Several physicians who were interviewed readily admitted that they had done abortions on women who had German measles. The confessions were secretly taped, a rather grandiose authoritarian gesture since the doctors made no attempt to deny the abortions.

California Attorney General Thomas Lynch announced that the state had prepared charges against twenty-one physicians and was preparing charges against another twenty for performing illegal abortions. *The San Francisco Chronicle* broke the story before any indictments had been handed down in an article that noted the law had rarely been enforced. This was considered the largest legal crackdown on doctors in California history and perhaps in the history of the United States. Since the restrictive laws had been passed, very few licensed physicians had been accused of performing illegal abortions.

On the heels of the hospital raids came an announcement that the California State Board of Medical Examiners was filing disciplinary charges against two prominent San Francisco physicians, Paul J. Shively of St. Luke's Hospital and Seymour Smith of San Francisco Memorial Hospital, for performing abortions on women with German measles. The abortions they had done had also been approved by hospital abortion committees. The two men faced revocation of their licenses. Shively and Smith admitted they had performed therapeutic abortions on women exposed to rubella.

Overnight the San Francisco medical community rallied around the accused physicians. Dr. George Herzog, president of the San Francisco Medical Society, described Shively and Smith as "top obstetricians in town and in the state" and, when asked if he had performed any abortions on women exposed to rubella, replied, "I'm sorry I haven't, because this is a distinguished company of doctors. They are humanitarians." Herzog said that doctors throughout the city were in a furor and aroused to a battle-ready pitch. Within days the city's obstetricians and gynecologists voted ten to one to support the two accused doctors. The San Francisco Medical Society met soon after the indictments were announced and voted 104 to 10 to call for broader abortion laws.

Despite support within the medical community, the immediate effect of the controversy was to halt all abortions in the city. By the end of May, lawyers for the San Francisco hospitals insisted that abortions be halted until the law was cleared up. Most physicians had stopped doing them anyway. Pregnant women exposed to rubella were forced to go elsewhere for abortions. Those who could afford to do so traveled to another state or out of the country, but poor women who had been exposed to German measles simply had to run the greatly increased risk of giving birth to a severely deformed child.

Doctors organized a statewide California Committee on Therapeutic Abortions to fund the defense of their colleagues who had been charged with illegal abortion. The committee immediately voted to embark on an educational campaign to promote greater public understanding of the need for liberalized abortion laws. Most of the committee members were San Francisco physicians, but also serving on the board was the Reverend Lester Kinsolving, a founder of the New York–based Clergy Consultation Service, the group that had pioneered in abortion referrals.

A reform bill in the works in the California legislature since 1963 had been killed twice in committee, primarily, as its current sponsor Representative Anthony Beilenson noted, because so little support had been forthcoming from the 22,000 members of the California Medical Society. Virtually overnight, however, Beilenson found himself with the support he needed to push through the bill, and in 1967 a liberalized bill passed the California state legislature.

Meanwhile the accused doctors received suspended sentences, which they later appealed in court and won. The California State Board of Medical Examiners, after much dilly-dallying, finally reprimanded one doctor and suspended the licenses of eight others for ninety days.

Dr. McNulty's attempt at cracking down on illegal abortions by licensed doctors had backfired miserably, and he soon resigned from the California Board of Medical Examiners. Instead of solidifying disapproval of abortion, his action had spurred a response on the part of those who wanted reform.

Physicians across the country, many of whom had bent the abortion laws themselves, were alarmed at the events in San Francisco. For years so-called legal abortion had been the exclusive domain of the medical profession, and law enforcement officials had confined themselves to going after illegal abortionists. Now it seemed that physicians' unspoken immunity had been shattered. No one could feel safe until the issue was resolved.

Physicians, who fifty years earlier had used abortion to solidify themselves professionally, would now break ranks publicly over the very same issue. From now on they would be at the forefront of the drive to reform the abortion laws. Not surprisingly, given their history with abortion, their support would at times be halfhearted and ambivalent, but for their own good they could no longer ignore the growing concern over restrictive abortion laws. At last the stage was set for reform.

Part II

IN THE
LOWER COURT

5

Suing the State

Eight weeks passed between the first meeting of McCorvey, Weddington, and Coffee and the filing of the case, not a lot of time in terms of what was needed to prepare a legal case—but too much time for McCorvey, who still hoped against the odds that she might be able to get an abortion. During those weeks, Weddington and Coffee found themselves moving from the task of theorizing about defeating the state's abortion laws to the challenge of actually doing something about them.

The Christmas holidays of 1969 slowed everything down, and researching the case took time. Before they began their research, Coffee and Weddington met several more times with Norma McCorvey and the Does. The Does were no problem, committed as they were to the case, but Norma was somewhat worrisome. She was having difficulty caring for herself and had gone underground, staying, to use her own words, in a succession of "flophouses for hippies" and with various female friends.

Coffee and Weddington often had trouble contacting her, and they worried that she would change her mind about being a plaintiff but not bother to notify them of her decision. Theirs was not a family law case, where a lawyer needed regular contact with the client to check on family finances or the children's welfare. Once the facts of the abortion case had been established, there was little reason to be in touch with McCorvey. Still, either Coffee or Weddington, usually Weddington, called her whenever there was something to report or, as was more often the case, when nothing was happening. They stayed in touch with her mostly to reassure themselves that she was not having second thoughts about the case. And they did that less and less as they became preoccupied with preparing the case.

The Texas abortion law consisted of six separate articles:

Article 1191. Abortion
If any person shall designedly administer to a pregnant woman or knowingly procure to be administered with her consent any drug or medicine, or shall use towards her any violence or any means whatever externally or internally applied, and thereby procure any abortion, he shall be confined in the penitentiary not less than two nor more than five years; if it be done without her consent, the punishment shall be doubled. By "abortion" is meant that the life of the fetus or embryo shall be destroyed in the woman's womb or that premature birth thereof be caused.
Article 1192. Furnishing the means
Any person who furnishes the means for procuring an abortion knowing the purpose intended is guilty as an accomplice.
Article 1193. Attempt at abortion
If the means used shall fail to produce an abortion, the offender is nevertheless guilty of an attempt to produce abortion, provided it be shown that such means were calculated to produce that result, and shall be fined not less than one hundred nor more than one thousand dollars.
Article 1194. Murder in producing abortion
If the death of the mother is occasioned by an abortion so produced or by an attempt to affect the same, it is murder.
Article 1195. Destroying the unborn child
Whoever shall during parturition of the mother destroy the vitality or life in a child in a state of being born and before actual birth, which child would otherwise have been born alive, shall be confined in the penitentiary for life or for not less than five years.
Article 1196. By medical advice
Nothing in this chapter applies to an abortion procured or attempted by medical advice for the purpose of saving the life of the mother.

Weddington and Coffee decided they would challenge the constitutionality of Articles 1191 through 1194 and 1196. Article 1195, which referred to destruction of the fetus during the process of birth, could be read as a straightforward malpractice law, so they felt no challenge was necessary.

The two women were grateful that the Texas abortion statute, enacted in 1859, was what reformers referred to as an "old-style" law, compared with the "new-style" reform laws that had been written in the late 1960s. The Texas law was unusually restrictive and permitted abortion only to save the mother's life, not even in cases of incest or rape. In contrast, the new reform legislation typically added therapeutic exceptions—to preserve the mother's physical or mental health, to prevent serious fetal deformity, and to terminate pregnancies resulting from rape or incest. In theory these new laws were supposed to make abortion more widely available. In practice they made it less accessible since complicated administrative procedures, such as residency, age, and consent requirements, hindered the abortion process, especially for women who did not know how to cut through red tape.

The constitutionality of some of the so-called reform laws was already being challenged in courts, at considerable time and expense. With an old law, a court challenge could be straightforward and uncomplicated, or so the two women hoped. They would not have to spend a lot of time and money amassing statistical evidence that the laws were being administered in a discriminatory fashion, nor would they have to pay expert witnesses to attest to the fact that consent or age requirements denied women access to abortion. Instead, they could base their challenge on a single, straightforward issue, the idea that the Texas abortion law was unconstitutional.

Coffee and Weddington could not have undertaken the case had they been required to spend much money on it. Their only source of funds was personal, and neither woman earned much money. Since both were now working at full-time jobs, Coffee at her law firm and Weddington as Ft. Worth's first woman assistant city attorney, all research would have to be done in their spare time. The subject of fees never came up with their clients. The Does were employed but did not earn very much and lived in a tiny one-bedroom apartment, and Norma McCorvey had no home and was barely making ends meet working part-time as a waitress or bartender. Had the case been undertaken by a major law firm, even on a pro bono basis, considerably more money and manpower would have been devoted to its preparation. A law firm would assign several associates or junior partners to do the initial research; the women had no one but themselves. Fortunately, their expenses were minor, consisting only of some nominal court fees.

Legal research is not unlike looking for a needle in a haystack, and although it has been made easier in recent years by desktop computers and Lexis, a legal database that produces almost instantaneous results, it still tends to be tedious work. One begins with a theory—in Coffee and Weddington's case the idea that the current Texas abortion law was unconstitutional—and then looks for material, either in the form of important law journal articles, precedent-setting cases, or in their case, since material was sparse, prior cases of any kind, to support the theory. Coffee and Weddington spent hours combing bibliographies and indexes for clues to cases or journal articles that might be relevant.

The use of the courts to attack the constitutionality of a law was a recent development. As a legal tool, it came into widespread use during the 1950s and 1960s, an era of expansionism in civil rights. Lawyers who chose to challenge laws were often required to mine new territory within the Constitution, to seek connections where none had previously existed. It was exciting and even exhilarating work, but it also required creativity and thoughtfulness and sometimes more than a little daring. Above all, of course, the results had to be persuasive.

Both women believed, as did most lawyers working on abortion, that any constitutional challenge to the abortion laws would be based on the Fourteenth Amendment, which guaranteed equal protection under the law. Beyond this, Coffee and Weddington had little idea whether there were other grounds for overturning the laws. They began by looking for other abortion cases, ones that might support their theories or provide new ones.

The American legal system, based on the English common-law system, relies heavily on precedent—that is, previously decided cases. Most judges are reluctant to reverse a body of decisions pointing in one direction. Not all cases, though, are considered precedent setting. A court pays more attention to cases decided in its own state than to those decided in another state where the laws might be different, although an important decision by another state's high court carries weight, especially if the court is respected for its opinions.

Coffee and Weddington found surprisingly little to go on. Few suits had been brought involving abortion, and even fewer were important enough to set precedents. No abortion case had yet come before the Supreme Court, and only a few state courts had dealt with the issue. They found only one recorded case in Texas.

Watson v. *the State of Texas,* decided in 1880, involved a young woman named Mattie Shook, who became pregnant by a man known only as Watson while living with him, his wife, and his children. Because he was a physician, Watson told Shook he would give her a medicine that would cause her to miscarry. Despite taking ergot, the drug he prescribed, even more frequently than he had ordered, she failed to miscarry. A note describing Mattie's condition was sent to the doctor's wife, reputedly from Mattie's fiancé but actually from Mattie herself, and this led to the court case. Mattie Shook testified against the physician.

A lower court found the man guilty of "designedly" administering an abortifacient, an illegal act under the Texas antiabortion law, but a Texas appellate court reversed the lower court on technical grounds. The court's reluctance to punish the abortionist twenty years after abortion had been outlawed in Texas was interesting and even persuasive, but the case was of little help to Weddington and Coffee, based as it was on a technicality rather than on any constitutional grounds.

Another case, which had been heard by the Supreme Court, proved to be much more important. Even though it did not deal with abortion, it provided them with the constitutional grounds they were seeking to build their case. *Griswold* v. *Connecticut* was a challenge to a one-hundred-year-old Connecticut law that forbade the sale of birth control devices.

The case was instigated on November 1, 1961, when Estelle Griswold, executive director of the Planned Parenthood League of Connecticut, and Charles Lee Buxton, a respected physician and head of obstetrics and gynecology at Yale University, opened a clinic in New Haven, Connecticut, from which they planned to provide people with birth control information and dispense contraceptives. They also hoped to provoke some kind of legal action that could be turned into a court challenge to Connecticut's archaic law. Within days of opening the clinic, Griswold and Buxton were arrested for giving birth control information and instruction to a married couple. They were tried in the Connecticut courts, where they lost and from which they appealed to the Supreme Court.

Two respected and talented women, Harriet Pilpel and Catherine Roraback, originally handled the *Griswold* case, but when it became apparent the case was headed to the Supreme Court, Planned Parenthood acquiesced to the commonly held belief that women should not argue before the Supreme Court and looked for male legal counsel. They found Fowler Harper, a law professor at Yale and First Amendment specialist who believed the case could be argued on the ground that denying a doctor the right to discuss and inform patients about birth control interfered with his right to free speech. The lawyers decided to structure their case around the First and Fourteenth amendments.

They also toyed with the idea that the case involved privacy but felt it was too shaky and unestablished a right to use it. Even though they were mounting a test case designed to challenge the Connecticut law, they owed their clients the best-possible defense. They would have done nothing further about privacy had Fowler not seen a law journal article by the respected New York University law professor (and later dean) Norman D. Redlich entitled "Are There 'Certain Rights'. . . Retained by the People?" It suggested an alternate interpretation of the Ninth Amendment, which was traditionally read as reserving to the states any powers not specifically ascribed to the federal government. Redlich suggested that the Ninth Amendment reserved unspecified rights to the people, not the states. His thinking meshed neatly with the idea of a privacy right, and after reading Redlich's article, Fowler was convinced that they should use the Ninth Amendment and, more important, should base their defense on the idea of a privacy right. Even though the Constitution said nothing directly about privacy, Fowler, along with many other constitutional scholars, was increasingly certain that a privacy right could be inferred. The grounds of the *Griswold* case were expanded to include all possible constitutional references to privacy: the First, Third, Fourth, Fifth, Ninth, and Fourteenth amendments.

In two earlier challenges to the Connecticut birth control law, *State* v. *Nelson* and *Poe* v. *Ullman*, decided in 1939 and 1961 respectively, the issue of privacy had been touched upon. In *State* v. *Nelson*,

J. Warren Upson, Nelson's lawyer, had filed a pleading in which he had argued that the right to decide to have children, and concomitantly the right to use contraception, were natural rights with which the state should not be permitted to interfere. *Poe* v. *Ullman* was appealed to the Supreme Court. Reluctant to become embroiled in the birth control controversy, after hearing the oral arguments, the Court side-stepped the issues and declined to decide the case on grounds that it presented no real controversy. Justice William Douglas wrote a strong dissent that echoed Upson's thinking about natural rights and privacy.

It was not until Justice Douglas wrote the *Griswold* opinion in 1965 that he and the High Court finally articulated the privacy right. The Connecticut statute prohibiting the use of birth control was unconstitutional, he wrote, because its enforcement violated "the zone of privacy created by several fundamental constitutional guarantees." Among the grounds he cited as support for a right of privacy were the First, Third, Fourth, Fifth, Ninth, and Fourteenth amendments.

The privacy right looked good to Weddington and Coffee. If they followed the thinking in *Griswold*, they would have not one but several solid constitutional grounds on which to base a woman's constitutional right to abortion.

The *Griswold* case seemed so uniquely tailored for the development of an abortion right, in fact, that at the time it had been rendered, it had set off speculation in scholarly circles that the Supreme Court might be using the case as a signal to civil rights lawyers, an indication that after years of rejecting abortion cases, the Court was at last willing to hear one. Tom Emerson, the Yale Law School professor who took over the *Griswold* case when Fowler died in 1963 and argued it before the Supreme Court, wrote about this theory. In an article entitled "Nine Justices in Search of a Doctrine," Emerson suggested that no other explanation was adequate to describe why the Court had taken a case like *Griswold*. At minimum the nation's top court wanted to hear cases of national scope, and the Connecticut birth control case certainly did not qualify. No other state had a law even remotely similar to Connecticut's archaic law banning the use of birth control.

Nevertheless, reasons existed not to rely entirely on *Griswold* to build their case. For one thing, it was at the time and had remained one of the more controversial cases the Court had ever decided, garnering some of the most unqualified praise and severe criticism of any Supreme Court decision in years. Constitutional scholars were sharply divided over the existence of a privacy right. The decision's defenders applauded the Court for having acknowledged a right they believed existed even though it was not specifically written into the Constitution, while its critics were appalled to think that the Supreme Court had created a right where, in their eyes, at least, none had existed previously. They could not believe that a right not mentioned anywhere in the Constitution—and one about birth control no less— could be enshrined alongside such treasured values as freedom of speech or equal treatment under the law. Even some scholars who acceded to the idea that privacy was a constitutionally protected right still felt that the idea of marital privacy, let alone sexual privacy, went too far.

It was true, as the loose constructionists (those who thought the Constitution was subject to broader interpretation) maintained, that the Constitution said nothing directly about marital privacy, birth control, or, for that matter, abortion; but privacy was not an entirely new constitutional concept. Without giving it a name, the Supreme Court had been deciding privacy cases for decades. Many jurists traced the concept of legal privacy to Justice Louis Brandeis's famous dissent in the 1928 case *Olmstead* v. *United States*, in which he wrote that the American people had the "right to be let alone." Douglas seemed to have anticipated this criticism because in the *Griswold* opinion he listed several notable Supreme Court rulings that had supported a right to privacy—*Pierce* v. *Society of Sisters*, which established the right of parents to educate their children as they saw fit, and *Meyer* v. *Nebraska*, which established the right to teach a foreign language.

Another drawback to using privacy was its newness. Even apart from any controversy surrounding it, privacy was a relatively undeveloped area of the law. No one could predict how the right would fare with time, whether it would take hold as an established constitutional principle or fade away within a few years. No one even knew the best way to present it in the courtroom—possibly to a judge who was not familiar with, or inclined to accept, a new legal concept. Countering this drawback was the fact, revealed in even the most cursory review of family law decisions, that privacy (whether or not it was called that) was still the pillar that held up many family law cases.

In a sense, Weddington and Coffee had no other viable ground for the establishment of an abortion right. They decided to use it.

As for the specific amendments that Douglas had listed in the *Griswold* opinion, they, too, seemed well suited to an abortion case strategy. Coffee and Weddington had originally thought they might base their case entirely on the Fourteenth Amendment, but experts with whom they had talked—especially Harriet Pilpel, who had pioneered in the birth control area—felt that a better tactic would be to give the Court as many potential grounds as possible for deciding the case and let it choose from among them.

Prior to *Griswold*, lawyers had tended to go into court with one solid ground on which a decision could be based, but once Douglas had described privacy as a fundamental right protected not by one amendment, but by "penumbras" from several amendments and even the entire Bill of Rights, constitutional lawyers changed their approach and tried to offer as many grounds as they could think of for finding a law unconstitutional. Weddington and Coffee thought the strategy might work equally well in a federal three-judge court.

Support for using an array of grounds also came from another source. A young University of Alabama law professor named Roy Lucas, eager to make a name for himself in abortion reform, published an article in the June 1968 *North Carolina Law Review*, in which he described several potential grounds for legalizing abortion, most notably the First, Fourth, Fifth and Fourteenth amendments.

Lucas was the first to write about the grounds for a constitutional challenge, but it would not be fair to say that this line of thinking originated with him. The idea of developing constitutional grounds to challenge the abortion laws was very much in the air, particularly among East Coast abortion lawyers such as Harriet Pilpel, ACLU lawyer Melvin Wulf, and New York Law School professor Cyril Means, with whom Lucas had contacts. Nevertheless, Lucas's article had become something of a bible for constitutional scholars working on abortion, one that Coffee and Weddington would have had trouble overlooking in their research since there were so few sources to turn to. In our talks, however, neither Weddington nor Coffee could recall having relied on Lucas's article, but even if they did not use it directly, it seems unlikely that they would not have been influenced by it, if only by hearing about it secondhand.

Once Coffee and Weddington had decided on the potential

grounds, they actually spent little time mulling them over. Theirs was not the kind of case that invited intense scholarly research; a far more important concern was that they get their case under way while Norma McCorvey was still pregnant. The two women read enough about each amendment to make sure they understood its application and to decide whether or not to use it.

The First Amendment protected free speech, including people's right of association. Some jurists felt the abortion laws interfered with the freedom of association between a woman and her physician, but many legal scholars thought it was a weak basis for overturning the abortion law, even though Douglas had written extensively about First Amendment rights in *Griswold*. Pilpel disliked using the First Amendment, for example, and Emerson thought it was a poor line of reasoning, one that did not provide a "favorable opportunity" for pressing forward in abortion reform. Coffee and Weddington were not eager to tie an abortion right to physicians any more than they had to, but they saw no reason to exclude this argument.

The *Griswold* opinion also relied on the Third, Fourth and Fifth amendments. The two women decided almost immediately to discard the Third Amendment. Although it dealt with privacy by denying the government the right to quarter soldiers in people's homes during peacetime, it had no real tie to abortion.

They planned to use the Fourth Amendment, which protected citizens from unreasonable search and seizure, and the Fifth Amendment, which protected people from self-incrimination, largely because both had been mentioned in *Griswold*. In the opinion, Douglas had questioned the extent to which the state would have to go to enforce the anticontraception law, asking, "Would we allow the police to search the sacred precincts of marital bedrooms for telltale signs of the use of contraceptives?" The idea of doing that, he continued, "was repulsive to the notion of privacy surrounding the marital relationship." A parallel situation occurred with laws restricting abortion, Coffee and Weddington felt, in that enforcement of the abortion laws involved invading the privacy of the physician's office. The *Griswold* opinion held that the self-incrimination clause of the Fifth Amendment protected the privacy right by creating a zone of privacy around citizens that protected them from government intrusion; Coffee and Weddington would use it.

Their own contribution was to include the Eighth Amendment, which forbade cruel and unusual punishment. Both women knew that no judge was likely to rule that denying women abortions was cruel and unusual punishment, but they thought its inclusion made a poignant point nonetheless.

They were less certain about using the Ninth Amendment, even though Douglas had included it in his majority opinion and it had been the focus of a concurring opinion by Justice Arthur Goldberg. Their reluctance to use it was based mostly on the fact that they knew so little about it. Often considered the amendment that created states' rights, the Ninth was rarely used. Neither woman had seen Redlich's article that had influenced Fowler to use the Ninth Amendment in the *Griswold* defense, nor did they know that the Ninth was generating excitement in academic circles, where constitutional scholars were beginning to talk of putting it to more expansive use. They only knew that *Griswold* was one of the rare occasions when the Ninth Amendment had been used to overturn a state law, and that did not seem to bode well for their purposes.

In Texas, where abortion was already viewed as a states' rights issue, the Ninth Amendment was interpreted as reserving to the states all powers not specifically granted to the federal government. Coffee and Weddington were sure that even if they could prove that the present law was unconstitutional, the state of Texas would still be able to make a strong claim that the writing of a new law was up to the state legislature. And the state's lawyers might even argue that the court had no business striking the law, that this, too, was the province of the legislature. (Opponents would always maintain that abortion should be regulated by the states; they viewed any kind of federal court ruling on the issue as anathema.) Using the Ninth Amendment to strike the abortion laws would, as far as the state was concerned, be like waving a red flag in front of a bull. Despite this, both women saw that the Ninth Amendment offered a substantial ground for recognizing the right to privacy and decided they had to use it.

The constitutional amendment that offered the most support for overturning the abortion laws, at least in the eyes of many legal experts, was the Fourteenth. Generally, it guaranteed every person equal protection under the law. Specifically, the due process clause of the Fourteenth Amendment required that laws be written clearly enough for the average person to understand. A law that was vaguely written, for example, was unconstitutional because it caused confusion about who was protected by it and the circumstances under which protection was extended—the very thing physicians objected to about the abortion laws.

They argued that they were forced to interpret the laws each time they performed an abortion. Physicians claimed confusion arose over what constituted a life-threatening illness because the laws offered no clear-cut guidelines and, as a result, were unevenly applied. Some physicians interpreted the law in its strictest sense and did abortions only when a woman's life was truly threatened, while others stretched the law to cover situations that might or might not be life-threatening—instances where a woman claimed her mental or physical health was in jeopardy, for example. From the physicians' point of view, therefore, the Fourteenth Amendment offered the best basis for overturning the abortion laws.

Coffee was afraid, however, that any ruling based on the Fourteenth would leave control of abortion in the physicians' hands rather than in the hands of women, where she believed it belonged. If they got a ruling based on the Fourteenth Amendment, she feared there would be nothing to stop the Texas legislature from writing a new, crystal-clear law, possibly with the assistance of physicians, that still left the abortion decision in the hands of doctors—and undermined the right of women to decide for themselves.

Coffee, who wanted at least to make a stab at establishing a woman's constitutional right to abortion, had no trouble persuading Weddington to share her view. Both women had come to believe that a woman had a right to control her own body, which included the decision to terminate a pregnancy, but they were less sure that the general populace or even a liberal court would share that conviction. So rather than risk everything, they opted to follow a more conservative course of action and include the Fourteenth Amendment with all its potential risks to women.

They developed a strategy in which they would stress those amendments that addressed a woman's right to abortion in their oral arguments but would also be prepared to fall back on the Fourteenth Amendment if necessary. In part, they chose this strategy because it would enable them to use two major decisions that were handed down as they were preparing their own cases. These involved abortion laws that had been declared unconstitutional on grounds of vagueness, but in each lawsuit the courts had also had something interesting to say about women's rights to abortion.

In *People* v. *Belous*, handed down in September 1969, Dr. Leon Belous, an obstetrician-gynecologist practicing in Los Angeles, was indicted for abortion. The case drew nationwide attention in part because the physician involved was so respected, but also because this was one of the rare occasions when the law interfered with a physician's right to practice medicine. In this instance the physician had not even performed the abortion himself but had merely referred a patient to an illegal abortionist.

A former naval commander in the medical corps during World War II, Belous was chief of obstetrics and gynecology at Cedars of Lebanon Hospital when he was indicted. He had long thought physicians were hypocritical in their treatment of women who requested abortions, and although he did not perform them, he had begun openly to refer his patients to skilled illegal abortionists. Belous, who appeared frequently on local radio and television shows, made his views widely known.

Early in 1967 Belous was contacted by a couple who said they desperately needed an abortion and threatened to seek one on the black market if that were all they could obtain. Initially Belous said he could not help, but then he relented and met with the woman to examine her and confirm her pregnancy. He referred her to a Dr. Karl Lairtus, a licensed physician from Mexico who had recently moved to California. Belous wrote a prescription for an antibiotic and encouraged the woman to see him for a postsurgical check-up.

She contacted Dr. Lairtus and arranged to undergo an abortion in his office. While she was resting in his office after the surgery, the police, who had been tipped off by another patient, raided the office and arrested Lairtus. They seized his notebooks, which led them to an entry naming Belous as the referring physician. Belous was also arrested and charged with being an accomplice to an illegal abortion.

A three-year legal struggle ensued, during which Belous was supported by the American Civil Liberties Union as well as his own counsel. In the first trial, a municipal court judge dismissed the case on grounds that Belous's office had been searched illegally. The district attorney then convened a grand jury and reindicted Belous on the woman's testimony that he had referred her to an illegal abortionist. Belous was convicted by a Roman Catholic judge in Superior Court, and on appeal his conviction was upheld in an appellate court, in which two of the three sitting judges were Roman Catholic. Belous then took his case to the California Supreme Court. He insisted that his defense be made on constitutional grounds, specifically a woman's right to receive medical care.

On September 5, 1969, in a four-to-three decision, the California Supreme Court ruled that the California abortion law was unconstitutional on grounds that it was vague under the due process clause of the Fourteenth Amendment. The court declined to say that abortion should be regulated in any way except for the fact that it should be performed by a licensed physician. Noting that 178 deans of medical schools had filed a friend-of-the-court brief supporting Belous and a more liberalized abortion law, the California court commented that the law had "always recognized that the pregnant woman's right to life takes precedence over any interest the state may have in the unborn." The present state law, the court said, must be rejected "as an invalid infringement upon the woman's constitutional rights."

Proponents and opponents alike were surprised by the unequivocal note struck by the *Belous* decision. No one had anticipated such a broad ruling or such a clear-cut victory for pro-choice forces. From Coffee and Weddington's perspective, however, the most important thing about the decision was that for the first time ever, a court had directly addressed the issue of a woman's constitutional right to abortion. More important, the court stated that her right was based on privacy.

The *Belous* case also marked a turning point in abortion reform. Previously reformers had focused on the state legislatures as a means of changing the abortion laws, but now they read the California Supreme Court decision as a sign that they might make more progress in the courts. Many reform lawyers would jump ship from the state legislatures and chart a new course that would send them sailing straight into the federal courts. Within the next year or so, the Supreme Court was going to receive a lot of requests to docket abortion cases.

The other case, *U.S.* v. *Vuitch*, involved a licensed physician, one who practiced in the nation's capital. C. Milan Vuitch, who was licensed in Washington, D.C., Maryland, New York, and Virginia, had been operating several abortion clinics, one within blocks of the White House. Vuitch was a flamboyant, essentially antiestablishment character who had performed abortions in Yugoslavia before they were legal there. He emigrated to the United States after marrying an American woman. In 1957, having retrained as a physician here, he performed his first abortion in the United States. Vuitch felt that a loophole in the Washington, D.C., law permitted abortion to preserve a woman's health as well as her life, and that the abortions he was doing were legal. He invited arrest by openly performing abortions in his clinics and by taking referrals from problem pregnancy counseling services and physicians all over the country. So sure was Vuitch of his rights that he openly courted a test case. On May 1, 1968, while he was operating on a patient, his office was raided.

Because Washington, D.C., was federal territory, Vuitch was arraigned in federal court. His first court challenge was successful. On November 10, 1969, Judge Arnold Gesell of the U.S. District Court of the District of Columbia ruled that the Washington, D.C., law was unconstitutional because of vagueness. He further declared that the law provided "no clear standard to guide either the doctor, the jury, or the Court. . . . There has been, moreover, an increasing indication in decisions of the Supreme Court of the United States that as a secular matter a woman's liberty and right of privacy extends to family, marriage, and sex matters and may well include the right to remove an unwanted child in the early stages of pregnancy."

The *Vuitch* ruling was important because it was the first time a federal court had overthrown an abortion law. Abortion reformers across the country took heart because now not one but two abortion laws (at opposite ends of the country, no less) had been overturned on the grounds that they were unconstitutional. While Coffee and Weddington still had grave doubts about using vagueness as a reason to overturn the abortion laws, they no longer had any doubts about whether the courts were willing to tackle abortion. *Belous* and *Vuitch* gave great impetus to their case, and they knew it.

Like most pro-choice reformers, and like many women, in fact, Coffee and Weddington tended to dismiss arguments about the fetus's rights, which were, they felt, always inferior to the woman's. Still, they knew that the subject of fetal rights was almost sure to be raised by the state at some point during the hearing, and they had to be prepared to respond to it.

Based on the Constitution, birth appeared to be the point at which a human was entitled to the legal rights of a person. (This was also the case in most religions, they knew, but they did not want to broach the issues of religion in court if they could avoid them.) The

79

Fourteenth Amendment defined a person as anyone born or natural-ized. It was true that property and other rights had been accorded to fetuses, but the assumption of these rights had always been dependent upon live birth. There were no cases where rights were granted to a fetus purely on the basis of its being a fetus, for the simple reason that, in the eyes of the law, at least, it was not yet a person.

While the issue of whether or not a fetus was a person was relatively clear-cut from a legal standpoint, it was far less so else-where, especially among philosophers and ethicists. On the one hand, Coffee and Weddington worried that the state would raise nonlegal—and perhaps emotionally explosive—issues of fetal rights. On the other hand, if they themselves stayed with purely legal arguments and did not acknowledge the emotional element, they might also lose the support of some women.

Any woman who has ever been pregnant, even unwillingly, can attest to the fact that her feelings for the unborn fetus in her womb are far more complicated than any law can possibly allow for. Many people who fully supported a woman's right to abortion were not so clear about whether the fetus had no rights at any stage of pregnancy. Weddington and Coffee were all too aware of the shades of gray that colored the abortion issue generally and the issue of fetal rights specifically. They knew they would have to walk a tightrope while balancing the unemotional stance of the law and the emotional views of most persons.

Because of this, they decided to approach any discussion of fetal rights cautiously, using only the broadest possible terms in order to give as many people as possible room to support a woman's right to abortion. In part, this decision was made out of respect for each individual woman's right to decide when an abortion was appropriate for her; in part, it was done out of political savvy. The two lawyers even agreed that, if pushed, they would acknowledge that some limits could be placed on the abortion right.

At this early stage of preparing the case, neither woman was thinking in terms of total reform, anyway. The idea that the state or, for that matter, physicians, would have nothing to say about the regulation of abortion was still unimaginable to Coffee and Weddington and most other reformers working on liberalization. Everyone seemed to agree that even if a woman's right to abortion could be established, it would still be a limited right, one the government could and would regulate, if only in the woman's best interests. The government, for example, could require that abortions be done only in a hospital or before a certain stage of pregnancy, in order to protect a woman's health. As they got deeper into the abortion issue, Coffee and Weddington would each come to believe that the woman's right was unequivocal and should not be infringed upon by anyone; but they knew this was too radical a view to present in court—or anywhere else publicly, for that matter.

Only one other issue remained to be discussed—the discrimination women suffered because of the restrictive abortion laws. Weddington felt strongly that she wanted to stress this. Imbued with a deep sense of social justice, she was acutely aware of how unmarried, pregnant women were treated in our society, the fact that they were forced to drop out of high school or to attend alternate schools, that they could not participate in school activities. Many colleges and universities would not admit unmarried, pregnant women. Employers discriminated against them in their hiring practices, and of course, many of these same prejudices applied to married, pregnant women. Weddington felt strongly that unless women could control when they bore children, they could not fully control their own lives, and she wanted to emphasize this as she prepared Norma McCorvey's case. Coffee readily agreed that these were important issues.

The two women worked well together despite the considerable differences in their personalities. Weddington, although not a particularly outgoing person, looked like an extrovert next to Coffee. She also wanted more outside support for their decisions and approached several of her former law professors at the University of Texas, as well as such New York reformers as Harriet Pilpel and Cyril Means. Coffee, perhaps because of her greater legal experience, felt less need to rely on outsiders and was more wary of doing so.

Although Weddington was not naturally given to dealing with abstractions, the two women soon decided that she would research the merits of the case while Coffee tackled the procedural legal issues such as standing and mootness, with which she was more familiar. If Coffee minded or even realized that Weddington was taking over the more glamorous aspect of preparing the case, she never acknowledged it even to herself.

* * *

Coffee soon determined that their case properly belonged before a three-judge court. These special courts, composed of three judges from one federal appellate circuit, had been established by the Three-Judge Court Act of 1910 in response to the accelerated economic expansion throughout the United States since the end of the nineteenth century. Three-judge courts were also an attempt to resolve a struggle between the federal government and the states over who would regulate the burgeoning interstate commerce—or to be more specific, an attempt to thwart the federal judges' powers to interfere with the states. The thinking was that three judges would act with greater caution than one and would thus serve as a check on one another's powers.

In 1937 another three-judge court act, as laden with political overtones as the first, required three-judge courts to hear all cases involving challenges to the constitutionality of state laws. (A companion law made them responsible for hearing challenges to federal laws.) Although these laws were ostensibly part of President Franklin D. Roosevelt's efforts to reform the courts, in reality they were a response to fears that federal district judges acting alone would strike down his New Deal legislation.

From the beginning, three-judge courts were an anachronism in the legal system. Shortly after they were established, other laws were passed that eliminated the problem of a single federal judge usurping the states' powers, but the three-judge courts continued to exist even though they were rarely used until the 1960s. That was when civil rights lawyers discovered that they provided a unique forum for striking down discriminatory state and federal laws. At a time when the Supreme Court was proving to be especially sympathetic to civil rights suits, the three-judge courts provided direct access to the top court in the land by allowing, in certain instances, specific parties to lawsuits to bypass the federal appellate court.

Between 1955 and 1959, the average number of cases heard annually by three-judge courts numbered a paltry forty-nine. From 1960 to 1964, as the civil rights movement gathered strength, the average annual caseload expanded to ninety-five. In 1970, at the height of the civil rights movement, three-judge courts heard 162 cases on civil rights alone. In 1973, the year of the *Roe* v. *Wade* decision, 183 civil rights cases were argued in front of three-judge panels.

The direct route of appeal to the Supreme Court was not the only reason Coffee and Weddington were happy that their case would be heard by a three-judge court. Once a three-judge court was convened, the judges were obligated to hear the case as soon as possible, even if doing so meant an interruption in their normal schedule. Because the judges had to suspend their regular work, they liked to dispense with the cases as quickly and efficiently as possible. They were eager to avoid evidentiary trials and preferred to try cases on the law whenever possible. Short briefs were encouraged.

Not everyone in the reform movement was happy with the haste that typically surrounded a three-judge court. In Georgia and New York, where abortion cases were then being tried before three-judge courts, lawyers were fighting a losing battle to force the courts to hear evidence they believed would strengthen their cases. The courts, less than enthusiastic about the political overtones of some of the evidence—depositions taken from women who had undergone illegal abortions, for example—were declining to hear it.

But the idea of being able to move quickly through the system up to the Supreme Court, if it came to that, held greater appeal to Coffee and Weddington with each passing week. The *Belous* and *Vuitch* cases, with their widespread publicity, had created a sense of urgency over abortion. The nation's attention grew more intense with each successive decision, and anticipation was building for a Supreme Court decision that would settle the issue. Coffee and Weddington were beginning to feel as if they were in a horse race, and having the right to go into a three-judge court seemed a little bit like winning the pole position.

They were also not unhappy that their cases fell under the jurisdiction of the progressive Fifth Circuit, a bench that had proven particularly receptive to civil rights cases. Legal experts would later laud the justices of the Fifth Circuit as the real heroes of the civil rights movement, noting that it was they who had assumed responsibility for the day-to-day enforcement of the decisions handed down by the Supreme Court.

One small point still bothered Coffee: Now that she had Norma McCorvey, who was pregnant, did she still need John and Mary Doe, the young couple who had volunteered themselves as plaintiffs a few months earlier? Weddington thought the Does' case was weak because Mary Doe was not pregnant, but Coffee wanted to keep them and file two separate suits, one with McCorvey and another with the Does. The two cases would eventually be combined, she realized, but she felt that filing two separate suits would improve her odds of drawing liberal, or at least sympathetic, judges. The judge in whose court a case was filed was, as a rule, appointed to the three-judge panel.

To the extent that she could manage it, Coffee also wanted a well-rounded case. Ideally she would have liked to have a physician on the case, but none had come forth to offer his services, and she had not pursued this. But at least her plaintiffs would include a pregnant, single woman (who by herself might be more easily discriminated against) and a married couple who was established and respected in the community.

Many jurists thought that only a physician could sue to liberalize the abortion laws, since they (and illegal abortionists) were the only ones who could be punished under the law. The woman who attempted to obtain an abortion was, in all but a few states, immune from prosecution. If she could not be prosecuted, she could not be injured—at least legally—by the law. Since one has to suffer a direct injury under the law in order to sue, lawyers had for years backed off from abortion cases involving pregnant women plaintiffs because they thought such cases could not be won.

Coffee and Weddington were convinced, however, that only by using a woman as a plaintiff could they establish that the laws outlawing abortion denied women their constitutional rights. They believed they could make a case that the woman was injured by the state's abortion laws, and that, as she had no other form of relief, the court had no choice but to consider her interests.

In late February 1970 Weddington and Coffee were still working on the case, almost obsessively checking and rechecking facts and technical legal points. They might have taken even longer had Coffee not received a call from Ruth Eyre, a reporter at the *Dallas Times Herald*, one of the two major Dallas dailies. She had heard of their case and wanted to write about it.

The fact that the press was about to break the story when they had not yet filed the case set Coffee in motion. She sat down one night after work and typed out the pleadings. In one of our conversations, she would muse that she did not know why she had rushed to file the case before the reporter broke the story rather than one or two days afterward. But perhaps it was the kind of pressure she needed at that point to prod her into action.

The typographical errors stood uncorrected; all legal phraseology was checked and rechecked. Coffee spent every spare minute of the next few days writing the original pleadings, which listed the plaintiffs' complaints and the legal action they sought to remedy these complaints. Since Weddington did not live in Dallas and was working full-time, she could not help.

On Tuesday, March 3, 1970, Coffee gathered up all the papers and carried them to the federal courthouse to file the original pleadings on the two separate suits, *Roe* v. *Wade* and *Does* v. *Wade.*

The plaintiffs asked for a declaratory judgment stating that the abortion statutes of Texas were unconstitutional and an injunction restraining Henry Wade, the chief law enforcement officer of Dallas County, from enforcing the laws. They claimed that the Texas statutes were unconstitutional on grounds that they were vague and abridged their right of privacy under the First, Fourth, Fifth, Eighth, Ninth, and Fourteenth amendments.

The first reaction came, not surprisingly, from the conservative *Dallas Times Herald,* which ran an editorial on Friday, March 6. Noting that the abortion laws were "badly in need of intelligent overhaul," the paper still found itself opposed to the suits: "We have no sympathy with the attempt of a married couple and of a single woman to get the existing abortion law declared unconstitutional by a Dallas federal court." Specifically, the paper took issue with the fact that the plaintiffs were "disguising their identities with fictional names. . . ." The newspaper's real objections to the cases, however, seemed to be that so serious a social problem was being tossed into the hands of a few judges.

6

The State Responds

On March 16, 1970, District Attorney Henry Wade was officially served papers notifying him that he was being sued by plaintiffs Jane Roe and John and Mary Doe, who were seeking a court order to prevent him from prosecution of future abortion cases. If law enforcement officials could not enforce the abortion laws, then Jane Roe would be free to obtain an abortion from a licensed physician.

Wade had been district attorney of Dallas County since 1950, when he had run as a young, upstart lawyer. Everyone—politicians and voters—acknowledged that he ran a tight ship. In fact, Wade's staff was unusually good for a district attorney's office. Several of Dallas's crack criminal lawyers had done a stint with the chief at one time or another. His office was considered an excellent training ground for a criminal lawyer. Wade was also famous as the prosecutor of Lee Harvey Oswald, President John F. Kennedy's assassin, and Jack Ruby, who had killed Oswald before he could come to trial.

If Wade, the father of three daughters and two sons, had any personal animosity against abortion, it never showed. A Democrat, he had supported Adlai Stevenson, and his wife was a professional volunteer whose primary cause was poor and homeless people. Wade was a self-made man with Calvinist roots and values. Like most Texas men of his upbringing and class, he was no admirer of feminists, but there were signs he did not dislike them and may even have had a grudging respect for them. During juror selection for Jack Ruby's trial, another lawyer urged Wade not to accept a woman who insisted she was "Ms.," not "Miss," but Wade rejected the idea, saying, "Naw, she'll be just fine. Those women libbers want to be tough as men."

For several years Wade's office, like most district attorneys' offices across the country, had instigated virtually no abortion prosecutions. District attorneys typically prosecuted an abortionist only when a complaint was filed by a police department, and that only happened when a woman showed up, usually at a large metropolitan hospital, with a badly bungled abortion and was willing to talk to the police about what had happened to her. Few women, even those who were seriously injured or maimed, were willing to press charges and risk having their plight become public knowledge. In the 1960s most women who underwent illegal abortions were unmarried, and pregnancy for an unmarried woman carried severe social stigma for her—and for the child, if she chose to bear it.

When a woman did press charges, the case invariably became a cause célèbre, and one such case every few years served to keep illegal abortion under control in a community. These notorious suits also served to paint an image in most people's minds of illegal abortion as a dangerous, risky procedure, a notion reformers did little to refute.

When I began to look into this aspect of abortion, several pro-choice reformers suggested that illegal abortion was not as dangerous as it had been depicted during the reform movement. Admittedly, an image of tens of thousands of women being maimed or killed each year by illegal abortions was so persuasive a piece of propaganda that the movement could be forgiven for its failure to double-check the facts. The exaggeration was also a safe one. Since these were illegal activities, no records were kept, and the death and injury rate was an impossible statistic to pin down. When a woman required medical treatment as a result of an illegal abortion, her physician often disguised the facts on her medical record so as to spare her any embarrassment.

Birth control expert Linda Gordon has investigated the idea that the rate might not even have been as high as the eight thousand to ten thousand deaths that were attributed annually to illegal abortion. She concluded that abortions done after the mid-nineteenth century were not particularly unsafe or life-threatening, largely because women had stopped using abortifacients, toxic chemicals that affected the body's entire system, to terminate pregnancies. Abortifacients were the most popular, as well as the most dangerous, method of abortion. By the end of the nineteenth century few women were using abortifacients, largely because the regular physicians had successfully driven the midwives out of practice and brought pharmacists under their control, to the point where medicines were administered and sold only under the direct orders of a physician.

Another factor that may have reduced the dangers of illegal abortion was suggested to me by several physicians. As abortifacients fell into disuse, surgical abortions replaced them. The restrictive laws passed between 1860 and 1880 did not alleviate abortion so much as drive it underground. And if one stands by the accepted medical belief that the surgeon who does the greatest number of operations and is thus able to maintain and even hone his skills is the best qualified, then women have probably been better off in the hands of competent but "illegal" abortionists who did hundreds of the minor surgeries every week than with the family doctor who did one abortion a year. Even the new techniques, such as antisepsis in the mid-1800s and vacuum aspiration in the mid-1960s, found their way to the offices of illegal abortionists.

The failure to strictly enforce the abortion laws, then, was at least partly a reaction to the public's changing perception of abortion. People heard less about disastrous abortions because fewer women were subjected to them. Fewer cases were prosecuted, and people became more receptive as a result to the idea of liberalizing the abortion laws. The change in the public's attitude, in turn, contributed to a growing disinterest on the part of law enforcment agencies, who had never been very concerned with pursuing what was essentially considered a victimless crime.

Even though it was not actively enforcing the Texas abortion law, the D.A.'s office could not be described as receptive to a challenge to it. In the 1960s most states' law enforcement agencies, including the Dallas District Attorney's office, looked upon the numerous civil rights challenges that began coming their way as frivolous. They resented the time they took up.

Nonetheless, given the times, Wade's office had been expecting some kind of attack on the laws that discriminated against women. They thought perhaps women would strike out against protectionist labor laws. No one thought the abortion law would be challenged, and it came as a shock when it was. There had been no sense among the conservative, mostly male lawyers in the D.A.'s office that any major discontent had been building among women regarding abortion. Besides, they tended to view the state's abortion law not as discriminatory against women so much as a statement about the moral standards society wanted to uphold. As a result, just as Weddington and Coffee had hoped, Wade's office was totally unprepared for their attack on the state's abortion laws. And from the minute *Roe* v. *Wade* and *Does* v. *Wade* were filed, Wade and his staff recognized that these were serious challenges and, therefore, potentially significant cases.

The attorney general's office quickly learned that Coffee and Weddington were reputable, capable lawyers, and that Coffee had clerked for Judge Sarah Hughes on the Fifth Circuit. The pleadings were carefully thought out and well written. However, this is not to say that anyone in the district attorney's office thought for a minute that the abortion laws stood a chance of being overturned. They did not, and they were sure they would prevail in any courtroom. Still, it was clear this was no frivolous lawsuit.

None of this helped anyone's mood in the D.A.'s office when Wade was served the papers. Wade's lawyers, who usually went to trial for murder, armed robbery, or rape, did not want to waste their time on a challenge to a nearly defunct, century-old state law. It was typical of Wade, however, not to slight the case, not least because a federal lawsuit against him had recently slipped through the department's hands. Wade had learned of it only when a judge called him and asked if he knew he was being sued for $50,000 and that no one in his office had responded to the complaint. After that, Wade assigned one of his brightest assistant D.A.'s to work full-time on federal lawsuits brought against county officials.

The abortion suit went to John Tolle, hand-picked by Wade to handle the federal cases. After what had happened to his predecessor, Tolle knew that Wade was looking over his shoulder. To add insult to injury, Wade always pretended to confuse Tolle, who had straightened out the whole mess, with the assistant D.A. who had created it. Wade never let an opportunity pass to remind Tolle and anyone else within earshot of the day when he, Henry Wade, district attorney of Dallas County, almost had to pay $50,000 out of his own pocket because one of his employees had not taken care of business.

With Tolle at the helm, Wade was not in any danger. Tolle, who would later become a federal magistrate in Dallas, was one of the more competent lawyers in an office that was not suffering from incompetency. A native Dallasite, he only decided to go to law school at age thirty, after serving in World War II and working for a few years in his father's tavern. He attended Notre Dame as an undergraduate and Southern Methodist University Law School. Recalling that the Catholic church had not yet actively begun its antiabortion campaign (and his own feelings were not well-enough formed to influence him one way or the other), Tolle told me that being a Roman Catholic did not affect his handling of the case. Lower key and seemingly less aggressive than most prosecutors, Tolle was nonetheless an accomplished trial lawyer. He was a blunt-spoken man of wry humor, someone who was capable of asking the woman he loved to marry him during the summer he graduated from law school because, as he noted during the proposal, what with law boards and job hunting, the summer was shot anyway.

Tolle thought he could build a case around the right of the fetus to legal protection. He would cite tort cases (ironically, the same tort cases that pro-choice lawyers relied on to build their cases) showing how postnatal damages had been awarded to prenatal fetuses. On occasion, when a fetus was presumed to have been injured in the womb, some courts had awarded them damages, although the payments and inheritance rights were always conditional upon live birth.

Tolle also believed, mistakenly as it turned out, that the abortion restrictions had been around for a long time in the common law, and that however much they were ignored, there was a long-standing precedent for their existence, one that a court of law would not find easy to overturn. It was one thing, he believed, to ignore the abortion laws, another to eliminate them. He did not think public morals had changed so much that people would be willing to enshrine abortion among our nation's protected rights.

The idea of a privacy right had not sufficiently permeated the district attorney's consciousness, and it never dawned on Tolle to prepare a defense against a claim that women were entitled to abortions on that ground. Besides, privacy was not exactly the kind of legal right to which prosecutors were inclined to pay much attention. Their lives were much more affected by the *Miranda* ruling, for example, which touched on every single criminal proceeding they handled, than by a ruling that overturned an obscure Connecticut law on birth control and thereby, in the eyes of a few legal scholars, created a new right of sexual privacy. "Privacy" would strike most prosecutors as a soft, sissified kind of law when compared with the hard-hitting, reality-filled law they dealt with every day. Illegal search and seizure they thoroughly understood, but the idea of a right of privacy for the most part eluded them.

To prepare the case, Tolle surveyed the medical literature on abortion. He concluded there was nothing new that would lead him to believe an attack on the abortion laws would succeed. The physicians to whom he talked always agreed that the fetus was a separate being from the woman. Indeed, if that were the question, there was little chance that any physician would disagree with Tolle's thinking. The fetus was indeed a separate being from the woman; no serious scientist would dispute that biological fact. Tolle did not think, as many women did, that such a simplistic question only begged the issue, which was the degree of control a woman was entitled to exert over this being that existed inside her body.

After surveying the issues that he saw as defining the case, Tolle came to the conclusion that the best approach was to argue that the fetus was a separate human being with every bit as much right to live as the woman in whose uterus it was carried. Once the fetus's right to live had been established, he thought, then the woman obviously had no right to control it. If he had to give ground anywhere, he might yield to the point of admitting that the rights of the fetus had to be balanced against the rights of the woman. Never did he think, nor could he imagine, that any court would accept the notion that the woman's rights might prevail over those of the fetus.

On March 18 Judge John R. Brown, chief of the United States Court of Appeals for the Fifth Circuit, named the justices who would form a three-judge panel to hear the two cases, which were consolidated.

On March 23 Tolle responded to the complaint against his

boss. In what was called Wade's "original answer," Tolle wrote that the facts of the case were unproven, that the defendant did not know that Roe was unmarried, that she wanted to terminate her pregnancy, that she suffered from economic hardship, or even that she, as far as he was concerned, was a real person.

The district attorney also stated that the plaintiff Jane Roe lacked the standing to sue because the Texas abortion statute affected only those persons who performed abortions, not the women on whom they were performed. No woman could be prosecuted under Texas law for obtaining an abortion, legal or illegal; only the person who performed an abortion could be prosecuted. As a result, the district attorney argued that Jane Roe could not have suffered any legal injury because of the Texas abortion laws. The statement clearly revealed the district attorney's position on what might turn out to be the most controversial issue in the case: As far as the state of Texas was concerned, Jane Roe might have a complaint about the restrictions the abortion laws placed on her personally, but under Texas law, she had no one—no government official or agency or court—to whom she could complain legally.

Finally, Tolle contended that the Texas abortion laws were not vague or unconstitutional. Implied but not stated was an assumption, widely held by law enforcement agencies and others who opposed legalized abortion, that if the abortion laws had been on the books for a century without a serious challenge, that alone was proof they were not vague or unconstitutional.

The next day the state of Texas, a party to any suit in which a state law is challenged, moved to dismiss *Does*, the case involving the married couple, on grounds that no "actual, justifiable controversy" existed. Interestingly, the attorney general did not file a similar motion in *Roe*, Norma McCorvey's case, presumably because it was not so sure that she, who was at least allegedly pregnant, did not have standing to sue the state of Texas.

The charge of no controversy was the same one employed by the Maricopa County lawyers in the Finkbine case six years earlier. For a lawsuit to be valid, it must involve some actual, legally recognized controversy; people cannot sue simply because they do not like a law; they must be able to prove that a law injures them directly in some way. Courts do not waste their time and the taxpayers' money on suits that do not involve real injuries.

The charge that their plaintiffs had no standing to sue was the one that Coffee and Weddington had most feared, primarily because it could end their challenge to the abortion law before it even reached the court for argument. It was with some relief, then, that they learned someone wanted to intervene on their case. An intervenor is someone who, because of a related interest, asks to join a lawsuit already in progress. If permission to intervene is granted by the court, the intervenor is then given full status as a plaintiff.

The prospective intervenor was a licensed physician named James Hallford, who had been indicted by District Attorney Wade on two criminal accounts of abortion. Hallford, then in his late forties, was a graduate of Southwest Medical School. At some point in his career, Hallford's medical practice became devoted entirely to abortion.

No one I talked to about Hallford knew for sure why he started doing abortions. He told one of his lawyers that he had become concerned about illegal abortion in 1958 when, as a medical student at Parkland, a large metropolitan teaching hospital in Dallas, he had seen several women brought in each week suffering from illegal abortions at the hands of unskilled abortionists. He observed that most of the women were poor and could not afford a "good" abortion. Hallford observed that most women had already made up their minds to get an abortion by the time they came to him, so, for him at least, the issue boiled down to whether he would provide his patients with an abortion that was safe and antiseptic or let them risk an unsafe, possibly septic surgery at the hands of an untrained abortionist.

I could not ask Hallford personally about his life as an abortionist because he left the Dallas area without a trace about ten years after the case. No forwarding address could be located for him; his lawyers no longer had contact with him (although one had successfully defended him against drug charges brought by the local medical association a few years after the abortion case); and no professional association knew his whereabouts.

Whatever his motivation, word had gotten around Dallas that Hallford would do abortions, that he was a licensed physician, and that his fees were reasonable. As one of the city's primary sources of illegal abortion, he was a prime target for a legal crackdown.

Hallford was indicted on charges that he had performed abortions illegally on two occasions about the time that Coffee and

Weddington were preparing to file their abortion suits. In such cases it was usual for the district attorney to file multiple indictments. That way, if one did not hold up in court, there was a backup.

The doctor was not given any notice of an impending raid, which many people read as a sign that the district attorney was getting ready to crack down on illegal abortion even before the case was filed. Although law enforcement agencies did not generally go out of their way to let hardened criminals know they were about to be arrested, they sometimes took a gentler tack with licensed physicians who discreetly ran private abortion clinics, giving them warning so they could close down temporarily if they chose to do so and thereby avoid arrest.

Hallford's attorney was Fred Bruner, a man who knew his business well from having worked in the D.A.'s office for several years. Assisting him was a young lawyer named Roy Merrill, who had worked in the district attorney's office in Lubbock, Texas.

Hallford's lawyers were planning to mount the defense that most physicians used when charged with abortion—namely, that the abortion law was vague and therefore unconstitutional. Hallford would claim that he was unable to differentiate between those cases that fell outside Article 1196 of the Texas law, which stated that abortions could be performed on medical advice from a physician in order to save the woman's life, and those that were not covered under this section.

Nothing less than Hallford's medical license was at stake. If found guilty, he would lose not only his medical license, but also his professional standing within the community. To exonerate him, therefore, his lawyers were seeking any tactic short of permitting their client to plead guilty.

Merrill, who did most of the legwork on the case, was engaged in a series of ongoing talks with Prosecutor John Sparling, which were held in the judge's chambers. At first Merrill hoped he and Sparling could cut a deal and, to this end, had suggested that constitutional issues might be at stake. He implied that he might ask for an injunction to stop District Attorney Wade from further prosecution of the case until this was cleared up.

State Judge Jerome Chamberlain, who was in charge of the case, told Merrill he had no chance of getting an injunction to prevent

Wade from prosecuting any more abortion cases. Merrill thought the judge and the D.A.'s office were taking an unusually tough stance on this case, a fact he found painful because he had become close to his client.

Merrill had spent hours with Hallford going over the case. He found the doctor quite likable, and most important, the young lawyer believed his client's motivation for doing abortions was honorable. He hated to think there was little he and Bruner could do to save Hallford's license or, worse, keep him out of jail. Having pulled all the strings he could think of to save his client, he was becoming resigned to an unhappy outcome when Bruner called him one day and said he had a new strategy in mind that they should discuss.

A few weeks earlier Bruner had suggested to Merrill that constitutional issues might be involved but had not spelled out what they were; when the judge dismissed the notion in so peremptory a manner, Merrill considered the issue settled.

Now he was pleasantly surprised to learn that his boss had been doing some research on his own. It was clever but not uncharacteristic of Bruner to make a suggestion like this. Unlike most criminal lawyers, who read relatively little law outside their specialty, Bruner liked to look at the big picture and took pride in keeping up with the theoretical side of the law. Now he had obtained copies of *People* v. *Belous* and *U.S.* v. *Vuitch*, the same two abortion cases Coffee and Weddington had found.

Bruner briefly described the two decisions to Merrill and then handed him the opinions so he could read them for himself. If Merrill agreed that they formed the basis for an argument that the charge against their client was unconstitutional, they would reopen the issue with the judge.

Bruner particularly liked the *Belous* decision because it came from the California Supreme Court. Like many other lawyers, he admired that court for its forward-looking decisions and considered it to be a shaper of social policy in the United States. If the California Supreme Court thought abortion was a ripe issue, Bruner believed the U.S. Supreme Court would not be far behind in its thinking. Word was out that U.S. Supreme Court brethren paid attention to the opinions of the California Supreme Court. And with these two decisions, Bruner no longer had any doubts that abortion was a constitutional issue.

Merrill studied the cases and got back to Bruner right away to tell him that he agreed with his idea. The more he read about the circumstances of the two cases, in fact, the more he saw a parallel between their plaintiffs and his client. Confident there was a good chance that the crime of which his client was accused was unconstitutional, he called Judge Chamberlain's chambers to request a meeting with the judge and the prosecutor.

When consulted this time, Judge Chamberlain agreed that the case properly belonged in a federal court. Although he knew it would infuriate the prosecutor to see an indicted abortionist slip through his fingers, Chamberlain said he had no choice but to pass this case on to a federal court rather than hearing it as a criminal case. Feeling that a major victory had been won, Merrill was elated.

The next day, while preparing to request a three-judge court for their client, Merrill heard about *Roe* v. *Wade* on the radio.

As far as he was concerned, the fact that another case had already been filed was his second break. As soon as he arrived at work, Merrill talked to Bruner, who agreed that they should at least talk to the lawyers on *Roe* v. *Wade*. Within minutes Merrill was on the telephone talking to Coffee about their cases. He pointed out something she was already well aware of—namely, that she did not have anyone representing the medical profession, let alone anyone accused of abortion. Merrill did not have to plead his client's case very strongly. Coffee saw the merits of Merrill's proposal to have his client join her case as an intervenor. She said she would have to check with her co-counsel, but since both women had discussed this problem at great length, it would only be a formality.

As it turned out, the arrangement suited everyone. Coffee and Weddington had a stronger case, and Bruner and Merrill had found a way—temporarily, at least—to stave off a jury trial for their client. But even if Coffee and Weddington had declined to let Hallford intervene, Bruner and Merrill would have filed a petition challenging the Texas state law, and their case would probably have merged with *Roe* v. *Wade*.

On March 19, two weeks after the original complaint was filed, Hallford officially applied to intervene in *Roe* v. *Wade*. Five days later he was granted permission to do so by the court. Merrill and Bruner requested and got a postponement of the trial against their client pending the outcome of the federal case.

From the district attorney's point of view, Hallford's entry into the case changed things little. Tolle still did not think he stood a chance of losing, and if you polled the average person on the street in Dallas, he or she would probably have agreed.

Although Tolle did not think Coffee and Weddington would file a false affidavit or sue without a real plaintiff, he still wanted to depose Jane Roe. The more he could learn about her, the better his defense would be. In any lawsuit, parties try to force disclosure of information—facts, deeds, or papers—in the other party's possession so they can better defend their position. This often drawn-out process is called "discovery." One frequently used technique of discovery is deposition, in which a witness is questioned under oath by the other party's lawyers.

Tolle's primary motivation for deposing Jane Roe was to see for himself how pregnant she was. He was not overly confident that McCorvey had no standing to sue, but if he could establish that she was too pregnant to undergo an abortion, he could ask for the case to be dismissed on those grounds. Given the time it took to prepare a federal case, Tolle thought it reasonable to look into this. He knew he was supported by many legal experts on both sides of the abortion debate in his belief that such cases were inevitably moot because pregnancy was a self-terminating condition.

His other motive for deposing Roe was that he might uncover something in her character that would make her an unsuitable plaintiff. Perhaps she was not as poor as she claimed, or perhaps she lived with a man who was willing to support her and the child. If he deposed her, her true identity would probably be revealed, not only to him but to a news-hungry press corps. If they were nosy enough to follow up on the case, they might do his dirty work for him, and if she were unwilling to have this happen, she might order her lawyers to drop the suit. Either way, he came out ahead. On March 27 Tolle filed a formal request to depose Jane Roe on April 11 in his office.

For a week, while Judge Sarah Hughes privately weighed her response to this request, Coffee and Weddington stewed. They were afraid they might not be able to get in touch with Norma if she had to be deposed. A bigger worry, though, was that she would back out rather than risk having her identity revealed. The two women began to feel that the case was slipping through their fingers before it had even begun.

They contacted Norma to explain what was happening and were pleased to hear that she felt strongly enough about the case to be willing, if there were no alternative, to be deposed and take the consequences. Coffee and Weddington promised they would try to arrange something short of a deposition.

They decided to ask for a meeting with the district attorney in the judge's chambers and submit information regarding their client's identity. If the information were officially revealed "in camera," to use the legal expression, it was still possible that McCorvey's identity could be kept secret. Both lawyers hoped that would satisfy everyone.

The district attorney's request to depose Jane Roe ultimately did not carry much weight with Judge Hughes, who saw no reason to force a woman suing for an abortion to reveal her identity. Although she denied Tolle's request to question Jane Roe, Judge Hughes did express concern about the use of an alias. While not unheard of, they were somewhat rare. Believing that she should satisfy herself, her fellow judges, and, one presumes, the historical record by insuring that Jane Roe was a real person, Hughes ordered Linda Coffee to submit an affidavit in which Roe testified under oath that the facts of her case were as presented.

Linda Coffee interviewed her client in her law office. The affidavit, a telling document as much for what it does not say, still stands as one of the few definitive biographical statements about Norma McCorvey. Later, when Norma began talking to reporters, it was sometimes difficult to sort out the different versions of her life that emerged in the press. The affidavit remains a poignant report not only on her but also on the plight of all poor, unwed mothers.

III. FACTS

1. Plaintiff Jane Roe is an unmarried woman.

2. Because of economic hardships and social stigmas involved in bearing an illegitimate child, Plaintiff wishes to terminate her pregnancy by means of an abortion. . . .

3. Plaintiff's life does not appear to be threatened by the continuation of her pregnancy.

4. Plaintiff has been unable to secure a legal abortion in Dallas County because of the existence of the Texas Abortion Laws.

5. Her inability to obtain an abortion has caused Plaintiff to suffer emotional trauma.

6. Plaintiff cannot afford to travel to another jurisdiction to seek to secure a legal abortion under safe, clinical conditions.

7. An abortion performed by a competent, licensed physician under hospital or clinic conditions is a safe and simple procedure which presents less danger to the pregnant woman, particularly in the first trimester of pregnancy, than does ordinary childbirth.

8. An abortion outside of the clinical setting by unqualified personnel is extremely dangerous and often results in death, maiming, sterility, and infection.

Nowhere in the record is Jane Roe's true identity revealed, nor is any mention made of her claim that she was raped. Once the crisis of whether or not to depose Jane Roe was resolved, the case moved along fairly smoothly from the points of view of both parties.

In mid-April Coffee wrote a motion asking for a summary judgment. Such a motion is a legal pleading to the effect that in the absence of any factual disputes, there is no need for a jury trial—and thus no need to call witnesses or hear evidence. Such a judgment could only be issued when there is no dispute over the facts of the case—that is, when the questions raised are purely legal and can be decided on the issues involved.

Coffee had determined that the motion for a summary judgment was in order because of a rumor she had heard. As a former law clerk on the Fifth Circuit, she had maintained a pipeline to the court. Her primary source of information was a clerk of Judge Hughes who kept her abreast of the scuttlebutt on current cases. He relayed the information that Judge Irving Goldberg, a panel member, reportedly had been heard to say that he did not want a lengthy trial and saw no need for expert witnesses or indeed witnesses of any kind. He wanted to review this case purely on the issues involved.

Coffee and Weddington were pleased to pick up this bit of court gossip since it reinforced their belief that they need not go to the time and considerable expense of providing expert witnesses. They also read it as a sign that their client probably would not have to testify. And even though most legal experts would say this was wishful thinking on their part, they also chose to take it as a sign of encouragement, believing that the judges might be predisposed toward their case. Although Coffee wrote the motion for a summary judgment, it was filed in Hallford's behalf, probably a bit of subterfuge designed to allay any suspicions regarding the source of the information. If so, the ploy was unnecessary because it was not at all unusual for a three-judge case to be decided on the merits without hearing evidence.

The motion for a summary judgment was denied and a hearing was held, although no witnesses or further evidence was presented by either side.

Dr. Hallford's lawyers filed a short brief in his behalf in mid-April. In it, among other things, they issued a plea for damages, a ridiculous request for someone charged with criminal activity. This irritated John Tolle, who, in response to what he considered one ludicrous motion, filed another ludicrous motion: a request for a jury trial. It was impossible to have a jury trial in a federal appellate court, but then Tolle thought it was impossible for Hallford to hope to be awarded damages. As far as the district attorney's office was concerned, Hallford was lucky not to be in jail already. Judge Goldberg, in whose court these requests were filed, was amused by them both and equally quick to recognize their preposterous nature. He denied Tolle's motion for a jury trial.

On April 22 Coffee reluctantly amended *Roe* v. *Wade* to a class-action suit. Although she loved class-action suits, she did not feel that the abortion case needed to be a class action. The advice to amend the suit had come through Sarah Weddington from some New York abortion reformers to whom she had occasionally talked. They had expressed their concern that a federal court might hand down an important abortion ruling that would not apply to all women. Coffee felt that any ruling would have to apply to all women since the courts could hardly rule that Norma McCorvey could have an abortion but that no other Texas citizen could. Usually mild-mannered, Coffee resented what she deemed to be an intrusion on her case. Perhaps she sensed it was an omen for the future, or perhaps she was merely being possessive about what she felt belonged to her.

All that remained now was for all parties to file briefs. Briefs written for three-judge courts are only a few pages of straightforward factual material, unlike the longer, more detailed, and occasionally brilliant briefs that are delivered to the Supreme Court. Tolle prepared a brief representing the views of the district attorney, while Coffee stayed up late several nights typing her brief. On the same old manual typewriter at which she had prepared the original pleadings, she pecked out eighteen pages in which she merely restated the facts of the case and the arguments for overturning the restrictive law. The women's group at the Unitarian Church submitted a short amicus curiae brief in support of Roe and the Does.

All avenues of legal dispute having been used up by both sides, an oral hearing was set for May 22, 1970.

7

Reform,
Dallas Style

When Coffee and Weddington began working on *Roe* v. *Wade*, they did not know anyone else in Dallas or even in Texas who was working on abortion reform. In fact, they had no contacts anywhere in the country with other reformers. They did not know about any national groups organized around abortion reform, although one, the Association for the Study of Abortion (ASA), had been in existence since 1964. An educational rather than a lobbying group, it focused its early attentions mainly on doctors and other professionals whose lives would be affected by reform. Another group, more oriented to the average woman, was in the early stages of organization. The National Association for Repeal of Abortion Laws (NARAL) held its first public organizational meeting in February 1969 at the Drake Hotel in Chicago just as Coffee and Weddington were most immersed in preparing their challenge to the Texas law.

Grass-roots groups working to pass reform laws had come and gone in several states, most notably Colorado, North Carolina, and California, all of which had passed liberal reform laws in 1967, "liberal" meaning that for the first time abortions could be done to preserve a woman's health as well as her life. A year later, in 1968, Georgia had passed a reform law, and a repeal bill was introduced in New York in December 1969. In only one neighboring state, New Mexico, were reformers actively involved in reform, and New Mexico's recently passed reform law would go into effect in 1969, shortly before the Dallas reform movement took root.

Although abortion reform was in the air across the country,

Texas was hardly receptive to it. Texans were too chauvinistic and firmly entrenched in their own ways to seek any kind of social change. In a state that had eagerly sought annexation to the United States during the ten years from 1836 to 1846 when it was an independent republic, it was not surprising to find a large number of citizens who maintained a fierce loyalty to states' rights—and abortion was viewed from the start as a states' rights issue. If changes were to be made in the abortion laws, states' rights advocates argued, they should be made through the legislatures and not the courts—especially not through a federal court that had no business meddling in the states' affairs. Coupled with this was an equally portentous feeling about the emerging women's rights movement. Even though feminism, which like abortion reform was more an idea than a reality in the late 1960s, had barely made its way to Texas, the mostly male legislators who ruled the Austin statehouse did not like it. No one would catch them catering to any "libber" causes.

Of all the Texas cities, politically and fiscally conservative Dallas, best known to most Americans as the place where John F. Kennedy was assassinated, was least likely to give rise to a reform movement. For years it had been viewed as a breeding ground for the most unbending and radical kind of political conservatism. Despite its outward image, though, inner changes were occurring, changes that were mostly promoted by concerned Dallasites who were embarrassed over the city's image in the wake of the assassination. Liberals who had long since abdicated political control to the conservative establishment now thought the time was ripe for a swing to the left politically. And although they were not looking for a radical cause, as abortion was considered to be in 1969, they were more open than they had been in years to the kind of social reform that typically accompanied a swing to the left.

As nearly as any of the participants could recall, abortion reform in Texas began in late fall 1969, when Virginia Whitehill, a Planned Parenthood board member, responded to a request from the local Unitarian church for someone to speak to them about abortion.

At that time the Unitarians were the only Protestant denomination to have taken a strong stand on abortion. In 1963 their general assembly had passed a resolution condemning the restrictive abortion laws as an "affront to human life and dignity." They supported legalized abortion to protect a mother's life and physical or mental health, in cases of rape or incest, serious fetal deformity, and whenever a "compelling reason, physical, psychological, mental, spiritual, or economic," existed.

Despite their early concern, little happened in Unitarian circles until 1969, when abortion became a more pressing church concern. Another churchwide resolution was passed that year in support of the clergy, many of whom were Unitarian, who were working with the Clergy Consultation Service on Abortion, a New York–based organization with local branches that provided coun-seling—and referrals—to women with problem pregnancies. In keeping with the growing sense of militancy about abortion rights, many Unitarian clergy also began to preach about women's rights and abortion. The Women's Federation, the national Unitarian women's group, voted to make abortion a number-one priority in their programs. The Women's Auxiliary of the Dallas Unitarian Church had been studying the issue of abortion for about a year when these resolutions were passed in 1969. Linda Coffee had been one of their guest speakers, and now they wanted to hear from a representative of Planned Parenthood.

Virginia Whitehill had never before given a speech, but she was naturally gregarious and interested to learn more about abortion, so she volunteered to talk to the Unitarian women. Her interest in abortion stemmed from her volunteer work at Planned Parenthood and her equally active membership in Zero Population Growth. She had been unable to interest the local Planned Parenthood in the abortion issue, and this she attributed to a fear of their losing the public monies that had been pouring in during the past few years if the organization began lobbying for a political cause. In fact, neither PP nor any other group involved in population control had ever shown much support of abortion rights for women. However logically aligned the interests of birth controllers and advocates of women's rights seemed to be, the interests and goals of the two groups were essentially incompatible.

Feminists promoted individual choice. They believed women should control their own reproduction, including having whatever means were available to terminate an unwanted pregnancy. In contrast, the highly influential birth control and population activists, who believed the world population was growing at an alarming rate, sought stability above all else. Their goal could be and eventually was summed up in one deceptively jingoistic slogan—zero population growth—which meant that the birth rate should correspond directly to the death rate. Where feminists wanted to redefine and reshape men's and women's roles, birth controllers firmly supported the nuclear family, which they saw as a key to maintaining stability. Putting control of reproduction in the hands of individual women was the last thing they wanted, since they advocated national and even worldwide controls on population growth. As a result, even though birth control and population activists supported the use of various forms of birth control, abortion was never one of them. For example, during the 1960s U.S. nonmilitary foreign aid went only to countries that followed a stringent program of family planning, the guidelines of which were established by the State Department. Abortion was not part of the package.

Population and birth controllers believed a relationship existed, on the one hand, between poverty and a high birth rate. If women had fewer children, poverty would vanish or be diminished. Feminists, on the other hand, thought better health care, especially prenatal health care, could help women and children who lived in poverty-ridden areas. They thought it was discriminatory to ask or expect poor women to have fewer children simply because they were poor.

Despite her active memberships in Planned Parenthood and Zero Population Growth, a powerful population control group throughout the late 1960s and 1970s, Virginia Whitehill still found herself interested in abortion. She did not see any conflict between granting women the right to obtain abortions and attempts to regulate population growth. In fact, she feared that the drive to reduce the population would reach only the educated, more aware women. She thought poor women would pay no attention because they were not consciously attuned to anything as sophisticated as a movement to control the population. Yet these were the very women Whitehill thought should have access to birth control and abortion.

Whitehill prepared a speech that consisted mostly of statistics—on the number of illegal abortions, the number of abortion-related deaths (as high as ten thousand a year, according to some experts)—all of which pointed to the need for abortion reform. Pat Cookson, another Planned Parenthood volunteer, agreed to accompany her on her first public-speaking engagement.

Whitehill proved to be an adept public speaker. She had a natural talent for persuading people to her point of view and spurring them on to action, not that the Unitarian women needed much persuasion. While Coffee had talked to them in relatively abstract terms about the legal action that was needed to overthrow the state's abortion laws, Whitehill made the issues surrounding abortion personal. She had described how any one of the Unitarian women—or one of their daughters or a sister or a good friend—might desperately want and need to terminate a pregnancy and be unable to do so, except under frightening, unsafe, and humiliating circumstances. She told the churchwomen that while they were among the privileged elite who might be able to arrange for a "legal" abortion, most women, especially poor women who did know how to operate within the system, were unable to terminate a pregnancy even when it occurred under the direst of circumstances, such as rape or incest. It is the personalizing of an issue like abortion that leads to grass-roots activity, and Whitehill managed to make abortion a very personal issue indeed as she talked to the Unitarian women.

The Unitarian women responded enthusiastically to her cry for reform, but they also knew they had gone as far as they could with abortion within the confines of the church. Her invitation to speak had come at the end of a year of study of abortion, and besides, the Unitarian women's group was neither a single-issue nor a political organization. Still, a few women within the group could not give up the idea of taking some action on this pressing issue. They clustered around Whitehill after her speech to ask what could be done. Someone suggested that they organize a new, separate group around the issue of abortion. The idea produced great excitement. Telephone numbers were exchanged, and promises were made to call immediately and begin setting up the new group.

Within days the telephone lines were buzzing as the women began to organize. They were not inexperienced at this; most of them had volunteered considerable time for various liberal and civil rights causes. Also, they were not typical abortion reformers. What set them apart was that they were all middle-class housewives and not particularly disgruntled ones at that. Supported by their husbands, they were women who chose to volunteer rather than work at paying jobs. Although intellectually sympathetic to many elements of the equal rights movement, feminism per se held no appeal for them. In fact, some of them opposed it. They had read Betty Friedan's book and found it thought-provoking, but it did not enrage them. It did not provoke them, as it did some women, to leave their husbands and children and embark on a search for a lost identity. True, their marriages seemed to be breaking up at the same rate as everyone else's, and they rejected the exaggerated sex roles thrust on them in the 1950s, but their rebellion against the feminine mystique was much gentler than most feminists experienced. They firmly rejected the radical path, not because their husbands would object or because they were ignorant of it, but because they truly were middle-of-the-road reformers.

Yet it was women like these who formed the broad base of support necessary for a theoretical issue like abortion to be translated into action. They formed a true grass-roots movement, one that was neither radically oriented nor professionally organized. In large part their success could be attributed to their being in the right place at the right time. When they began to organize, the time was right and they were in the right state to make the most of their mainstream attitudes.

At the nucleus of the group was Virginia Whitehill, whose petite, delicate blond looks and beautiful clothes belied her political savvy and intellectual toughness. She had graduated from Mt. Holyoke College in 1950 with a degree in history, to which she attributed her lifelong interest in current and historical events. Left with two small daughters to rear after an early marriage ended in divorce, she had moved in with her parents in Pelham Manor, New York, a Westchester community north of New York City, and had taken a job in the city with the Rockefeller Foundation. She worked there about two years, until 1959, when she married an old high school friend, James Whitehill, a Princeton graduate who worked as a manufacturer's representative. It was while working at the foundation that she formulated many of her ideas on population control. John D. Rockefeller had always been interested in population control, and he could be said to have bequeathed his interest, along with the funds to do something about it, to the Rockefeller Foundation, which subsequently and peripherally handed it on to Virginia Whitehill. Her experience at the foundation—better than a master's degree, she would recall—left her with a strong, continuing interest in population control and philanthropic work.

Virginia and James Whitehill settled in Dallas after their marriage. Shortly after arriving, they joined a local Presbyterian church as a means of getting acquainted, and Whitehill was invited to join the women's group. To her horror, the group's primary activity consisted of rolling bandages for cancer patients—a task Whitehill found condescending. She was sure that a machine could better perform the task anyway. Miffed at being asked to do this kind of work, she withdrew from the church group and began volunteering at Planned Parenthood. When the women's movement began to organize in the 1960s, Whitehill was interested in that, too. She believed in equal treatment for all people and her husband supported her in that belief. She joined NOW when it formed.

The president of the Unitarian women's group also played an active role in organizing the new abortion group. Ellen Kalina, an attractive dark-haired woman, was reared a Roman Catholic and had five children by her first husband before she joined the Unitarian church and began to reevaluate her attitude toward women's rights and contraception.

Another Unitarian, Pat White, the mother of several children, also helped with the initial organizing and offered her house for the early meetings. As program chairman of the Unitarian women's group, she had been responsible for inviting the guest speakers who came to talk to the group about abortion.

Within a few weeks Doris Hensarling (who would in 1976 divorce and take back her maiden name of Middleton) had joined the core group of reformers. Middleton, whose can-do spirit made her a female counterpart to President Jimmy Carter, would have been one of the founding members of the Dallas reform group but for her love of music. Her husband and three children attended the Unitarian church while she stole off to the Episcopalian church because she enjoyed the ritual and music. When she learned about the group that was forming around the abortion issue, she joined immediately. More than anyone else in the group, she was sympathetic to the feminist philosophy, but at the same time Middleton firmly believed that radical politics alienated legislators and that in a state like Texas they would not work. Well aware of her power, she nonetheless proudly viewed herself as a behind-the-scenes worker.

The group's most immediate needs were for money to operate and a place to meet, but before the women could work on these things, they had to settle on a name for their fledgling group. They spent many hours trying to find just the right name—one that would not, they hoped, irritate people before they had a chance to present their case. The name would go through several incarnations, but in the organizing stage they settled on the Dallas Committee to Study Abortion, which bore a marked similarity to the oldest and most prestigious nationwide abortion-reform group, the Association for the Study of Abortion. It was fitting since both ASA and its smaller counterpart in Dallas had as a common goal a desire to interest and inform people about abortion. Of course, the members of both groups were also optimistic that anyone who studied the abortion issue closely would conclude that liberalized laws were needed.

Whitehill took it upon herself to try to raise money for the fledgling group—an effort that met with success almost right away. Within a few weeks of the night when she spoke at the Unitarian Church, she had two pledges, each in the amount of $50. One came from the Council of Jewish Women and was arranged by Carolyn Tobian, a member of a prominent family active in political and religious circles in the city who would also join their group. The second came from the Women's Auxiliary of the Dallas Unitarian Church.

Unused to raising money, Whitehill soon realized that getting the first contribution was the hard part. After that, she got braver. Thumbing through her address book, she began calling anyone she thought might be remotely interested in helping out. Since she was, by her own admission, probably the only woman in Dallas who belonged to both NOW and the Junior League, Whitehill had many contacts on all levels of Dallas society. Furthermore, although a firm believer in liberal causes, she nonetheless maintained memberships in several conservative groups. Partly she did so because the conservative memberships helped her stay in touch with what other people were thinking, as well as what the opposition was doing, but she also joined these groups because she was a firm believer in single-issue politics and believed—accurately, as it would turn out—that even within the membership ranks of the more conservative groups she might muster support for some of her more liberal causes. When Whitehill began soliciting funds for the abortion group, she called liberals and conservatives alike, confident of the abortion issue's broad appeal.

Whitehill did manage to raise $500—a lot of money in 1969—from one conservative contributor, a Dallas society matron not known for her interest in either liberal or radical causes. Whitehill talked to her about the need to support abortion reform because it would help control the population and prevent famine in Third World countries. In contrast with her approach to the Unitarian women, she was careful not to put the issue into personal terms. The woman agreed to contribute $500, but within moments of hanging up the telephone she called Whitehill back. In the high-pitched, girlish voice for which she was known, she whispered, "Ginny, this is not one of those women's libber groups, is it?"

"Oh, no," Whitehill replied, "I think it's just about one issue. Now if other people who are working on this want to work on other issues in other groups, we can't stop them, but this is just for one issue." Thus reassured, the woman put her check in the mail. Once Whitehill saw that she could raise money from people who would not necessarily support women's rights but would support abortion rights, she determined to do what she could to keep the Dallas Committee to Study Abortion a single-issue group.

Finding a place to meet proved to be more difficult than raising money. People could donate money anonymously, but the organization that offered a meeting room to an abortion rights group would be perceived as being firmly in the pro-choice camp—and abortion was rapidly becoming a highly controversial topic. During their first few organizational meetings, the women stored their files and supplies in their dining rooms and met in each other's living rooms. Eventually Pat White's home became the group's headquarters, and their mailings bore her return address on Ridgeview Circle. But the women knew—or hoped—the day would soon come when they would need a public meeting place. They had begun to plan their first public meeting for February 1970 and already believed they would turn out enough interested persons to require a public hall or meeting room.

The women found out just how controversial abortion was when they began calling various local organizations—Planned Parenthood, Zero Population Growth, the churches—to ask if the group could donate a meeting room and some office space. Many of the people they talked to whispered support but were unwilling to take so public a stand as lending them a meeting place. Reverend Dwight Brown, the Unitarian minister and a man who would prove to be one of their staunchest supporters, offered a meeting room and an office in the Unitarian church.

By January 5, 1970, enough money had been raised for the fledgling group to draw up a budget. The women had raised $1,022 in dues and contributions and had spent $203.96 in printing costs to prepare their first mailing. Whitehill had donated $31 in postage.

They had also begun to establish important contacts with politicians and were regularly recruiting new members. Among their important political contacts was Texas State Senator George Parkhouse of Dallas, who in 1967 introduced a senate bill to reform the Texas law. As was the case in most states that passed reform laws between 1967 and 1968, it was modeled after an abortion law written in 1959 by the prestigious American Law Institute as part of a proposed model penal code. The ALI law, which became known as the "therapeutic abortion law," was conservative, conforming to the kind of abortions that many doctors were doing anyway. The fact that it permitted abortion only in cases of rape, incest, severe fetal deformity, or when the woman's physical or mental health was threatened meant that many women who needed abortions would be denied them. No attempt was made to establish or protect a woman's abortion right. There was no suggestion, for example, of abolishing the hospital therapeutic abortion committee that kept control of abortion in the hands of physicians and away from women. In addition, many of the states that passed laws modeled along ALI lines added residency and consent requirements.

Although Parkhouse managed to get the bill out of committee, he was unable to muster the two-thirds vote needed for consideration by the full senate. Interested as the senator was in abortion reform, he was not especially receptive to the newly formed Dallas Committee. He had initiated reform long before the "ladies," as he thought of them, came along, and he saw no reason to go out of his way to curry their favor. When Parkhouse retired after the 1967 legislative session, the women thought there might be no one in the Texas legislature interested enough to work on abortion reform.

The legislature met in 1969 before the group had gotten organized, but the women had noticed that a relatively new member of the house of representatives, James Clark, was sponsoring an abortion bill in that chamber. Elected to the legislature in 1966, Clark had taken over an abortion bill from a departing colleague. It was just the kind of bill that junior legislators got stuck with, but Clark's interest in abortion proved to be genuine, tied as it was to his more general interest in family law. His willingness to work in abortion reform stemmed from a visit to a state school for severely retarded persons, which had left a deep impression on him. Clark saw a connection between those "poor souls" and abortion rights that he described in the following way: "I don't think that the same God that gave us rationality to learn these things [how to do abortions] intended us to do nothing with the information. The Catholics would jump on me. They would say we must work to take better care of the children. Well, we've had thousands and thousands of years of Christian tradition, and we haven't done it yet."

Clark was handed an ALI-type bill, now viewed by most reform groups, including the Dallas women, as too conservative, primarily because it did little to give women any greater access to abortion. The bill had restrictive provisions involving residency and consent requirements that were not part of the ALI-model bill. Clark made a few changes to liberalize the bill even further so that it would provide more women with access to abortion than was the case with the ALI-type bills, and even though he suspected the bill was doomed from the start, he submitted it for committee review. He was warned by fellow legislators that even if his bill made it out of the house, the senate intended to substitute the less liberal and more favored ALI format. As it was, Clark's bill never made it out of committee.

When the Dallas Committee learned about Clark's efforts in behalf of reform, they contacted him and were delighted to discover that he was eager to work with them. Over the next two years Clark and the women reformers would become true allies, with Clark carrying their bills into the legislature and the women providing the kind of backup support that he needed to push the bill through the legislature. They organized letter-writing campaigns, gave testimony, undertook research, and, under his auspices, learned how to lobby other legislators. Clark provided the women with a much-needed entrée to his colleagues.

About the same time the women began to work with James Clark, two Texas state senators, Tom Creighton and Don Kennard, picked up the banner from retired Senator Parkhouse and introduced new abortion legislation in the senate. The women worked with both men but never formed the close ties with them that they did with Clark.

Clark was a rare man in the 1960s in that he was willing to listen to what women wanted and then try to help them get it. He spoke out in favor of granting women autonomy very early, at a time, in fact, when the idea was still shocking and radical. In 1969 Clark was telling anyone who would listen that people needed to "recognize a woman's right to do what she believes is right with her body."

Such solid support was not always forthcoming from the prefeminist, male-dominated abortion-reform movement. Many of the high-powered male doctors and lawyers working on reform in such peripheral groups as Planned Parenthood and the American Civil Liberties Union were not so quick to support and work for abortion reform in the mid-1960s. The ACLU took up the reform banner in the late 1960s, mostly because of the persistent urging of a strong feminist faction within the group headed by Judge Dorothy Kenyon of New York, who in February 1967 wrote an irate letter to the New York Civil Liberties Union about their reluctance to tackle abortion. Noting that the mostly male committee and board members considered abortion to be a social rather than a legal problem, one that was too controversial to handle, she nevertheless continued to push the ACLU to become more actively involved with the abortion issue. Roy Lucas, who had moved to New York from Alabama, also began to push, and by 1968, under the auspices of the ACLU, he was working with several prominent New York physicians to develop a test case. (Nothing ever came of the case because those working on it had a falling-out over goals.)

Members of ASA and NARAL, the groups that had spearheaded reform on the East Coast, were at odds with one another over how liberal the new abortion laws should be. Lawrence Lader, a founding member of ASA, had broken with the group partly over an administrative policy decision that limited the powers of board members (of which he was one) and also over how confrontational the group would be. Lader wanted to lobby for changes in the abortion laws; ASA had opted to remain a nonprofit, nonlobbying educational group. They were willing to compromise with reform rather than repeal, if necessary, whereas Lader, who founded NARAL after he left ASA, wanted total repeal. Even within ASA and NARAL, though, there were schisms between those members who wanted total repeal, which would leave the abortion decision entirely in the hands of women with no government regulation, and those members who thought some regulation was necessary.

On February 11, 1970, the Dallas Committee to Study Abortion held its first public meeting. Fewer than one hundred persons, the vast majority of them women, attended. Although few of the women attending the meeting would know this, in their midst was Mary Doe, the plaintiff in *Does* v. *Wade*.

If the agenda was serious that night, the atmosphere was congenial and informal. The meeting opened with a reading of the Texas law on abortion and some discussion of Clark's bill. The women learned that the Texas statute was an old-style restrictive law first written in the mid-1800s and revised once in 1925, the kind that was common in most states. Only a few states had passed the newer reform laws.

Clark sent a report describing his legislative efforts. Noting that, in his opinion, the 1969 bill in the Texas legislature had failed because of lack of public support, he said he hoped this would not be the case in the next session, since the Dallas group would be there to support him. He suggested that the group look into sponsoring an opinion poll to establish statewide support for changing the law and pledged to follow up on their efforts with legislative support and press activity.

Next on the agenda was discussion of the recently passed New Mexico reform law. Hoping to benefit from someone else's experience, the Dallas women had established some contact with a reform group there. The New Mexico reformers felt they had not worked closely enough with the medical establishment in seeking support for their bill and urged the Texas women to enlist the support of regional physicians as soon as possible. This prompted the Dallas group to ask for volunteers to set to work on a campaign designed to enlist the support of the Texas Medical Association as well as individual doctors.

The group then turned to what would become one of their major ongoing concerns, what they could do to interest and educate the public about the need for abortion reform. They knew they had to put together an information packet, something that stated their position clearly and could be used to interest others in their reform efforts and to lobby legislators. Several women volunteered to begin work on a pamphlet, while another offered to write the Association for the Study of Abortion to see what materials they could supply. At that time ASA was the most active publisher and disseminator of informative and unbiased materials on abortion and abortion reform, and they gladly gave consent for others to use their materials. The Dallas Committee also decided to sponsor a public forum that would invite debate on both sides of the issues. Mary Doe and Barbara Richardson, the club reporter for the *Dallas Times Herald*, agreed to head up this project.

The liveliest and most prolonged discussion of the evening revolved around the stand the Dallas reformers would take on reform versus repeal. The abortion liberalization movement had initially started as an attempt to reform restrictive state laws, but as grass-roots and single-issue activist groups began to organize throughout 1969 and 1970, repeal became a hotly debated topic of discussion. The Dallas group, like most others, was divided over the issue. Some who favored reform did so for purely practical reasons, because they believed this was the most they could hope to achieve. They argued that they stood little or no chance of persuading legislators or courts to repeal all the abortion laws, thus leaving abortion totally unregulated and available on request by individual women. They also believed that only with reform could they build a strong, broad base of support to change the laws. They argued that even though most people wanted abortion reform, the majority did not yet favor repeal. The idea was still too new and radical.

Another faction that supported reform did so more for philosophical and emotional reasons than for practical concerns. They felt that a woman's right to abortion had to be balanced against a fetus's right to survive and that (unless a woman's life were at risk) after a pregnancy had progressed to a certain stage—many drew the line at three or four months or quickening—the right to abortion should be limited by law. Women were not morally free, they felt, to have abortions under any circumstances at any stage of pregnancy. They feared that total repeal would encourage abortion for what they viewed as frivolous reasons—because a woman wanted to preserve her beauty, feared the rigors or pain of childbirth, felt she could not support a child financially, or wished to attend graduate school or pursue a career. Many thought these were not valid reasons to abort a fetus and believed the state had a right to restrict abortions under these circumstances.

Perhaps because they had already been studying abortion for several months, most of the women who had organized the Dallas reform group supported repeal. They felt it was the only action that would truly ensure a woman's abortion right. Repeal represented several things to them. First, it was a guarantee—the only guarantee, they felt—that women could control their own reproduction, that they alone would decide when and under what circumstances they would terminate a pregnancy.

Second, repeal meant that abortion would no longer be controlled by physicians except to the extent that any other surgery was. In studying the history of abortion, they had discovered the passage of restrictive abortion laws a century ago had subjected abortion to unusual medical controls that occurred with no other surgery. No other prospective surgical patient was expected to get several or even one psychiatric opinion or to seek permission from an entire committee prior to undergoing surgery. And certainly no other surgical procedure had a residency or consent requirement. Abortion was subject to these kinds of controls, the women argued, largely because physicians had played such an important role in writing the restrictive state legislation.

Most important, they felt that repeal was the key to giving women—especially poor women—access to affordable abortions. If repeal were enacted, the women stated, clinics and even paramedics could provide low-cost abortions for poor women. Technology had advanced to the point where abortions could be done safely by trained paramedical personnel. Postoperative complications were very rare. In Japan, Scandinavia, and several Eastern European countries, abortions were routinely done on an outpatient basis. Clinic abortions always were cheaper and involved less red tape than hospital operations. Repeal would also eliminate the degrading and by now despised hospital and psychiatric certification, which was still a practice in most states' reform laws.

The discussion rose to an emotional pitch when some of the women who favored reform insisted total repeal would only open the door to late abortions, which many found morally repugnant. Those who supported repeal replied that almost all abortions were done within the first trimester, that only a minuscule number—one-half of one percent—were done after the fourth month. Of those, some were admittedly performed on women, mostly teens, who were negligent in responding to the early signs of pregnancy, but the vast majority were done on women who encountered life-threatening medical complications during the course of their pregnancies. Besides, they argued, few women had abortions for frivolous reasons. Most made a responsible and often painful decision to undergo abortion.

The repeal faction also built a strong case showing that reform was not working. In many reform states, the number of legal abortions had not increased after reform laws were passed, largely because those laws contained so many restrictions. A woman had to be over a certain age, or had to have lived in a state for a certain number of months, or had to have her husband's or parents' consent, in order to qualify for a legal abortion. Women could exercise little discretion regarding their reasons for abortion in states with laws patterned after the ALI-model law, which permitted abortion only in cases of rape, incest, grave impairment of the woman's physical or mental health, or gross deformity of the fetus.

Worst of all, in reform states the illegal abortion rates had not often gone down. In Colorado, for example, fifty legal abortions were done in 1966, the year before the new laws were passed. Ten thousand legal abortions were done in 1967, the year its reform law took effect, but there were still an estimated 8,000 illegal abortions. The situation was similar in California, where 10,000 abortions were done legally after reform and 90,000 illegally. In Maryland, another state that had passed an ALI-type law, in one year an estimated 12,000 to 15,000 illegal abortions took place. Examples like these, uncovered by the Dallas reformers in their research, were enough to indicate that most reform laws were not working. Furthermore, with legality the price of abortions (both legal and illegal) had risen and now averaged between $600 and $700, thus causing many disillusioned reformers to refer to the reform legislation as "rich ladies' laws." In New York City, hospitals were reportedly guaranteeing physicians who agreed to do abortions $2,400 a day.

Basically, the repeal faction's argument boiled down to the fact that the reform laws were complicated, and that the more complicated the law, the less access women would have to abortion. In addition, reform laws obviously would be more open to attack than no laws at all.

Representative Clark supported repeal. Having tried to work with a model-ALI law, he was well aware of the limitations of reform. He believed that reform was still too restrictive, that it would be like putting a "bandage on a gaping wound . . . an attempt to deal with five percent of the problem. . . . We really need to recognize a woman's right to do what she believes is right with her own body."

The repeal forces won out, and the Dallas Committee voted to support total repeal, thus putting themselves in the forefront of abortion reform, along with some of the more radical pro-abortion groups in the country such as Pat Maginnis and Lana Phelan's Society for Humane Abortion in California and Redstockings in New York.

The last item of business at the first meeting was a talk by a Mr. Wray Morehouse, an abortion counselor from Illinois and California who was establishing a referral office in Houston. He described the stories of several women who had undergone criminal abortions. Contained in the notes of the meeting was the observation that "Mr. Morehouse's telling it 'like it is' lent a touch of realism to the subject of our concern."

A little surprisingly, Morehouse's case histories prompted no similar need among those present to share their experiences about abortion. Some of the women who were there that night must certainly have had abortions, and everyone present surely had known someone who had undergone an illegal abortion, but such intimate details of members' lives were not exchanged then or ever among the group members. Perhaps it was not so surprising after all, when one considered that an illegal abortion, particularly one that was gotten alone and under humiliating circumstances, was often among a woman's most painful memories. Such experiences simply could not be dredged up lightly or publicly. But part of the reason no one came forth with a personal story was that the subject was still taboo even among the very people who were trying to change the laws.

Virginia Whitehill, who became the unofficial spokeswoman for the group, soon discovered just how painful women's experiences with illegal abortion were. On several occasions after she spoke, women came up to her to talk about their own illegal abortions. They usually said they had never talked to anyone before about their experiences but were breaking their silence out of a need to thank her for what she was doing—for working to make sure that no woman would ever have to go through what they had suffered.

Whitehill also discovered there was something even more painful than an illegal abortion, and that was surrendering a child for adoption. Several times after she gave a speech, Whitehill was taken aside by a tearful woman who had given up a child for adoption to be told that abortion would have been much easier. These women said that unlike the pain of abortion, which healed eventually, the suffering over having given up a child went on forever. Occasionally, too, she was taken aside by a woman who had undergone a horrifying illegal abortion and needed to share the experience with someone.

Throughout the spring of 1970 the Dallas women dedicated themselves to working on abortion reform. They studied the materials from ASA, which were distributed to members. They also read other materials on abortion, most notably *The Search for an Abortionist* by Nancy Lee; Lawrence Lader's *Abortion;* another book also entitled *Abortion*, published by the Roman Catholic Church to explain its view; *Abortion in the United States* by Mary Calderone; and *Abortion: Law, Choice, and Morality* written by Roman Catholic social scientist Daniel Callahan. Their reading helped shape their views on the subject and provided them with information they needed to prepare their own literature.

The Dallas Committee immediately began to prepare several mailings, which consisted of their own fliers and materials obtained from ASA. In the beginning, before they obtained ASA reprints, they simply sent out their own fliers, rough, one-sheet leaflets that were typed rather than typeset and cheaply printed on Kraft paper. One, written in the form of a letter, was a poignant plea for support of repeal:

> Eighty percent of therapeutic abortions are performed on middle-class white women who can well afford the hospital charges, the doctors' fees, and the psychiatric examination establishing their "emotional instability." The woman possessing some sophistication and education is not defeated by the intricacies of review by doctors' committees and psychiatric examination (though her abortion is often unreasonably delayed), but the poor woman is most often confounded by the red tape. According to Dr. Keither [sic] Russell, chairman of the California Medical Association's

committee on maternal and child health, "This is not a poor woman's law. That's one of its main failures to date." Richard Lamm, Colorado legislator who led the fight for reform, admits, "We had a cruel law. We still have a cruel law."

In an analogy they would use again and again, the group compared criminal abortion to Prohibition:

> The situation is analogous to the bootleg liquor traffic that flourished during Prohibition at great risk to the consumer and at great profit to the bootlegger. In the case of abortion, the damage is compounded because it is inflicted on two innocent victims, the woman and the unwanted child. If legal, reasonably priced abortions were available, there would be no need for law enforcers to blink at the criminal abortionists because an urgent, desperate need would be adequately and legitimately met by society. The hypocrisy and discrimination built into our present system would be ended.

Following an example of East Coast reformers, they organized a chain letter, urging people to write their legislators and show support for reform by attending statewide hearings at the University of Texas: "This is a time for those interested in justice and compassion to act. . . . Please make at least four copies of this letter or compose your own letter to send to others. Please don't break the chain, as time is running out! Share this information with as many individuals and organizations as possible."

The Dallas Committee's early fliers and pamphlets were not so hard-hitting or sophisticated as they would later become. Without any real competition from opposition groups, for example, reformers had not yet become cautious about the language they used to describe abortion. Like most other reformers at this stage of the movement, the Dallas women interchanged the terms "fetus" and "child"; not for another year would they insist on using only the scientifically correct terms "embryo" and "fetus" to describe an unborn young from age one to eight weeks and after eight weeks until the moment of birth respectively. They had not yet begun to use the term "pro-choice" and still referred to themselves as "pro-abortion," a term they would later realize was inaccurate and even find repugnant. With a similar disregard for semantics, the Dallas Committee's early brochures also bore the bold title *Abortion by Choice*, which was later changed to *Motherhood by Choice*.

The literature revealed a tie reformers felt existed between the need to reform the abortion laws and the tragedy of unwanted children. In early brochures they plaintively asked: "How long are we going to accept the sentimental mythology that once a child is born, he is automatically loved and cherished?" The theme of the unwanted child never proved to be particularly persuasive, perhaps because abused children were a far more complicated issue than this reference implied; at any rate, this early theme was soon dropped from the literature.

Another theme, influential in the early stages of abortion reform but less so later on, was the notion that abortion could be used to solve the population problem. Whitehill and several other women in the Dallas group thought that abortion was a useful tool in controlling population growth, but they firmly believed it should not be used on anything but a voluntary and individual basis. Their view put them at odds both with Planned Parenthood, the leading and most established population control group, which advocated sterilization but not abortion as part of its Third World population control program, and with feminists, who felt that poverty was not necessarily the cause of overpopulation and considered campaigns to sterilize women while denying them access to abortion highly discriminatory.

On May 4, 1970, a newsletter, accompanied by a packet of information, went out from the Dallas Committee to all persons on their mailing list. The newsletter advertised their upcoming events—two discussion sessions, the public forum set for Tuesday, May 19, a movie, plans for a speakers' bureau—and reported on the activities of the membership, fund-raising, and letter-writing committees. The latter had been busy writing to members of the Texas Medical Association's Special Committee on Abortion Laws. The newsletter was accompanied by a packet of information that consisted mostly of ASA reprints.

Their most ambitious project was the public forum, now called an Ecumenical Dialogue on Abortion. It was held at eight P.M. at the Northaven Methodist Church. Speakers included Virgina Whitehill;

Dr. Claude Evans, chaplain at Southern Methodist University; State Representative James Clark; James T. Downs III, M.D., an obstetrician and member of the Texas Medical Association's abortion committee; Shirley Levin, an attorney; Dr. Edward Rydman, a marriage counselor; and the Reverend Paul Schott, president of a local Jesuit preparatory school.

Reverend Schott, in particular, had been invited to present the opposition's point of view. Genial and articulate, a fair and intellectual debater, he often shared a podium with Whitehill at her invitation. The day would eventually come, however, when she would ask him to join her in a public debate and he would refuse, without offering any reason. Whitehill would always believe that the Church, increasing worried over the success of the reform movement, had ordered Schott to stop appearing with her. As they failed to round up widespread support from Catholic laity, the Church hierarchy closed the door on open debate on abortion.

Another panelist, the Reverend Claude Evans, also would play an important role in the Dallas group and in Texas abortion reform in general. As a chaplain whose flock consisted of the entire student body of Southern Methodist University, Reverend Evans had seen and heard more than his share of tragic stories about abortion, many of them firsthand from the women he counseled. He had been involved in debate with other university faculty about the university's role as a parent in absentia, a debate that had been centered on whether the university was obligated to inform parents when it knew that a student was seeking or had obtained an abortion. Evans strongly felt that informing parents was a betrayal of the students' trust. This and his natural sympathies propelled him into abortion-reform activism. He became an early member of the steering committee of the Dallas group and was always one of its staunchest and most energetic reformers.

The importance of the presence of the clergy on the podium that night and in abortion reform could not be underestimated in a state like Texas, located in the middle of the Bible belt. In most areas where abortion reform had gained a foothold, the bulk of the opposition could be expected to come from the Roman Catholic church. In Texas, however, the Church was not particularly powerful; most of its members there consisted of poor Hispanics, and the real source (potentially) of religious opposition, were there to be any, lay with the Protestant churches, both fundamental and mainstream.

It was a calculated decision on the part of the Dallas Committee to hold their first public event in a church.

One hundred seventy-five persons attended the forum, which consisted of a brief panel discussion followed by a lengthy question-and-answer session. Representative Clark opened the meeting by calling for an individual's right to do what his or her conscience dictated—"what one feels God intended for him." Speaking of the recent defeat of his abortion bill, which he attributed largely to organized efforts on the part of the Catholic church, he said, "The spirit of inquiry is not the situation in Austin. . . . I have never seen an issue with so much intemperance, bigotry, and controversy." Adding that "it was only in this century that the pope decided abortion was contrary to the law of God," Clark urged people to make their feelings known to their legislators.

Father Schott responded by stressing that there was "a moral position which Catholics do support and defend—the moral right of the fetus." He said the removal of all laws on abortion could "give the state the right of decision which could have devastating effects" on such things, for example, as mercy killing.

Whitehill drew the greatest amount of applause, however, when she noted that despite opposition to abortion, which some religions saw as a form of murder, few religions had "come out against the killing of young men in wars over real estate." To tumultuous applause, she added: "Some call this postnatal abortion."

The Dallas Committee was thrilled with the turnout at the public forum. Like most of their early efforts, it was even better received than they had expected. They made plans to step up their activities and intensify the campaign to persuade people to support abortion reform. Busy as the women were with their own agenda, though, in May something happened that electrified them and lent enormous credibility to their reform efforts. In early March the Dallas Committee had learned that Linda Coffee, working with another young lawyer named Sarah Weddington, whom they did not know, had filed two abortion suits. The cases were scheduled to be argued in the federal district court on Friday, May 22, just four days after the ecumenical forum. The Dallas Committee would most definitely be in the courtroom on the day of the oral arguments to show their support. In fact, they would even telephone as many women as they could to encourage them to attend the hearing and show their support for abortion reform.

8

The Dallas
Hearing

May 23, the day of the oral arguments in the Fifth Circuit Court, was merely overcast, but it could have been pouring rain and Coffee's and Weddington's spirits would not have been dampened. Both women were surprisingly self-confident considering their youth and inexperience. This would be Weddington's first courtroom appearance, and *Roe* v. *Wade* was certainly the biggest case Coffee had ever handled.

The two women met early on the morning of the hearing to review their arguments. Coffee would lay the groundwork with a discussion of the technical, procedural issues involved, but both women were eager to drive home the idea that a woman's right to abortion was constitutionally protected. This was the crux of their case.

They would be sharing their arguments with Fred Bruner and Roy Merrill, counsel for Dr. Hallford. Although the lawyers had talked with one another several times over the past few months, they would be meeting that morning in person for the first time. Since their primary responsibility was to their client, Bruner and Merrill planned to argue that the laws were vague and overbroad, the typical defense when a doctor was accused of illegal abortion. These were constitutional issues, too, but a ruling that the Texas law was vague or too broad did nothing to establish a woman's constitutional right to abortion. Eager to cover as many bases as they could, Coffee and Weddington were not averse to having these arguments made so long as they got to present the view that women had a constitutional right to abortion.

The hearing was to be held in Judge Hughes's courtroom in the Dallas federal courthouse. Outside the main entrance on Ervay Street, large, shiny brass letters proclaimed the building's odd dual usage: United States Post Office and Courthouse. Occupying a full city block, the building had been constructed in the 1930s by WPA workers.

The first floor bustled with the usual activity of post offices everywhere, and only on the second and third floors, where the judges' chambers and the courtrooms were located, did the building take on the somber aura one associates with courtroom proceedings. White marble rose halfway up the white plaster walls, interrupted by the heavy oak double doors of the courtrooms. Unlike the post office, where civil servants and citizens mingled across open doors and counters, the marble walls and closed doors of the courthouse acted as a barrier between those who came for justice and those who were charged with dispensing it. Voices were eerily muted as if they came from some lofty, far-off place. Walking on the barely worn granite floors, I automatically slowed and lightened my pace, a fruitless attempt to reduce the echo of my footsteps, which were by far the loudest noise to be heard. A child would know without being told not to frolic in these halls.

The courtroom was packed, primarily with women and the press. Whitehill and her band of reformers had done well rounding up spectators, and most of the seats were filled with interested, pro-choice women. (Outside, five women carrying placards that proclaimed "My body, my decision" and "Compulsory pregnancy is a cruel and unusual punishment" picketed the courthouse throughout the proceedings.) Print reporters, chattering like magpies among themselves, crowded into the other unoccupied seats. By nature far more curious than the average observer, they spent the entire half hour or so before the hearing bouncing theories and prognostications off one another. Notably absent were any television people. Portable videotape cameras had not yet revolutionized the evening news with live, on-site reportage, and since the television stations had nothing to show, they were not much interested in the case. Rumor held that one judge's wife was present in the courtroom, but rumor often held that when an important case was being heard. The Does were present, Norma McCorvey was not.

At eight months, McCorvey's pregnancy would be difficult to conceal, but Coffee and Weddington were not eager to have their plaintiff in the courtroom for other reasons. They did not know how thoroughly the state had investigated her background, whether, for example, they had found out who she was, how pregnant she was, or anything about how she lived. Her presence might trigger prejudicial comments about her lifestyle or unmarried status or strengthen any arguments the state planned to make along these lines.

Keeping McCorvey out of the courtroom was not difficult. She was so unavailable—usually taking up to three or four days to locate—that had they wanted her present at the last minute, they probably could not have arranged it.

The Fifth Circuit three-judge court was called to order promptly at ten A.M. Coffee and Weddington were lucky their case was being heard on the Fifth Circuit. On its bench throughout the 1960s and early 1970s sat some of the most learned, experienced, and even-handed jurists in the nation. Until *Roe* came before the court, the Fifth Circuit was best known for having undertaken the sometimes painful implementation of the *Brown* v. *Board of Education* decision, which had ordered the desegregation of American public schools. Described by one court watcher primarily as the "pace horse for the development of race relations," the Fifth Circuit, which at that time encompassed Alabama, Florida, Georgia, Louisiana, Mississippi, and Texas (it has since been subdivided), actually had a turf more complex and diverse than that of any other federal circuit. Its justices routinely handled maritime, border and immigration, land speculation, and gas and oil law.

The members of the abortion case panel had been announced several months earlier. All three were Dallasites. In one chair sat William McLaughlin Taylor, whom intimates called Mac. Appointed to the federal bench in 1966 by President Lyndon B. Johnson, Judge Taylor had encountered his first controversial case shortly after he took his seat. In the nation's first case of its kind, he upheld a school's right to refuse enrollment to three long-haired male youths. The decade-long Dallas school desegregation case began in Taylor's courtroom in October 1970. Within a year Taylor had ordered the busing of 7,300 students, a plan that was later overruled in the Fifth Circuit Appeals Court. A second plan, which Taylor also approved, was rejected by the Supreme Court. Taylor reopened hearings on the case a third time but withdrew when criticism surfaced over the fact that his former law firm had defended the school system.

Taylor was known for his fairness and patience, the latter a rare trait on this particular panel of judges. An experienced litigator, he prided himself on never having held an attorney in contempt of court. One law clerk recalled: "He was very willing to sit there and let the attorneys put on their cases. But he never lost sight of the fact that it was not the lawyers' cases, but the litigants' cases." Taylor's background before going on the bench had mostly been in trial law, and with criminal charges pending against their client, Bruner and Merrill considered him a most welcome addition to the panel.

The sole woman on the panel was Sarah Tighman Hughes, who could, it had been said, "strut sitting down"—a reference to the fact that Hughes more than compensated for her small physical stature with a peppery personality. Having achieved national recognition as the judge who swore in Lyndon Johnson after John F. Kennedy's assassination (something she did not consider the highlight of her career), she shortly thereafter shocked people with her scathing denunciation of Dallas as a city that tolerated a "climate of hate."

Hughes's other foray into the national limelight had occurred in 1935 when she was nominated to a district judgeship. A state senator who opposed her nomination said she "ought to be home washing dishes," to which she retorted that the senator would not have been elected to his position if "his charming wife had been home washing dishes instead of campaigning for him." To further reinforce her point, Hughes invited the national press to her home to take pictures of her at her kitchen sink.

Hughes never wavered in her support of women, although she preferred to think of herself more as a role model for what young women could do rather than an active feminist. When Whitehill once confessed to Judge Hughes that she was feeling depressed over the lack of response to abortion reform, Hughes admonished her: "Why, Ginny, I wanted to put women on juries in the 1930s, and Texas didn't let them sit until 1954. Don't you dare give up."

President John F. Kennedy appointed Hughes to the federal bench in 1961. Opposition to her appointment arose, ostensibly on grounds that at age sixty-one she was too old; actually, those who opposed her appointment did so because they resented her political activism while on the bench. Insulted that either reason should be grounds for keeping her off the federal bench, she decided to fight for the job. A lifelong liberal Democrat with ties to House Speaker Sam Rayburn and Senator Ralph Yarbrough, Hughes called in years of political favors that were owed to her; as a result, her nomination sailed smoothly through the Senate.

Hughes was right about not being too old for the job: the federal bench got over twenty years of good service from her, years in which she refused to relinquish her overtly political activities. Coffee and Weddington would have been pleased to have any woman on the panel, but as they stared at the small red rose embroidered on Judge Hughes's robe, they knew this was a judge they would have chosen themselves had the decision been up to them.

The remaining judge, the man who would dominate the hearing, was Irving Goldberg, a feisty personality widely admired for his intellectual prowess on and off the bench. Being subjected to rapid-fire questioning by Justice Irving Goldberg, who was always one step ahead of everyone else in the courtroom, was an experience lesser lawyers preferred to avoid if possible. Even the brightest Dallas lawyers liked to tell themselves that it was hard for anyone to look smart when Judge Goldberg was doing the questioning.

He was an intensely private man; little was known about his life off the bench. Prior to his federal appointment in 1966 by President Johnson, Goldberg had spent most of his professional life practicing law in Dallas. He was deeply involved in the civic and philanthropic life of the city and in 1968 was awarded the prestigious Brotherhood Citation of the National Conference of Christians and Jews.

Coffee and Weddington were more than willing to take the risk of looking stupid, however, to have someone with Goldberg's leanings and integrity on the panel. He was the Fifth Circuit's most consistent liberal and had, in the words of one Fifth Circuit scholar, shown "unwavering support for enforcement of civil rights and liberties." However, Judge Goldberg was above all else a practical liberal who sought solutions that worked; that might serve them well.

From Coffee and Weddington's point of view, the panel looked as if it had been hand-picked for them, and indeed, many people were willing to believe that Fifth Circuit Chief Judge John Brown had weighted the panel in favor of the abortion-reform forces. It is highly unlikely that he did any such thing. First of all, the Fifth Circuit at that time was judicially active and liberal; second, there were guidelines about the choice of judges for a three-judge court. Since Coffee had filed two separate cases, which were assigned to two different judges, the judges in whose court the cases fell were automatically appointed to the panel when the cases were consolidated; that accounted for the presence of Taylor and Hughes on the panel and left Brown with only one justice to appoint with a free hand. That had to be a circuit judge, and Goldberg was an obvious choice since he lived in Dallas. Nevertheless, the makeup of the panel provided the two young lawyers with an enormous psychological boost.

Since Coffee was handling the legal technicalities of the case, she would speak first. Her arguments were of the utmost importance. Any challenge to a state law, particularly one brought in a federal court, is regarded as a serious matter, largely because the Constitution contains guarantees that are designed to protect the states' autonomy from the federal government. When such cases are brought before a federal court, special legal barriers are imposed to insure that the federal government interferes as little as possible with the affairs of a state. For example, before the court could weigh whether or not McCorvey was legally entitled to an abortion, it had to consider such things as whether she had any right to sue the state of Texas over its abortion law and, if she did have a right to sue, whether she had a right to sue in a federal court. The federal courts were obligated to let the states resolve such issues either through the state court systems or through legislative action whenever possible.

A federal court could step in only under rare circumstances, when, for example, as Coffee would now argue, a state was infringing upon a citizen's basic, fundamental rights as guaranteed in the Constitution. It was now Coffee's job to persuade the court to look beyond these limitations on its right to interfere with the affairs of a state to render a decision on the merits of the case, that is, whether or not her client (and by implication, all women in Texas) had a right to control her own body.

Coffee began by discussing the kind of relief the court could grant her clients. It could grant declaratory relief, essentially a statement indicating that it found the Texas abortion law to be unconstitutional. It could also grant injunctive relief, a more effective remedy, in which it would, in effect, order the state of Texas to stop enforcing its abortion law.

Although the assumption was made that a state would follow any ruling by a federal court, this was not necessarily the case, particularly in the emotionally charged 1960s when state laws were routinely challenged in federal courts. For this reason, the granting of injunctive relief was considered a more serious legal action than the granting of declaratory relief. Depending upon one's leanings (that is, whether one was an ardent states' righter or a believer in a strong federal government), an injunctive order directed at state officials could be seen as insult added to injury (the injury being the declaratory relief) or an added incentive to obey a federal court ruling. The federal courts were understandably reluctant to issue an injunction to a state if they could avoid doing so.

Coffee believed that both kinds of relief were necessary if her client and the women of Texas were to have any real access to abortion. If the court granted only declaratory relief, she feared that the status of the Texas abortion law would be left in limbo, and that doctors and hospitals would not be willing to perform abortions until the matter was resolved. That would not happen until the state legislature rewrote its abortion statutes, something that could take months or even years. Furthermore, there was no guarantee that the new law would not be even more restrictive than the original.

If the court issued injunctive as well as declaratory relief, however, abortion would become legal virtually overnight in Texas, since law enforcement officials would be under court order not to enforce the law. Coffee was certain that this would guarantee access to abortion. Without the threat of prosecution, many hospitals and doctors would perform them gladly.

In order to convince the court that her client was entitled to both declaratory and injunctive relief, however, Coffee had to persuade the judges that the abortion right was constitutionally protected and that it fell into the category of fundamental rights that were afforded special protection. For example, First Amendment rights involving free speech and assembly were so protected.

Coffee believed that another federal case, *Stanley* v. *Georgia*, had extended the same special protection to the right of privacy. But because she was on less secure ground with the privacy argument (the right to privacy was so new that it was impossible to know whether the judges accepted it as a right, let alone as a specially protected right), she began to discuss the First Amendment right to abortion. She explained how the right of free association between a doctor and patient was impinged upon by the current abortion law. Doctors, for example, did not feel free to advise their patients on abortion.

It quickly became apparent to everyone present in the courtroom that the judges had no interest in pursuing the First Amendment as the source of the right to abortion. Judge Hughes interrupted Coffee to ask, "What First Amendment rights?" Judge Goldberg redirected the questioning, asking Coffee whether she thought the same argument that injunctive relief was required could be made if the Ninth Amendment were involved.

Although mention of the Ninth Amendment was somewhat surprising to her, Coffee seized the opportunity to reframe the argument around a concept in which the justices were apparently interested. "I don't think it makes any difference in our case," she replied, "because whether you say that the rights involved are First Amendment rights or Ninth Amendment rights, I feel they are so important that they deserve the special protection that has been accorded to First Amendment rights. In other words, they involve fundamental human freedoms, which I think recent cases have indicated are beginning to be given the same priority treatment that First Amendment rights have always been afforded."

The court next turned its attention, as Coffee had known it would at some point during her argument, to whether any other remedy (such as remanding the case to a Texas state court) existed short of declaring the Texas abortion law unconstitutional. If so, the judges would be inclined not to rule and instead give the state a chance to fix its own law without federal interference.

Could Dr. Hallford have taken his case to a state court? Coffee acknowledged that he could have but said she did not think it was fair to make the rights of women to obtain abortion contingent on a doctor's defense of himself in a criminal case. Was the law separable—that is, could it be rewritten by the state legislature or courts in such a way as to remove any unconstitutional portions? What if, for example, the section permitting abortions only to save a woman's life were removed? Would that make the law more acceptable? Coffee insisted it would not, reminding the court that in any event this had not been the intent of the original framers of the law. She added, "I think the statute is so bad that the court is just really going to have to strike it all down. I don't think it's worth salvaging."

To which Judge Goldberg responded: "You think sixty-three years of unconstitutionality should have worn everyone's constitutional patience. Is that what you're saying?"

"I think so," Coffee answered. "I think the state of Texas had plenty of time to construe this statute, if it can be construed in a constitutional manner." That ended the time allotted for her argument.

The spectators in the courtroom had grown restless during Coffee's argument, although the judges and other lawyers had paid close attention to what she said. This impatience was not entirely due to the nature of her arguments, either. Despite her brilliant legal mind, Coffee was not a particularly effective or dramatic speaker. She had a distracted and somewhat disorganized way of speaking. Her diffidence was another barrier to understanding her presentation, and she looked worried. But the bottom line was that the topics she discussed were not glamorous or provocative. Important as they were to the outcome of the case, to the untrained legal ear they were little more than pedantic legal details.

Whitehill, for one, could not stop thinking how messy she looked. It bothered her that Coffee did not appear to have taken the time to comb her hair. Whitehill, who valued appearances, thought Coffee looked disheveled. (Indeed, Coffee might have looked even more disheveled had Fred Bruner, who accompanied her to the courthouse, not walked her into a drugstore and bought her a pair of hose so that she would not appear with a run in the ones she was wearing.)

The spectators, especially the women on the Dallas Committee, knew how important this case was, and frankly they had been hoping for a little more drama, or perhaps more flair in presenting the arguments, something that would make exciting reading in tomorrow's newspapers and interest even more people in their cause. They were not disappointed when Weddington began to argue her half of the case.

Although less confident of her legal prowess than Coffee, Weddington was an excellent public speaker. Calm and serene once it was her turn to speak, she managed to sound expert—and self-assured. She began by announcing that her argument would cover the "justification which the state alleges for the state abortion statute, that is, the protection of the life of the child, and . . . whether or not there are substantial constitutional issues involved."

Weddington continued: "I would like to draw the court's attention to the fact that life is an ongoing process. It is almost impossible to define a point at which life begins or perhaps even at which life ends. Certainly life in its very general matter is present in the sperm, it's present in the ova. This potential of life depends on a set of circumstances which must then occur."

Her argument was one that reformers used increasingly when confronting those who claimed that human life was present from the moment of conception. Why limit the onset of human life to conception? Why not go back even further and say that it was present in every sperm and every ovum? Did people want to outlaw birth control because it destroyed potential life?

Although Weddington was prepared to cite several cases in which courts had found that fetuses did not have the legal rights of a person, she never got the chance. For the second time, Judge Goldberg asked counsel to address the issue of whether abortion could be based on a Ninth Amendment right, as well as whether the state had any compelling interest in regulating abortion. Did the state, for example, have any reason to require that all abortions be done in a hospital or that they all be certified by one or more physicians? He also asked Weddington whether she thought there should be differing standards for married versus single women.

Weddington agreed that health standards were involved and that nonlicensed medical personnel should not be permitted to do abortions, but she added: "I cannot see any justification for regulating the abortion when it is done by a doctor." She also said she did not see how denying unmarried women, who, she noted, formed the majority of those requesting abortions could serve any compelling state interest.

Judge Goldberg asked if she knew whether there was any relationship between access to abortions and promiscuity. Weddington said there was none that she knew of.

He continued to press this point, asking whether she knew of any research on the subject, to which Weddington replied, "Not to my knowledge, other than the fact that [such young women] are already promiscuous when the statute is in effect, and in fact, these are some of the girls who need this right and who have the most socially compelling arguments why they should be allowed abortions—the young still in school, those unable to shoulder the responsibility of a child—these girls should not be put through the pregnancy and should be entitled to an abortion." Weddington felt strongly about this issue, and it showed in her response; her voice took on an orator's eloquence.

Goldberg next asked whether the fact that the state might have to pay for many of the abortions for young women should be a reason to deny them the right to abortion. It was a reasonable question in light of the fact that Texas shouldered one of the nation's largest welfare rolls and that Medicaid payments for obstetrical care had recently been reduced in Texas. Weddington said she thought the state might have more of an interest in eliminating the welfare payments to support children after they were born.

Her argument concluded when Goldberg asked her whether she thought the Texas abortion statute was more vulnerable on the Ninth Amendment basis or on grounds of vagueness. Without hesitation she replied: "I believe it is more vulnerable on the Ninth Amendment basis."

A large, impeccably tailored man with a gallant and somewhat imposing personality and years of experience in criminal courtrooms, Fred Bruner managed to control and shape his arguments more successfully than any of the other lawyers who came before the court that day. Determined to waste no time in turning the argument back around to his client's interests, Bruner began by expressing his regret that Weddington found the law more vulnerable on the Ninth Amendment because he "was about to argue on the vagueness of the statute."

With the court's encouragement, he proceeded to do so: "It's the position of Dr. Hallford . . . that not only is this language vague and hard to understand for the man of common intelligence, but even doctors themselves cannot interpret the language of the statute, and in Dr. Hallford's affidavit, he states that even hospitals and doctors cannot determine what they should or shouldn't do, what is permissible and what is not permissible under the language of this particular statute." To further support his argument, Bruner cited several recent cases—*Belous*, *Vuitch*, and *Babbitz*—in which courts had overturned the law on grounds of vagueness.

In summary, Bruner addressed an issue that had concerned the justices throughout the arguments—namely, whether declaring the Texas law unconstitutional would permit anyone—even scurrilous, unskilled abortionists—to perform abortions. Unlike most states, Texas had no law restricting abortion only to licensed physicians, and the court had shown concern that overturning the law might mean anyone could perform abortions under any circumstances. Bruner declared: "I think the very fact that . . . this abortion law [is] on the books of Texas has driven women to [illegal abortion] in the state today, and that if the abortion law of the state of Texas were declared unconstitutional, it would give women the right, the constitutional right, to go to a doctor or to a qualified person who had the right surgical instruments and have this matter done at their wishes. . . ."

Throughout his testimony, but especially in his summary, Bruner had shown himself to be an adept criminal lawyer. Not only had he managed to reassure the judges about something that might prove to be a major stumbling block for them, the fact that their ruling would free anyone in the state of Texas to do abortions, he had also managed to end his argument on a small but meaningful note of drama.

What Merrill lacked of Bruner's suavity he made up for in earnestness. His task was to attack the other major weakness in the Texas abortion law that could conceivably affect Hallford. Because of the way the Texas abortion law was written, the burden of proof was on the doctor charged with illegal abortion. The defendant had to prove he had not committed a crime; it was not up to the state to prove he had, as was usually the case in criminal prosecutions. Merrill argued that placing the burden of proof on the defendant was a clear violation of due process under the Fifth, Ninth, and Fourteenth amendments.

So concisely did he present his argument that he required less than the seven and a half minutes allotted to him. The justices listened carefully and did not interrupt Merrill once.

* * *

Plaintiffs' counsel had completed their arguments, and it was now time for the attorney general, who was automatically a party to any suit that challenged the constitutionality of a state law, to defend the Texas abortion law. Despite months of delay on the state's part and the fact that the D.A.'s office had done all the work, the attorney general's office seemed ill-prepared for the task at hand.

The attorney general had not been surprised to hear that the abortion law was being challenged. His staff knew the abortion issue was ripe for a challenge and had expected some kind of legal action sooner or later. This did not mean, however, that the lawsuit was welcome.

The Texas attorney general's staff was beleaguered with civil rights suits in the late 1960s. At times they averaged fifty-two cases per lawyer. The numerous civil rights cases were considered a thorn in their side because they took up so much time and manpower for what were deemed inconsequential reasons. One prisoner, for example, had managed to file seventeen separate lawsuits involving possible violations of his civil rights. And if prisoners were a problem, students were even worse. Across the nation they had torn up campuses and towns, and even in staid Austin mobs of students from the University of Texas had swarmed over the Capitol grounds. Lawyers from the attorney general's office had stood at the windows of their seventh-story office and watched what they could only view as out-and-out (and, in their view, inexcusable) anarchy.

By the time *Roe* v. *Wade* was filed, though, the attorney general's men were optimistic that the pendulum of public opinion was swinging back to a law-and-order stance. People were tired of having their courts tied up with frivolous civil rights challenges from long-haired kids, draft protestors, and other dissidents. No one understood what women had to be so unhappy about. As the sixties drew to a relatively quiet close, the attorney general's office had gotten its second wind; they would be more than happy to take on anyone who wanted to challenge the state's abortion laws. They were sure the case would be an easy victory for them.

The state could have decided not to respond to the challenge. It would have been a simple matter to let a law that was relatively unenforced anyway become officially defunct. When a woman had sued to establish her right to march with the Texas A & M band, the attorney general had declined to defend the law that kept her out of the band. But no one, at least no one in the attorney general's office, thought legalizing abortion was as simple an issue as letting a woman march with the boys if that was what she wanted to do. Abortion involved life-and-death issues—specifically, the life of an innocent fetus that could not defend itself. No one was surprised when word came down from Attorney General Crawford Martin himself that the state would defend its abortion law.

Like all federal cases, *Roe* v. *Wade* fell under the auspices of the enforcement division, headed by Robert Flowers. Flowers turned the case over to Jay Floyd, his assistant chief, because he knew Floyd would recognize its importance. He had great respect for Floyd, not least because he believed Floyd to be one of the most meticulous lawyers he had ever known. Floyd's pencil holder held perfectly sharpened pencils, and his files were color-coordinated. His desk drawers were organized, unheard of for an overworked assistant attorney general. A specialist in liquor law, Floyd had prepared a huge notebook, always on his desk, containing every law written in that field.

Each morning Floyd began work the same way, by moving the files of the cases he would be working on that day from a windowsill to his desk. As he checked each case's progress, he moved the file back to the windowsill. If he had to recheck a case, he moved the file back to his desk and then back to the windowsill again. Floyd worked rapidly and rarely required assistance. He wrote his own briefs, composing them as he typed and rarely preparing more than one draft.

Flowers left his people alone once he had assigned a case, asking only to be updated on an informal basis; but *Roe* v. *Wade* intrigued him, and it seemed to have personally interested the chief, too. Attorney General Martin had told Flowers he thought not defending the abortion law would be like not defending the murder law. Besides, he was tired of people suing public servants like Henry Wade, who were only trying to do their jobs.

Flowers, too, had given the case considerable thought. He felt *Roe* v. *Wade* was an open-and-shut case, one the state could win easily. As far as he was concerned, from the moment of conception the chromosome structure was in place, the gene structure was in place, and life had begun. Any defense of the Texas abortion law would be based on the fact that the womb was food and shelter, just like a baby in its home. To destroy an infant in the womb was murder, the same as when a three-month-old infant were killed in its cradle.

One thing, Flowers knew, would prevent the state from using this defense: this view was religious or philosophical rather than legal. The law did not view abortion in this way. Flowers knew the state could not go into court and claim that abortion was murder for the simple reason that legally it was not. Neither Texas law nor, for that matter, the laws of any other state held that abortion was murder. It was always a lesser crime, usually manslaughter.

Flowers believed that a great number of those who opposed the legalization of abortion shared his view. If his assessment was correct, then there were many people out there who not only did not want abortion legalized, but would support a move to restrict it further. He thought the time was ripe to assert a claim on behalf of the fetus. If the state built its defense around the idea that abortion was murder in the moral sense, at least, Flowers believed people, including the judges who would hear the case, would understand and accept his argument regardless of how the Texas law was written. Once everyone agreed that abortion was a grave moral wrong, surely the Texas abortion law would stand.

Thus, Flowers was optimistic that the state would not only defend its abortion law successfully, but that it might even be tightened further as a result. If he could get a ruling that the law was designed to protect fetal life, Texas would have the toughest abortion law in the country.

Flowers had discussed his views on abortion with his boss, Attorney General Crawford Martin, who liked the idea and gave him the go-ahead. Floyd, a busy man, had no objections to being presented with a ready-made defense—one with which, as it happened, he agreed. He had not yet had time to talk with John Tolle, who was handling the case for the district attorney's office, but he assumed the D.A.'s people would go along with this defense. Floyd could not spend too much time on the case, so he let Tolle do most of the work of preparing the defense. The two men exchanged a few cursory letters over the next few months but never met to coordinate their defense or work out a mutual strategy. They would be meeting for the first time when they presented the oral arguments in defense of the state.

Floyd was nervous when his turn came to argue. He had stood up earlier out of turn, because he had mistakenly thought it was his time to speak. Now he would have to begin his arguments with an apology, to be sure the justices understood that he had meant no harm by speaking out of order. Despite his nervousness, he was confident he could make short work of the case. Neither he nor anyone in the attorney general's office could imagine that the court would seriously consider declaring the abortion law unconstitutional. Besides, there were serious jurisdictional problems with the case, such as whether Jane Roe or any woman had a right to sue for legalized abortion. After all, the law was not directed at them; no woman in Texas was ever party to an abortion suit, so she could not claim to have been injured by the law.

Floyd began by pointing out that it was the state's position that the court had no reason even to hear this case since, as far as he could see, none of the plaintiffs had any standing to sue. He believed—the state was arguing—that the case was moot. None of the court papers had made any reference to how far along Roe was in her pregnancy, but since the suit had been filed in March and it was now the middle of May, assuming that the defendant had been at least a couple of months and possibly several months pregnant when the case was initiated, it now stood to reason that she was either no longer pregnant or was too far along in her pregnancy to undergo an abortion even if the court agreed she could have one. Her case presented no real controversy; there was nothing to litigate; in other words, the case was moot. As for the Does, their case had never presented any real controversy since, as far as he knew, Mary Doe was not pregnant, nor had she been when the case was filed. The original motion filed by her attorneys had made this clear. She and her husband therefore had no standing to sue.

This was the argument Coffee and Weddington had feared. It was the reason they had amended *Roe* v. *Wade* to a class-action suit. As plaintiffs in a class-action suit, Jane Roe and Mary Doe were suing not merely for themselves, but on behalf of all other women who might find themselves similarly situated—pregnant and in need of an abortion. Nevertheless, they waited nervously to hear how the justices would respond to Floyd.

Fortunately, his argument seemed to carry little weight with the court. Judge Goldberg reminded Floyd that some of the children involved in school desegregation cases had graduated from college by the time their cases were litigated. Did this mean that they were not entitled to attend desegregated schools? Judge Hughes indignantly asked: "What would give them standing in a case like this to test the constitutionality of this statute? Apparently you don't think that anybody had standing."

Coffee and Weddington breathed a sigh of relief. They had safely passed the hurdle that had prevented so many others from bringing abortion cases into court. Of course, the judges could always change their minds when they deliberated, but for the moment they did not appear receptive to the argument that the case was moot, that Roe or any other pregnant woman had no recourse in the courts simply because pregnancy was a self-terminating condition.

Sensing correctly that he had lost this round, Floyd moved on to the First Amendment issues, declaring that he failed to see how a right to abortion could be found anywhere in the constitution, but especially in the First Amendment.

Judge Goldberg quickly replied, "We agree with you on that." But then he asked Floyd to address whatever constitutional grounds might be found in the Ninth Amendment and the issue of vagueness.

At that point Floyd's defense began to unravel. He had not prepared to rebut the plaintiffs' claim that abortion was constitutionally protected, so he pressed ahead with the only argument he had prepared—namely, that the state had a compelling interest in protecting the fetus. In doing so he made a major mistake, one that was probably fatal to his defense of the Texas abortion law. Floyd cited *Belous*, the case in which the California Supreme Court had ruled that the woman's right to abortion was based on privacy; the *Belous* decision had been considered an unequivocal victory for pro-choice forces. Floyd continued: "Now, Your Honors, there have been many, many arguments advanced as to when an embryo becomes a human being. There have been religious groups that have joined in the controversy, and it's my understanding, and I'm not setting forth the Catholic faith—"

Floyd's point was lost on everyone except Goldberg, who interrupted to ask if Floyd was trying to say that the state's compelling interest extended to the point of conception.

"That is correct," Floyd answered.

"I don't see how that's getting you anywhere."

"But the point is," Floyd continued, "that the state's interest—is that it may be a consideration of whether or not murder occurs, that is, if this embryo is considered a human being."

Goldberg again tried to find out whether Floyd was arguing

that an embryo should be considered a human being from the moment of conception.

"Yes, Your Honor," he replied, and then he did something a lawyer should never do: he began to hedge on his defense. "Now I'm not advocating this, I'm saying there's some controversy in regard to this, that at no matter what stage of pregnancy, the embryo is a human being." Floyd continued, "There is controversy to that effect. Medical practitioners disagree, and speaking of medical advances, we have now reached a point, I think, where a medical practitioner can operate on an unborn child, perform surgery. The state must give consideration to these various interests and opinions in deciding whether or not it has an interest in the subject matter."

Judge Goldberg responded, "Well, the state has asserted its compelling interest to the extent that it makes any abortion under any condition practically illegal."

"Except to save the life of the mother," Floyd added.

Judge Hughes, who could stand no more of the confusion, interrupted: "But don't you know what that means? The case which you quoted held that [the law] was too vague and indefinite—the *Belous* case knocked the statute on that ground."

"That is correct," Floyd said, "on the right of privacy—there's no question about that."

"Well, then," Hughes reiterated, "your case isn't authority for your argument."

"No, the *Belous* case—I'm not saying it's authority, I'm getting to the right of privacy."

Floyd went on to say that privacy meant only the right to be left alone and nothing more. It had nothing to do with abortion, in his view. He had obviously known where he was going with the *Belous* reference but had still made a mistake by relying on a case that did not ultimately support his view.

Judge Goldberg pounced on the word "privacy," noting that in his view it was a bad word to use in this area. "But apparently everybody wants to use it. . . . I just know privacy won't do, but I know what you are talking about." He then tried unsuccessfully to pin Floyd down about whether a woman's death had to be imminent for an abortion to be acceptable. Floyd declined to make what he viewed as an essentially medical judgment.

His time up, Floyd sat down. His argument had not been successful. It had been weak, and after the mistake of citing *Belous*, he had never recouped enough to save his defense of the Texas abortion law.

John Tolle was left with a touchy task: in fifteen minutes he had to pick up the pieces of his co-counsel's shattered defense *and* build a solid case for the state. He had put considerable time and effort into the preparation of this case, and like Floyd, he believed that the state had a right to protect fetal life. Unlike Floyd, he had limited his examination of abortion to the purely legal issues. That he now planned to do the same thing with his oral argument would prove to be his greatest strength. Tolle's argument would be the most intellectually enticing, if not ultimately the most persuasive, that would be heard in the courtroom that day.

He wasted no time disputing the plaintiffs' right to sue, nor did he attempt to refute Weddington and Coffee's arguments directly; rather, he tried to make the court see them in a different light. He began with the difficult issue of states' rights. Noting that he did not disagree with Weddington's statement that no one knows when life begins, he went on to say that even in the absence of answers to this difficult question, the state still had "a right to protect life . . . in whatever stage it may be in . . . and if there is no absolute fact as to when life occurs, then it becomes, I think, a legislative problem as to when they're going to set an arbitrary time."

Finally the state had scored a point. The idea that abortion was most legitimately a concern of the state and not the federal government had to have been on the minds of the judges that day. Throughout the 1960s states' rights had become a highly controversial issue, particularly as the federal courts, following an example set by the Supreme Court, had proven increasingly open to expanding individuals' civil rights, often at a cost to the states' powers to regulate their affairs.

States' right supporters maintained that changes in the social fabric of the nation should come from the individual states and not from the federal courts, which were seen as overstepping their powers when they ruled on matters such as the constitutionality of state laws. In contrast, those who led the drive to expand individual civil rights (and they were well aware that their best chance for success lay with the receptive federal courts) argued that letting each state establish its own guidelines on such important issues as voting, educational, and prisoners' rights would result in a patchwork of laws that would vary from state to state and prove to be highly discriminatory. If Americans valued equal educational opportunities, then surely the only course of action was to protect that right for all citizens. And this was the task most effectively accomplished by the federal government, they argued. For example, it would not be possible, or moral, to desegregate the schools in some states but not in others. Often lost in the debate over states' rights was the fact that the Constitution was designed to protect individuals from government tyranny, whether state or federally instituted, and that governments on all levels existed only to serve the people.

Nevertheless, the principle of states' rights was part of the system of checks and balances that had been carefully woven into the Constitution, and it must, as an ideology, be respected. For over two centuries, therefore, the federal courts had challenged the authority of the states only rarely and then with the greatest caution. Several recent cases, in fact, had warned the federal government away from excessive interference in the affairs of the states. In 1959, in *U.S.* v. *Livingston*, the Supreme Court had written: "Regard for the interest and sovereignty of the state and reluctance to needlessly adjudicate constitutional issues may require a federal district court to abstain from adjudication if the parties may avail themselves of an appropriate procedure to obtain state interpretation of state laws requiring construction." Several cases warned against the federal courts interfering in state criminal proceedings, for example, or from seeking to adjudicate a case that could be handled in a state court.

But the *Livingston* decision also contained a warning about the degree to which federal courts could justifiably abstain from state concerns, noting: "Though never interpreted by a state court, if a state statute is not fairly subject to an interpretation which will avoid or modify the federal constitutional question, it is the duty of a federal court to decide the federal question put to it." Not to do so might subject the litigants to unnecessary strife and expense.

Indeed, despite Tolle's claim that the matter of abortion properly belonged in a state legislature, the three judges still thought they had a "federal" question to deal with—namely, whether or not the present Texas law denied women a basic constitutional right. Goldberg pointed out that protecting life at any stage of development seemed not to have been the intention of the framers of the Texas abortion law. Seeing room for a possible compromise, he asked Tolle, as he had Coffee and Weddington, whether striking the phrase "to save the life of the mother" might not make this law viable. Tolle replied, as they had, that he did not think this would be true to the original intention of the law. But where the two women had argued that the law could not be saved because it was so unconstitutional, Tolle said he felt the law was constitutional the way it was written, thereby eliminating any need to remove anything from it.

Tolle pressed harder, saying, "I believe that we're talking about rights. I think that the most persuasive right that the plaintiffs urge, as was held in the *Babbitz* case, and all the cases refer to it quite heavily, is the right of privacy, for want of a better term, and there you get to the point where the state has to regulate conflicting rights—whether the state has got an interest in the life of the unborn child sufficient to regulate the woman's right to privacy. This is a very difficult question, and I think that it is properly a legislative question.

"I don't think the state has to have a law at all regulating abortion. I believe the field is such that it can regulate it constitutionally. I personally think, and I think the state's position will be and is, that the right of the child to life is superior to that woman's right to privacy."

Tolle's argument was as good a defense as could be offered of the state's compelling interest in regulating abortion: the state had to balance two rights, that of the fetus to survive and that of the woman to privacy. In doing so, it could certainly find that the woman's right to something called privacy—a word Tolle diminished simply by the way he said it—was inferior to that of the fetus to life.

The idea of balancing rights was not new. A well-known legal concept, it was what most people thought of when they thought about justice. Although rarely viewed in this way, all our liberties are gotten at the expense of an individual or group. Every time a court rules for something or someone, of necessity it also rules against something or someone else. The protection of the rights of the accused, for example, are often obtained at the expense of some of the public's right to protection from possible criminals. The right to affirmative action for a minority is obtained at the expense of the majority. Even the right to sexual privacy that was guaranteed to individuals in the *Griswold* decision was obtained at the expense of society's right to impose one overall moral standard on sexual behavior. Now Tolle was suggesting that the court could also balance the right of the fetus, or baby, as he referred to it, to survive against the right of the woman to privacy.

The only thing surprising about Tolle's defense was that it had not been used earlier.

States had previously tended to defend their restrictive abortion laws on grounds that the fetus *ought* to be granted the full legal rights of a person, but that was asking a lot of a judicial system that had never granted a fetus personhood and had actually denied it in virtually every case that had ever arisen. In most states, no death certificate was required for a fetus (Texas required one only after five months). Fetuses had never been permitted to claim benefits such as workmen's compensation that were normally given to children.

No property or other inheritance rights were granted prior to live birth. Indeed, prior to live birth it was impossible to prove that a fetus was entitled to inherit anything. A widow impregnated by a man other than her husband could falsely claim to be pregnant by her husband in order to claim an inheritance for her child. The timing of the child's birth would, of course, help to establish its inheritance claim.

No tort recovery had ever been made in Texas (or in most other states) as a result of injury to a fetus that was not born alive. In cases dating back to the fourteenth century, damages for the killing of a fetus were denied on grounds that the cause of death could not be proven. The fetus might have died from natural causes in utero five minutes prior to being assaulted, and in a case involving the death of a very young fetus, there would not be a body at all. As recently as 1970, the California Supreme Court, in *Keeler* v. *Superior Court*, found that a husband who assaulted his pregnant wife, thereby causing the death of their thirty-five-week-old fetus, was not guilty of murder. According to the court, a fetus was not considered a "human being, in the legal sense." Its destruction involved a significantly lesser penalty. Even in the few recent wrongful death cases where parents had been awarded damages for stillborn or miscarried fetuses, several prominent jurists pointed out that what was really being compensated was the mental anguish of the parents. In the eyes of the law, a fetus was not defined as a legal person, nor had it been in hundreds of years of common-law history. It would be difficult for any court to reverse so long-standing a precedent.

Of course, Tolle was applying a bit of legal sophistry by arguing not that the fetus be granted the rights of personhood, but that its rights be balanced against those of the woman, since if the fetus's rights were considered at all, it would in effect be granted de facto personhood. Tolle was wise not to make this the crux of his argument when he could achieve the same thing by a more round-about route using a widely recognized and respected legal tradition, that of balancing rights.

Unfortunately, since Tolle spoke last, Coffee and Weddington would have no chance to respond to his rather persuasive argument. They would not be able to refute his implication that women sought abortions frivolously or out of convenience, or that the decision to abort was one that could be or frequently was made lightly, all of which was not true for the vast majority of women. Even a woman who badly wanted an abortion, and could not be dissuaded from getting one, typically experienced some ambivalence over her decision.

Most women view abortion only as the lesser of several painful choices, less painful certainly than carrying a fetus for nine months and giving it up for adoption at birth, never to see it again or know its destiny, never to know whether it is cared for or loved. Adoption, so frequently suggested as an acceptable alternative to abortion, leaves most women with a lifelong heartache and is a solution that is not without its trauma to the child, too. Abortion is certainly less painful for many women than trying to rear a child who cannot be nourished emotionally or provided for materially. And for women who already have several children, it is often less painful than bringing another dependent into the world who will deprive the rest of their needs.

Coffee and Weddington would not be able to rebut Tolle's argument by pointing out that when abortion was viewed in terms of the realities of daily life, privacy could hardly be considered a frivolous or insignificant right, that it was, rather, something that went to the heart of a woman's entire existence. Much of the course of a woman's life—not only at the moment she wanted an abortion, but over several decades and possibly for the rest of her life—hinged on her right to terminate a pregnancy when she needed to. Her right to decide when to have a child affected everything—her ability to mother the children she already had or would later have, to get an education, and to hold a job that might be her only means of economic support, as well as her marital happiness and overall social and emotional well-being.

Then, too, in any discussion of balancing rights, some consideration would have to be made of the numbers of women, mostly poor, who had died or been maimed physically and emotionally as a result of illegal abortions. Women would continue to be subject to the same fate if abortion remained illegal. If one lesson could be learned from the history of abortion throughout time and in all cultures, it was that outlawing abortion never prevented women from obtaining them; it merely sent them underground for them. The message, for those who chose to see it, was an important one. In this respect, the woman's life also could be said quite literally to hang in the balance with regard to abortion.

Nor would the two lawyers have an opportunity to point out that while fetal life was indisputedly human, it was not the same kind of human life that existed in a fully developed, sentient, already born person. Antiabortionists liked to point out that human life began at the moment of conception, that from the second an ovum and spermatozoon combined, the genetic structure or framework for a human being was in place.

Bernard Nathanson, an early pro-choice activist-physician who ran New York City's largest abortion clinic after that state legalized abortion, and who subsequently became a leading spokesperson for the antiabortion forces, took to stating after his conversion that the only difference between a one-month-old fetus and a nine-month-old fetus was weight and mass. Following his lead, antiabortion activists soon made the similarity between the developing fetus and a baby one of their most persuasive arguments against abortion, staunchly maintaining that a fetus was nothing more than a complete but smaller version of a baby, even though such thinking flies in the face of accepted biological evidence.

To understand why a fetus is not merely a small baby, one need only to consider the development of its organs, many of which are either absent or underdeveloped in the early stages or do not perform the same functions prior to birth that they will after birth. A fetus's liver, to take just one example, initially produces blood, a function that will later be taken over by its bone marrow. No matter how much a fetus may resemble a baby, its lungs do not breathe for it, nor do its stomach, intestines, bladder, and bowel digest and excrete for it as they will do later. These functions are performed by the placenta, an organ formed in the woman's uterus during pregnancy for the sole purpose of supporting the fetus.

Antiabortionists also made much of the fact that brain waves could be recorded at around eight weeks, as if that sign alone were incontrovertible proof that the fetus was a sentient being. But this analogy, too, is misleading. Before twenty-seven weeks, biologists tell us that brain function is a subcortical activity; that is to say, it is purely reflexive. Based on the best understandings of fetalogists and neonatologists, the young fetus does not feel pain, nor is it in any way a sentient being.

Rather than thinking of life as beginning at the moment of conception, biologists tend to think of it as existing on a continuum, an image that is appropriate since no one can say for sure when life begins and ends. It is true that a genetic "blueprint," as biology professor Garrett Hardin preferred to call it, exists from the moment of conception, but much has to happen for that construction guide to become human enough to emerge from the mother's womb a fully developed person.

One might even say that the odds are against its doing so. In its first week of development, before the blastocyte has implanted on the wall of the uterus, as much as 40 to 50 percent of all pregnancies are aborted spontaneously. Biologists agree that human life starts out as a single cell, develops into a multicellular unit, and only gradually travels down the road toward becoming a full human being, and they also agree that along the way there are many wrong turns that can be taken, developmentally speaking.

In hinting that the woman's right to privacy had to do with convenience or selfish whims, Tolle took up a strand of thinking that antiabortionists would soon develop more fully—namely, that not only women's minds but also their bodies were hostile to fetuses. Nathanson would describe the fetus as "an uneasy tenant" in the mother's womb, a place that offered an "immunological sanctuary" from, among other things, the mother, "whose white blood cells mount an attack" to reject the fetus.

Like the earlier analogy of the fetus to a baby, this was an image that transposed (largely male, antiabortionist) wishful thinking into reality and, in this case, in doing so, attempted to deny the dynamic interaction between the woman's entire being (not just her uterus) and the fetus that was crucial to the latter's development. Modern science has dispensed with the concept that a fetus is merely an appendage of a woman, but it does not view it as a separate agent, either. Furthermore, even though a fetus becomes capable of survival outside a woman's body several weeks before birth, as feminist historian Rosalind Petchesky has noted, its premature existence is neither easy nor normal. The undeniable fact is that the fetus is meant to finish developing inside a woman's uterus until the moment of birth. Complex and complicated reasons exist for it to do so, all operating to the fetus's benefit. Antiabortionist longings aside, modern biological science has yet to invent—and in fact is a long way from inventing—a laboratory substitute for the woman's womb.

Beverly Wildung Harrison, a Christian feminist ethicist who has perhaps thought and written more cogently on the subject of ethical behavior toward the fetus than anyone else, points out that all such comparisons and analogies of a fetus to a baby, although seemingly bathed in scientific fact, are actually ethical and moral arguments clothed in scientific language. The fetus may be like a baby in some respects, but it is emphatically not a baby. Although antiabortionists like to point out that the fetus is now a medical patient, we must realize that however wonderful these advances in medical treatment are, it is still a fetus and not a human baby that is being treated. The idea that the fetus is in fact a baby simply does not hold up scientifically, nor does the suggestion that the womb is a hostile environment for the fetus. Despite this, the analogies are highly seductive, and many jurists and physicians have fallen under their sway.

Tolle's argument actually hinted at more than it said, and had he carried it through to its logical conclusion, it is doubtful he would have concluded that the rights of the fetus were in fact more powerful than those of the woman. Few people of any religious or moral persuasion were truly willing to say that the rights of an unborn fetus that could not survive outside the womb were more valuable than those of a sentient, fully developed, adult woman.

Despite its inherent weakness legally and philosophically, Tolle's argument carried great weight emotionally, if not in the courtroom, then among antiabortionists and those whom they sought to persuade—through any means—to their point of view. His argument foreshadowed one of the strongest messages the antiabortion movement would present to the public. And his argument did not fall on deaf ears in the courtroom. Coffee and Weddington felt he had done some damage not only with the eloquence of his argument, but also because his was the last voice the court would hear on the subject. However, the two women remained optimistic that their view would ultimately prevail.

The proceedings were almost over, but first the intellectually indefatigable Justice Goldberg had one more question for the plaintiff's attorneys. What, he asked, would happen if only District Attorney Henry Wade were enjoined to stop prosecuting illegal abortionists? Would every other district attorney in the state also be prevented from enforcing the law, or would they be free to go ahead with prosecutions? Only Henry Wade had been mentioned in the court documents; none of the other district attorneys throughout the state had been cited.

Stunned at the implications of what she was hearing, Weddington asked Justice Goldberg to repeat the question. Then she answered: "It was my understanding that since the attorney general's office had chosen to come in, and since they are now a party-defendant to the suit—"

Justice Goldberg interrupted: "Are they a party-defendent?"

"Well, I thought by—"

Judge Hughes jumped into the fray. "I don't believe they have intervened." Turning to Floyd, she asked, "Has the state intervened?"

Floyd jumped to his feet and practically shouted, "No!"

John Tolle also leapt up and said, "If the court please, I believe we can cite another example. In the *Buchanan* case, the court's injunction ran against Henry Wade only, and I don't think it binds anyone else."

Goldberg turned back to Weddington and asked: "Do you have any response to that?"

She replied, "We goofed."

It was another bad note on which to end the arguments.

9

The Dallas
Decision

Unlike Supreme Court decisions, federal court rulings are typically issued with little or no fanfare. They are virtually never read aloud in the courtroom but are instead quietly made public, often only in typed manuscript form, by the clerk's office, which in the abortion case was in New Orleans, the seat of the Fifth Circuit. The *Roe* decision was a routine announcement. After slightly less than a month's deliberation, the judges released their opinion on June 17, 1970. Copies of the decision had been mailed to the lawyers on the case. Other copies were placed in three press boxes—one for the *Times-Picayune* and the others for the wire services—in the clerk's office.

The opinion, only thirteen pages long when printed, began by addressing the jurisdictional issue of standing: Did Jane Roe and the other plaintiffs have a right to sue? The court found that Jane Roe and Dr. Hallford had standing, but the Does did not. Their case was dismissed. The court reasoned that since Mary Doe was not pregnant, she and her husband's case presented no real controversy. One of the ground rules for bringing a lawsuit is that it must present real controversy.

Turning next to the merits of the case, the court again ruled in favor of the plaintiffs. They found that the Texas abortion law was unconstitutional: a woman's right to abortion was constitutionally protected. In a concise paragraph that formed the heart of the opinion, the judges wrote: "On the merits, plaintiffs argue as their principal contention that the Texas abortion laws must be declared unconstitutional because they deprive single women and married couples of their right, secured by the Ninth Amendment, to choose whether to have children. We agree."

Roe v. *Wade* was the first decision in which the woman's right to abortion had been the primary issue. Other recent decisions had touched on the woman's right but always in a way peripheral to the primary issue of the doctors' right to do abortions. In *Belous*, a narrow decision (four to three) by the California Supreme Court, the court had written that the "fundamental right of the woman to choose to bear children follows from the Supreme Court's and this court's repeated acknowledgment of a 'right to privacy' or 'liberty' in matters related to marriage, family, and sex." But the issue in *Belous* was the doctor's right to do abortions, not the woman's right to decide when to undergo one. Similarly, in *Vuitch*, Judge Gesell had found that a woman's mental and physical health could be considered when making the decision to end a pregnancy, but again, that direction was intended to serve as a guideline for the doctor, not the woman. *Roe*, however, was not about the physician's rights; it was entirely about the woman's rights, and as a result reformers hoped it would carry special weight not only with other courts, but also with the public.

The Dallas judges did not limit the woman's right in any specific way, although they did comment that the right to abortion was not "unfettered." They pointed out, for example, that a desire to insure medically safe and competent abortions, as well as a possible concern for the quickened fetus, were two interests a state might have in regulating abortion.

The court's findings also applied to both single women and married persons, something Coffee and Weddington had been worried about after Goldberg had asked so many questions during the oral arguments about a possible tie between promiscuity and women's access to abortion. The days when courts attempted to enforce specific sexual morals were on the wane, but Coffee and Weddington knew it was still conceivable that the court might decide to give only married women access to abortion. The *Griswold* decision on birth control had been widely interpreted as applying only to married persons, and not until 1972, two years after the Dallas decision, would the Court, in *Baird* v. *Eisenstadt*, find that the right to privacy in matters of birth control extended to single as well as married persons.

* * *

Coffee and Weddington were thrilled but only moderately surprised at the decision. All along, they thought things were moving in their favor. They knew they had drawn a good and quite probably sympathetic panel of judges. Then the arguments had gone well for their side, and in contrast the state had not done a particularly good job of defending its abortion law. Coffee had been impressed with John Tolle's arguments, but she still believed the right of a woman to decide for herself when to terminate a pregnancy was more persuasive than the concept of balancing the rights of the fetus against those of the woman.

Ironically, the attorney general's office would not have disagreed with opposing counsel's assessment of the case, although they saw matters in a slightly different light. As far as they were concerned, the selection of judges known for their libertarian leanings had not helped their cause. They thought the arguments revealed that the judges had more or less made up their minds in advance. There was all that talk from Judge Goldberg during the oral arguments about the Ninth Amendment, the way he kept asking counsel to comment on it. They would not air their disappointment publicly at the time but years later would still recall with bitterness their feeling that nothing they said or did in the courtroom had any effect on the deliberations that followed.

Others who followed the case did not consider the state's view of the deliberations so outlandish. Rumors that the case had been decided in advance circulated for years within the Dallas legal community, and theories of how this came to be were repeated to me fifteen years later with as much clarity as if the case had been decided only a few days earlier. The most popular version held that since Coffee had clerked for Judge Hughes, the two women had probably discussed the case, or that at minimum Coffee had learned what Judge Hughes's views on abortion were and knew that any challenge to the abortion laws would be welcomed by her. Some people even suggested that Judge Hughes might have encouraged Coffee to bring a test case to the Fifth Circuit.

When I asked Coffee about the rumors, she denied them, saying that had Judge Hughes been inclined to encourage a case in this way, which, Coffee emphasized, she was not, she would not have been likely to choose Coffee as her vehicle: Coffee had not been one of her favorite clerks. Coffee further recalled how busy the Fifth Circuit was in those days, so busy that no one, neither judges nor clerks, had time to spend in the kind of extraneous conversations that uncovered the judges' views of issues other than those that were related to the case before the court. Furthermore, knowing Judge Hughes's views on abortion was no guarantee that she would turn out to be the judge who would handle an abortion case. Such rumors, tantalizing as they may be to mull over, must be recognized for what they are: the kind of legal folklore that inevitably builds up around any landmark case.

Unfortunately, little is known about the deliberations that led to the *Roe* decision. The opinion was issued per curiam, that is, written by the entire court rather than one justice, an action that suggests, if nothing else, a high degree of unanimity among the justices. All signs point to the fact that there was little debate among the justices, although not for the reasons suggested by the state's lawyers. Irving Goldberg, the only justice still alive when I researched this book, declined to discuss the court's deliberations with me, except to say, "We deliberated, that I know. We hadn't made up our minds in advance."

The official court record, stored in a federal repository in Ft. Worth, was purged of any personal notes, memos, or drafts of the opinion, but Judge Goldberg believed there would have been little of this anyway, because of the way *Roe* and most other three-judge cases were handled throughout the 1960s. He recalled that most of the Fifth Circuit justices preferred to do circuit work and, as a result, tried to dispatch three-judge cases as expeditiously as possible.

The fact that the Ninth Amendment came up several times during the oral arguments suggests only that the judges had begun researching the case prior to the hearing. From their research, they had obviously discovered that they were interested in exploring the Ninth as the source of the abortion right, should such a right be found to exist. One Dallas newspaper report attributed the court's interest in the Ninth Amendment to the fact that the Dallas judges had tracked three federal court decisions on abortion—*Belous*, *Vuitch*, and *Babbitz*—in the weeks prior to hearing their abortion case.

The three cases undoubtedly influenced the Dallas judges to find a constitutional ground for an abortion right, but it was the *Babbitz* decision, a per curiam opinion issued by a three-judge panel in Wisconsin just three months before the Dallas judges began their deliberations, that dealt most directly with the woman's abortion right, even though the case involved a physician. In that opinion the court found, among other things, that the Wisconsin abortion law was unconstitutional on grounds that it violated a woman's right to privacy as guaranteed by the Ninth Amendment. The court further declared that any state interest in the fetus was outweighed by the rights of the woman.

It was the use of the Ninth Amendment, according to many legal scholars, that was the most interesting aspect of the Dallas decision. Although it was sometimes included in the list of possible constitutional grounds, no one seriously believed it had much potential for establishing an abortion right. In his article on the constitutional grounds for abortion, for example, Roy Lucas had relegated the Ninth Amendment to a footnote, stating: "Several theoretically feasible but unnecessary constitutional theories are omitted from this discussion. First, whether a physician or an organization could claim a First Amendment right to inform patients as to the whereabouts of competent abortionists. Second, whether the Ninth Amendment, of its own thrust, permits of a fundamental right to abortion."

Most persons thought the woman's right to abortion would be found in the Fourteenth Amendment—specifically, in the due process clause of the Fourteenth Amendment, which stated that the rights guaranteed to all individuals in the Constitution could not be violated or withdrawn except by due process of law. But there were reasons not to rely on the Fourteenth Amendment; it was in many people's eyes a tarnished amendment, especially when applied to a case like *Roe v. Wade.*

The difficulty lay not with the concept of procedural due process, which was firmly embedded in the amendment, but with substantive due process, a more elusive legal concept. Procedural due process referred to a specific set of procedures (such as informing someone of the crime with which he was charged or of his right to counsel) that had to be applied whenever someone was deprived of a basic liberty. Substantive due process involved broader issues of liberty, such as privacy and the right to an equal education. The government—federal or state—had to show a compelling reason before it could infringe upon these liberties. The Dallas court, though, like the Wisconsin three-judge panel, had clearly rejected the use of the Fourteenth Amendment. Its reasons for doing so could be traced to a judicial dispute over the Fourteenth Amendment that dated back virtually to the moment the amendment had been adopted.

The Fourteenth Amendment, added to the Constitution after the Civil War, was designed specifically to protect the rights of black ex-slaves. By the late 1800s the Fourteenth Amendment, or at least the due process clause, was being subjected to uses its shapers had not foreseen.

At the close of the nineteenth century the United States was in the midst of an enormous and unprecedented economic boom in which huge fortunes were made overnight, often on the backs of exploited workers. The plight of the workers became a cause for social concern, and a drive was begun to improve their situation. At the urging of social reformers, state legislatures began to pass protective labor laws. Inevitably, since so much was at stake for the employers, these new laws were challenged in the federal courts, where the employers soon discovered they had a sympathetic ear. The federal courts and the Supreme Court regularly struck down legislation that was designed to protect workers; in most cases they used the Fourteenth Amendment as their grounds. In the wake of several decisions in which the Supreme Court supported the right of big business to get even bigger, the Court lost popular support and was subject to widespread criticism. Even the Constitution became a target as people charged that it worked for the rich robber barons, but not the poor wage earner.

Matters came to a head in 1905 in *Lochner* v. *New York*, a case in which the Supreme Court ruled that a recently passed New York law that limited the number of work hours in a bakery to sixty per week was unconstitutional on grounds that it violated substantive due process under the Fourteenth Amendment by interfering with the right of an employer to contract freely with his employees. In protest, Justice Oliver Wendell Holmes wrote a famous dissent that would provide the philosophical basis for eliminating substantive due process: "A constitution is not intended to embody a particular economic theory. . . . It is made for fundamentally differing views, and the accident of finding certain opinions natural and familiar, or novel, and even shocking, ought not to conclude our judgment upon the question whether statutes embodying them conflict with the Constitution of the United States."

In reaction to *Lochner*, people's animosity toward the Supreme Court intensified, reaching a frenzy and making the Court as unpopular as it had been since the infamous *Dred Scott* decision of half a century earlier. Of the debacle of the *Lochner* decision, constitutional scholar Laurence Tribe would write eighty years later: "Out of the language of an amendment written to liberate former slaves, the Justices of Cleveland and Harrison thus forged shackles to hobble government efforts to protect the health and welfare of American workers."

To its discredit, the Court did not immediately back off from its unpopular interpretation of the Fourteenth Amendment, but within a few years *Lochner* had become a code word for the demise of substantive due process. It would no longer be used regularly to decide cases, especially those involving, as Holmes noted, "economic theory." The debate over substantive due process lay dormant until 1965, when *Griswold* v. *Connecticut* came before the Warren Court.

When *Connecticut* v. *Griswold*, the case challenging the Connecticut state law that made the use of contraceptives illegal, came before the Court, the justices agreed the Connecticut law was a bad one. What they could not agree on was how to go about declaring it unconstitutional. In the lower court, the defendants' counsel had argued, among other things, that marital privacy was protected by the First Amendment, but Justices Hugo Black and Potter Stewart felt otherwise. In the weekly conference to discuss the cases argued the previous week, Black quipped that as far as he was concerned the First Amendment protected the right of assembly, and recognizing the right of a married couple to assemble in bed was a new one to him. While observing that he found the Connecticut law "uncommonly silly," Stewart agreed.

The real issue for Black and Stewart, however, was the similarity they saw between *Griswold* and *Lochner*. Both cases required opinions that could only, as far as they were concerned, be based on judges' personal values. In other words, any decision in *Griswold* would have to rely on substantive due process, which the Supreme Court had decided it would no longer use to decide cases.

Justice William Douglas said he believed First Amendment rights were exactly what was involved. If the Court could find that the right to travel was part of the right to assemble, as it had, then this more personal right was surely entitled to the same protection. Noting that Douglas seemed at minimum to be further along in his thinking about the case, Warren asked him to begin drafting an opinion.

A fast worker, Douglas was soon circulating a draft, the most salient feature of which was that it relied on the First Amendment. This heavy reliance on the First Amendment upset Justice William Brennan, who believed in the right to privacy but did not think it was protected by the First Amendment. Brennan suggested that Douglas take another look at *Lamont* v. *Postmaster General*, a case decided earlier that term in which Brennan had written that "the protection of the Bill of Rights goes beyond the specific guarantees to protect from congressional abridgement those equally fundamental rights necessary to make the express guarantees fully meaningful."

Douglas liked Brennan's concept of privacy and subsequently rewrote his draft, relying heavily on Brennan's idea that certain rights were protected by several different amendments rather than one. Instead of relying exclusively on the First Amendment, Douglas now wrote that the right to marital privacy was also protected by the First, Third, Fourth, Fifth, and Ninth. He stated, "Specific guarantees in the Bill of Rights have penumbras, formed by emanations from those guarantees that give them life and substance."

In shaping the argument in this way, Douglas also believed he was circumventing the issue of substantive due process that Black and Stewart had raised at the weekly conference. Acknowledging that some of his brethren thought that substantive due process was an issue, he reminded them, "We do not sit as a superlegislature to determine the wisdom, need, and propriety of laws that touch economic problems, business affairs, or social conditions."

To support his claim that familial privacy was a legitimate and basic freedom worthy of constitutional protection, Douglas pointed to other comparable cases over the past sixty years since *Lochner* in which the court had ruled on privacy—and had, in many instances, relied on substantive due process to do so.

The vote in *Griswold*, which was handed down on the last day of the 1964 Term, was seven to two, with Justices Black and Stewart dissenting on grounds that *Griswold* was a resurrection of substantive due process. They argued that substantive due process should no more be applied to cases involving personal liberties than to those involving economic liberties—and perhaps even less so since the former involved indeterminable issues of public morals.

Justice John Harlan wrote a concurring opinion in which he reiterated a theme he had developed in a lengthy dissent in *Poe* v. *Ullman*, an earlier attempt to overthrow the Connecticut birth control law. In it, he expressed his view that the Fourteenth Amendment was a reasonable basis for deciding such cases. It was part of the Constitution, after all, and was furthermore the best standard for deciding when state laws were constitutional. Harlan also observed that the rejection of one line of reasoning, such as due process, would hardly be enough in any event to keep judges' personal views out of their opinions.

Chief Justice Warren and Justice Brennan also voted with the majority to overturn the Connecticut law, but Warren found Douglas's opinion overbroad, so he joined a concurring opinion written by Justice Arthur Goldberg, as did Brennan, who had been planning to write his own concurrence but found it too embarrassing to do so after Douglas borrowed so heavily from his *Lamont* opinion.

Goldberg, aware that the problem with substantive due process had not been, and perhaps never would be, resolved, opted to look for an entirely different constitutional basis for protecting privacy. He found it in the Ninth Amendment. Usually interpreted to mean that those powers not specifically delegated to the federal government were reserved to the states, the Ninth Amendment could, Goldberg wrote, also be interpreted to mean that any rights not reserved to the federal government were reserved to the people.

To support his theory that the Ninth Amendment could be used to strike a state law, he tracked the history of the amendment in his unusually eloquent concurrence. The Ninth Amendment, Justice Goldberg stated, was written almost entirely by James Madison, who introduced it to Congress, where it was passed with "little or no debate and virtually no change in the language." It "was proffered to quiet the expressed fears that a bill of specifically enumerated rights could not be sufficiently broad to cover all essential rights and that the specific mention of certain rights would be interpreted as a denial that others were protected." In *The Federalist*, where Madison had talked about the Ninth Amendment, he had written that "no language is so copious as to supply words and phrases for very complex ideas." Applying the standard that was used to protect other basic rights,

Goldberg wrote that the protection offered by the Ninth was so fundamental that it could only be abridged when a state showed a subordinating compelling interest. The idea of constitutional protection of privacy that Douglas had painted with such a broad stroke had, by Goldberg, been neatly narrowed: marital privacy was protected under the Ninth Amendment.

From the Dallas judges' point of view, the most important aspect of the Goldberg concurrence must have been that it provided them with a way around the still controversial issue of substantive due process. Although the *Griswold* opinion would stand as a legal landmark on several counts, it must not, at least in the eyes of the Dallas judges, have fully resolved the issue of whether substantive due process could be used to decide cases involving constitutional rights. Rather than write a weak opinion that might not stand up under further judicial scrutiny, the Dallas court, like the Wisconsin court in *Babbitz*, opted to follow Goldberg's lead and rely on the Ninth Amendment as the basis for the abortion right. Quoting extensively from Goldberg's concurrence, the Dallas court wrote: "The essence of the interest sought to be protected here is the right of choice over events which, by their character and consequences, bear in a fundamental manner on the privacy of individuals. The manner by which such interests are secured by the Ninth Amendment is illustrated by the concurring opinion of Mr. Justice Goldberg in *Griswold* v. *Connecticut*."

In addition to finding the Texas abortion law unconstitutional on grounds that it violated the woman's right to privacy under the Ninth Amendment, the Dallas court also ruled that it was vague and overbroad. In making this assessment of the law, the judges did look to the Fourteenth Amendment, stating that the law failed "to provide Dr. Hallford and physicians of his class with proper notice of what acts in their daily practice and consultation will subject them to liability." The court asked:

> How *likely* must death be? Must death be certain if the abortion is not performed? Is it enough that a woman could not undergo birth without an ascertainably higher possibility of death than would normally be the case? What if the woman threatened suicide if the abortion were not performed? How *imminent* must

death be if the abortion is not performed? Is it sufficient if having
the child will shorten the life of the woman by a number of years?
These questions simply cannot be answered.

The grave uncertainties . . . under the related abortion
statutes are more than sufficient to render the Texas abortion law
unconstitutional under the due process clause of the Fourteenth
Amendment.

The only setback—a major one—for the plaintiffs was the judges'
refusal to issue an injunction to back up the declaratory relief. Coffee
had considered an injunction, which would order the state to stop
enforcing its abortion law, vital to winning the case. Only with such
an order would women truly have the protection they would need to
obtain abortions in Texas. The court indicated, however, that it
would consider an injunction tantamount to excessive interference in
the affairs of a state, particularly since Dr. Hallford, the intervenor,
was involved in a criminal prosecution. While the court acknowledged
that there were occasions when a federal court was obligated to
intervene to settle a constitutional issue, they did not feel that this was
one of them.

The court noted that while Texas had taken no action to revise
its abortion law, the fact remained that the state could hardly be
accused of acting in bad faith. It was barely enforcing the law, and the
plaintiffs had not been harassed—two actions that might have
warranted action by the court.

Coffee had argued that the fact that First Amendment rights
were infringed upon was enough to create a need for an injunction,
but the court had not bought her argument that the abortion right had
anything to do with the First Amendment. Citing *Porter* v. *Kimzey*, a
Supreme Court ruling that stated "the door is not open to all who
would test the validity of state statutes . . . by the simple expedient
of alleging that prosecution somehow involves First Amendment
rights," the court even chided her a bit for suggesting that it did.

Had Coffee confined her argument to the newer (and admittedly less established) judicial theory that privacy was a fundamental right, would she have had a stronger argument that injunctive
relief was required? Certainly, where fundamental rights were found
to have been infringed, federal courts had tended to issue injunctions.
An injunction had been issued, for example, in *Babbitz*, the Wisconsin

abortion case. But *Roe* was different, largely because of Dr. Hallford's criminal prosecution, and the opinion made it quite clear that this weighed heavily in the judges' minds. It was entirely possible that the Dallas judges would not have seen fit to issue an injunction under any circumstances.

Pleased as Coffee and Weddington were with the overall opinion, they were unhappy over not having gotten injunctive relief. Coffee, in particular, never came to terms with the court's refusal to grant it. Even though she realized injunctive relief was "a very sensitive point" and that the judicially active Fifth Circuit had greater reason than most federal courts to tread lightly where states' rights were involved, she still felt it was unrealistic for a federal court to expect a state like Texas to comply with a ruling that involved only a declaratory judgment. For her, the question was not so much whether the federal government should respect Texas, as whether Texas would respect the federal government. Her ominous feelings were soon confirmed.

Part III

ON APPEAL

10

The Appeals

Within hours after the decision was announced, District Attorney Henry Wade called a press conference at which he rather jubilantly announced: "Apparently, we're still free to try them, so we'll do just that." He was referring to the fact that the Fifth Circuit Court had refused Coffee and Weddington's request for an injunction ordering him to stop enforcing the abortion law. In effect, Wade was issuing an open invitation to the Dallas County police to crack down on illegal abortion. Furthermore, the example set by his office would be followed by district attorneys across the state of Texas.

The next day, Texas Attorney General Crawford Martin held a press conference in Austin to announce that the state would appeal the Dallas decision. In a way, Martin's reaction was more understandable than Wade's. The attorney general's office at least had built its case around its moral opposition to abortion; Wade's reaction appeared to have more to do with protecting his image as a tough law enforcer than anything else since, like law enforcement officials across the country, he had been less than diligent for years about enforcing the abortion law. About a year earlier, though, the situation had changed when a federal judge had overturned the Washington, D.C., abortion law, and the nation's capital had become an abortion capital overnight, providing abortions not only to women who lived in the district, but also to women from all over the country. District Attorney Wade had no intention of letting that happen on his turf.

The two press conferences merely added to the confusion that followed the decision. Was abortion legal in Texas or was it not?

Could doctors and hospitals perform them or not? Inquiries poured into law enforcement offices. Wade's office did its best to discourage all abortions by telling everyone who asked that, at least as far as the district attorney was concerned, (1) the law was still what it had been before the ruling, (2) the statutes were still on the books, (3) the decision was under appeal, (4) no injunctions were issued by the federal judges against the district attorney that would preclude prosecution or following the state law, and (5) the district attorney was still prosecuting Dr. Hallford. John Tolle was assigned to act as liaison between Wade's office and any hospitals that sought further clarification.

What this all meant was that the decision had changed nothing. If anything, abortions would now be less accessible than they had been before the ruling. Texas women were not going to be able to obtain the abortions to which they were constitutionally entitled. Coffee and Weddington were frustrated and at least a little angry, although they blamed neither Wade nor Martin. They might have liked them to work a little less diligently, but they understood that both men had to cope with public opinion, too. Besides, as lawyers they knew what was happening. They had fired the first round, and now Wade and Martin were firing the second. The third and, they hoped, final round was up to them. They needed to take their case to a higher court.

Fortunately, one result of the ruling had been to put Coffee and Weddington—especially Weddington, who was the more outgoing of the two—in touch with the pro-choice network that was rapidly taking shape across the country. As word of the *Roe* decision filtered through the legal world, congratulations and offers to help began to pour in, mostly from New York, where many groups were actively seeking reform, but also from lawyers around the country who were working on other abortion cases. Many of the lawyers wanted copies of the brief and the decision. Weddington and Coffee were happy to send copies of the decision to other lawyers, but the brief, only a few pages long and hastily hand-typed by Coffee, who had been racing to file *Roe* v. *Wade* before a local reporter broke the story, was not worth sending out. In return, they sought advice about the next step— where they should take their case on appeal.

The two women also were not displeased to discover that the decision and the publicity that ensued made them minor celebrities in Dallas. Deluged with invitations to speak before local groups, they soon realized they would have the forum they needed from which to address the problems that remained with the Texas abortion law, the most pressing of which, they now knew, was the fact that the judges' ruling was not going to be respected by local law enforcement officials. Hospitals and doctors who were, in theory, free to do abortions were not about to start doing them. They also knew they would need to raise money to mount an appeal, and their newfound celebrity might help them do that.

Wherever they took an appeal, the first step was to find out whether their clients were, in fact, willing to continue with the case. Throughout all the publicity, Norma McCorvey managed to maintain her anonymity. Besides, she had just had her baby and was recuperating from childbirth and the much more painful decision to give her child up for adoption. McCorvey was quite naturally preoccupied with matters other than the decision—especially since the decision had not been of any help to her. Weddington called her to talk about the idea of appealing the case. McCorvey thought the case was settled and could not understand what was left to do, but she had become very attached to Weddington and, to paraphrase her own words, would have trusted Weddington with her life. She readily agreed, therefore, to appeal the case.

In contrast, the Does, who had come to view themselves as symbols of the reform movement, had managed to speak out publicly, although they still maintained their anonymity. Because of their activities in the pro-choice movement, they had contacts with the press and agreed to be interviewed provided their identities were not revealed. In an interview with Barbara Richardson of the *Dallas Times Herald*, they explained that although they had lost their case, they still felt as if the Dallas judges had ruled in their favor anyway. They wondered if "the judges might have thought that our society is not ready for that drastic a social reform." Considerably more sophisticated about the law than McCorvey, they were eager to appeal and understood exactly what was at stake.

Given the go-ahead from their clients, Weddington and Coffee's next problem was where to take the appeal. Everyone agreed an appeal was proper, but opinion was divided as to where the case most properly belonged. Some people thought they had to go to the next highest court, the Fifth Circuit Appellate Court, while others thought they might have a direct route of appeal to the Supreme Court. The appellate process, "inherently ponderous," in the words of one expert, is also not unlike working one's way through a mine field: in neither situation is there room for mistakes. Deciding where to take an appeal, or even whether the case merits one, is not always easy—and taking a wrong turn at any stage can be disastrous. The women had heard about several abortion cases rumored to be destined for the Supreme Court where lawyers had filed improper appeals and, in doing so, had irrevocably lost the right to appeal. The Wisconsin case *Babbitz* v. *McCann* would probably have been heard by the Supreme Court rather than *Roe* v. *Wade* (it had raised almost identical issues) had errors not been made in preparing the appeal.

Sometimes even experienced lawyers are unsure where to take an appeal, so Coffee and Weddington knew they needed some expert help. Although they discussed the problem with just about any lawyer who called to talk to them about the case, they again relied on the expertise of Page Keeton, dean of the University of Texas Law School; Bernard Ward, a professor who was well versed in Supreme Court procedures; and John Sutton, whom Weddington had worked for during and after law school. While they were preparing *Roe* for the lower court, these men had suggested that they might fall into the relatively rare category of cases that had a direct route of appeal to the Supreme Court, and now they were exploring that possibility.

Meanwhile, Coffee and Weddington made plans to file an appeal with the Fifth Circuit Court of Appeals. Better to file an appeal, they reasoned, in a court in which they were sure the case belonged than try to go directly to the Supreme Court and lose any chance of appealing in the lower federal court. Bruner, who was also planning to appeal on behalf of his client, filed for Dr. Hallford on July 23; Weddington and Coffee followed suit on behalf of their clients the next day.

Shortly after they filed their appeal in the Fifth Circuit, they learned that they did indeed have a right to appeal directly to the Supreme Court. Although people often speak of "appealing" a case to the Supreme Court, actually only a few special classes of cases come to the Supreme Court via appeal. Most come via a writ of certiorari. (Apart from their different names, though, requests for certiorari and appeals go through essentially the same process to reach the Court.) At that time, cases in which a three-judge court had been asked for and had not granted an injunction were entitled to direct appeal. Coffee and Weddington had never given any thought to laying out their case in such a way as to enhance their chances of taking it to the Supreme Court, but it now seemed that what they had initially viewed as a setback—the court's refusal to grant injunctive relief— would prove to be a decided advantage.

To set the appellate process in motion, the appellants need only file a simple notice of appeal with the court in which the case originated. In three-judge cases, the appeal must be filed within sixty days of the final decision. This they did on August 17, 1970.

The appellants were Norma McCorvey (who filed again as Jane Roe), John and Mary Doe, and Dr. James Hallford. The party that originates an appeal is the appellant regardless of whether he or she was a defendant or plaintiff in the lower court. The next step—often a time-consuming one—is to prepare a jurisdictional statement, a special brief that must be filed within sixty days of the appeal. This is a comprehensive, sometimes lengthy document, in which the appellant presents written arguments on behalf of the case. Ostensibly these are designed to persuade the court to hear oral arguments or at minimum to affirm or dismiss the case, as one prefers.

The appellee, as the other party is called, has thirty days to respond to the jurisdictional brief. Knowing that his response will not change the Court's consideration of the case, he may decide, as Texas did, not to file a responding brief. All this means that a case will not be "ripe for consideration," as the Court likes to say, for a minimum of 150 days in a three-judge case (120 days in most other cases, which have different deadlines for filing).

While Coffee and Weddington were in the throes of preparing a Supreme Court appeal, they received some help from an unexpected source.

The women were never sure how Roy Lucas heard about them, probably the same way other lawyers had—through the legal grapevine. In any event, Weddington picked up the telephone one day to find him on the other end of the line. Like the many other lawyers with whom they had talked, Lucas at first seemed only to want to wish them well and find out how their case was going. When they told him about both appeals, he offered one excellent suggestion, that they file a motion in the Fifth Circuit Court to hold that appeal in abeyance pending any action by the Supreme Court. They were grateful to him for the advice.

A difference soon emerged, however, between Lucas and the other movement lawyers who had called. While attorneys such as Harriet Pilpel and Cyril Means were helpful, they seemed to recognize and respect the fact that the case belonged to Coffee and Weddington, and they offered advice only when asked. Lucas, however, gradually let it be known that he was interested in working with them in a more direct way. He presented himself so persuasively that they found him nearly impossible to refuse.

For one thing, his credentials seemed impeccable. He described the many cases he was handling across the country, including *Vuitch*, recently decided in a federal district court in Washington, D.C., and now, like *Roe*, headed to the Supreme Court. He sent them copies of the article he had written while still in law school—the first ever to outline the potential constitutional grounds for establishing women's right to abortion.

Most important to two young, inexperienced lawyers, Lucas held out the promise of resources and badly needed funding. Although they were willing to continue working for little or nothing, they knew expenses were not minor. They certainly hoped to spend less than the $240,000 that *Brown* v. *Board of Education* reportedly cost to bring to the Supreme Court; nonetheless, one of their primary concerns was money. They would need it for the printing costs (the Supreme Court seemed to want everything in duplicates of forty) and for research. As director-general counsel of the James Madison Law Institute, which was mostly funded by civil rights activist-lawyer Morris Dees and Joseph Sunen, owner of Sunen Contraceptives, Lucas told Weddington and Coffee that he could provide both. He would help personally with fund-raising, and the institute maintained contacts with lawyers working on abortion cases across the country, often submitting amicus curiae ("friend of the court") briefs, which were used to help support important cases. It had an extensive collection of abortion briefs upon which a model for the Supreme Court might be drafted.

The impressive board of directors for the James Madison Institute read like *Who's Who* in civil rights and included such illustrious names as Yale Law School Professor Tom Emerson, who had argued *Griswold* in the Supreme Court; New York University Law School Professor Norman Dorsen, who had helped to establish the rights of illegitimate children and was a familiar face at the High Court; University of California Law School Professor Norval Morris; Tufts University Sociology Professor Edwin Shur; Stanford Law School Professor Anthony Amsterdam; Yale Law School Professor Charles Black; and Professor Clark Byse of Harvard Law School.

Lucas's offer to Coffee and Weddington, when he finally got around to making it, was to handle the appeal for them. Although at the time, as Coffee would later recall in our conversations, Roy Lucas looked like welcome help, she and Weddington wavered back and forth over whether to accept his offer. On the one hand, they were keenly aware of their own inexperience—and scared to think that the burden of abortion rights for all American women rested on their shoulders. On the other hand, they were extremely proud of what they had accomplished in the Fifth Circuit Court, and they wanted to take the case to the Supreme Court by themselves. Like many other pro-choice reformers, they were beginning to develop a sense that this was somehow uniquely a woman's issue—and to them, that meant women should take responsibility for it.

Despite their feelings, however, they suffered from the lack of any powerful female role models within the pro-choice movement. Like most other civil rights movements, the abortion movement was initially dominated by men—powerful physicians and constitutional lawyers who formed an independent old-boy clique within the abortion network. So competent and highly esteemed a lawyer as Harriet Pilpel, who had originated much of the strategy behind the constitutional right to abortion and who as counsel to Connecticut Planned Parenthood had developed the *Griswold* case, had not argued *Griswold* in the Supreme Court; that honor had been claimed by her male co-counsel, Tom Emerson.

Lucas was not above playing on the women's insecurities by pointing out what he considered to be flaws in the way *Roe* had been handled at the federal court level. For one thing, the use of aliases bothered him, and he suggested they might pose a problem for the Supreme Court, too. The fact that no evidence had been presented in the lower court was another potential problem. It might give the Supreme Court a reason to send the case back to the lower court to develop the record. He hammered home the difficulties and importance of preparing a brief of Supreme Court caliber. It was a pipeline to the justices' minds and might be all that several of them would read about abortion.

Had Coffee and Weddington had more experience, they would have known that while aliases were not common, they were not unusual, either. (The Supreme Court would not question the use of aliases, as indeed most courts did not in an era when protecting a woman's reputation from social stigma was a serious matter.) They also would have known that throughout the 1960s, three-judge panels frequently declined to hear evidence, preferring instead to render an opinion strictly on the merits of the case. As for preparing the brief, it did seem like an enormous task, one that might require resources and funding beyond their ability. Weddington felt the lack more strongly than Coffee. From the start, when East Coast reform lawyers had strongly urged that the case should be amended to a class action suit, Coffee had resented what she viewed as unnecessary interference from outsiders. She would always believe that she and Weddington could have gotten along quite well by themselves. Her only reservation about outside help was that she planned to continue working at her job and was not sure how much time she would be able to devote to the case.

About the time Lucas was raising these issues with Coffee and Weddington, several Supreme Court rulings seemed to signal a new trend that they feared might affect *Roe*'s chances of being heard. The Court remanded several important cases, including two from Texas (one involving the state's sodomy law and another involving an obscenity law), back to the lower courts so the record could be more fully developed there. The Court was reportedly trying to stem the flow of civil rights cases, and one method of doing so was to deny standing until all proper avenues of appeal at the state level had been exhausted. Both Texas cases involved criminal proceedings, as did *Roe*, which fueled speculation among the local press that the *Roe* appeal would also be sent back. Coffee and Weddington worried that they should have originated their case in a state court rather than before a federal three-judge court, and this simply added to the pressure they already felt to let Lucas handle the appeal.

In his efforts to persuade them to sign on with him, Lucas played up his experience. Although he had hardly been out of law school any longer than Weddington and Coffee, he managed to sound more worldly and experienced—how New Yorkers often managed to sound to the rest of the country. He seemed to know everyone who was actively or even peripherally involved in abortion reform on both coasts, and he had impressive ASA, ACLU, and NARAL ties. Lucas also had a way of speaking about Supreme Court justices as if he had some sort of personal pipeline to them, and he even implied that the Court preferred to hear arguments from the numerous "good" lawyers in New York and Washington, D.C., rather than two country bumpkins (although he did not, of course, say this directly).

Even if Weddington and Coffee had been inclined to do a background check on Roy Lucas (which they were not), they would have found little to alert them to potential trouble. His interest in abortion appeared to be both serious and genuine, dating back to a summer in 1969 he spent in England between his junior and senior years of law school. The liberal British abortion law had just been passed, and people in his circle were talking about little else. From home Lucas got word of another exciting boost to the reform cause, a recently published article written by former Supreme Court Justice Tom Clark, in which he had come right out and said that women had a constitutional right to abortion. The article was widely hailed by pro-choice reformers as a signal that the time was ripe to bring an appeal before the Supreme Court.

Lucas also had met and married the first of his three wives, a woman named Uta Landy, who was herself intensely interested in abortion reform. Her interest fed his, and Lucas returned to the United States and his senior year of law school imbued with the possibility of changing the abortion laws in his own country.

In the course of developing his interest in abortion reform, he made sure he met the right people. Harriet Pilpel was especially impressed when he called on her one afternoon to ask her advice on his article—so impressed that she began to mentor him through the movement. In the words of one lawyer who knew them both, she lionized Lucas, and under her auspices he was able to obtain many more plum committee assignments than anyone else of his years and experience.

It was difficult not to like Lucas. He was charming, intelligent ("damned bright," according to Lawrence Lader), handsome, extremely personable, and smooth talking. Several years after the *Roe* decision, when most of his law practice consisted of helping abortion-service providers, Lucas's willingness to fly to his clients at the drop of a hat (for a hefty fee) caused the providers to refer to him only half-jokingly as their "knight in shining fusillage."

Admittedly, Lucas was overly aggressive, but then young lawyers were expected to be. Later his brashness and self-serving attitude would begin to wear thin with other movement activists, but it had not yet done so when he contacted Weddington and Coffee. Had they checked him out, they would have found nothing to dissuade them from working with him. After much wavering back and forth, Coffee and Weddington finally decided to let Lucas work with them, although they believed the deal they struck with him left them fully in control of their case.

When Weddington called McCorvey for the second time in several weeks to tell her that her case was being appealed to the Supreme Court, and that she and Coffee might even go to Washington, D.C., to argue it, a flabbergasted McCorvey could only stammer, "God, the Supreme Court of the United States. My God, all those people are so important. They don't have time to listen to some little old Texas girl who got in trouble." Weddington assured her that they did and quite possibly would.

Although Attorney General Crawford Martin had announced that he would appeal, no one in his office had much time to devote to preparing an appeal, and the opportunity to do so might have been lost had Assistant District Attorney John Tolle not begun preparing an appeal as soon as the decision was handed down. Strictly speaking, the case no longer involved Henry Wade and his staff. Since the attorney general was charged with responsibility for defending the laws of the state, the case was now officially his to contend with. The district attorney's office typically bowed out at this stage, but Tolle had developed a special interest in the case and hoped to continue working on it. The attorney general's people were so overburdened that, by their own admission, they often let cases slip through the cracks by failing to take appropriate legal action within the required time. Determined not to let this happen with *Roe*, Tolle decided to go ahead and initiate an appeal. Later he and Floyd could talk about working together. Tolle believed if they joined forces, they could build a better case in the appeals court.

Like everyone else working on *Roe*, Tolle was at first unclear about where to take the appeal. He soon determined that the state's appeal properly belonged in the Fifth Circuit Court of Appeals. The basis for the appeal was that the state did not believe its abortion law was unconstitutionally vague or overbroad. The state, unlike the plaintiffs, had no right to a direct appeal to the Supreme Court; instead, it could only take the case to the next highest federal court.

On July 10 Tolle had filed the first appeal in the entire case with the Fifth Circuit Court of Appeals. When he notified Assistant Attorney General Jay Floyd of his action, Floyd wrote back, thanking him and indicating that the attorney general's office would handle the case from here on out. A disappointed Tolle realized he would no longer be working on the abortion case.

Throughout the summer and fall of 1970, Lucas and the Madison Law Institute took over much of the work on *Roe v. Wade*, which largely consisted of arranging for the lower court record to be submitted to the Supreme Court and getting the jurisdictional statements printed in multiple copies and delivered to the Court.

On October 30, 1970, Lucas was notified by the Fifth Circuit clerk that the record had been submitted to the Supreme Court. In November Lucas was told that the docket fee was due at the Supreme Court. That meant the case was being docketed, and, if all went well, the justices would soon consider whether or not to take the case.

In fall 1970 one of the cases that came in on appeal to the Supreme Court was *Roe v. Wade*. The Court dealt with it as it did all other cases.

Petitions for certiorari and appeals are distributed to all the justices for review. Although each considers the applications separately, the justices do not discuss all 3,800 requests that come their way each year at conference. In about 70 percent of the cases, they agree that a case is frivolous or before their court improperly, and it is removed from the agenda without further discussion. The remainder are put on a list to be discussed at conference. A minority of four votes are needed to take a case.

Constitutional scholar Norman Dorsen has said that he would not be surprised if Justice Harry Blackmun had been influential in the decision to take the case. One can even reconstruct what might have happened at the conference when *Roe* v. *Wade* was first discussed. In favor of hearing an abortion case were undoubtedly Justices William Brennan, Thurgood Marshall, and William Douglas, the Court's stalwart liberals. They were all that remained of the Warren Court's liberal majority that had expanded civil and minority rights so diligently throughout the 1960s. On the opposite side, literally and figuratively, were probably Chief Justice Burger, in his second term, and Justice Potter Stewart, an Eisenhower appointee and strict constructionist who had generally opposed expansion of civil rights. A surprising member of the bloc that opposed liberalizing the abortion laws was Justice Byron White, a Kennedy appointee. White, who had been Robert Kennedy's number-two man in the Justice Department, was known to be tough on both crime and civil rights violations. His opinion on women's rights was unknown, but he could reasonably have been expected to join the liberal bloc. Instead, he opposed liberalized abortion. Justices John Marshall Harlan and Hugo Black had died within weeks of each other shortly before the Court reconvened, so only seven justices were sitting, one more than the minimum needed for the Court to conduct any business.

There remained Harry Blackmun, the most junior justice, who had joined the Court the previous June. Blackmun's leanings on abortion were unknown. (Justices do come to the Court with a history of political activity, but their past voting records are not always the best evidence of how they will react or vote once they have joined the Supreme Court. In fact, Supreme Court justices in recent years have more often than not proven to be disappointments to the presidents who have appointed them.) The third choice of President Nixon, after his two earlier nominees Clement Haynesworth and Harrold Carswell had failed to win consent from the Senate, Blackmun had maintained a low profile since coming on the Court. He was a midwesterner, a fact that was reflected in his pragmatic approach to everything, including the law. After attending Harvard Law School, Blackmun had worked in private practice for sixteen years; when appointed to the Eighth Circuit, he developed a reputation as a hardworking, capable jurist. The experience in his life that carried the most weight on this case, however, was the period between 1950–59 when he had served as resident counsel to the Mayo Clinic, nine years that were, by his own account, among the most exhilarating in his life. Blackmun was at Mayo during the exciting pioneer years of heart surgery, and what he witnessed there left him with an enduring, almost reverential respect for physicians.

Blackmun was the only justice with any serious medical experience. If he said the case was important and deserving of the Court's attention, that undoubtedly would have carried considerable weight with the other justices.

Only 5 percent of all cases were scheduled for oral argument. Despite these poor odds, pro-choice reformers badly wanted a case to be heard by the Supreme Court. Reformers worried that if the decision were left up to the individual states, the abortion laws would end up in a constant state of revision, as state legislatures alternately loosened and tightened the laws in accordance with the vagaries of their political constituencies. And of course, the ultimate issue revolved around the fact that if women had a constitutional right to abortion, as most reformers and the majority of Americans now believed they did, then it would not do to deny women access to abortion in one state while permitting it in another.

Most pro-choice reformers believed the Supreme Court would have to hear an abortion case sooner or later. In fact, the race was on to get a case heard by the Supreme Court. By the time the Court appeal on *Roe* v. *Wade* was filed, eleven states across the country had local cases pending, twenty cases challenging state abortion laws were before three-judge courts, and five, counting *Roe*, were on the docket in the Supreme Court. The Dallas reformers in particular wanted "their" case to be heard.

Coffee and Weddington could only hope that *Roe* would be chosen. Sometimes their hopes ran high, although in their less optimistic moments they could not imagine that theirs would be the one. Other cases probably had a more fully developed record from the lower court or had included expert testimony, or perhaps they simply presented the issues in a more clear-cut way than *Roe* did. They fretted that they should not have used anyone but Norma McCorvey as an appellant, and then they buoyed themselves up with the thought that their clients were an unusually well-rounded roster of appellants. But then again, maybe the Court would only hear a case on one of the new, so-called reform laws. It could be used to strike down new and old laws in one blow, if the Court chose to do so.

The opposition was not unhappy with the possibility of a Supreme Court decision. Although they firmly believed that this was an issue best resolved by the states and even though most of the lower court decisions had not gone their way, they could not imagine that the highest court in the land would condone abortion. At worst, they thought the Supreme Court might permit abortions in instances where it was needed to protect a woman's life and health.

The Court was unusually backlogged throughout 1970, and it was not until early May 1971, near the end of the term, that the announcement came that the Supreme Court was indeed prepared to hear an abortion case. In fact, they had voted four to three to hear two cases: *Roe* v. *Wade* and *Doe* v. *Bolton*, the latter a case challenging a new reform law in Georgia.

Sarah Weddington, in 1980,
accepting an award after
speaking at the convention
of the National Federation
of Democratic Women.
(UPI/Bettmann Newsphotos)

Sarah Weddington, in 1979,
when she was a senior political advisor to President
Jimmy Carter.
(UPI/Bettmann Newsphotos)

Linda Coffee, in 1972, shortly after she argued *Roe* v. *Wade* in the Fifth Circuit federal court. *(UPI/Bettmann Newsphotos)*

Norma McCorvey, in 1985, in her office where she works as an apartment building manager. *(UPI/Bettmann Newsphotos)*

Sherri Finkbine at home in 1962, during the period when she was trying to obtain a legal abortion in Arizona. Finkbine's request for an abortion when she learned that she might be carrying a thalidomide-deformed fetus played an important role in setting off the nationwide controversy over abortion reform. *(UPI/Bettmann Newsphotos)*

California physician Dr. Paul J. Shively, *left*, with his attorney Robert Lamb, during his hearing before the state's Board of Medical Examiners for illegal abortion. Dr. Shively was placed on probation and Dr. Seymour Smith, the other doctor involved in the case, was reprimanded. The doctors' case, like Finkbine's, served to awaken people to the need for abortion reform. *(UPI/Bettmann Newsphotos)*

Virginia Whitehill, around 1970 when
she undertook to reform abortion laws
in Texas.

Doris Middleton, who played an active
behind-the-scenes role in organizing
Texas abortion reform, in 1987.

Ellen Kalina Lewis was active in the women's group at the Unitarian Church and later served as the first president of the Dallas abortion reform group.

Judges Irving S. Goldberg (1982) and Sarah T. Hughes (1981), Fifth Circuit Court of Appeals. Two of the three judges who heard *Roe* v. *Wade* argued in 1970 in Dallas. *(Randy Grothe/ Dallas Morning News)*

New York University Law School professor Norman Dorsen, a well-known constitutional lawyer who specializes in civil rights, in 1987. He argued *Vuitch* in the Supreme Court and was the lead lawyer in *Roe* v. *Wade*.

Supreme Court Justice Harry Blackmun, *center*, who wrote the *Roe* v. *Wade* opinion, in April 1970, shortly after the announcement of his nomination to the Supreme Court. He is flanked by his sponsors, Senators Walter Mondale, *left*, and Eugene McCarthy, *right*. *(UPI/Bettmann Newsphotos)*

Abortion reform rally, St. Louis, 1970. Across the country women registered their dissatisfaction over present abortion laws with public marches and rallies. *(UPI/Bettmann Newsphotos)*

On January 22, 1985, the twelfth anniversary of the *Roe* v. *Wade* decision, antiabortion reformers knelt on the steps of the Supreme Court in protest. *(UPI/Bettmann Newsphotos)*

11

The Opposition

Not until mid-1970 did the opposition, stimulated no doubt by the Dallas decision and subsequent word that the Supreme Court was going to hear an abortion case, finally awaken to the need to organize against abortion reform. At that time, virtually the only opposition to abortion came from the Catholic church hierarchy. Even lay Catholics were caught up in the move to liberalize abortion. In 1962 about half of all Catholics disapproved of abortion to protect the woman's health or in cases where the fetus would be severely deformed. By 1969 only one-third of all Catholics disapproved of abortion for these reasons, compared to one-fifth of the general non-Catholic population that disapproved.

Throughout most of the mid- to late 1960s, those opposed to abortion sat smugly by watching the reform efforts, confident that nothing would come of them. How could reform happen in a society that could not even say the word? Abortion liberalization looked like a doomed cause if ever there was one. Newspapers refused to cover the subject. Magazines—especially women's magazines, which could have been (and later became) a powerful ally to the reform movement—never wrote about it. Almost no books were available on abortion. Lawrence Lader's *Abortion*, which had awakened many people to the need for reform, was not published until 1966. His book did not generate much interest on the part of publishers, and few other books followed his; those that were published were usually directed at a professional readership. Even Alfred Kinsey, director of the Indiana University Sex Institute and chronicler of the changing sexual lives of Americans, did not think to include abortion in his 1958 book *Pregnancy, Birth, and Abortion* until after he attended a 1954 conference on abortion sponsored by Planned Parenthood. His research involved a very small sampling of women, around three hundred, who were willing to acknowledge having had abortions, but the book was the first to present concrete data on abortion.

Illegal abortions were barely whispered about by the women who had them, even though most experts estimated that over a million American women a year underwent illegal abortions. That eight to ten thousand women died each year from complications was the nation's least-discussed, if not best-kept, dirty little secret.

Apart from the fact that no nationwide forum existed from which to hold a public discourse on abortion, antiabortionists also believed the reform movement was its own worst enemy and that it would bring about its own demise soon enough without any help from others. The movement was beset with internal power struggles and even public squabbling in the early 1970s, as feminist reformers tried to appropriate abortion as an exclusively "woman's" issue, thereby alienating (or so the opposition believed) many middle-of-the-road reformers. And finally, if the idea of legal abortion was not radical enough, then surely the public would find the newly emerging idea of abortion-on-request—or abortion-on-demand, as antiabortionists liked to call it—totally repugnant.

The opposition, however, had not been dormant. Wherever state legislatures had attempted to pass reform laws, the Church had spoken out against them, usually with success. Sermons were preached, and although the Church denied it, mail campaigns had been organized. James Clark attributed his failure to get passage of a liberal reform law in Texas almost entirely to the Church's opposition. Clark had been confident that he had at least enough votes to get the bill out of committee, but his hopes were dashed when legislators began backing off, largely because the Church instigated a mail campaign that produced more mail—and mail that was more hateful and vindictive—than Texas legislators had ever seen on one subject.

Despite its success in stopping state legislatures, the Church seemed unable to slow the trend toward liberalization. Since 1967 eleven state legislatures had passed reform laws, and in the first six months of 1970, three large states—Alaska, Hawaii, and New York—had enacted so-called repeal laws. The state of Washington was on the verge of repealing its restrictive laws in November through a referendum on abortion, known as Referendum 20.

In Hawaii Roman Catholics had even contributed to the law's passage. The bill was ushered through the state senate by a Catholic senator and further helped along by a nun, who, although personally opposed to abortion, offered riveting testimony in favor of the repeal bill because she felt that abortion should remain a matter of individual choice. The only opposition to the bill came from the 30 percent of the island population that was Catholic, and several legislators publicly protested their heavy-handed tactics in trying to defeat the bill. Governor John Burns, a Catholic who attended mass every morning, permitted the bill to become law, although he did not sign it. He issued a lengthy statement in which he expressed a view that echoed the thinking of many liberal Catholics at the time, explaining that he could "never let his private political and religious convictions influence his judgment as governor of all the people." As a result, despite his personal misgivings and considerable pressure—including many threats—he had not vetoed the law.

Liberal Catholics—and even not so liberal ones—tended to agree that any decision regarding abortion should be based on an individual's personal morality, and that Catholics should not impose their views on others. Underlying this cautious attitude, of course, was a reluctance to challenge the traditional separation of Church and State and growing fears about overpopulation.

Repeal (instead of reform) was surprisingly palatable to many lay Catholics anyway, who argued that it was preferable to liberalizing state laws on abortion. This view, initially espoused by priest-activist-legislator Robert Drinan of Massachusetts, held that abortion would be a less complicated issue—as well as a matter of individual conscience—if the states had no laws on the subject.

The Catholic church's second defeat occurred in New York, where another repeal law went into effect on June 1. The Church had raised only token opposition to the passage of the law several months earlier, believing that the large Catholic population and its ongoing presence as a political force in that state would be enough to prevent passage of a liberal abortion law. To its shock, the Church discovered that more than its presence would be required to stop the legalization of abortion and by that time it was too late to do anything further.

But the most surprising and serious defeat was the Dallas decision. Within the legislative domain, the Church could use an array of tactics to influence legislators, but it was powerless to do anything to prevent court decisions. Threats, taunts, and tantrums simply did not work with judges, and decisions of courts, once rendered, were more likely to stand unchanged than were legislative decisions. Even more disheartening was the fact that the decision had been handed down not by a small, inconsequential local court, but rather by a widely respected federal court that provided a direct line of appeal to the Supreme Court. By now the Church recognized that if the Texas case had not been accepted by the Supreme Court, some other case would have been. Abortion had become a national issue; worse, a national consensus on the need to legalize abortion was taking shape.

The Church was a far less powerful presence in Texas, a bastion of Anglo-Saxon and German Protestants, than in Hawaii or New York, so there was little it could do to influence the decision on a local level. In fact, the response of Texas Catholics was remarkably low key. Even though the Texas abortion law would be in limbo for at least six months and possibly longer, local representatives of the Church announced that it would not get involved in attempts to abolish or liberalize the Texas abortion law. Graham Callan, a lawyer and former legislator who headed the Texas Catholic Conference, voiced the increasingly popular view among Catholics, saying, "Personally, I feel that no law would be an improvement over either the existing law or the liberalization approach. As a lawyer, I thought the old law was simply a bad law; as a church man [liberalization] would have been a bad law, too."

Mrs. Peter J. Collara, president of the Catholic Women of the Dallas Diocese, went so far as to say that the decision confirmed her faith in the judicial system, adding: "I think this decision is the only one the court could have made." Pointing out that the present abortion law was rarely enforced anyway, she continued, "You couldn't prosecute under those terms. [The law was] really too vague and broad. Why have a law you can't enforce? . . . We Catholics hold that the decision is made before conception, not after."

Only two somewhat militant and presumably Catholic-backed groups materialized in Texas. In August, two months after the Dallas decision, a group headed by a young, Catholic public relations expert named Patrick Roper announced plans to open an interdenominational branch of the American Council of Medical and Social Education in Richardson, Texas, where Roper lived. The all-too-euphemistically named organization, whose sole purpose was to combat abortion, was to be officially headquartered in Washington, D.C. Roper announced that the tax-exempt and nonprofit organization expected to operate with a first-year budget of $7.9 million, which would enable it to open similar offices in two hundred locations around the country. At the time of the decision, the group's major activity had been the production of an antiabortion film, *The Right to Live*, featuring actress Loretta Young. Roper had enlisted the aid of several antiabortion physicians in Richardson and Dallas to work with his group. Despite his energy and what appeared to be the promise of major funding from some unnamed source, little more was heard from Roper on the subject of abortion after his initial press conference, and in the words of one physician whose support he had enlisted, the group had "died on the vine."

The second group, the Sons of Thunder, had been organized as the Dallas Ad Hoc Committee for Life and sometimes used a Spanish version of its name, *Los Hijos de Tormento*. With a mostly youthful affiliation of both sexes, it claimed about one hundred members nationally and thirty to forty active members in Dallas. The group's first official act had been a sit-in at the Dallas Planned Parenthood offices several months before the decision. Shortly after the oral arguments, on a Sunday in early June, in what was one of the earliest, if not the nation's first, acts of abortion-related violence, the Sons of Thunder vandalized the George Washington University Student Health Services office in Washington, D.C., because abortions were allegedly done there. After the decision, when the local media was eager to talk to anyone who wanted to speak out about abortion, the Sons of Thunder gained a short-lived voice, but like Roper's group, it quickly faded.

The Church's surprisingly low-key attitude toward abortion could be attributed in part to the fact that it had been surprised by both the remarkable growth of the pro-choice movement and the Dallas decision. But many people felt the Church's unexpected acquiescence was related to the sense that there was little it could do to stem the interest in liberalizing the abortion laws. It had not escaped the notice of experts and laity alike that the Catholic church was in a period of serious decline.

Vaticanologists traced the decline to Vatican II, held during the winter of 1965, and the expectations it raised—especially among a growing contingent of liberal Catholics—for a more open church.

Most promising was the idea of collegiality among the bishops, something that held great appeal for the independent-minded Americans. Collegiality meant the pope would no longer rule as an absolute monarch but instead would share power with the bishops, welcome news to Americans because it meant they would have more of a voice in running the Church and, they hoped, a hierarchy that was more responsive to the revolution in Catholic thinking that was already well under way in their country.

This revolution, which paralleled an upheaval in social values that was occurring throughout American society, encompassed many issues but in its heart revolved around the twin issues of war, specifically the Vietnam War, and sex, specifically the need and right to use birth control. Throughout the 1960s, partly out of a fear over excessive population growth around the world, American Catholics felt so strongly about birth control that they widely disregarded the Church's teachings on it. When Vatican II showed promising signs of opening the Church to debate, their hopes were raised that birth control would be one of the subjects toward which the Church would display an open mind. The Church's teachings on birth control were not infallible, so it was realistic to think that the pope, with the support of the bishops, might change his mind about it. After all, it was only in 1869, after several hundred years of viewing abortion benignly, that the Church made it a sin subject to excommunication.

People's hopes were dashed, however, within only a few months of Vatican II, when, against the advice of medical, theological, and population experts as well as some of his own bishops, the pope decreed that the Church's teaching on birth control would stand unchanged. His refusal to budge on birth control led even more disillusioned American Catholics to walk away from the Church, leaving at least the American branch as powerless as it had been at any time in the past century.

This powerlessness was confirmed publicly in 1967, when the federal government decided to do something about the supposed looming population crisis. That year, for the first time in its history, the government began subsidizing birth control activities, an action it would not have dared to undertake when the Catholic church was still a powerful lobbying force. In an effort to formalize and centralize its birth control funding, the Tydings bill, which called for an expenditure of $1 billion over five years for birth control research and services to poor people, was introduced.

In August 1970 the bill passed the Senate with little dissent, causing Senator Thomas Eagleton, who had ushered the bill through the upper house, to announce with premature optimism: "In a time of great controversy over important social and political issues, unanimity has been reached in recognition of the desirability and need for noncoercive family planning services." That same month, the Pentagon formally approved abortion on all U.S. military bases around the world, regardless of local laws, and also announced its intention to provide family planning services to all military personnel and their families who requested it.

Wall Street Journal reporter Norman C. Miller attributed the unusual degree of unanimity in the Senate on the Tydings bill to the fact that so little opposition was raised by the Catholic church. No one was talking about it publicly, he wrote, but both politicians and the Church hierarchy seemed to agree that the Church's power had been considerably diminished by Vatican II. One layman on the Church commission that attempted to persuade the pope to relax the rules on birth control did go on the record, saying, "I doubt very much that the bishops will try to exercise their influence on a subject on which their flocks are hopelessly split. They sense that they wouldn't be backed up by many Catholics."

The Church might have continued to play a diminished role had not another issue come along that held at least the promise of restoring it to its former power. That issue was abortion. The Church discovered that while it could not wield the influence over its members that it would have liked regarding birth control, abortion was another matter. Polls showed that most Catholics, even those who used birth control and favored liberalized abortion laws, still believed abortion was wrong—at least personally. Not as adamantly opposed to it as the Church would have liked, the laity nonetheless did not view abortion as simply another method of birth control, as some of the more radical pro-choice reformers were beginning to insist it was.

Abortion began to look like the one issue where the Church could get the right and the left together. Even antiwar leftists might rally around the Church on abortion; some Catholics who opposed the war in Vietnam because it killed innocent young men saw a parallel in the way abortion also took innocent lives—those of unborn babies. The Church would later gather in the fundamentalists, who made up a poor underclass that also opposed abortion, but for the moment it was enough to use abortion to round up straying Catholics.

The passage of the Tydings bill through the House of Representatives became the testing ground for this newfound power. The Church mustered all its strength and still considerable lobbying power to halt the bill. In the process it began to develop the rhetoric it would use throughout its campaign to stop legal abortion. Reverend James McHugh, spokesman for the U.S. Catholic Conference, the national umbrella group of the bishops, fretted publicly that the funding of birth control would inevitably lead to the funding of abortions. "There are," he maintained, "some people who believe that abortion is merely another form of contraception." In a tactic designed to woo those Catholics who thought abortion should be a matter of individual choice, Church spokesmen suggested that the new liberal laws were actually an assault on individual freedom. A Church representative commented: "Coercion of the individual takes place when overzealous welfare workers, medical personnel, maternal and child-health specialists attempt to pressure an individual mother or couple to avoid further childbearing."

Pleased with the defeat of the Tydings bill, the Church determined to flex its muscles even more on abortion. The National Conference of Bishops, officially an administrative arm of the American bishops but unofficially its lobbying group, would coordinate the campaign. Apart from this, a grass-roots campaign would be organized through various nonsectarian committees. Church-sponsored groups could usually be recognized by the tag line "right-to-life," which appeared somewhere in their names. A variation on the right-to-life committees was the Voice for the Unborn, which would represent the Church's antiabortion activities in Washington.

In August 1970, still limping from legislative defeats in New York and Hawaii, to say nothing of the Dallas decision, members of the newly formed right-to-life movement convened at Barat College in Illinois. Their agenda was to develop a national strategy and new, tougher tactics for dealing with the pro-choice movement. Thirty-seven states sent representatives. They would become active in any state in which a legislative change in the law was being contemplated or in which a court challenge was pending. For the immediate future, they targeted New Jersey and Pennsylvania, where reform bills were pending in the legislatures, and Washington, where the referendum, the nation's first on abortion, was scheduled for November. A reform bill had been defeated in the legislature, largely due to the Catholic church's efforts, but the referendum, a compromise measure after the defeat of the bill, could not be stopped, and the Church was singularly determined to beat back this second attack on one state's abortion law. Finally, still smarting from the New York defeat, the right-to-life movement also targeted New York, where it planned to mount a massive campaign to repeal the brand-new reform law. A fall 1970 gubernatorial campaign would offer the perfect battleground on which to wage this renewed attack.

Various other tactics were devised for use nationwide and even in states with no abortion activity. Hospitals that performed abortions would be picketed, and women entering clinics to obtain abortions would be harassed. In August 1970, when the Pentagon had announced that military hospitals were to perform abortions for service personnel even in states and countries where abortion was illegal, military hospitals were added to the list of places to picket.

Petitions were circulated to collect the signatures of persons opposed to abortion. Special affiliates of right-to-life committees were formed. One offshoot of Voices for the Unborn, for example, was called Nurses Opposed to Referendum 20, or NO. Right-to-lifers threatened to withhold support from the United Fund until assured that hospital money was not used for abortions.

The right-to-life activists developed a strategy for targeting pro-choice candidates for defeat when they ran for reelection and in doing so brought single-issue politics to the forefront of American political life for the first time in decades. A candidate who was pro-choice was slated for defeat except when the slate contained two pro-choice candidates, in which case the incumbent candidate was slated for defeat in order to eliminate the person with the most seniority. In 1970 and for the next few years, an unusually large number of legislators received invitations to speak at Roman Catholic churches, where they were always questioned closely about their views on abortion. The Right-to-Life Party, organized in late 1969 during the New York campaign to liberalize the abortion laws, ran candidates of its own across the country, although these candidates rarely took a position on anything other than abortion. (They also failed to garner any significant number of votes.) In fall 1971 New York priests in six churches preached against the election of R. Bradley Boal, a prominent Westchester legislator and chairperson of the Committee for Legal Abortion. He was narrowly and unexpectedly defeated, as were many other excellent liberal legislators throughout the country.

While such stalwarts of the movement as Planned Parenthood and the Association for the Study of Abortion diligently refrained from lobbying (laws prevented nonprofit organizations from lobbying for political causes), the Church, also nonprofit, became increasingly blatant in its lobbying efforts. It regularly used the pulpit to rail against the evils of abortion, often scheduling its attacks for special Human Life Days (and Months) that it decreed. During these theme periods, special efforts were made to raise funds, and sermons were preached against abortion. Special masses were dedicated to "respect for human life." An Iowa chapter of Citizens Concerned took "memorial" donations for a Monsignor Patrick Byrnes, and another Iowa diocese appealed directly for funds to be sent to the Family Life Bureau, a department of the National Catholic Conference of Bishops.

During one California political campaign, the Church brought Republican registrars into the churches on Sunday morning to reregister mostly Democratic Catholics as Republicans. The effort was a response to the Democratic party's state platform, which contained a pro-choice plank. One sunny August Sunday in St. Barbara's Church in Santa Ana, 530 voters switched their party affiliation. Even after the scheme was exposed by Edmund G. Brown, Jr., the Democratic candidate for secretary of state and himself a Catholic, fourteen more churches were scheduled to have Republican registrars present on Sunday mornings in September. The Church subsequently denied it had contacted the Republicans, but the Republicans claimed they had been invited in.

It was in Washington State, however, during the referendum campaign, that the Church mounted its most massive and calculated campaign against abortion. For the first time, it planned to enlist the support not only of Catholic laypersons, but also of the large rural fundamentalist vote. It was an alliance that would prove to be extremely fruitful in the future, if not in this particular campaign.

The Voice for the Unborn announced that it would spend $300,000 to oppose Referendum 20. An East Coast public relations firm was hired to orchestrate the campaign. One of their most persuasive or, depending upon one's point of view, offensive tactics was to plaster the state with antiabortion billboards featuring a giant picture of a four-month-old fetus cradled in a human hand and the slogan "Kill Referendum 20, not me."

In a letter to state Church hierarchy, Thomas A. Connolly, archbishop of Seattle, urged his priests to solicit funds on behalf of the Voice of the Unborn and also ordered every priest to attend a seminar on abortion. In response to advice given by "technical advisors," the Church would operate its campaign on two levels, the letter continued, the first being the "broadly inclusive citizen organization" and the second "the Catholic Church's program of activity." The second level, he pledged, would do what it could to expedite and facilitate the first.

Even before the election, people began to protest the tone of the antiabortion campaign, and much of the criticism was directed at the Church. One editorial writer spoke of the "bitter battle" that had resulted since the "Catholic Church has moved in with massive guns and ammunition in an effort to discredit the bill." In a letter to the editor, a woman expressed her anger at having to explain the billboards to her four-year-old son. Despite the money and energy poured into opposing abortion, it was legalized in Washington.

The Catholic church's increased antiabortion activity forced pro-choice people to respond, and unfortunately, after 1970, they devoted as much time to countering the opposition as they did to promoting liberalized laws. A NARAL bulletin sent to all members summarized the situation: "The opposition is a threat because 1) it has substantial funds, 2) it operates within a powerful, influential, and established organizational framework with a communications network that can command quick and obedient action, 3) its arguments are built around emotionally loaded words that confuse the uninformed, and 4) its approach encourages a religious polarization damaging to a democratic society."

NARAL considered the financing of antiabortion activity by the Church a major cause for alarm. Like most pro-choice groups, NARAL was officially a lobbying group and was not therefore tax-exempt. Like other pro-choice groups, it suffered a rather hand-to-mouth existence and resented the resources of the very rich Catholic church. In addition, the Church's broad-based ability to raise money would always far exceed anything that could be done by small, single-issue pro-choice groups.

NARAL encouraged its local chapters to reach out to the many lay Catholics who were still deeply ambivalent about abortion (as well as their Church's activities to combat its legalization). The organization kept reminding its members that the Church's campaign was largely the work of the hierarchy and suggested organizing abortion-repeal groups made up of lay Catholics. Catholic Women for Abortion Law Repeal had been influential and active in the New York reform campaign. In Pennsylvania a Catholic repeal group left a blank petition in an obstetrician's office and without any active lobbying managed to round up over two hundred signatures. In Washington, to counter the Catholic nurses' organization, a group calling itself Catholics for Individual Responsibility Concerning Abortions organized and issued the following statement: "As Roman Catholics we endorse Referendum 20 because we believe it is possible to be against abortion in our personal beliefs and practices and yet support reform of Washington's archaic abortion laws. . . . We shouldn't continue to legislate our concepts of morality on others just as we do not wish them to legislate their concepts of morality on us."

Protestant churches could also be encouraged to sign petitions to counter the Catholic influence. In answer to the Catholic church's Abortion Sunday, one Pennsylvania clergyman sent a letter to all Protestant clergy in the state in which he pointed out that "one communion has launched a well-financed and coordinated campaign to preserve the present Pennsylvania law on abortion" and called upon his colleagues to circulate petitions among their congregants in support of a reform law.

By the end of 1970 the Catholic church had shown that it was willing to go to great lengths to oppose abortion. It proved to be fearless about lobbying legislators and as willing to use threats as persuasion. Its greatest frustration continued to be the court decisions, which were now coming with increased frequency. But if there was no way to prevent them, the Church soon determined that it, too, could use the courts. In late 1971 Professor Robert Byrn, professor of law at Fordham University and founder of the Metropolitan Right-to-Life Committee, went into the New York State Supreme Court to have himself named legal guardian of Baby Roe, a fictitious fetus representing all unborn fetuses between four and twenty-four weeks scheduled to be aborted in New York hospitals. In January 1971 State Supreme Court Judge Francis X. Smith granted Byrn the injunction he sought, one that in theory would halt all abortions in the state. Abortions were not halted, however, and a month later a New York State Appellate Court overturned the ruling. The case took on the overtones of a three-ring circus, and few took it seriously.

The Church had managed to round up sizable support among its ambivalent Catholic laity, but it had alienated as many Catholics with its strident and overtly political tactics. Despite this, the Church was relentless in its opposition to abortion and would continue its efforts to keep it illegal right up to and even after the Supreme Court decision.

12

Renewed Vigor

After the Dallas decision, the women reformers enjoyed a sense of renewed vigor as they refocused their reform efforts. The decision was a big step forward, and although it gave reform the boost needed to gain widespread support, it soon became obvious that the ruling was not going to be enforced. The Dallas Committee decided they must continue the fight to repeal the Texas abortion laws and, if necessary, to push a liberal abortion bill through the Texas state legislature.

On Whitehill's agenda, in particular, was an introduction to Sarah Weddington, whom she thought might be of value to them in achieving their goals. Weddington's performance at the Dallas trial had made a deep impression on her and the other Dallas reformers. Here was a young woman, barely out of law school and in her first professional courtroom appearance ever, who handled herself beautifully in front of three fairly formidable federal judges. If she had been frightened, it had not shown. She had displayed an impressive amount of self-assurance throughout the arguments. The group was also impressed with what it could only describe as her ladylike demeanor. Ellen Kalina would recall that her main impression of Weddington had been of someone who was a "real southern belle."

Such things mattered to the Dallas reformers. They were especially concerned now that feminists, after several years of focusing on other important issues, were beginning to work more actively in the pro-choice movement. Many reformers on the East Coast, like Lawrence Lader, embraced feminism. He had recently written that only feminists could supply the kind of anger that was needed to move the country toward repeal, which was what most pro-choice activists now wanted. In his book *Abortion II*, a memoir of the reform movement, he would write: "We had to have the support of the mass feminist movement, literally [to] bring women 'into the streets' for repeal." Yet the kind of feminism Lader and others in the East Coast reform movement were espousing held little appeal for the more conservative Dallas reformers.

Ironically, it was only a year earlier that feminists, who were also coming into their own as a social and political movement, had begun to use militant tactics. The first major confrontation occurred in New York in February 1969 when a group of women disrupted an abortion hearing by the Joint Legislative Committee on the Problems of Public Health. When the chairman could not regain control of the meeting, he recessed it to another room, after calling in the police to stand guard and keep out the protestors. Angry and insulted at being treated in such a manner, the women staged a sit-in outside the meeting room.

A month later the radical New York feminist group called Redstockings, furious at a federal court's refusal to hear testimony by women who had suffered through illegal abortions, held a public deposition at the Washington Square Methodist Church in Greenwich Village. For the first time American women spoke publicly about their experiences with abortion. Throughout the year New York feminists picketed whenever there was a need—marching, for example, at the American Medical Association meeting that summer. Increasingly, pro-choice activism was being associated with feminism, and with radical feminism at that.

Whitehill and her group were troubled by the feminists' approach. They were sympathetic to some degree because they knew that politics had played a major role in delaying long overdue reform in New York, but they felt that their reform effort was moving along more smoothly in Texas because they had not couched their argument in feminist terms. Texas feminists were increasingly making themselves heard on the subject of abortion, and the Dallas reformers were growing alarmed. Philosophically, they stood shoulder to shoulder with the feminists; tactically, they were miles apart.

Whitehill suspected that Sarah Weddington might be excellent for helping them ward off the feminist threat. Younger than most of the committee members, she could hold her own against the feminists, who were her generation. A lawyer, a skilled orator, yet attractive and feminine in just the right way, she was also a good person to press their cause to everyone else. She would project the image they needed and would not threaten either side of the debate.

Several days after the oral arguments, Whitehill called Weddington to introduce herself and tell her about their group. She and Weddington decided to meet. Whitehill and Pat Cookson, another group member, drove the forty miles to Ft. Worth, where Weddington lived with her husband, Ron, to have lunch and get acquainted. The two women left the meeting more impressed than they had been during the oral argument. They could definitely see Weddington playing an important role as spokesperson for abortion reform in Texas.

Weddington, for her part, had shown considerable interest in their fledgling organization and seemed eager to work with them. She told them she and Coffee were planning to appeal the case and would need money and support to do so. She, too, was discouraged by the Texas law establishment's reaction to the decision and wanted to work on legislative change. Weddington also made it clear that she believed in working within the system and would resist the use of militant or radical tactics to change the abortion laws.

In contrast, the women were far less impressed with Coffee. During the oral arguments, they had trouble following what she was trying to say (as would practically anyone who was not a lawyer), and they found that her speaking manner left much to be desired. A shy woman, Coffee lacked Weddington's innate poise and exceptional oratorical skills. Intellectually in tune with the needs and desires of women, perhaps even more so than Weddington, she still lacked the ability to capture an audience's imagination the way Weddington did.

Although the women made no conscious decision to cut out Coffee, they began to show off Weddington more and more to the exclusion of Coffee. They wanted her to be their representative, the movement lawyer. Coffee, who had started the cases and was considered lead counsel by the Dallas judges, faded more and more into the background.

The Dallas Committee more or less stagnated through the steamy Texas summer, waiting for the annual burst of energy that always accompanied fall to resume their reform efforts. Elsewhere around the country the debate over repeal grew more heated, and by late summer the group, which favored repeal over reform, issued a position statement reiterating their belief that repeal was the best way to protect the abortion right:

> We affirm the right of every child to be wanted. We affirm the right of every woman to have full legal control of her procreative functions. We recognize that abortion is both requested and practiced in Texas today. We have organized for the purpose of education, believing that the laws of the state of Texas should be changed. We favor repeal rather than modification of the existing laws.

For all their fears about feminism, it was a statement that put them in the same camp with their more radical sisters, although it drew no criticism from the media or anyone else in Dallas.

They joined the National Association for the Repeal of Abortion Laws, a group Lawrence Lader had started in December 1968. An exchange of letters shows that they also wrote NARAL to find out whether it knew of any pro-choice statements made by Catholic clergy. NARAL reported back that it knew of no such statements.

The Dallas group would devote a considerable chunk of its time and energy in the coming year to soliciting endorsements for the pro-choice position. Throughout the summer they mulled over the value of actively seeking church support. Whitehill felt that the abortion issue was only temporarily dormant within the Catholic church, and that the group should round up support from Protestant clergy to counter the Catholic backlash that she felt was inevitable as the abortion debate continued to heat up. She noted that New York activists had sought religious endorsements and reminded the group that the Clergy Consultation Service had been in the forefront of reform. Whitehill believed it was a tactical error to leave the churches out of any public debate in a state like Texas, where religion played so important a role in people's daily lives and in politics.

Most of the other members of the group disagreed with her. They felt it best to leave the churches out of the debate or, at minimum, not to pressure them into taking any kind of position.

Before the group could resolve its differences, the churches began to confront the issue of abortion on their own. In Texas, at least, their interest in abortion reform was not so much tied to a genuine desire to help women as to a desire to separate themselves from the widely publicized Catholic view on abortion. Religion—especially evangelical, fundamental Protestant religion—had always been the backbone of Texas life, and the Catholic church was relatively weak and powerless. So when the Catholic view on abortion began to take on overtones of *the* religious view, it was enough to spur many local Protestant preachers into action. Speaking of the need to educate his congregation about abortion, Dr. Lee Porter, pastor of Houston's Bellaire First Baptist Church, said: "They thought it [opposition to abortion] was the American way of life, but really it was the Catholic interpretation."

The only problem was that the Protestant denominations had no official view, a situation they would obviously have to remedy right away. The Unitarians had taken a stand, but they were the exception. In November 1969, after the Texas legislature defeated the first reform bill, the powerful Baptist General Convention had gone on the record, stating that in their view the present restrictive law denied people "the benefit of the best medical judgment" and failed to deal with the problems of rape, incest, and fetal deformity. It was hardly an outspoken liberal view, but it was a start. The Baptists added that "meaningful and necessary changes in abortion laws have been delayed in Texas as the result of a strong and well-organized lobby"—a pointed reference to the Catholic church's opposition. Several Baptist preachers added their names to the Dallas Committee's list of endorsements.

In April 1970, two months before the Dallas decision, the United Methodist Church, speaking for its ten million members nationwide, announced that it felt abortion should be removed from the criminal codes and "made available only on request of the person most directly involved." The Methodists went even further, saying they favored "cheap and easy" abortion to "stem the flow" of the population crisis.

In June the Presbyterians issued a statement indicating that they supported abortion in cases of rape, incest, fetal deformity, and where the "physical or mental health of either mother or child would be gravely threatened, or the [sic] socioeconomic condition of the family." Issued in the midst of the repeal-reform debate, the Presbyterians were careful to add that their endorsement, otherwise surprisingly liberal, should not be taken to mean that they supported abortion-on-demand.

In July the Lutheran Church of America, the largest and most liberal of the two Lutheran denominations, issued another surprisingly liberal statement: "People have a right not to have children without being accused of selfishness or betrayal of the divine plan, and every child has a right to be a wanted child. On the basis of the evangelical ethic, a woman may decide responsibly to seek abortion."

Once the national decision-making bodies of the Protestant denominations began to advocate abortion reform, the Dallas group decided to solicit the help of local clergypersons, even though many of the local churches did not necessarily agree with their church's official stand. Their effort was spearheaded by the Reverend Claude Evans, chaplain at Southern Methodist University, who opened many doors to rectories when the Dallas women needed help in establishing contacts. He had been personally sympathetic to the movement from its start. In May 1969 Evans had announced that he was organizing a Dallas branch of the Clergy Consultation Service started a few years earlier in New York. By mid-October he had enlisted the aid of eighteen local ministers from eight denominations, and the service was ready to start operating.

A week before the Dallas decision and two weeks before the Texas Methodist Church voted to support legal abortion, Evans had preached a sermon calling for abortion reform. "If my daughter found herself pregnant, if she concluded that there was not enough mature love between the two to support the demands of parenthood, and if she came to me early enough, I would move heaven and earth to find a respectable physician who took such work as his obedience to the promise of God that man is meant for a community of love. In a given situation," he continued, "one must make a choice. War or abortion could be the lesser of evils. And most importantly, children must be wanted, must know they are wanted." Despite his continuing misgivings about any but the earliest abortions, Evans continued to work closely with the Dallas Committee.

The churches lent a much needed stamp of acceptability to abortion reform. Once the major Protestant denominations took a stand, the Dallas women had an easier time obtaining other endorsements. By

1971 they had added to their list of endorsements the local chapter of the National Association of Social Workers, the Dallas Child Abuse Committee, the American Public Health Association, and Planned Parenthood of Dallas, the latter endorsement undoubtedly due at least in part to Whitehill's work with that organization. The most important endorsement they sought—and ironically the toughest to get—was that of the Texas medical establishment. However much physicians wanted clarification on the present abortion laws, they were not prepared to obtain it at a cost of their own professional power.

The Texas Medical Association had begun to study abortion as early as June 1967, when Dr. Howard Dudgeon, Jr., then president of TMA, appointed a special committee of nine male physicians, headed by Dr. Hugh W. Savage. Their purpose was to study abortion, specifically, ways in which the Texas abortion laws might be modernized. A year after the committee was assembled, it polled the 9,338 members of the Texas Medical Association for their views on abortion. An unusually high 53 percent of the membership responded. Of this group, 4,435 physicians favored a change in the present law, and only 536 physicians opposed any changes at all. The highest rate of approval—a margin of ten to one—was for abortions done to preserve a woman's physical or mental health, when the fetus was believed to be severely deformed, and in cases of incest and rape. Abortions done for socioeconomic reasons were approved of by a margin of only three to two.

Despite this overwhelming support for more liberal abortion laws, the TMA issued a conservative recommendation that endorsed abortion to protect the woman's physical and mental health, in cases of rape and incest, and for gross deformities of the fetus. Nowhere in the committee's report did the members say anything about the woman's right to control her reproduction. Their emphasis was on the freedom the physician needed to "do his professional duty in consultation with his colleagues and in a manner consistent with the ethics of his profession, without fear of molestation by either the law or the *patients* [italics added]." Even though the Dallas reformers and others across the country were calling for nonhospital abortions done by paramedical personnel, the Texas physicians insisted that they be done only in hospitals, and that five physicians be consulted in the decision. The Dallas reformers particularly hated the fact that the therapeutic abortion committee was not eliminated.

When Representative Clark took over the abortion bill in the Texas House of Representatives, he approached the TMA with some proposed changes he had in mind for the bill. His strategy was to elicit whatever support he could get from the TMA without pushing the physicians too much. At a meeting with the Special Committee on Abortion in January 1969, Clark began by saying that he did not want the doctors to sponsor the bill. All he was looking for was some support for his bill, and to this end he wanted them to examine some proposed changes in the bill—the same kind of bill, he reminded the doctors, that Senator Parkhouse had sponsored, one that was essentially patterned after the conservative ALI-model law.

Clark asked the TMA to consider three changes: first, that the therapeutic committee be reduced from five to three physicians; second, that a residency requirement clause be eliminated; and third, that the age of consent be reduced to fifteen. The physicians agreed to the first and last change but would not agree to lifting the residency requirement. They insisted that any woman who wanted an abortion in the state of Texas must be a resident for at least ninety days.

Forearmed with Clark's experience, the Dallas Committee began to lobby the doctors in a similar manner. They planned to meet with them, one or two at a time, over lunch, during which they hoped to outline their position in an informal way and also to get feedback on it. After the amount of social repartee that precedes any business conducted over lunch in Texas, they launched into their abortion talk. Although they tried to present issues in as nonthreatening a way as possible, the women (to their credit) did not tone down their views for the mostly conservative doctors. They emphasized the need for total repeal without any of the old-style restrictions such as committee approval, age, and consent of residency requirements. The women had carefully researched their subject and were armed with statistics showing how well abortion reform was working in other states. After the New York reform law took effect in July 1970, the Dallas women used the disarray that seemed to have followed it to emphasize how much simpler it would have been to repeal the law rather than pass a new one. They pointed out the difficulty hospitals and doctors were experiencing in administering the reform law and reminded the physicians that abortions were successfully done in free-standing clinics with little red tape in Japan and several Eastern European countries.

The women were adept at pointing out that polls showed that a majority of woman—not feminists, but all kinds of women—wanted a change in the abortion laws, thus subtly reinforcing the idea that two could play the power game. Implied but not stated was the notion that although doctors might exercise considerable power over women's lives, they did so only through a certain amount of complicity on the part of women.

The doctors were also not above a veiled threat or two. They sought constant reassurance that the Dallas reformers were not "bra burners" or "women's libbers," and of course implied in their pokes at feminists, the Dallas women soon realized, was the message that if they were good "girls"—in other words, not feminists—then their recommendations would be considered. And if they were not . . . well, the implications of that were clear, too: No assistance would be forthcoming for the "ladies" from the "good" doctors.

Despite the doctors' blatant sexism and disinclination to help, the Dallas women did not give up on the possibility of obtaining a medical endorsement; it was too important to them to let the issue drop. They managed to tolerate the condescension of the physicians and at the same time get their points across. A carefully worded letter sent to Hugh Savage in April 1970 enunciated their view that only repeal of existing laws would address "the heart of the problem" in language that made their position quite clear.

They wrote that "80 percent of therapeutic abortions are performed on white women" and "95 percent of college-educated, unwed pregnant women end their pregnancies with abortion." They expressed their belief that the fact that so many therapeutic abortions involved white, educated women pointed to a violation of the Fourteenth Amendment—another not-so-subtle way of informing the doctors that they were discriminating against poor and minority women.

However much they might have to bow to the inevitable, the physicians were in no rush to relinquish their power over women's lives; it was in their best interests at the time to sit back and watch the legislation take shape rather than becoming active participants in it. The Texas Medical Association's cooperation would always be limited, as was the cooperation of doctors across the country.

* * *

Having fully succeeded with the clergy and only partly succeeded with the physicians (actually, the debate was ongoing), the Dallas women next turned their attention to ways in which they could lobby the mostly male state legislators. This was a major undertaking in a state like Texas, where lobbyists were more populous than oil wells. There were four or five lobbyists for every state legislator, and neither profession was particularly supportive of women at the time. It was into this macho-male fray that the Dallas Committee was planning to leap when the next Texas legislative session began.

The women felt they had no choice: if they could not achieve what they wanted through the courts, they had to work through the state legislatures. And it seemed like a waste of time, especially with the Dallas decision having proven to be so ineffective, to sit by and wait for the next court decision. Besides, even if the Supreme Court issued a broad ruling outlawing abortion overnight, everyone agreed that the states would still write new laws on abortion, and the reformers wanted to be part of that political process.

Despite their experience lobbying the physicians and the churches, and the many endorsements the women had obtained over the past few months, working with the state legislators would be their first major, coordinated lobbying effort. Scared and thrilled at the idea, the women were eager to get started. Their confidence had grown considerably over the past few months, and as Whitchill kept reminding them, lobbying was "just a matter of thinking through logically what has to be done and then doing it."

Thanks in part to James Clark and also to their own efforts, the women had been developing important contacts since they had begun to organize. Now they would set about turning these contacts into allies. Gus Mutscher, speaker of the Texas House of Representatives (a job that was by many people's estimate more powerful than that of governor), had promised to help them not only by escorting their proposed bill through the committee, but also by making sure that opposition bills died there. A powerful Baptist lobbyist, Phil Strickland, associate secretary of the Texas Baptists Christian Life Commission, helped out on several occasions by sharing a list he had compiled of the senators and representatives and their known views on abortion. He put one mark beside the names of those thought to be pro-choice but wavering in their support and another beside those who were Roman Catholic and presumably could not be brought around to vote for abortion reform under any circumstances.

Their lobbying efforts took several forms, from supplying legislators with data on abortion to showing off their endorsements, but an important, albeit ceremonial, activity was the personal visit to a legislator's office. The Dallas women took care to look like "ladies" when they called on the legislators: white gloves and suits were the order of the day. Whitehill, an Easterner by birth and especially sensitive to charges raised by the opposition that outsiders were campaigning for abortion reform in Dallas, took special care when she lobbied. Unable by her own admission to work herself up to a full Texas drawl, she still did her best not to sound eastern. She began every meeting by emphasizing that although Texas was her adopted state, she loved it very much and wanted nothing but the very best for it. Only after several minutes of praising the great state of Texas did she launch into her spiel on abortion.

Whitehill and the Dallas women had spent months prior to their lobbying efforts making sure they understood the various positions on abortion reform, who was for them and why. They had taken the time to study the opposition's views so they could refute them intelligently. They might look and act like ladies headed to a charity committee meeting, but they were intelligent, articulate women determined to make sure their opinions were heard and understood. In part, they did this by giving a current (and therefore nonthreatening) context to their views. For example, Texas had recently enacted a progressive and highly acclaimed Family Law Act. The women pointed to this accomplishment and told the legislators they hoped they would be as progressive about abortion.

They also devised ways of approaching what everyone euphemistically called the "religious issue," a reference to the Catholic church's opposition to abortion. The women were not above trading on the anti-Catholic feeling that seemed almost indigenous to Texas, a state settled by Anglo-Saxon Protestants who had carried their evangelical puritanism west with them and made it their unofficial "state" religion.

Texas also took states' rights seriously and separation of Church and State very seriously. Members of the clergy were barred from holding office in the state legislature. The women learned to phrase their comments in a kind of code that was clearly understood by the legislators to whom they spoke. They emphasized, for example, that restrictive abortion laws seemed to support the view of one particular (unnamed) religion.

The women knew that the legislators, including several Protestants with large Roman Catholic constituencies, had been scared away from the 1969 reform bill, when the Church had organized an unexpectedly forceful mail campaign that pleaded, begged, and threatened the legislators if they voted to liberalize abortion. The Dallas women worked hard to win the support of several key legislators who, were it not for this pressure from the Church, would ordinarily have supported the liberalization of abortion. By turning the current Church position on reform to their advantage, they attempted to assuage legislators' fears by assuring them there was a way they could support abortion reform and still be reelected. Reminding the legislators that the Church had taken the position that no law was better than a reform law, the Dallas women assured the worried legislators that repeal would please everyone.

Despite strong odds against their success, the women became skilled lobbyists who knew how to persuade, how to counter argument with argument, when to push, and most important, when to leave well enough alone. The real test of their strength would not come, however, until abortion was put to a vote, and that would not happen for several more months.

During one of their many trips to Austin throughout 1970, several members of the Dallas Committee were sitting in the balcony of the state house. During a break in the floor action, they began mulling over their budget, always a major source of concern. Their primary expenses were mailing costs, since they spent considerable time and effort preparing and distributing information on abortion. This time they had run up a $700 printing bill, and with far less than that in their checking account, they had no idea how to pay it.

Until she spoke to them, no one had noticed an elegant, dark-haired woman in her mid-forties sitting close enough to overhear their conversation. In what they would learn to recognize as her softspoken but direct manner, she said, "I'm so interested in what you all are doing with this abortion reform. I would love to help you out in some way."

Unaware that she was talking to the only daughter of one of Texas's richest oil men, Whitehill answered jokingly, "Well, we have this huge printing bill and absolutely no idea how we're going to pay it. You could help us with that."

"How much do you need?"

"Oh, it's a lot, but a contribution would help."

"Well, how much is it?"

"The whole bill is $700."

"I'll pay it. I'll write you a check for more if it will help."

Thus began the relationship between the Dallas Committee and Ruth McLean Bowers. Bowers, the mother of five children, some of whom had married Catholics and did not approve of her work in abortion, offered far more than monetary support, although over the next few years she was a financial angel to the Dallas reform group. As useful as her money were her power and social connections.

Since they had organized over a year ago, the Dallas women had failed in their attempt to win support from the influential old-money Texas establishment, particularly the women. And now that abortion was becoming a hot feminist issue, the society women were even less interested in having anything to do with it.

Despite the rebuffs, the Dallas Committee had long wanted to organize a statewide committee of prestigious persons who supported humane abortion reform. Bowers, who lived in San Antonio, organized a lunch at her country club, to which she had invited the kind of women whose support the Dallas women had been hoping for. The women came from all over Texas, and when Ruth Bowers made it clear that she not only supported this cause, but was lending her name to a statewide committee that was forming, Texas society followed suit.

Bowers rounded up nearly thirty endorsements from women all over the state. Her name, along with Whitehill's, was listed as state coordinator right below those of the committee members. The women on the statewide committee lent little besides their names, but this was enough to open many more doors, and it also carried some weight with the politicians.

Over the next year, of the core group that made up the Dallas Committee, various women came and went, lending time and support when they could and dropping out when a pressing family problem prevented them from doing much. Ellen Kalina, the group's first president, moved to Washington State and became involved in efforts to change the law there. Ruth Bowers, Virginia Whitehill, and Doris Middleton became the anchors around which the group revolved, with Sarah Weddington helping out whenever she could.

Their numbers were never large, a fact they carefully guarded from the opposition. At their June 1970 meeting the Dallas Committee had a slate of fourteen positions, of which only three were filled. Sometimes, as at their August meeting, as few as seven people attended. They could claim a core group of twenty-five to thirty women but they had built up a mailing list of four thousand. By comparison, NARAL, the predominant nationwide reform group, averaged about eight hundred active and eighty organizational members, of which the Dallas Committee was one.

The Dallas group had picked up an enormous amount of experience and political know-how over the past year. They had sponsored or participated in numerous organized forums and public dialogues. Their speaker's bureau routinely supplied speakers to radio and television shows where abortion was discussed. They had written and disseminated their own pamphlets and many other materials on abortion all over the state to large numbers of interested persons. Most important, they had become skilled lobbyists and were often called upon to testify at committee hearings in the Texas legislature.

Despite their growing political clout, one of their favorite activities was to pile into someone's car or, more often, Reverend Dwight Brown's van, and drive to some other city to "see what they could stir up." Ft. Worth, only forty miles away, was a popular place to work, but they also routinely drove the several hundred miles to Houston—often stopping at small towns en route.

Once they arrived in a town or city, they hit the streets like other good campaigners, passing out literature and talking to anyone who would listen. At the time the women thought nothing of crisscrossing the entire state of Texas; but years later Whitehill would say that if she were ever born again, she would like it to happen in Rhode Island, which in its entirety was smaller than Harris County alone, in which Houston was located.

The women often worked at Doris Middleton's house, because she had the space to accommodate their major activity, preparing and sending out mailings. A large room off the dining room furnished with only a Ping-Pong table was ideal for spreading out their papers and envelopes. When a major mailing was going out, the women never hesitated to enlist their children and their children's friends, who thought folding sheets of paper, licking stamps, and sealing envelopes had its own charm. Only one inconvenience was attached to the use of Middleton's home. The table had to be completely cleared off and all supplies stowed away each night because her husband, a conservative Republican, disapproved of what they were doing.

The Dallas reformers were probably more similar than not, a factor that undoubtedly contributed to their unusual degree of congeniality. All were middle class, educated women. They ranged in age from the early twenties—a young University of Texas graduate student named Victoria Foe—to the mid-forties, but most of the women were in their mid- to late thirties. Apart from Ruth Bowers, no one in the group enjoyed great wealth, and several strained their pocketbooks to make voluntary contributions to the group. Most were native-born Texans or had long ago adopted Texas as their home. Most had children.

Their interest in abortion, although intense, never became very personal, a factor that also undoubtedly contributed to their success as lobbyists. For them, the abortion issue revolved around a desire to help other women, particularly those who were less fortunate than themselves. They felt strongly that the abortion laws discriminated against poor women, that, to paraphrase the words of one psychiatrist, the only difference between a legal and illegal abortion was $300 and whom one knew. They were well aware that the abortion rate across the country for private patients was four times greater than for ward patients.

They got along well with one another, and their disputes were, for the most part, ideological rather than personal. Everyone in the group seemed to have been endowed with an uncommonly generous spirit that enabled them to resolve their differences without too much friction—certainly without the political infighting and inflated egos that seemed to plague the East Coast reform movement. Or perhaps their compatibility was simply a function of the fact that they were so much alike. Ironically, however, when they were finally put to the test, they proved to be strangely and unnecessarily unwilling to compromise.

The Dallas decision galvanized women all over Texas into action over the abortion issue, particularly when they learned that even though abortion was legal, they would not be able to obtain one in the state of Texas. Within a few weeks of the decision, pro-choice groups had formed in Austin, Houston, and Galveston. By the end of 1970 the various organizations, at the instigation of the Dallas Committee, were attempting to form an umbrella group, which they had tentatively named the Texas Abortion Coalition, or TAC.

From the beginning, unfortunately, TAC was sabotaged with political, hidden—and not so hidden—agendas. The basic problem seemed to stem from the fact that the newly formed groups were more feminist in their orientation than the Dallas group. Most of the women in the newer groups had arrived at their interest in abortion via the women's rights movement, a sharp contrast to the Dallas women's more elitist origins in the population control movement.

That the Houston group was controlled by radical-Marxist feminists also caused friction with the more mainstream Dallas women, who by this time felt proprietary not only about the abortion issue, but also about the methods they were using to bring about change. The Dallas women were completely convinced that working within the system was the only way to influence Texas's male, mostly conservative legislators. In particular, they were angry when one of the Houston women in TAC ran for mayor on the Communist ticket. She had gotten a lot of publicity for including a pro-choice plank in her platform—an effort the Dallas women found unforgivably ill timed since, after months of lobbying by Dallas Committee members, the Texas legislature was on the verge of passing what would be the nation's most liberal repeal law.

Despite the conflict in ideologies, the various groups set out to work amicably together in TAC. They selected a motto for their statewide campaign—"Abortion is a personal decision"—and by mid-December 1970 plans were under way for several activities and events. An Austin press conference announcing the formation of TAC went off so successfully that for the first time a local television station covered a pro-choice event.

A flurry of letters were exchanged, each detailing what the various local groups were doing to get TAC organized. From Houston Debbie Leonard wrote that her group was writing a statement of public support for liberalized abortion that would be published, along with a long list of individuals' names, in newspapers in mid-January. Evelyn Sell wrote Sarah Weddington that the Austin women were working on a chain letter that could be used statewide. The Dallas women were charged with responsibility for preparing leaflets that could be used statewide to promote the pro-choice position.

The Dallas women dominated the initial organizational effort. Whitehill and Weddington respectively were named acting honorary chairwoman and chairwoman of TAC. With Doris Middleton in place as acting treasurer, the Dallas women were placed securely at the helm.

Plans were under way for a public hearing to be held on January 30, 1971. Legislators would be encouraged to attend, and those who could not, to send letters and telegrams of support. A newsletter would be started to report on the hearing and other activities. Local groups were busy planning regional events to be held in the two days prior to the large public hearing in Austin. The steering committee would meet January 9 to work out details of the public hearing and other items on their agenda.

The first signs of disharmony had appeared at an earlier steering committee meeting held in Houston on December 12, 1970. A motion was passed unanimously to sponsor the public hearing, but a heated discussion arose when someone from the Dallas Committee suggested that no antiabortion representatives should be permitted to speak and that even the pro-choice speakers should be controlled. It was further suggested that only a brief question-and-answer session be permitted after each speaker's allotted time. The proposals irked the feminists, who saw them as an attempt to prevent radical women from presenting their views. The Dallas women denied this was their goal but made it clear that they did not think the presentation of radical or strident views would serve the abortion cause well. Eventually a vote was taken and the motion to limit the speakers passed.

The next item on the agenda, to hold the public hearing in Austin on January 30, passed unanimously. The feminists also wanted to sponsor a legal walk and a mass rally at the state house, the kind of action that was getting so much publicity for pro-choice reformers in other parts of the country. After showing the strength of their numbers, the women would disband to meet with legislators in their offices. The Dallas women vehemently opposed the idea of the walk and the rally. Initially, they objected on grounds that few legislators would be in their offices on a Saturday, but their real reason—that such activities were too strident, smacked of radical feminist tactics, and therefore might offend the mostly male legislators—eventually came out. The Dallas Committee increasingly saw feminism as a threat to the pro-choice movement.

Both sides had sound reasons for their views, but these quickly got lost in the rhetorical struggle that followed. The feminists pointed out that militant tactics were working on the East Coast. New York would never have passed its reform law, they argued, had it not been for the highly visible radical tactics of New York feminist groups.

In their defense, the Dallas women argued that they had not only made a decision not to employ radical tactics, but had based their decision on what they believed was an accurate assessment of the state of politics in Texas, which was not, they reminded the feminists, anything like New York. They pointed out that they had worked hard to bring some incredibly chauvinistic legislators around to a pro-choice point of view. They knew only too well that they were condescended to by the physicians and state legislators and even by some of the clergymen with whom they worked. But the bottom line was that they were making progress—slowly and tediously, but it was progress all the same.

In fact, they maintained that their view was every bit as liberal as that of the feminists. They wanted repeal rather than reform. What they did not want was to undo their work with what they considered unduly militant tactics. In Texas rallies and marches were associated with long-haired student rebels and radical politics, and Texas legislators had had enough of that, having experienced a decade of student unrest over the Vietnam War. The Dallas reformers did not think the pro-choice movement could benefit by being associated with feminism if the women's movement insisted on using militant tactics and civil disobedience.

As the argument grew larger and more explosive, it became obvious that the bottom line for the Dallas reformers was that they did not want the abortion movement linked in any way with feminism, although they did not mind individual feminists working with them. The feminists, for their part, resented what they viewed as a heavy-handed, elitist approach to reform. By 1970 the war between the sexes had escalated to the point of deep alienation, and after so many years of compliant acceptance in so many areas of their lives, with so little to show for it, many women were itching for a fight.

They could not care less if their actions on abortion or anything else offended a bunch of male legislators; in fact, so much the better if they did. Having tried nicely to wrest some of the power from men, they were ready to move on to stronger tactics if this was what was required for women to emerge in society as equals.

The majority of the women present were neither as radical as the feminists nor as conservative as the Dallas Committee, and they saw nothing wrong with a legal walk and rally in front of the state house. Unable to resolve the question in a way that pleased the two groups at opposite extremes, the women unanimously accepted a notion to table the question of the walk and rally until later in the agenda. Then they wisely broke for lunch, giving themselves a brief cooling-off period.

In stark contrast with the morning session, the rest of the meeting moved along uneventfully. There was some maneuvering about whether to headquarter the organization in Austin or Dallas. The Dallas women wanted it in Dallas for the simple reason that they believed it would permit them to exercise greater control over what they viewed as a dangerously radical element. Although their conservative politics were clearly in the minority at this meeting, they wanted to make TAC work, and a compromise slowly came about. The steering committee agreed to put the statewide coordinating center in Dallas. Shortly after that, the group also voted 21–10 to sponsor the legal walk and rally in Austin. Despite such important and obvious victories as control of the officerships and headquarters, the Dallas women went home unhappy.

Not everyone thought the Dallas women were right to be so concerned about control. Several other members of the steering committee urged them to ease up on their opposition to the feminist proposals. One woman, who confessed to feeling uneasy initially about a march, said that her fears were allayed (and by implication, she thought those of the Dallas Committee should be as well) when she learned that the march was actually going to be a legal walk, and that the rally would be an extension of the hearing with moderate speakers. She also pointed out that the Sunday papers could not carry anything but the morning events anyway, so there would be no pictures of female radicals milling about the Austin state house.

Miriam Kass, a *Houston Post* reporter who had covered abortion from the start of the reform movement in Texas, also wrote Whitehill urging the Dallas Committee not to close doors to groups more radical than hers. Basically sympathetic to the Dallas women, Kass said she could understand Whitehill's worries about abortion reformers being stereotyped as hippies, but nonetheless she thought that if the women were to get anything done, TAC must be open to all. She cautioned the Dallas women against wasting their time keeping one group out rather than seeking to balance the radicals with moderates.

Her advice was not taken, and the schism was not healed. After the January 9 steering committee meeting, the Dallas women indignantly withdrew from TAC.

Although no one felt good about the split-up, the Texas women could console themselves with the knowledge that they were hardly alone in their failure to work together. Their petty (and sometimes not so petty) bickering and even full-scale power struggles were a microcosm of the kind of internal strife that plagued the pro-choice movement. One woman who was present at all the TAC organizational meetings would later comment that from the beginning there obviously had been great schisms on a personal and impersonal level. In retrospect, it seems a shame that the Dallas reformers could not bring themselves to accommodate feminism. Their efforts would not have been seriously hindered—and might even have been helped—by employing some of the radical feminists' tactics.

After withdrawing from TAC in early January 1971, the Dallas women turned their full attention to the repeal bill they were hoping to see passed in the Texas legislature that year. James Clark had not run again, but the abortion bill had been taken up in the house by Representative Sam Coats. It was sponsored in the upper house by Senators Tom Creighton and Don Kennard, the latter being the chairman of the Senate Public Health Committee.

Over the past year the women had convinced these three men and many other legislators that repeal would be better than reform. They made sure that all the legislators had received material detailing how the so-called reform laws were not working out, as well as a legislative update on the status of abortion in Colorado, which was currently trying to replace its reform bill with a repeal bill. Weddington had drafted a model repeal bill, which the sponsors accepted with few changes. On March 11, 1971, the repeal bill was introduced in both houses, accompanied by seventeen pages of explanatory text.

Angry that they were unable to stop the bill, the opposition went into high gear, charging that the bill amounted to abortion-on-demand. The bill's sponsors immediately began countering the opposition's criticism, insisting that no one could demand an abortion from a physician, and that this bill merely made the decision a private one between a patient and her physician. They stressed repeatedly that one-third of all illegal abortions were done by physicians anyway, a fact that should by itself indicate the need to rewrite state laws. And of course, hanging over the legislature's head was the fact that a federal court had just found their state law unconstitutional.

Six days later, on March 16, 1971, the *Dallas Times Herald*, which supported moderate reform, railed against the idea of repeal, calling it "morally repugnant" and warning that if the proposed bill passed, physicians would be able to perform abortions "with no more than the written consent of the prospective mother."

A floor hearing was scheduled for March 29. The Dallas women took on the task of orchestrating the hearing. They would decide who would speak and for how long. By now they were old hands at this, having testified numerous times themselves at committee hearings.

Among the speakers they lined up were Lucas and Weddington, who would address the issues of constitutionality, an especially important topic in light of the recent Dallas decision. The women had met Lucas in January when he had come to Dallas several times to help with fund-raising efforts for the Supreme Court appeal. On January 29 they had sponsored a fund-raiser for him. Lucas was now listed as lead counsel on *Roe* v. *Wade*, and press releases also described him as lead counsel on *Vuitch*, the Washington, D.C., case that would probably be heard by the Court in the coming year.

Although the Texas Medical Association had not yet indicated it would support repeal, and would not do so officially until a week before a vote was scheduled to take place on the floor of the state senate, Dr. Hugh Savage also agreed to testify about the medical issues of abortion, as did B. T. Hollins, a Houston obstetrician-gynecologist.

Representing the clergy were three ministers, Claude Evans, Phil Strickland, and James Campbell, of the Methodist, Baptist, and

Presbyterian denominations respectively. The "social-psychological" aspects of abortion would be addressed by Whitehill, representing the Dallas Committee to Study Abortion, now officially renamed the Texas Citizens for Abortion Education; Betsy Mandel, representing Child and Family Services in Austin; Robert White, a professor of psychiatry at the University of Texas; and Mrs. Horace Robbins, identified only as a Catholic laywoman who had served on the Governor's Commission on the Status of Women. Ten minutes were allotted for a film entitled *The Unfinished Story* and six minutes to personal testimony by three women who had undergone abortions but whose names were not listed on the agenda.

The icing on the cake, as far as Whitehill was concerned, was the testimony by then-legislator (and later governor) Richard Lamm of Colorado, who had been instrumental in passing that state's reform law in 1967 and now did not like it, favoring repeal instead. Whitehill, who had met Lamm through her activities in Zero Population Growth, was convinced that he and he alone could persuade Texas legislators that they could vote for repeal and get reelected. She had personally asked him to come to Texas to testify and had gotten the Dallas Committee to pay his airfare.

In a handwritten letter he sent her when the hearing was in the planning stages, he counseled the Texas reformers to "go for repeal only," warning that "reform is not only no compromise, but is counterproductive." Lamm advised Whitehill not to underestimate the importance of the hearing and advised the Dallas Committee to put only its most conservative people in the spotlight. These might not be the key people, he noted, "but you must show that the middle citizen is on your side, not only Unitarians, civil libertarians, women's lib, etc." Lamm specifically recommended that the Dallas women use the most conservative clergy and physicians they could find who still agreed with their position. He warned against emotional or extreme witnesses, saying this was where the opposition always erred when it testified before legislatures, choosing to send people who offered emotional and often not very rational testimony.

Despite Lamm's excellent advice and their hard work in setting up the hearing, which was successful, the bill was only narrowly voted out of committee. The Senate Public Health Committee voted five to four to send the bill to the floor. The five yes votes were Protestants; the four no votes, Catholics; and four other members of the committee, who represented heavily Catholic areas, did not attend the meeting.

Senator Creighton announced that he would call for a count as soon as he had enough votes to pass the bill. That moment never came, and the bill died on the floor—two votes short of the two-thirds vote needed to obtain a floor vote. The House bill died in committee.

Sorely disappointed but refusing to be deterred, the Dallas women vowed they would be back next year and for as many years as it took to pass a liberal abortion bill. Having learned just how frustrating legislative politics could be, though, they fervently hoped that the Supreme Court would render a decision that would eliminate the need for them to pursue the fight any longer in the legislative arena.

13

Preparing for
the High Court

When the Texas legislature failed to liberalize abortion yet again, Weddington turned her attention to preparing for the Supreme Court oral arguments, now scheduled for mid-December. After the Dallas decision, Weddington had taken a job as assistant city attorney (the first woman to hold the position) in Ft. Worth but had resigned nine months later upon learning that the Supreme Court was going to hear *Roe*. Coffee worked with her when she could spare the time from her practice. They read other cases and any other materials they could find on abortion, trying to absorb as many facts and ideas as possible, all of which would have to be honed down to a few essential points to be made in the justices' presence during the thirty minutes they would have to argue the case.

When the Supreme Court announces that it will hear a case, it indicates either that it has jurisdiction or that it will postpone consideration of jurisdiction until it has heard the merits of the case argued. In *Roe* v. *Wade*, the Court had postponed jurisdiction, a sign to counsel that they should address jurisdictional issues early in the brief and at the start of the oral argument. Coffee and Weddington knew this meant they would have to deal with the issue of mootness yet again and also probably with whether the case should have been taken into a state court before approaching a federal one.

The two women hoped they would be able to share the argument. They had been told that the Supreme Court sometimes let two lawyers who had worked together on a case split the oral arguments, and they intended to ask permission to do so. Their plan was to divide the arguments the same way they had in the lower court, with Coffee arguing the procedural issues while Weddington tackled the merits of the case.

Meanwhile matters appeared to be proceeding smoothly at the James Madison Law Institute. While none of the money or other support they had been promised was forthcoming yet, Lucas had altered the letterhead of the James Madison Law Institute, a somewhat promising sign, to list Sarah Weddington as executive director of the southwest office.

He had prepared a budget for the case, which he was circulating in an attempt to raise money. He estimated printing expenses for the brief at $6,000 and set aside a matching figure for the appendix; $15,000 would be needed for the amicus briefs. Other expenses were relatively minimal: $2,500 to pay for printing the brief and record from the lower court, $3,000 to print a reply brief (which was never done), $3,500 in travel costs, and $2,000 for a miscellaneous and contingency fund. The largest expense in the $69,000 budget was $31,000—$25,000 to be used to pay the James Madison Law Institute staff and $6,000 for "additional research assistants." Lucas's fund-raising efforts on *Roe*'s behalf yielded little, however, and he repeatedly pushed Weddington to raise money, reminding her that since *Roe* was a "Texas case," the money should rightfully come from Texans. Weddington did raise the needed money for the appeal, from Ruth Bowers, who wrote a check large enough to cover most of the expenses of taking *Roe* to the Supreme Court.

Welcome assistance also came from the New York chapter of the Association for the Study of Abortion. The scholarly group was ideal to guide two inexperienced young lawyers through the maze of complicated legal maneuvering that led from Dallas to the Supreme Court, to say nothing of the complex and sometimes confusing maze of East Coast abortion politics. A nonprofit organization, ASA did not lobby but functioned as a resource center for the most up-to-date information and thinking on abortion.

Regarded as an important source of unbiased information by journalists, scholars, and government agencies, ASA staked its reputation on its integrity. For example, like other pro-choice and antiabortion groups, ASA put considerable effort into researching an estimate of the number of illegal abortions done each year. It was an almost impossible statistic to determine since records are not usually kept of illegal activities. Even more important, the estimate had political overtones. Pro-choice groups naturally wanted to arrive at as high a figure of illegal—and potentially life-threatening—abortions as they could, while antiabortion groups were determined to play down the figure in an effort to deemphasize the need to legalize abortion.

In one pamphlet, ASA had relied on the most frequently used estimate of one million illegal abortions per year. When Jimmye Kimmey, a former Barnard professor, became the executive director of ASA in the fall of 1966, the booklet was in the process of being revised. As she was preparing it for the printer, Kimmey expressed her concerns about accuracy to Christopher Tietze, a founder of ASA and head of the World Population Council. Was this estimate of illegal abortions accurate? she wanted to know. Tietze thought it was too high and suggested that the real number of illegal abortions was more like half a million. The booklet was revised using the latter figure.

ASA put much of its money into legal research that would prove enormously helpful to Weddington and Coffee. The group had funded several major opinion polls over the years. When they learned that a case was going to be heard by the Supreme Court, they funded the research and writing of an important article by New York Law School Professor Cyril Means, which delved into the history of the abortion right. Means's work provided new insights into the reasons the states had passed restrictive abortion laws during the late eighteenth century.

ASA also gave Weddington and Coffee access to some of the country's top experts on abortion. The group had been founded several years before abortion became a controversial topic mostly by lawyers and doctors who were interested in studying abortion in an unbiased way to see what changes in the law might be warranted. The women would have the benefit of legal counsel from abortion experts such as Harriet Pilpel and Cyril Means. As counsel to Planned Parenthood in Connecticut, Pilpel, a leading figure in the birth control movement, had worked on several major cases, including *Poe* v. *Ullman* and *Griswold* v. *Connecticut*. Other members, such as Christopher Tietze, Alan Guttmacher (head of Planned Parenthood), and Dr. Robert Hall, a leader in the New York reform movement, would provide medical advice. Hall had worked with Roy Lucas and the ACLU to develop a test case involving New York physicians (which never came to fruition), and he had also been one of the first physicians to propose in the mid-1960s the then startling idea that the abortion decision should reside with the woman and not with her physician. Many of the ASA members also belonged to the ACLU, and this gave Weddington access to their files and expert legal counsel, should she want it.

Most important, perhaps, was the fact that ASA's orientation was toward judicial rather than legislative reform. Pilpel, who had put considerable thought and energy into the issue, believed women had a constitutional right to abortion; she thought it resided in either the Fourteenth or the Ninth Amendment. ASA had been on the lookout almost since its founding for cases that could test Pilpel's theories. The group was convinced that the abortion right, like the right to birth control, would be established in a series of cases rather than one. Courts, especially the Supreme Court, were not prone to broad decisions, and as a result ASA was geared for a series of individual skirmishes rather than one big battle.

ASA's mistake, if it can be called that in hindsight, was to focus too closely on the potential disadvantages of a loss rather than the advantages of a victory. Perhaps overly concerned with how much any single defeat in a court might hurt the overall cause, they sought an ideal plaintiff—and such creatures rarely exist. In examining potential cases, they also weighed how a loss might affect women's struggle for equality or, for that matter, abortion reform in state legislatures—and in the process found most potential plaintiffs wanting. Consequently, when *Roe* was appealed to the Supreme Court, ASA members were no closer to developing a test case than they had been when first organized, but other cases were working their way up through the judicial system.

Even though several things—McCorvey's differing versions of the rape, the use of aliases, the insubstantial record in the lower court—would probably have kept ASA from taking the case had it been offered to them, they realized that *Roe* was going to be heard in the Supreme Court whether they wanted it to be or not and wisely thought it best to have at least some influence over the case. ASA members were impressed with the way Coffee and Weddington had handled the case in the lower court; they thought it had been argued very well and were pleased to see the decision based on the less controversial Ninth Amendment rather than the Fourteenth. They approved of Coffee and Weddington's handling of the touchy issue of

Norma's claim that she had been raped and thought the two women had shown excellent judgment in keeping any reference to a rape out of the official court records. In short, ASA decided to throw its weight behind *Roe*.

As Weddington became better acquainted with ASA members, she also learned more about Roy Lucas, and what she learned, unfortunately, did little to put her mind at ease. ASA, which had funded some of Lucas's research, had recently stopped working with him. Jimmye Kimmey, who felt that Lucas had great potential, also recalled that she "had to watch out with him, that with the best will in the world, he could convince himself that what he was doing was right no matter what." Lucas also had a falling-out with Pilpel, his mentor in the movement. Several ASA members tactfully conveyed ASA's disillusionment with Lucas to Weddington, more to warn her to be careful in her dealings with him than from any vindictiveness. Weddington, who always liked to put things in the best possible light, was forced to concede that Lucas's fall from favor with the East Coast establishment was tied to something more than large egos and in-group politics.

She had also become increasingly anxious over Lucas's failure to send her a draft copy of the *Roe* brief. Due July 15, it was scheduled to go to the printer around June 15. When early May arrived and Weddington had seen nothing, not even a rough copy of a draft, she grew even more concerned. Whenever she talked to Lucas, he reassured her that everything was going smoothly. His staff was reportedly hard at work on the brief, and she would be receiving it any day. Weddington and Coffee, however, grew increasingly suspicious and worried. Had Weddington not already scheduled a trip to New York to meet with ASA members and work on the oral arguments, one of them would have planned a trip simply to check out the situation at the James Madison Law Institute.

Upon arriving at the James Madison Law Institute, Weddington was dismayed to learn that the *Roe* brief had not even been started. The staff appeared to be hard at work writing amici curiae briefs on other abortion cases but was doing nothing about her case. Lucas was rarely around to supervise or prod them in any event. Having only recently severed his ties with ASA, he was now in the midst of a battle to stay afloat in NARAL.

No one activity or event led to Lucas's fall from grace with the East Coast movement. Instead, a combination of factors—most notably his increasing interest in making money in the movement and his aggressive personality—had simply worn people out. The split with NARAL was due to philosophical differences as well as personality conflicts. As various states had legalized reform, Lucas had begun to do more and more work for "providers," as persons who provided abortion services, usually through clinics, were called. Certain restrictions in the new reform laws, as well as resistance on the part of local hospitals, medical associations, and law enforcement officials, meant that providers were constantly in need of legal counsel in the early days of liberalization. Lucas soon made it clear that he was their man—for a price that many in the movement considered scurrilously high. Other movement lawyers also represented providers and took fees for their work, but few charged—or were accused of charging—such high fees as Lucas did. That, coupled with his high style of living, had earned him more than a few enemies in the movement.

Lucas's mistake was to continue working actively in the reform movement, particularly in NARAL, after he started working for providers. NARAL's founder and guiding light, Lawrence Lader, who was himself something of an autocrat but had devoted years to the movement without taking a salary, felt strongly that no one in the movement should be making money on abortion. In many ways Lader's view was unrealistic, especially after abortion became legal. It was one thing not to make money referring women to illegal abortionists, another not to make money once abortion itself became legal. The opposition, however, constantly harped about the huge profits to be made in abortion, especially in abortion clinics, which would become their particular target. As a result, even after several states had legalized abortion, Lader continued to insist that movement people—that is, NARAL people—should not earn money on the reform effort.

When Lucas failed to mend his ways, Lader led a contingent, composed mostly of New York reformers, to drum him out of the organization. Lucas was NARAL's legal counsel and was also running for a committee position in the upcoming fall elections. An attempt was made to remove his name from the nominating slate. The power struggle would not culminate until just before the national meeting in

October 1971, when a faction of out-of-state reformers protested his removal, and much of Lucas's energy throughout the summer was devoted to mustering his defense. Eventually, a compromise was worked out whereby the membership would be invited to vote on Lucas's nomination by a special mail ballot. It was only a stalling tactic; Lucas was out by early fall.

Within a few days of arriving at the institute, Weddington realized that if the *Roe* brief were going to get done, she would have to do it herself. Fortunately this was a situation where Weddington was at her best. An associate once noted that she was, above all else, an excellent pinch-hitter, someone who "evaluates things very quickly and always seems to know what she is going to do. When put to the test, she always performs." She called her husband, Ron, who had stayed behind to run their recently opened law practice in Austin, to ask if he would come to New York and help her. He readily agreed. Weddington's visit, originally scheduled for a few days, stretched out to eleven weeks, and Ron Weddington spent five weeks working on the brief at the Madison Law Institute.

ASA found them housing in a sparsely furnished, third-floor walk-up near Gramercy Park. By night they were the only tenants; by day the building was an abortion referral service. They enjoyed a pleasant walk through Washington Square Park to the James Madison Law Institute, which was located in a row house (rumored once to have been the home of e.e. cummings) tucked away at Four Patchin Place, a tiny cul-de-sac off Sixth Avenue in the West Village.

The brief was easier to write in New York, home to several of the nation's finest law libraries. Mostly, though, Weddington worked out of the institute's library, which contained many model and actual briefs on abortion cases. In addition, Weddington had compiled her own collection of research material.

Lucas was not thrilled with Weddington's presence, nor she with working under his auspices, but they managed to get through the days and weeks without open warfare, not because their personalities were compatible (they were not), but because they shared a dislike of confrontations. The situation was helped by the fact that Lucas was out of town much of the summer. When he was in town, he was preoccupied with his struggle to remain a presence in the abortion movement.

Lucas repeatedly suggested to Weddington that if she would only pitch in and help with other projects, he and his staff could work on the *Roe* brief. Possessed with a quiet streak of stubbornness and a determination to do a job right, she simply ignored him and went ahead with her own work. With or without Lucas's presence, the institute was frantic with work that summer. Frequently, everyone worked through the weekends, no mean feat in New York's stifling summer heat. Weddington recalled that there was time to form some friendships. The staff planned several outings to Jones Beach, and once they stole away for an entire weekend at Lake George, where a staff member had a summer house. In addition, Sarah and Ron Weddington spent several weekends in Pelham Manor, New York, visiting Virginia Whitehill's parents.

More important than the camaraderie was the way the staff pitched in to help one another when they had a deadline to meet. Weddington would work on someone else's project, and others, in turn, would help her out. A young law student working at the institute for the summer checked citations and did a lot of the research on *Roe*. The business manager lent a hand with proofreading and offered moral support when the work seemed overwhelming. Apart from her husband, who was content to let her run her own case, she was the only person working on *Roe* full-time.

Weddington wrote most of the women's history section herself. Ron Weddington wrote the section on constitutional rights, incorporating much of Lucas's article as he went along. Means's article was published in time for most of it to be incorporated into a section on the history of abortion. Although the gist of his argument—that abortion, long a common-law liberty, had only become illegal in an attempt to protect women's health—was later superceded by newer research indicating that a few other motives (the desire to control women's reproduction and the doctors' drive to achieve professional status, to name but two) had contributed to the restriction of the abortion laws in the late eighteenth century, his article caused a stir in pro-choice circles. It was not widely known that for centuries, under common law, women had been entitled to terminate pregnancies prior to quickening. Lucas read drafts of the brief at various stages, as did Norman Dorsen, who had consented to be the lead lawyer on the brief since Weddington and Lucas had not been admitted to the Supreme Court bar.

In addition to using Cyril Means's article, Weddington and her husband also visited his summer home in Gloucester, Massachusetts, so he could work with her on the briefs and coach her on the oral arguments. Stopping by Gloucester to visit Cyril Means became something of a tradition within the movement. A few months before the Weddingtons visited, Representative Richard Lamm read Means's article and came to Massachusetts to seek his advice on Colorado's reform activities.

The brief and the oral argument were each major undertakings, ones that would have occupied several lawyers nearly full-time in any law firm. Anthony Lewis, author of *Gideon's Trumpet* and a columnist who writes frequently about the Supreme Court, has written of the process of preparing a case for the Court: "The shaping of the facts and issues into a Supreme Court argument is the job of the advocate. The brief and argument that finally appear are only the visible part of the iceberg—the end of a long process of selection and decision and imagination."

Despite the pressure on her to complete the already overdue brief in a relatively short amount of time, Weddington enjoyed the work, particularly the writing. She was confident of her research and writing skills, having trained as an English teacher in college and then having done a lot of writing and research in her two-and-one-half years working for the American Bar Association after law school. She tended to draft at the typewriter, but other sections of the brief were handwritten, and in the end she sat down with scissors and cut and pasted together everyone's work until she had organized the brief in a way that pleased her. Weddington and the James Madison Law Institute staff worked equally hard preparing an enormous appendix. Designed as much to aid the work of future historians and lawyers as to impress the Supreme Court justices, it was nearly as major an undertaking as the brief itself.

Lucas mostly stayed away from the brief after Weddington took it over, but he was careful to maintain the appearance that he still controlled the case. Correspondence to the Supreme Court, for example, went out under his name. He requested an extension to August 1 to complete work on the brief when it became apparent in early July that the original deadline of July 15 could not be met. He corresponded with Texas Assistant Attorney General Jay Floyd, who had argued the case for the state of Texas in the Fifth Circuit and would now argue it before the Supreme Court. They agreed on a common index and worked out its contents. On July 7, without mentioning it to anyone, Lucas filed an appearance paper with the Court listing himself as the person who would argue *Roe* v. *Wade*.

On one day in the third week of July, Lucas sent three separate letters to the Court regarding *Roe* business: in the first he submitted the official record from the lower court; in the second, pages of the record that had been inadvertently omitted; and the third was a request for a second extension of the deadline to file the brief. Lucas wrote that even with the accelerated pace of writing and research, and working straight through the past two weekends, he could not get the brief to the printer before August 12. "The sheer work volume of assembling and digesting important materials," he noted somewhat officiously considering the circumstances, "has caused us to underestimate the time needed to complete a satisfactory brief."

By the end of summer the *Roe* brief was written. The arguments it contained had been worked and reworked, the latter largely the result of advice from Harriet Pilpel and other ASA members. It had gone to the printer, come back in proof form, been carefully proofed, and then gone out again for final corrections. In the end it was a serviceable if not brilliant brief, but then few briefs are brilliantly written—or even brilliantly thought out. Fortunately, neither is a requirement for the judicial process to work well. Forty copies of the brief were dutifully delivered to the Supreme Court on August 17.

Weddington's work load was lightened considerably that summer when ASA offered to handle the amici curiae briefs. An amicus curiae, or friend-of-the-court, brief may be filed by anyone who thinks a decision might one day have a personal effect on him or her. Persons wishing to file one request permission to do so of the court and counsel involved. As a courtesy, permission is invariably granted. The abortion cases attracted an unusually high number of persons and groups eager to file amici curiae briefs. Throughout August 1971 requests poured in to file them.

ASA had no intention of leaving the amici curiae briefs entirely to chance. They decided to "orchestrate" the briefs, much as a composer arranges symphonic music for an orchestra, a new idea at the time that has since been adopted in other important Supreme Court cases. Several ASA members were especially concerned about the fact that no expert witnesses or testimony had been presented to the three-judge court, and they wanted to see what they could do to set the record straight, so to speak.

Fortunately, ASA had in its executive director Jimmye Kimmey a person more than equal to the task. This tactful, intelligent former political science professor was the ideal person to organize such an enormous task. She knew the ASA membership intimately, including their professional contacts, and she tapped that network brilliantly. On advice of several ASA members, Kimmey decided that *Roe* needed, at minimum, a "religious" brief, one or more "medical" briefs (although she told me she encouraged a medical slant in all the briefs), and several briefs from professional groups, one of which, if possible, should be a "professional women's" brief. Each brief would supply another valuable piece of testimony or a perspective on abortion that ASA felt should be part of the official record.

Harriet Pilpel wrote the Planned Parenthood brief. Medical testimony was supplied by the American College of Gynecologists and Obstetricians, the American Medical Association, the American Public Health Association, the American Women's Association, the American Psychiatric Association, the New York Academy of Medicine, and an interested, seemingly ad hoc "group" of 178 physicians. Further testimony came from the California Committee on Therapeutic Abortion, which had organized to protest prosecutions of physicians and now claimed 5,000 members and offered 300,000 signatures; the California chapter of NOW, which had 20,000 members; and Zero Population Growth, with 300,000 members nationwide.

Kimmey and several other ASA members had also hatched the idea of organizing a brief consisting of personal testimony from prominent American women who had undergone abortions, something similar to the open letter published in April in France, in which such prominent women as Simone de Beauvoir, Catherine Deneuve, and Françoise Sagan acknowledged having undergone illegal abortions. Kimmey talked to several prominent American women who had gotten illegal abortions but was unable to convince enough of them to sign such a brief; she felt the idea died mostly because abortion was still enough of a taboo in the United States to dissuade women from taking so personally revealing a stand.

Another idea, this one for a "women's brief," did come to fruition. Among the groups supporting the brief were the American Association for University Women, which had only rather belatedly, in June 1971, taken a pro-choice stand (but which also had fifteen thousand members); the relatively new but already influential National Organization for Women (NOW); and the national board of YWCAs, among others. The brief was also signed by a long list of prominent American women: Jane (Mrs. Cass) Canfield, board member of the Margaret Sanger Bureau; Mary Daly, a prominent feminist theorist; Mary (Mrs. John) Lindsay, wife of the mayor of New York City; Eleanor Maccoby, a prominent Stanford University sociologist; Marya Mannes, author; Millicent McIntosh, president of Barnard College; Margaret Mead; Maurine Neuburger, former U.S. senator from Oregon and chairperson of the Task Force of the Citizens Advisory Council on the Status of Women; Jane Howard, author; Elizabeth Janeway, author; Marion Javits, wife of U.S. senator Jacob Javits; Alice Rossi, noted sociologist; Doris L. Sassower, former president of the N.Y. Women's Bar Association; and Harriet Van Horne, a popular columnist for the *New York Post*.

The women's brief was notable for claiming that the right to abortion involved personal autonony, the right of a woman to exercise complete control over her body. This meant, the brief stressed, that even if the fetus were found to be a legal person, a woman still could not be compelled to nurture it in her body against her will. It was radical thinking then, and still is, but most feminist lawyers today believe it is the only argument that truly supports the woman's abortion right. If feminists could bring another case before the Court, in order to strengthen *Roe*, they would probably shape their defense around this argument.

Kimmey and other ASA members also hoped to organize a "black" brief. Abortion was on the verge of becoming a sensitive issue among blacks, although it was not yet politicized to the extent it would be later when cries of black genocide emanated from the black community and the opposition capitalized on this concern. Despite some initial interest on the part of the National Council of Negro Women and other similar groups, the brief never got off the ground.

Rounding up people and groups to participate in the amici curiae briefs was not difficult. By the time *Roe* v. *Wade* had been accepted for argument in the Supreme Court, a majority of Americans supported liberalization of the abortion laws, along with a growing number of organizations, including most religions with the exception of Roman Catholics; all major medical and psychiatric groups, including the powerful American College of Obstetricians and Gynecologists; the family law section of the American Bar Association; the Task Force of the Citizens Advisory Council on the Status of Women; the American Civil Liberties Union; and Planned Parenthood.

Supervising and coordinating the briefs was a monumental task. Once Kimmey had assigned the briefs, she kept a close eye on the writers' progress and even on what was being written. One of her special concerns was the language used to describe abortion, and she made a major contribution in shaping the language in the briefs with her perceptive editorial comments. Her interest dated back to the moment when she had spotted a bumper sticker promoting the "Right to Life" movement. Kimmey instantly recognized that the anti-abortion movement had preempted the pro-choice movement with this new slogan. "Pro-life" was powerful; furthermore, it was an expression that could just as easily have been adopted by the pro-choice movement. Kimmey had long disliked what she considered to be an unfortunate and inaccurate description of those who wanted liberalized abortion: pro abortion. No women were "for" abortion. They were "for" the right to decide for themselves when to undergo an abortion. Women were, Kimmey decided after some thought, "pro-choice." To her relief, the label she coined stuck, and she promoted its use in ASA writing and then later in the amici curiae briefs. She also cautioned brief writers never to use the word "baby" when, in fact, they meant "fetus" and not to use the strident, hackle-raising expression "abortion on demand." Instead she recommended the less offensive and to her mind more accurate expression, "abortion on request." Kimmey read every amicus curiae brief with an eagle eye for the kind of language that was used, and to her credit, she was brave enough, in the face of some overblown egos, to suggest editorial changes that she believed would improve the arguments in favor of abortion.

The forty-two briefs submitted in support of abortion amounted to a massive effort not only in organization and writing, but also in the collection of signatures on the briefs themselves. In addition to working on *Roe*, Kimmey was coordinating the *Doe* v. *Bolton* amici curiae briefs, many of which were duplicates of the *Roe* briefs.

She recalled to me many years later how Margie Pitts Hames, lead counsel for *Doe* v. *Bolton*, had wanted signatures of physicians from every state that had enacted the ALI-model law—an enormous and also painstaking task. "We got an incredible number of signatures on those briefs," she said.

Perhaps because no organized effort was made to coordinate the amici curiae briefs in behalf of the state of Texas, very few antiabortion briefs were filed. Only four single-interest groups submitted briefs: Americans United for Life, "certain physicians and fellows of the American College of Obstetricians and Gynecologists," National Right to Life, and a group called LIFE—the League for Infants, Fetuses, and the Elderly.

In other areas, things were not shaping up any better for the Texas defense. Still beleaguered with civil rights cases, Assistant Attorney General Jay Floyd barely found time to return his appearance form to the Supreme Court, let alone write a brief. His boss, Robert Flowers, had become more interested in the case when he learned that the Supreme Court would hear it, and he produced several ideas for the brief.

Flowers had great admiration for Joseph Witherspoon, a prominent law professor at the University of Texas who had written extensively against liberalization of the abortion laws. Witherspoon was preparing a lengthy amicus curiae brief on behalf of the Association of Texas Archdiocesan Lawyers, a group independent of the Catholic church that handled individual cases. Flowers spent many hours in Witherspoon's office in deep conversation about the issues of abortion, hoping "just by osmosis . . . to absorb some of the brilliance of this man so I could portray some of it [in the state's brief]." The Texas brief, unfortunately for the state, would turn out to be far off the mark, consisting primarily of a claim of constitutional rights in behalf of the fetus and relying on antiabortion movement propaganda rather than scientific opinion.

If the state did not have time to prepare an adequate brief, it did find time for petty politics. In August, as the amicus curiae requests were coming in, Floyd wrote the Court clerk to protest the filing of several, most notably the Planned Parenthood and women's briefs. If the Court responded to this highly unusual complaint, no record appears in the files, and the briefs were filed.

In contrast with Floyd's protest was Norman Dorsen's gracious reply when Joseph Witherspoon wrote him seeking permission to file an amicus curiae brief:

> Dear Joe,
> Of course I consent to your filing an amicus in *Roe* v. *Wade* . . .

By early September, having already gotten at least one extension, Floyd realized he needed another. He asked the Court to extend the deadline for filing his brief yet again, this time until October 15, citing complicated issues "not only to the state of Texas, but to other states as well." Floyd had already called the Madison Law Institute to discuss the request, and Weddington's letter agreeing to the extension reached the Court two days before his did.

Weddington's letter is interesting for its tone, which seemed to indicate something of a superior-subordinate relationship with Lucas. Noting that he was out of the country, she was careful to add she had discussed the matter of the extension with him, and they had agreed to extend the deadline. She signed in behalf of herself and Lucas.

What happened on Lucas's return in early October was just as interesting. He wrote another letter to the Court, reconfirming what Weddington had already told them and identifying himself as "counsel for the appellants." The letter seemed to have no other purpose than to assert his role as lead counsel.

Both letters reveal something about the unspoken standoff that had developed between Lucas and Weddington over the summer regarding who controlled the case—or, to be more specific, who would argue it in the Supreme Court. Although Norman Dorsen had argued *In re Gault* and *Levy* v. *Louisiana*, two landmark cases in juvenile rights, and a half dozen other important cases before the Supreme Court, including *Vuitch*, the only abortion case to be heard by the High Court prior to *Roe* and *Doe*, he made no move to take over what he considered to be Weddington's and Lucas's case. Both Weddington and Lucas wanted to argue it, yet neither was absolutely sure who had the right or the power to argue the case, and neither dared risk a confrontation to settle the matter. Instead, the power struggle was played out in other, minor ways. Lucas, in his typically clandestine fashion, did not announce that he had listed himself as counsel to argue the case at the Court. And Weddington, characteristically evasive about an issue she did not yet want to deal with and also perhaps overly acquiescent (as her letter revealed) in the way that women sometimes are around powerful men, said neither yes nor no but simply went about her preparations, visiting Cyril Means so he could coach her on the oral arguments and permitting Harriet Pilpel to arrange several moot courts for her. Both undoubtedly hoped the issue might magically resolve itself without their ever saying a word to each other. But, of course, that was not about to happen.

14

Ladies' Day at Court

Weddington returned to Austin with one last dilemma still unresolved in her mind: she had to decide whether she or Lucas—or perhaps someone else entirely—was most qualified to argue *Roe* v. *Wade* before the Supreme Court. The case was scheduled for sometime in early December 1971. A request to the Court that she and Linda Coffee split the argument had been denied, but Coffee was not the problem. As far as she was concerned, Weddington had done most of the work on *Roe* v. *Wade* and was entitled to argue it. During the weeks Weddington spent at the James Madison Law Institute, however, she became increasingly aware that Lucas felt he should argue the case.

Lucas stepped up the pressure once Weddington returned to Austin. He insinuated their original agreement had been that he would argue the case, and after Margie Hames showed Weddington a letter in which Lucas had formally offered to make her a consultant, pay all expenses, and argue *Doe* v. *Bolton*, Weddington worried that she had perhaps turned over more of *Roe* than she had intended to. Having consulted with Coffee every step of the way on the case, she now turned to her with this problem. Although Coffee had not been directly involved in their dealings with Lucas, she could not recall any discussion about who would present the arguments. His offer, as she understood it, was to set Weddington up as executive director of the southwest branch of the James Madison Law Institute and to prepare the case for the Supreme Court—two promises he had failed to fulfill. Weddington's name had gone on a letterhead, but that was it, and he certainly had not made good on his offer to write the brief.

Weddington was keenly aware that her appearance in the three-judge court in Dallas had been her first ever in any courtroom, and that the oral arguments before the Supreme Court would be her second. She did not want to argue *Roe* if she could not do justice to the substantial issues involved. She also weighed whether she would be at a disadvantage as a woman. A woman's appearance as counsel before the Court was rare enough in 1970, so much so that when she had inquired about appropriate court dress, she was told that a floor-length, long-sleeved black dress was de rigueur. The idea that she could join the exclusive club of women who had argued cases before the nation's highest court held enormous appeal for Weddington, whose résumé was already dotted with an impressive number of firsts. But however impressed she was with her "firsts," she was too level-headed to let them interfere with her decision. By the time *Roe* v. *Wade* was accepted by the Supreme Court, Weddington was imbued with a sense of its importance not only to her personally, but to all women. It was for this reason that she questioned her ability to argue the case.

Most of the people to whom she spoke advised her to argue *Roe*. Pro-choice activists, particularly the women, believed that *Roe* was uniquely a woman's case and that a woman should most appropriately argue it. They reminded Weddington that Margie Hames was planning to argue *Doe* v. *Bolton* and that the Georgia law would be defended by Dorothy Beasley, an assistant attorney general of Georgia. Only the state of Texas, in what one person jokingly noted might one day be considered a strategic error, planned to send a man to argue the case. An appearance by a woman in the Supreme Court might indeed be rare, but it would be no novelty on the day when the abortion cases were argued.

Jimmye Kimmey strongly felt *Roe* was Weddington's case to argue, and so did Harriet Pilpel. This virtually guaranteed that ASA would throw its weight behind Weddington should such action become necessary. Weddington also knew that the Dallas reformers, several of whom had become close friends, would be sorely disappointed if she did not argue the case. They were looking forward not only to her day in court, but to theirs as well.

Apart from those who believed the case should be argued by a woman on feminist grounds, several East Coast abortion lawyers who knew Lucas expressed concern over his ability to handle a Supreme

Court argument, which called for both a high level of expertise and an appropriate dose of modesty. Some thought Lucas lacked the latter, that his arrogance and sometimes flippant manner might hurt in court.

Others, including Weddington, were impressed with Lucas's claim that he had argued *Vuitch* before the Supreme Court. The decision, handed down only months before *Roe* was argued, was viewed as a major pro-choice victory even though technically the pro-choice forces had lost. The Court had held that the Washington, D.C., law was not vague, but it had also found that abortion was permissible to protect both a woman's life and health. In many ways, *Vuitch* had laid the groundwork for *Roe*, and it had also been a ground-breaking case. Had Lucas argued it, as he claimed, it might have been a good idea to send him back into the Court with *Roe*.

But contrary to what he claimed, Lucas had not argued *Vuitch*—in any court. In a pattern that repeated itself in other abortion cases, Lucas had tried to argue *Vuitch*. When the case began to look big, Lucas contacted Dr. Milan Vuitch, the Washington, D.C., physician who was being prosecuted for illegal abortion, and began discussing his case with him in very much the same manner as he had with Weddington. That Vuitch had already engaged Washington attorney Joe Nellis as counsel seemed not to bother Lucas. Before Nellis, who had also represented Vuitch on other cases, realized what was happening, Lucas announced that he was joining him as co-counsel on the case. Vuitch was soon financing research Lucas did around the country on his behalf. He flew to Chicago to do some medical research and to Washington to learn more about the referendum.

The situation exploded shortly before the scheduled Supreme Court argument. According to Nellis, Lucas announced that Vuitch wanted him to argue the Supreme Court case or, at minimum, share the arguments with Nellis, something the Court was not likely to allow. Nellis objected. An experienced lawyer who knew his way around Washington, he now says he was more angry that a colleague had, in his opinion, engaged in the highly unethical practice of trying to steal his client than over the fact that he would lose his chance to argue a Supreme Court case. It especially grated on Nellis's nerves that Lucas seemed to think there was no problem with his behavior. Lucas's response then and now was that he believed everyone was entitled to the best-possible representation, and he considered himself to be the country's leading abortion lawyer. Only an angry threat from Nellis to file a complaint with the Supreme Court made Lucas back off. Lucas asked Norman Dorsen to argue *Vuitch* for him, and Dorsen agreed to do so. The Court let Nellis and Dorsen share the *Vuitch* argument.

Claiming that he had overslept, Lucas did not appear at the Supreme Court the morning of the arguments. Those who knew the circumstances surrounding the case thought it more likely that he was afraid to show up on the off chance that Nellis would carry out his threat. The fiction that Lucas had argued *Vuitch* would die hard, however; fifteen years later he still claimed that he had, and Weddington and many others still believed him.

Lucas seemed to have no doubts as to his ability to handle any abortion case anywhere in the country. In fact, he had developed a highly proprietary attitude toward abortion. It was not that he thought of it as his own personal crusade (although no one ever doubted his sincerity); rather, he was determined to be the lawyer responsible for changing the restrictive laws. In the final weeks before the argument, he grew even more determined to argue one of the cases, if not both. He called and wrote Weddington and Hames, pressuring them in every way he could think of. He told both women they risked setting back the women's movement twenty years if they argued the cases and lost. He said he knew the subject better than anyone in the country and had put in more time on it than anyone else, a fact that was not exactly accurate and would not necessarily have given him a prior right to argue the cases in any event. He claimed he had more experience in abortion than anyone in the country (also not true) and was the lawyer the Supreme Court would want to hear.

Their confidence finally battered by his persistent pestering, the two women separately sought advice from Cyril Means. Means had a keen but reasonably measured dislike for Lucas. He had, for example, dissuaded Nellis from filing a complaint with the Supreme Court over the *Vuitch* case on grounds that it would waste too much of Nellis's time. The law professor gave both women the same advice: Stand up to him and "tell the son of a bitch to go to hell." In our talks, Means reminisced that this was all Hames needed to hear, but that Weddington, fifteen years younger and considerably less experienced, found his advice much more difficult to follow.

As a result, Weddington continued to stall throughout the fall of 1971, never quite saying Lucas could argue the case but never directly telling him he could not, either. For a while, it looked as if both Lucas and Weddington might show up at the Court prepared to argue the case, but something happened just days before the argument to settle the issue. On November 21 Weddington received a copy of a letter Lucas had sent the Court, reaffirming his intention to argue the case. The letter infuriated her, and she resolved to argue the case herself.

For three days Weddington frantically tried to contact Lucas in New York to tell him of her plans. She left messages at the James Madison Law Institute and at his home. None were returned. Unable to reach him, she decided she could wait no longer before straightening out the matter with the Court. On November 24 the Court clerk received a letter from Linda Coffee, citing herself as general counsel and informing the Court that each of her clients (Jane Roe and John and Mary Doe) had requested that Sarah Weddington present the oral argument in their behalf. In what may have been an extraordinary precautionary measure lest anything else go wrong, Coffee for the first and only time in court records cited her clients by their actual names in addition to their aliases. She added that it was her understanding that all the other lawyers in the case had been informed of the change in counsel and consented to having Weddington argue the case. The last claim was an exaggeration since another letter, dated five days after Coffee's letter and written by Weddington to confirm her intention to argue the case, noted that she had not been able to get in touch with Lucas but did not feel she could wait any longer to settle the matter.

Last-minute spats among lawyers over Supreme Court arguments were not an everyday occurrence at the Court, but neither were they unheard of, and the Court clerk handled the situation with aplomb. A handwritten memorandum circulated at the Court described the situation and noted: "Letter from Lucas said he would argue. (Her clients want her to argue. I told her to call Lucas and work it out—that I said [sic] it seemed she had the prior right.)" Another note in the same hand but a different pen posed the query "Admitted?" beside Lucas's name, probably a reference to whether Lucas had been admitted to the Supreme Court bar, a necessary formality before one could argue a case. It probably did not escape the Court's notice that this was the second time in several months that Lucas had been the subject of a dispute in its court.

With the matter of who would argue the case behind her, Weddington focused her full attention on last-minute details. The first week of December, the Texas attorney general's office filed a motion to postpone the oral arguments. The official reason was that the state would prefer to have so important a case heard by a full court, and only seven justices were currently sitting; but more than likely the request was motivated by the fact that the state was not prepared. Weddington was relieved when the Court denied the state's request. Having worked virtually nonstop over the past few weeks to prepare herself intellectually and emotionally to argue *Roe*, she would have found a delay difficult, if not intolerable; her adrenaline was flowing.

The Weddingtons went to Washington, D.C., several days early, as lawyers arguing before the Supreme Court are advised to do (there is always the chance a case will come up earlier than its scheduled date). They also had to take care of some last-minute preparations there. They met with Margie Hames and her then-husband, William Hames, to discuss ways of dividing the issues in their two cases. Since *Roe* v. *Wade* was in essence a challenge to the constitutionality of state abortion laws, Weddington would argue the merits of the case, that is, the general legal issues, which, of course, sometimes overlapped the moral and ethical issues as well. In contrast, *Doe* v. *Bolton* was a challenge to the newer reform laws—specifically the restrictions such laws placed on women's access to abortion—so Hames would argue those questions. In addition, Hames would deal with the troublesome area of substantive due process if it arose.

Weddington also spent some time working in the Supreme Court library. This was her first realization that everyone at the Court also knew what a big case *Roe* was. Some of the people she met during her few days at the library were supportive and eager to tell her that they would be present for the oral arguments; others were cold and obviously disapproving. No one, it seemed, was neutral anymore on the subject of abortion.

The most important thing Weddington did during the week before the arguments was to participate in two moot courts. Moot courts are an excellent means of permitting someone about to argue a case before the Supreme Court to test arguments and receive expert feedback in return. Those who attend moot courts are charged to play the role of devil's advocates: they ask the toughest questions they can think of, just as the justices will do during the actual argument. But unlike a real court, if a particular answer does not satisfy, the moot court stops while everyone works to develop a better answer. Lawyers often hold moot courts as close to the argument as possible, to insure that any new material will be fresh in their minds when they enter the courtroom. Margie Hames declined to participate in one, not because she was feeling overly confident, but because she feared a moot court would frighten her even more than she was. Weddington, a natural performer since the days when she had participated in worship services at her father's church, was eager to participate in as many moot courts as possible and had even scheduled some herself with women from the University of Texas Law School.

The Washington, D.C., moot courts would be conducted, of course, on an entirely different—a more highly charged and expert—level than those in Texas. One court, held in a Washington hotel, consisted of activist women who were involved in the pro-choice movement. The other moot court, held in the National Lawyers' Club the day before the arguments, was organized by Harriet Pilpel and Cyril Means, who had done an outstanding job of rounding up an excellent sampling of the country's best civil rights lawyers, law school professors, and lawyers who had worked on abortion cases. Many of the lawyers who had worked on the amici curiae briefs for *Roe* and *Doe* participated. Joseph Nellis, who had argued *Vuitch*, the most recent abortion case before the High Court, was present; Norman Dorsen was not.

Since Weddington and the other lawyers were convinced that the state of Texas would base its defense on fetal rights, as it had in the lower court, a lot of time was spent on this issue. Previous court decisions, all of which showed that a fetus had never been considered a legal person, were reviewed. Nellis recalled lengthy discussions on how the Fourteenth Amendment had never contemplated the fetus as a person, how as a result the fetus had never been granted tort rights, inheritance rights, or any other kinds of rights except those contingent on live birth, the point at which the fetus became a legal person.

Much of the debate centered on how much to ask for. Most legal experts, including Pilpel and Means, thought the Supreme Court was ready to rule on abortion, but they could not believe it was ready to find that abortion was legal at all stages of pregnancy. Consequently, they urged Weddington to take whatever she sensed she could get. Implicit in this was a note of warning—the idea that perhaps she would do well not to ask for too much.

Another topic the moot court participants examined from every possible angle was privacy. Almost everyone present agreed that if the Court established an abortion right, it would rely on privacy as set forth in the Fourteenth Amendment as the basis of its decision, and they wanted to be sure that Weddington was well versed in all its aspects. (A few people hoped the Court would not rely on the Fourteenth but would instead find the right rested elsewhere, in the Ninth Amendment, for example.)

The lawyers, many of whom had argued cases before the Supreme Court or who had argued abortion cases in other courts, shared some of their techniques for playing to the justices. They told Weddington to aim her argument at the justice who had not yet made up his mind but might still be open to persuasion. She would not, of course, know for sure who that was. Other suggestions were to play to the justice's known areas of interest. Blackmun, for example, would undoubtedly listen most carefully to medically oriented arguments, while Douglas, Brennan, and Marshall would be receptive to arguments about individuals' civil rights.

She was also coached in tactics for handling a judge who tried to push her into a corner and make her say something she should not or did not want to say. The Court might, for example, take up the issue of whether the case was moot since Norma McCorvey had borne her child; Weddington must be prepared to show that the abortion right could never be determined if the Court followed strict legal procedure on mootness. She must show ways in which the Court had already redefined the issue of mootness—a task in which she would be helped by the Fifth Circuit Court opinion.

Everyone who participated was satisfied with the moot courts. Weddington welcomed the counsel of others and did not crumple under the sometimes sharp criticism that was offered. She was remarkably free of defensiveness, a trait that permitted her to use criticism to her advantage almost as soon as she heard it. Her streak of perfectionism also helped. If anything, Weddington had overprepared and as a result was confident of her ability to handle whatever anyone—moot court lawyers or Supreme Court justices—threw at her. The moot courts only reinforced her self-confidence. Weddington's performance during the moot courts also inspired confidence. Any lingering doubts in the minds of those present now vanished.

As the days dwindled to hours before the argument, Weddington's self-confidence was rivaled by a growing concern over the responsibility that rested on her shoulders with this case. Every spare moment in which she was not doing last-minute research or meeting with someone was spent rehearsing in her room at the Capitol Hill Hotel, which Texans still referred to as the "Bobby Baker hotel." She used an old speech class technique of arguing in front of a mirror to see if she was getting her message across. In her mind, Weddington argued to an imaginary Chief Justice Burger, trying to persuade him of what it would be like to be pregnant and not want to be.

She did not sleep well the night before the arguments. She would get into bed, remember a point she wanted to check, get up and look at it, and then repeat the process all over again with something else.

Even though her argument would not begin until ten A.M., Weddington was at the Court when its thirteen-ton bronze doors swung open the next morning. Like most visitors to the Supreme Court, she was initially taken by the grandeur of the physical surroundings. Most people are next struck by the smallness of the room where the Court sits. Such an important court is not expected to hold forth in so small a room. Weddington, ever the minister's daughter, saw the courtroom in another light: "Of course, I remember the majesty of the courtoom setting. When you enter at the back, there are the pews where the lay people sit. And they tell you not to chew gum and not to write and not to talk and not to put your arm on the back of the pews. It's just like church."

It was probably just as well that Weddington was unaware of the Court's view of this momentous day in her life. Court employees were jokingly referring to it as "ladies' day at court," and the "ladies" who were arguing the case were slightly irked, on their part, to discover that there were no toilet facilities for women in the lawyers' lounge.

Weddington was too busy throughout the morning to hear the jokes or even to get nervous. Seats had been reserved in advance for friends from Texas and people involved in the abortion movement, but it quickly became apparent that there were more Texans, activists, friends, and acquaintances than there were seats. Counselors were each entitled to six seats, and Weddington had persuaded Court personnel to allot her six extra ones for those who had traveled long distances to hear the case. Some law clerks turned over their seats to her, and Attorney General Crawford Martin, who would be sitting at counsel's table, graciously relinquished his extra seats to her. In all, she rounded up twenty seats for other people.

Virginia Whitehill initially thought she would not attend the arguments. Her father had recently died after a lingering illness, and she did not feel up to the trip. When Weddington had called to ask her if she would come to lend her moral support, Whitehill said no, she was too worn out and depressed to attend. After she hung up the telephone, though, her husband, James, who had overheard the conversation, talked her out of her decision. "You must go," he said. "You've done so much work on this. It's the big moment, and you can't miss it." As a result, Whitehill was in the courtroom. She came to Washington with Ruth Bowers, who despite her important contributions of time and money would have been too shy to attend alone. Both women were now good friends of Weddington, and it meant a lot to her that they were there.

Bowers's husband, a Texas politician, had gotten them good seats in the section reserved for the families of justices and court employees. While Weddington was crisscrossing the room in search of extra seating, Whitehill overheard a woman seated near her, she thought perhaps a justice's wife, explaining the Court proceedings to a friend. When the friend asked who the pretty young strawberry-blonde was, the reply came back, "Oh, I don't know. It's probably just one of the secretaries."

Many interested persons were present in the courtroom that day. Planned Parenthood and NARAL people were there, as were members of the ACLU. Harriet Pilpel and Cyril Means were present. So was Jimmye Kimmey. Joseph Nellis made it a point to be present. Charles T. McCormick, one of Weddington's law professors at the University of Texas, had flown in; he later sent her a note complimenting her on her argument. Also present from the University of Texas Law School was noted constitutional lawyer Charles Allen Wright. Scheduled to argue a case involving Howard Hunt later that day, within a few years he would become even better known as Richard Nixon's counsel in the Watergate scandal.

Jimmye Kimmey recalled the excitement she thought everyone felt that day at being present: "We all knew something important was happening. There was a kind of electricity." She also had special cause for pride when she saw the amici curiae briefs she had organized stacked up in front of the justices' seats on the bench. Amici curiae briefs, often biased and not necessarily full of strong points regarding the law, were sometimes ignored. Kimmey was thrilled to see this was apparently not to be the case with hers.

Absent that day was the woman who had lent her story, if not her name, to the case: Norma McCorvey. Weddington had talked with her about attending the arguments, but since they would only last thirty minutes and McCorvey would have no role to play, she decided, as did many Supreme Court appellants, not to be present.

McCorvey's counsel sat on the left facing the judges. At the table with her were Linda Coffee and Roy Lucas. Across from them on the right sat Assistant Attorney General Jay Floyd; his immediate superior, Robert Flowers; and Texas Attorney General Crawford Martin. Weddington barely got settled in her seat before the arguments began.

The honorable, the chief justice and the associate justices of the Supreme Court of the United States. Oyez, oyez, oyez, all persons having business before the honorable, the Supreme Court of the United States, are admonished to draw near and give their attention, for the Court is now sitting. God save the United States and this honorable court.

With those words, always used to call the Court to order, the velvet curtains (a recent Burger innovation) parted, and seven justices moved from behind the curtains to take their seats at the bench. Chief Justice Burger took his seat in the center chair, and the other justices, in descending order of seniority, sat on either side of him.

Four months after the deaths of Justices Black and Harlan, the Court sat with only seven judges, a fact that gave rise to speculation that it intended to deal with jurisdictional rather than constitutional issues in the abortion cases. Experienced court watchers considered the cases too important and controversial for a seven-man court to render a decision on the constitutional issues.

Pro-choice reformers felt and hoped otherwise; they were desperate for a Court decision that would settle the issue once and for all, especially now that the opposition had swung into action with such a vengeance. Reformers realized that the vote would be close, but they predicted it would go four to three in their favor. They believed Burger and Stewart would oppose any expansion of civil rights. Marshall, Douglas, and Brennan, the court's liberals, were undoubtedly with them, and Blackmun and White were the wild cards. But the reformers were fairly sure they had Blackmun on their side because so many physicians wanted to liberalize the abortion laws.

Despite the doomsayers who warned that the Court would not concern itself with constitutional issues, Weddington hoped that she would be able to get into them all the same. She particularly wanted to show the impact of pregnancy on women's lives, an issue she felt the Court was not as concerned with as it might be. She had reason to believe the Court would be interested in hearing the merits argued. Since it had decided to take the abortion cases, public pressure to settle the issue had only intensified. Many lower courts were rendering decisions, and although most of the decisions had resulted in liberalized abortion laws, not all had, and abortion was an increasingly divisive issue—the kind that the Supreme Court alone could resolve. The country needed a ruling on abortion just as it had needed one on school desegregation and prayer.

Chief Justice Burger led off the questioning. He first asked whether the Court's recent ruling in *Vuitch* had resolved any of the issues in her case, which did little to allay Weddington's fears that the Court might not address the constitutional issues.

Weddington described the ways in which the Texas and Washington, D.C., laws differed. The Washington law, she noted, permitted much greater leeway on the part of physicians in deciding which patients qualified for legal abortions; the Texas law permitted abortion only if a patient's life was in danger—not even in cases of rape or incest. Besides, she reminded the Court, the *Vuitch* ruling only applied to Washington, D.C., so it had not freed Texas doctors to perform abortions. Weddington also asserted that the case she represented challenged the total constitutionality of the law, whereas *Vuitch* had dealt with the constitutional issue of vagueness.

Stewart jumped into the fray at hearing this, saying that since Weddington was making a constitutional claim, there were many important questions to decide before the merits of the case could even be considered. When she agreed, he asked about Hallford's intervention, whether there was not some conflict since he had a criminal prosecution pending. (Bruner and Merrill, Hallford's original lawyers, were not in the courtroom.) Weddington answered that Hallford had come on the case after Mary Doe and Jane Roe had filed a class-action suit, and that he was not requesting any relief from his present lawsuit, only against future enforcement of the law. This was a bit of legal double talk, since any Court ruling that made abortion legal would bring Hallford's present prosecution to a halt.

When the Court was silent for a minute, Weddington seized the opportunity to tackle the issue of mootness, which she suspected would be the next question anyway. She noted that the injury claimed by her client differed from other injury cases in that pregnancy was unlike any other legal injury that could be sustained. Only women got pregnant. Pregnancy was also more intrusive than most other injuries. All this made pregnancy truly unique, something that might call for unique standards relating to mootness. Weddington said that this Court—and the Fifth Circuit Court—provided the only forum open to women since they were not party to abortion suits in Texas. Only physicians, not women, could be sued for illegal abortion. Having laid this legal groundwork, she talked more about the impact of pregnancy on women's lives, describing the discrimination they suffered in jobs and in education when unwanted pregnancies interrupted their lives and the emotional investment required over eighteen years to rear a child.

Weddington felt that her answers to Stewart's questions about jurisdiction had made an impression on him, but she sensed she was losing him as she talked about the impact of pregnancy on women's lives. She was not surprised; the idea that a woman could be injured by pregnancy or that pregnancy was destructive to some women's lives was fairly radical.

Weddington talked for a long time, about ten minutes, without interruption. Finally a justice rather gently broke in to ask if she would begin to discuss where in the Constitution the right to abortion might be lodged.

Weddington faltered for the first time. Perhaps because she had been coached to present as broad an array of rights as possible with the idea that the justices could choose among them or perhaps because she was not totally fixed in her own mind about where the right was lodged, she failed to answer the question as forcefully as she might have. Reminding the Court that the Fifth Circuit Court had found that the abortion right resided in the Ninth Amendment, she also quickly pointed out that under the common law, women had been at liberty to obtain abortions as they saw fit. And she brought up *Griswold*, the Connecticut birth control decision. Noting that she was "a little reluctant to aspire to a wisdom that the Court did not—was not in agreement on," she finally settled on the Ninth and Fourteenth amendments as proper places for the abortion right to reside.

Another justice asked if she were relying on due process under the Fourteenth Amendment. Weddington replied that the suit had originally been brought under that, and the equal protection clause, the Ninth Amendment, and a "variety of others."

Justice White sarcastically interrupted: "And anything else that might have been appropriate."

Weddington laughingly agreed, but she also sensed her mistake. Neither this nor her wavering over the grounds were fatal errors, and they might not even have been avoidable under the circumstances, but the strategy of presenting many grounds for the Court to consider seemed to be backfiring. The real problem, however, was that she had not handled the question deftly enough. She should have asserted each right strongly as she presented it. In arguing *Vuitch*, Norman Dorsen also had followed the strategy of presenting an array of grounds, but he had made a powerful argument for each one.

White broadened his line of questioning to ask whether the Texas statute imposed any time limit on when an abortion was performed—in other words, he wanted to know when Weddington felt a fetus was protected by the Constitution. Again she faltered, failing to give as definitive an answer as the situation called for; but she recovered quickly and asserted that "the Constitution, as I read it, and as interpreted and documented by Professor Means, attaches protection to the person at the time of birth. Those persons born are citizens."

Justice Douglas, who had until that moment appeared preoccupied with writing a note to one of his clerks, turned his full attention to the argument as soon as Stewart had begun his string of questions on jurisdiction. Now he brought up jurisdiction again, saying: "Well, so you're really—you're asserting that the pregnant woman has standing." He wondered aloud whether the doctor's standing affected the right to pursue this case. Weddington reminded him of a dissent he had written in an earlier case in which he had seemed to assert that the right to bring suit under similar circumstances existed.

Momentarily confused, the justice said that the finding in that case had been that the doctor could not bring suit.

"And which your dissent said was incorrect," Weddington quickly responded.

To which Douglas replied hastily: "Well, I repeat that it was."

The courtroom erupted in laughter. When it subsided, Weddington, sensing support for this line of argument, quickly added that even if Hallford were found to be an inappropriate party for relief, this should not affect the original suit brought by the women, who were, after all, still subject to an irreparable injury no matter what happened with doctors' abortion lawsuits.

One last issue—fetal rights—remained to be explored. One justice asked whether a constitutional defense of a fetus had ever been litigated in Texas. Weddington mentioned a case so recent that the Supreme Court had been unable to add it to the record. In *Thompson* v. *State*, a doctor who was being sued for abortion asked, as part of his defense, how the state could prove the fetus was alive at the time of the abortion. Some legal historians speculated that one of the reasons few legal systems ever considered abortion to be murder was the difficulty in proving that a body existed. One of the conditions for proving murder was the presence of a body. Even when an abortion was the ostensible cause of fetal death, it was impossible to know that the fetus had not died five minutes prior to the abortion. There could, in other words, be no presumption of life without proof, just as there could be no presumption of death without proof. For the first time ever, however, in *Thompson*, a Texas court had ruled, against precedent, that it presumed the fetus to be alive. The court also found that Texas had a compelling interest in protecting fetal life.

The *Thompson* ruling was exceptional, a break with hundreds of years of common-law precedent in which fetuses were found not to have rights prior to birth. In the area of trusts, estates, and wills, a fetus had no rights until live birth. Weddington cited a case from the Texas Supreme Court that held a fetus could not sue for prenatal injury prior to live birth. Thanks to Virginia Whitehill's habit of clipping abortion articles in several newspapers a day, she was even able to cite a case decided two weeks earlier in which the Iowa

Supreme Court had found that a fetus stillborn because of an accident had no right to sue for damages. Whitehill had clipped the blurb when she was in Iowa for her father's funeral and sent it to Weddington. Throughout her argument, in fact, Weddington had carefully referred to the unborn human as a fetus. The justices, however, were less clear about what to call unborn life. One justice inquired about the rights of "the unborn child . . . or whatever word you want to use for them."

Weddington had asked the Court clerk to signal her five minutes before the end of her argument so she could have a few minutes for rebuttal and summary, and now she was given that signal. She sat down.

It is not unusual for the courtroom to erupt in laughter during Supreme Court arguments, not because there is anything humorous about most cases, but because the justices, sympathetic to the tension that their courtroom prompts, occasionally add a note of levity. The historical record also shows they are receptive to an occasional jest by counsel. Texas Assistant Attorney General Jay Floyd, however, got off to a bad start, saying: "Mr. Chief Justice, and may it please the Court, it's an old joke, but when a man argues against two beautiful ladies like these, they're going to have the last word."

Expecting laughter, no doubt, he was greeted instead with pained silence from the spectators and the justices. Chief Justice Burger's face reddened, he looked as if he were about to say something, and then he nodded to Floyd to get on with his arguments.

A chastened Floyd turned immediately to the issues of jurisdiction, which should have redeemed his image with the Court and would have had he not focused on issues that the Court seemed already to have worked through with Weddington. Although no one would know until the opinion was handed down, many of those present believed Weddington had successfully maneuvered the issue of whether her plaintiffs had standing to sue. A gaping hole existed in her defense, however, over whether a federal court had any business interfering with a state's proceedings, especially criminal proceedings, before the plaintiffs had exhausted every possible avenue of action within the state. Floyd could have made a strong argument along this line, but instead of taking it up, he persisted in pointing out that the case was moot because Norma McCorvey, whom he carefully characterized as an unmarried woman, was no longer pregnant.

It was too much even for Stewart, who only half-jokingly responded that surely the Court could take judicial notice of the fact that there were, at any given time, unmarried, pregnant females in the state of Texas, again provoking laughter in the courtroom.

Floyd was reminded that this was a class-action suit. He replied that for a class action to be valid, one member of the suit had to be representative of the class and that McCorvey no longer was since she was no longer pregnant. He also argued, convincingly as it would turn out, that the Does had no standing to sue since they presented no present controversy.

When a justice asked how a woman in Texas could sue for the right to abortion, Floyd replied that he did not think it could be done at all, that "no remedy is provided." Sensing that he had finally seized the Court's attention, he continued, "There are situations in which, of course, as the Court knows, no remedy is provided. Now, I think she makes her choice prior to the time she becomes pregnant. That is the time of the choice. . . . Once a child is born, a woman no longer has a choice; and I think pregnancy makes her make that choice, as well."

A voice from the bench replied: "Maybe she makes her choice when she decides to live in Texas."

Again, the courtroom erupted in laughter.

Slightly miffed, Floyd asked, "May I proceed?" Then, in a feeble attempt to banter back, he added, "There's no restriction on moving, you know."

Although some of those present felt that the Court had mocked the counsel for Texas, something more important had happened. Floyd had approached the justices with an age-old assumption, namely that he and they belonged to the same old-boy network, one that excluded and even occasionally belittled women. And while there were undoubtedly men sitting on that bench who held some traditional values with regard to women, while they sat on the highest court in the nation, they were charged to treat all people equally. They succeeded in doing so to a greater or lesser degree depending upon the issues presented to them, but that day in court, in large part thanks to some presumptions of a male lawyer from Texas, they could not help but be reminded of their obligations.

Floyd continued to press on issues of jurisdiction, arguing that the case should be returned to the state because Dr. Hallford was involved in a criminal prosecution. He also said that the three-judge court had properly withheld injunctive relief, citing a ruling that said a federal court could properly issue declaratory relief while withhold-ing injunctive relief. From Texas's point of view, the issue should not really have been whether the state had improperly withheld injunctive relief, but whether they had properly granted declaratory relief. But Floyd seemed not to be moving in that direction until a justice asked him point-blank if he was saying that the Fifth Circuit was wrong to grant declaratory relief—if, in fact, the Texas abortion law was not unconstitutional.

Floyd faltered. He should have answered yes immediately and pressed the issue to the fullest. Initially, though, he said no, and only with prodding did he change his answer and say yes, he thought declaratory relief was wrong.

Another justice then asked whether the state had cross-appealed, an action that would affect the issue of relief. Amaz-ingly, Floyd was not sure whether it had. Several justices insisted the state had no right to cross-appeal since it had successfully staved off the injunction and in doing so had in a sense won the case.

A voice of logic finally prevailed in the courtroom, observing that what mattered was that the appellees were now before the Court because of a legitimate appeal by the appellants, so the case could proceed regardless of whether or not Texas had filed an improper appeal.

Another justice inquired as to Texas's interest in regulating abortion. Floyd cited *Thompson* v. *State*, the recent ruling that had asserted the state's right to protect the fetus, then quickly added, as if he sensed what might be coming next, "Whether or not that was the original intent of the statute, I have no idea."

"And yet Texas does not attempt to punish a woman who performs an abortion on herself?"

Floyd replied, "That is correct, Your Honor. And the matter has been brought to my attention: Why not punish for murder? Since you are destroying what you—or what has been said to be a human being." Floyd speculated on whether such a statute could be passed until he was interrupted by a justice informing him that no state punished the woman for murder.

Floyd replied that states nonetheless found doctors who did abortion to be guilty of murder.

"But that's ordinary felony murder, isn't it?" came the reply. A felony murder is a killing that occurs in the course of committing a felony, as when an arsonist kills someone (albeit not purposely) when he burns down a building or, in the case of abortion, when an abortionist kills a woman as he performs an abortion. It is a lesser charge than premeditated murder.

Floyd indicated that the state might also have an interest in protecting women. Gesturing toward the appellants' briefs, he said, "Those statistics have not shown me, for instance, that abortion is safer than normal childbirth. They have not shown me that there are not emotional problems that are very important resulting from an abortion. The protection of the mother may still be primary, but the policy considerations, Mr. Justice, would seem to me to be for the state legislation to make."

A sympathetic reply came back: "Certainly that's true. Policy questions are for the legislative and executive bodies, both in the state and federal governments. But we have here a constitutional question, and in deciding it, in assessing it, it's important to know what the state's interest is in the enactment of legislation."

Thus pressed, Floyd answered that the state's primary interest was to protect fetal life.

When, Justice Marshall wanted to know, did the state assert that life began? Did it begin in the first few weeks of pregnancy?

"At any time, Mr. Justice, we make no distinction."

"You make no distinction whether there's life or not?" Marshall pursued.

"We say there is life from the moment of impregnation."

"And do you have any scientific data to support that?"

"Well, we begin, Mr. Justice, in our brief, with the development of the human embryo, carrying it through to the development of the fetus, from about seven to nine days after conception."

"Well, what about six days?" Marshall asked.

"We don't know."

"But this statute," Marshall asked, now obviously enjoying himself, "goes all the way back to one hour."

Frustrated at being pinned down in such a manner, Floyd could only say, "I don't—Mr. Justice, there are unanswerable questions in this field, I—"

The spectators could no longer contain their laughter, and even Justice Marshall chortled: "I appreciate it, I appreciate it."

An obviously embarrassed Floyd said, "This is an artless statement on our part."

To which Justice Marshall politely replied: "I withdraw the question." There was more laughter.

"Thank you," responded a grateful Floyd, and then, still fumbling, he added, "That's really when the soul comes into the unborn, if a person believes in a soul, I don't know."

With the time that remained to him, Floyd attempted to eliminate as many grounds as possible for deciding that an abortion right existed. Acknowledging that the appellants were relying heavily on the Ninth Amendment, he made no attempt for some strange reason to refute this ground but instead said he thought the decision could not be based on either the First Amendment or privacy. Noting that *Griswold* had dealt only with marital privacy, he commented that if the Does were out of the case, as he and the state of Texas hoped they would be, there were no grounds for a privacy ruling. Floyd also cited several examples that demonstrated that marital privacy was not absolute, such as search and seizure laws; laws against fornication and adultery, as well as polygamy; and the fact that parents were required to educate a child.

Asked about the fact that the Texas abortion law made no exception in cases of rape, a situation in which a woman might find herself pregnant without having made the choice to be, Floyd could only answer that off the record, as he understood the state's policy, it was acceptable to "estop whatever has occurred immediately by the proper procedure in the hospital." In other words, a hospital could— without fear of reprisal—abort a woman who had been raped.

His time was up. Having just admitted that the state of Texas made exceptions to its own abortion law, Floyd's argument had hardly ended on a strong note. He had been on the defensive the entire time and had never been able to seize the initiative as he thought Weddington had done at several points during her arguments.

Weddington used her remaining five minutes to make a brief rebuttal, noting that the state had indeed erroneously filed an appeal with the Court.

Part IV

ABORTION POLITICS

15

Waiting

Weddington thought the arguments had gone well, although like most Supreme Court litigants, she kept reviewing the questions the justices had asked her, each time inventing better or more persuasive answers. Others who had observed her in court that day recall that she was splendid. She was admired not only for her intelligence, but also as a symbolic and unifying figure within the pro-choice movement. Maybe movement activists had not been able to pick the perfect appellant, nor had they gotten their day in court, as several had hoped, but after watching Weddington in the courtroom that December day, no one felt cheated. It was a moment of triumph that belonged to everyone who had worked for abortion reform.

Although only the Dallas contingent would come right out and say it, part of what had been impressive about Weddington was her feminine manner and appearance. Wearing her long strawberry-blond hair down over her shoulders, held back by barrettes, and dressed in blue, a color that flattered her porcelain complexion, she had looked lovely. She had also managed to display a demeanor befitting both her youth and the importance of the case. Weddington had answered the justices' questions not only intelligently, but with a certain serenity that recalled her roots as a minister's daughter. She was as cordial and calm as if she were entertaining a room full of her father's colleagues—persons to whom she deferred because of their position but with whom she was completely at ease because she knew and trusted what they represented.

After the oral arguments, a veil of lethargy settled over the reform movement. Because the Supreme Court conducted its work in private (the only branch of government to operate in such a manner), it was impossible to know what it would decide or even to predict when a decision would be handed down. Preoccupied with waiting, many people stopped working or became less active in the movement; even the pro-choice reform groups seemed to have difficulty getting their work done. One of the few persons to sense danger in this torpor was Lawrence Lader, founder of NARAL, who grew alarmed enough to comment publicly on the apathy, which perplexed him. Fifteen years later, when we talked about it, the Dallas reformers were better able to pinpoint what had happened. The Supreme Court arguments had felt like a climax to all their work, albeit a false one. The women were not smug, nor were they confident of victory, but they were exhausted, and the period of waiting for a decision—one that might, in fact, bring an end to all their work—seemed as good a time as any for a break. No one consciously planned to slow down, but it happened nonetheless.

The movement had simply worn people out. Abortion reformers often compared their struggle to the abolitionists' efforts to free the slaves, and in the context of the times, pro-choice reform was a natural extension of the civil rights movement of the 1950s and 1960s. But while these comparisons were accurate, abortion was also something more complex and involved than other social issues, at least for the reformers who were at the forefront of the movement. In the civil rights movement, for example, most people agreed it was wrong (regardless of how one felt personally) to discriminate against other human beings, whereas the lines between right and wrong could not be drawn so easily with abortion. A civil rights worker could look an opponent in the eye and in good conscience tell him that he was dead wrong, but most pro-choice reformers found it impossible to do the same to someone who personally found abortion repugnant.

Black and white children could be ordered to attend school together, but no one could tell a woman when she should or should not have an abortion. Nor could one person call another's personal feelings about abortion right or wrong. In fact, abortion reformers did counter the opposition by pointing out that no woman would be forced to have an abortion, but not surprisingly, such arguments fell on deaf ears. People's attitudes toward abortion were deep-seated and intensely personal, not particularly subject to persuasion from strangers.

The largely white, middle-class civil rights reformers at least had the advantage of arguing in someone else's behalf, while the largely female, white, middle-class abortion reformers were forced to argue in their own behalf—a difficult task at best and one that became more so as abortion became increasingly controversial. Even though the opposition was not as organized as it would be later, pro-choice workers were keenly aware that it existed. It breached their everyday lives in many unpleasant ways—the anonymous phone calls in the middle of the night, the shouted threats at public gatherings, the personal taunts when they tried to talk to individuals. Then, too, those who opposed abortion seemed to view it in biblical terms. They did not simply think the pro-choice reformers were on the wrong track; they thought they should burn in hell for their sins.

Among the Dallas reformers, only Sarah Weddington seemed to have been renewed by the oral arguments. Full of energy and drive, she returned to Texas to announce that she would run for state legislator. Although she felt the arguments had gone well, she knew that if the Court did not decide women's right to abortion was constitutionally protected, then the job of reforming the abortion laws would have to be done through the state legislatures. She wanted to be there, in the midst of that battle, too.

Actually, the period after the arguments had not seemed like a bad time for a break. Everyone with the exception of the Catholic church seemed to be moving rapidly toward a consensus that abortion was not only morally acceptable, but a necessity in a world threatened with serious population problems. In February 1971 the American Bar Association, whose last official act regarding abortion had been to back the American Law Institute–model law in 1959, announced its approval of another, more liberal uniform abortion act, one that gave unqualified approval for abortion for any reason up to twenty weeks. Another minor victory occurred when a Connecticut three-judge federal court in *Abele* v. *Markle* found that state's revised statute on birth control unconstitutional. Court decisions were pending in approximately thirty abortion cases around the country, and as reformers knew, court activity required less support (and certainly tolerated no lobbying) than attempts to change the laws through state legislatures.

The biggest boost to the pro-choice cause came in March when the Commission on Population Growth and the American Future released its report. Headed by John D. Rockefeller III and composed of congressmen, business and labor leaders, and educators, the commission issued a report that strongly supported the views of the pro-choice movement. Although abortion was still a crime in two-thirds of the states, the report formally recommended that the states liberalize their abortion laws so the decision to terminate a pregnancy would be a matter of individual choice. Assailing prohibitions against abortion as "obstacles to the exercise of individual freedom," the commission said women should be free to avoid unwanted childbearing and to control their own fertility. The commission also recommended that governments on every level make funds available to support abortion services. Commenting on society's reluctance to acknowledge sexual activity among teenagers, it further suggested that teens be given access to contraception.

The positive reinforcement pro-choice forces got from the commission's report was short-lived. It stirred up the opposition as much as any piece of legislation ever had. Within days the thirty Catholic bishops of New York passed a resolution criticizing the report. In presenting the bishops' statement to the press, Cardinal Terence Cooke commented: "This calls for a strong voice of protest." He announced that abortion would be the overriding issue at the bishops' spring meeting.

The bishops were reacting to more than just the commission report. The new reform law had been in effect in New York State for almost a year. During the first six months, almost 100,000 abortions had been performed, and estimates put the year-end total at 300,000; these numbers especially stung the Church hierarchy, which in recent years had wielded a great deal of political power in New York. Besides, New York State was a bellwether for the rest of the country. Other states looked to the examples it set, particularly on social issues. Although the right-to-life movement was targeting several states that were weighing a reform law, in only one state—New York—was a massive effort mounted to repeal a liberal reform law.

The New York bishops issued a pastoral letter denouncing abortionists and their "death-dealing trade." They went on to say:

"They even advertise their monstrous commerce beyond the confines of the state, thus making New York the abortion capital of America." Immediate excommunication, the statement reiterated, would be the penalty for any Catholic who deliberately procured an abortion or helped anyone else to get one.

So strong a reaction from the Church in a key state during a presidential election year was enough to alert the candidates to the abortion issue. Whether they felt they could not avoid dealing with it or simply thought it made an excellent target is impossible to say, but abortion became one of the most hotly debated issues of the 1972 presidential campaign. In fact, single-issue campaigns, rarely a part of the American political scene, emerged as a powerful force in the campaign. The national Right to Life party ran candidates whose only purpose was to defeat incumbents who favored abortion reform; their candidates typically had no platform other than their opposition to abortion.

Among the presidential contenders, a little noted exchange between President Richard Nixon, who was running for reelection, and the Democratic front-runner Senator Edmund Muskie, a Roman Catholic, provided the opening salvo in raising the abortion issue to the rough-and-tumble level of national politics. Appearing on the *David Frost Show*, Senator Muskie said that while he hoped the Church would be more liberal on birth control, he personally could not support liberalized abortion, at least not after the first six weeks of pregnancy and certainly not as a means of reducing the welfare rolls. In language that strongly echoed the Church's rhetoric on abortion, Muskie said, "I'm concerned about diluting in any way the sanctity of human life."

From his vacation retreat in San Clemente, California, Nixon responded by issuing a position statement that moved him, too, closer to the traditional Roman Catholic stand on abortion: "From personal and religious beliefs, I consider abortion an unacceptable form of population control. . . . Further unrestricted abortion policies, or abortion-on-demand, I cannot square with my personal belief in the sanctity of human life—including the life of the unborn. . . . A good and generous people will not, in my view, opt for this kind of alternative to social dilemmas. Rather, it will open its hearts and its homes to the unwanted children of its own, as it has done for the unwanted millions of other lands."

The press took little notice of the exchange between the two candidates. Not until the New York reform law was fully under siege did the media react and pro-choice reformers awaken to the need to revitalize their movement. By early 1972, with strong Church support, antiabortion reformers had managed to introduce into the General Assembly of New York a bill that would repeal the liberal abortion law.

The Donovan-Crawford bill would return New York to prereform days, making abortion impossible to obtain except to save a woman's life. Two years had passed since abortion reformers had been called upon to rally for abortion reform. That and the fact that Governor Rockefeller had promised to veto any repeal bill intended to undo the eighteen-month-old reform law lulled the pro-choice movement into a false sense of security. Even the press failed to correctly gauge the gathering strength of the antiabortion movement.

The first sign that something big was under way occurred in early April 1972, when abortion protestors announced plans for a big rally and march down Fifth Avenue. A few days before the rally, several suburban newspapers ran advertisements featuring a theme the antiabortion movement had adopted, that abortion was a form of genocide. One typical advertisement that ran in a New Jersey newspaper displayed a photograph of Adolph Hitler and a box score of deaths from wars and holocausts, which read:

Fourth place	Korean War	34,000
Third place	Vietnam	45,000
Second place	New York State	300,000
First place	Holocaust	6,000,000

The charge that abortion was a form of genocide, which had been made before but was now being used with increasing effectiveness by antiabortionists, was so shocking that pro-choice people at first were at a loss over how to react to it. It offended both Jews and gentiles.

The antiabortion rally was scheduled for Sunday, April 16, a day Cardinal Cooke had decreed as "Right to Life Sunday." Priests lectured from the pulpits while parochial school buses waited outside churches to take the marchers to Fifth Avenue. The rally turned out to be the largest antiabortion protest ever staged; newspapers estimated that ten thousand persons participated.

The pro-choice people had not planned a counterrally, but in *Abortion II*, Lawrence Lader reported that a small group, mostly members of the Women's National Abortion Action Coalition, gathered to demonstrate their views. While watching the opposition prepare to march, Lader endured a shocking encounter that crystallized in his mind how utterly driven these people were:

> The busloads unloaded on nearby streets streamed past us. They were mainly middle-aged people, prim and determined in blue serge suits and flowered Sunday dresses. When they saw our signs, their faces flushed and hardened. Most of them screamed, only one word, like a small explosion, "Murderer! Murderer!" The sound rolled up the street. In that half hour, there must have been a hundred faces thrust in front of mine with the same lacerating accusation. "Murderer!" I had debated abortion hundreds of times since 1968, but never had seen so much venom concentrated at one time.

Dreadful as Lader found it to be called a murderer, this was but one more calculated tactic in the well-developed antiabortionists' arsenal. Throughout the early 1970s right-to-life activists became increasingly adept at rewriting the terminology of abortion: the scientifically accurate words "fetus" and "embryo" were never to be used; instead, fetuses and embryos were to be described as "babies." Antiabortionists were taught to use the words "kill" and "murder" as often as possible when discussing abortion.

The march was timed to legislative activity. The New York General Assembly was scheduled to take action on the Crawford-Donovan bill within days. On Monday following the march, the same forces in reduced strength marched on the Capitol in Albany. A small group of antiabortion women burst onto the assembly floor and had to be forcibly removed.

Pro-choice reformers, for the most part, sat by calmly, confident that the bill would never get out of committee. The idea of undoing a piece of legislation that was only eighteen months old seemed ludicrous. They were further assured that even if the bill were somehow to get through the assembly, Governor Rockefeller would veto it.

Their confidence was shaken on April 25 when Governor Rockefeller proposed a compromise measure, one that would amend the new reform law to permit abortions until sixteen rather than the present twenty-four weeks. Finally, pro-choice people realized the threat was real. So far, the threat that Governor Rockefeller would veto any repeal legislation had been their best defense against the opposition. Now, under heavy pressure from the Church, he seemed to be wavering. They also knew that sixteen weeks really meant twelve weeks since physicians considered the vacuum aspiration method unsafe to use after the twelfth week and usually delayed any abortion not done before then until the sixteenth week, when the saline method could be used. A week later, on May 2, the totally unexpected occurred. The Crawford-Donovan bill was voted out of committee. It even seemed likely that antiabortion forces had enough votes to win in both houses. The pro-choice reform bill, only eighteen months old, was unraveling before their eyes.

Led by NARAL, reformers finally reacted and organized to combat the new threat, which only a few weeks earlier they had not considered real enough to warrant even a response. Thirty-five hundred dollars was raised to buy a full-page advertisement in *The New York Times*. The headline shouted: SAVE YOUR RIGHT TO ABORTION. Pro-choice forces boarded buses and traveled to Albany to lobby for the second time in two years for abortion reform. A committee of prominent pro-choice physicians, all active in the movement, was hastily pulled together to lobby legislators and the governor. Called into action were Bernard Nathanson, a NARAL founder and obstetrician-gynecologist who ran the largest abortion clinic in New York City; Alan Guttmacher, head of Planned Parenthood; and Christopher Tietze, director of the Population Council. In talking with legislators, the three men emphasized the dangers associated with abortions done between twelve and sixteen weeks and stressed the need to keep women's options open for a longer time.

On May 6 a pro-choice rally mustered a paltry 1,500 persons, although present to speak were an impressive coalition of supporters, ranging from Mary Lindsay, the mayor's wife, to Congresswomen Shirley Chisholm and Bella Abzug, to clergymen of several denominations involved with counseling services.

On the day of the rally, relatively good news arrived in the form of an announcement from Governor Rockefeller that he would compromise with an eighteen-week bill. But as if to counteract that was the bad news, a few days earlier, that President Nixon had repudiated the Population Commission, a not unexpected move since its findings had offended most conservatives and the Roman Catholic hierarchy. Unexpected and unprecedented, however, was a letter the president sent to Cardinal Cooke, in which he wrote that he wished to associate himself with "the conviction you deeply feel and eloquently express." Nixon continued: "This is a matter for state decision outside federal jurisdiction. . . . Historically, laws regulating abortion in the United States have been the province of the states, not the federal government. That remains the situation today, as one state after another takes up this question, debates it, and decides it. That is where the decision should be made."

Designed to spur on the repeal efforts (and not coincidentally to gather votes), the letter backfired as one New York politician after another denounced it as a transparent attempt on the part of a president standing for office to court the Roman Catholic vote. Republican legislator Constance Cook, who had sponsored the pro-choice reform bill in the New York General Assembly, pointed out that no evidence existed that Nixon had studied the abortion issue, which did not revolve around whether abortion was legal, but whether the state was going to support legalized abortion, a pointed reference to the fact that women would continue to obtain abortions with or without legalization.

Newspapers around the country covered the shocking instance of a American president aligning himself with a religion as well as his interference with a state's legislative process. *The New York Times* editorialized. "President Nixon's dismaying interference in the legislative process of this state in an effort to force repeal of the abortion reform law was a blatant misuse of his high position. . . . Historians should find it hard to locate a parallel instance of a President openly working through a particular church to influence the action of a state government." Governor Rockefeller, who headed Nixon's reelection campaign in New York, let his irritation be known by referring all calls to the White House.

By midweek the president's chief domestic affairs adviser, John D. Ehrlichman, was trying to smooth over the flap by claiming that the letter to Cooke was private and that permission to publicize it was the result of "sloppy staff work." He assured the governor that there had been no intention to embarrass him.

The damage was done, however, and the president, who had no past record either pro or con on abortion, was now firmly aligned with the right-to-life movement. Antiabortion forces jumped on

Nixon's statements and soon were reprinting his statements in their literature.

Lost in the shuffle was the much maligned Commission on Population Growth, which tried to buy an hour of television prime time to take its findings directly to the people and was turned down by all three networks. It appealed to the Federal Communications Commission on grounds that the refusal to sell it time amounted to a violation of the fairness doctrine that required broadcasters to provide equal time on conflicting issues. The appeal was rejected.

With all the tumultuous activity surrounding it, the voting in both houses of the New York General Assembly was tense. Debate began on May 10. The house voted 79–68, and the senate vote was 30–27 to overthrow the bill. By May 13, however, within hours after the vote, Governor Rockefeller vetoed the repeal bill, at which time he also issued a strong message regarding abortion rights: "I do not believe it is right for one group to impose its vision of morality on an entire society, nor is it practical for the state to attempt to dictate the innermost personal beliefs and conduct of its citizens. I can see no justifications now for repealing this reform and thus condemning hundreds of thousands of women to the Dark Ages again."

The attempt to repeal the New York reform law was a cliff-hanger that was followed by dozens of daily newspapers across the country. For the first time, the nation witnessed the sheer determination of those opposed to abortion, as well as the willingness of politicians to turn the issue into a political football.

All this was not enough, however, to lift reformers out of their apathetic state, despite other warnings that the reform movement was in jeopardy. A letter Virginia Whitehill wrote jointly to Sarah Weddington and Ruth Bowers passed on what should have been startling news that she had learned when she and Pat White attended a regional Planned Parenthood to do "some missionary work." At the meeting they had talked with Reverend Jack Singleton, chaplain at Texas Women's University, who had brought up the university's policy on abortion. For years this school, like many others across the country, had declined to act as parents in absentia for its students and had even gone to considerable lengths to protect its students' privacy. Now, with all the controversy over abortion, it was changing its policy and would be informing the woman's parents as soon as the school learned she was pregnant. The situation, he told them, was explosive. Whitehill urged Ruth Bowers, who had a personal interest in the school, to look into the matter.

In April 1972 another letter to Ruth Bowers expressed some of Whitehill's disillusionment with the reform effort. She complained about her travel expenses (Whitehill had remained, after Weddington, the group's most active spokesperson), noting that she and her husband had personally spent "an awful lot of money . . . which we are glad to do." Weddington had written Whitehill a check for $120 from the James Madison Law Institute funds, and Whitehill felt obliged to inform Bowers of this, since it was "her money." Whitehill wrote: "It is difficult sometimes, as we are not with endless resources, and have family obligations to see about. If you don't think the James Madison Institute should help me with travel expenses occasionally, please just say so, and I can manage." Whitehill also mentioned the mounting expenses for Weddington in connection with her work on reform.

Morale was low within the Dallas group for the same reason that it was among reformers elsewhere in the country. Key members dropped out or, in the case of Ellen Kalina, had moved away. In one letter, sent from her new home in Washington, Kalina, a former Catholic, expressed her dislike of the Church's tactics as well as her dismay over the anti-Catholic feeling that arose in reaction to the Church's interference in the abortion issue.

Pat White, who, like Ellen Kalina, had been involved with the Dallas Committee to Study Abortion since its inception, dropped out only a few months before the Supreme Court decision. She sent Whitehill a note explaining that after several years of heavy involvement with abortion reform, the time had come to put her personal life in order. Her mother had a heart condition and was going to require more of White's time. She also planned to remarry and felt she would be busy organizing her new life and "selling houses" over the next few months.

Despite the losses to the group, the core members—Whitehill, Weddington, Bowers, and Middleton—remained active. During the month of April alone, Whitehill had no less than five cities on her itinerary. Early in the month, she and her husband, James, traveled to Denver for a national Zero Population Growth meeting. She attended a regional Planned Parenthood meeting in Ft. Worth. No longer on the board of Planned Parenthood and unhappy in any event with what she regarded as their rather lukewarm support of abortion reform, she had nonetheless remained active in the organization, and at this meeting she hoped to make some valuable contacts, perhaps with women who would be interested in starting reform groups in their communities throughout Texas. Toward the end of the month, Whitehill flew to Lufkin, Nacogdoches, and Austin to speak on abortion, where she addressed students at the Stephen F. Austin College and taped two television shows. In a letter to her co-workers, she rated her travels as "good" and "worthwhile" and was especially pleased because the television show would be widely seen throughout east Texas and also because she had been able to establish some new contacts with other women working in reform.

Whitehill was the member of the Dallas Committee who maintained correspondence with several reform groups throughout the country. A letter she received from a member of an abortion-reform group called MORAL revealed that the same malaise that seemed to strike East Coast and Texas reformers was also afoot in the rest of the country. The letter began: "Things are rather slow, though I begin to feel a change in the general climate of opinion. For one thing, some church groups in Montana have begun to promote abortion reform, and are having meetings, films, panels, and such—all of which, you know, is a great help. MORAL is just barely struggling along, though; we have little money and enormous problems getting anything done. Even I've lost some fire—due to simple overwork, I think. I'm trying to keep afloat but have discovered my energy level has dropped—I'm sure you know (mixed metaphors aside) what kind of energy this sort of work takes."

The Dallas group knew. It was having trouble gathering enough support even to get out its regular mailings—the impact, Whitehill would observe in a letter to Ruth Bowers, who had paid for the mailing, of low morale. The women kept hoping the Supreme Court would reach a decision so they would at least know where they stood. Did several more years of work lie ahead of them, or were they to be rewarded for what they had already done with a Supreme Court decision vindicating their position on abortion? Letters exchanged by the various reform groups throughout 1972 and 1973, and many of their actions, revealed that the pro-choice reformers were all doing the same thing—biding their time, waiting for a Supreme Court decision that would either spur them into action with renewed fervor or settle the issue once and for all.

Throughout the spring of 1972, the one bright spot for the Dallas women in what seemed like an endless wait was Weddington's campaign for state legislator. She hoped to represent the thirty-five thousand people of Travers County in Austin and had kicked off her campaign on Monday, February 7, 1972, the same day that Sissy Farenthold, one of the few women prominent on the national scene, had announced she was giving up her seat in the state legislature to run for governor of Texas. Weddington did not campaign specifically on the abortion issue, but people knew about her role in *Roe* v. *Wade*, and it helped her more than it hurt her. As she had done in the only two courtrooms she had ever worked in, she managed yet again to espouse the principles of feminism in a way that was nonthreatening to both men and women. Most of her campaign workers were women (even her husband was working full-time in Farenthold's campaign), and most of her votes would come from women. Three men ran against Weddington; she defeated them all in the spring primary.

16

Deliberations

Normally the Supreme Court's deliberations are not known, but much attention was focused on the 1971 Term because it was viewed as a transitional court. After two years Chief Justice Burger had begun to make his imprint on the Court, and with the addition of another Nixon appointee, Harry Blackmun, at the end of the 1970 Term, Court watchers were eager to see how many, if any, of the liberal Warren Court decisions would be dismantled.

Some change was inevitable as old justices left the Court and new ones arrived to take their place, but one of the Court's great strengths was its relatively unchanging and apolitical nature. One of the rare times when that stability was threatened had occurred as the Depression was ending, when Franklin Delano Roosevelt tried to expand the Court from nine to fifteen justices, primarily to gain more support for his New Deal programs. In 1972 the specter of that era loomed large as President Nixon seemed determined to politicize the Burger Court. He had campaigned actively against the so-called liberal Court, largely as a way of appealing to conservative voters in the South (and, for that matter, a growing conservative bloc throughout the rest of the country) who had felt their rights and desires had been ignored and even trampled in the drive to expand civil rights for minorities. One of his campaign pledges was to appoint justices who would check the unbridled liberalism of the Warren Court, and with the deaths of Justices Hugo Black and John Marshall Harlan in fall 1971, he would have an opportunity to make good his pledge.

With the president having declared open war on the libertarian Court, the media now turned full attention on the Court's activities. For that reason, as much was known and written about the Court's deliberations in the abortion cases as any in recent history.

The Court normally discusses the cases for which it has heard oral arguments at its regularly scheduled Friday conference. During the week of December 16, 1971, when the abortion cases were to be discussed, the conference was pushed forward to Thursday to accommodate Justice Douglas's travel plans.

The agenda of the conference never varied. The first topic was always the written opinions, which would be released on the following Monday. Next came discussion of appeals and certiorari papers, and finally, in what was undoubtedly the high point of the meeting, there was discussion and voting on the cases that had been argued that week in court. The discussion of a case also followed a strict protocol. The chief justice spoke first, outlining the issues of the case. He was followed by the other justices in order of seniority. No justice ever interrupted another, and each could talk as long as he liked.

Burger was often unprepared for conference. He typically read summaries of the cases rather than the briefs. When the abortion cases came up for discussion at conference, he had difficulty summarizing them. In addition, his own position on abortion was unclear. A supporter of states' rights, he seemed to favor upholding the state abortion laws, but he also indicated he might find the Texas law vague. In contrast, White was adamant in his belief that the laws should not be struck.

Firmly in the opposing camp were Douglas, Marshall, and Brennan, who were reportedly ready to acknowledge a constitutional right to abortion, while Stewart and Blackmun, the Court's centrists, favored striking some but not all portions of the state's laws.

Once a vote had been taken, the senior justice in the majority assigned someone to write the case. Since the vote in the abortion cases appeared to be five to two in favor of striking at least some parts of the restrictive laws, Douglas, the senior justice in the majority, assumed he would assign the opinion. But later that same day, when a list of assignments was passed around, he and several other justices were surprised to see that the abortion cases had been assigned by the chief justice. Justice Blackmun would write the abortion opinion.

Douglas double-checked his notes; they showed he was in the majority and the chief in the minority. Brennan and Marshall agreed with him that the vote had been five to two, with only Burger and White firmly opposed. Three other cases also appeared to have been misassigned to minority judges. In one instance, Douglas had already assigned one case to Brennan during the conference. Another case was misassigned to Stewart, a member of the minority, who sent Burger a note declining to write the opinion.

The misassignments were probably not accidents. Several such incidents had occurred since Burger had taken over as chief. Some sources said Burger was either in the minority and had changed his mind, or he considered himself to be in the majority all along, even though this was not clear to the other justices. Others felt that Burger was trying, as he had in the past, to assert his right to assign minority cases.

Douglas had been annoyed on other occasions when the chief assigned cases he believed he, as the senior majority justice, should have assigned, but he had only confronted Burger on one occasion, a case the chief had assigned to himself despite being a minority of one. This time, though, Douglas was angry. He had been trying for years to get the Court to take on the abortion issue, and he knew how difficult it was going to be to get a solid majority opinion. Since he did not believe that Blackmun was firmly in the liberal camp, he saw this as an attempt to sabotage the case. It bothered him that Blackmun seemed to think the case revolved around physicians' rights to practice medicine freely rather than women's right to privacy.

Blackmun was also, in Douglas's eyes, a "Minnesota twin," an epithet attributed to Blackmun and Burger during the early months of Blackmun's tenure on the Court. Blackmun and Burger had grown up in the same blue-collar neighborhood in St. Paul, Minnesota, and although their paths had veered off in different directions after high school when Blackmun went to Harvard while Burger attended night school in his hometown, the press had made much of their supposedly similar backgrounds when Blackmun joined his fellow Minnesotan at the Supreme Court. The fact that their voting records had been remarkably similar during Blackmun's early months at the Court did little to diminish the idea of the "Minnesota twins." In 90 percent of the cases that came before the Court during his first term, Blackmun voted the same way Burger did.

Douglas showed up at his chambers on Saturday, December 18, and began drafting a scathing memo asserting his right to assign the cases. On Monday the memo was distributed to the members of the Court.

Burger responded on Monday, December 20, with a memo conceding his error in assigning two of the cases. As for the abortion cases, he felt the voting had been too vague to determine a clear majority, and that this was a case in which the written opinion would serve as the impetus for further debate. As a result, he had felt free to assign the opinion to Blackmun. Burger stood his ground and declined to let Douglas assign the opinion in the abortion cases, which were, he noted, "quite probably candidates for reargument" in any event. With only seven justices sitting, Burger was anxious about deciding so controversial a case, especially one that had become a major issue in the upcoming presidential election. More than anything, Burger would have preferred not to have the abortion cases before his court at this particular time. He wanted to decide them as narrowly as possible and would even be pleased to find a reason to send them back to the state courts.

Douglas let the issue of the abortion case assignments drop, in part because Blackmun was obviously so pleased with the assignment. He did begin drafting his own opinion on the abortion cases, one that he showed only to Brennan on December 22. On December 30, Brennan responded to Douglas's opinion with a ten-page letter of his own, urging him to give Blackmun a chance to circulate a draft. Brennan outlined his own view that abortion was a matter of individual liberty, and as such, was a woman's exclusive right.

Most new justices are expected to cut their teeth on fairly easy, noncontroversial cases during their first few months at the Court, and Blackmun was pleased finally to be handed so important a case. Tired of living under Burger's shadow, he saw this as a chance to make his own mark on the Court. Of course, he was also interested in the issues. Blackmun had once considered becoming a physician but had become a lawyer instead. Nine years of working as general counsel at the Mayo Clinic in Rochester, Minnesota, seemed to offer the best of both worlds. Blackmun felt his Mayo years also qualified him to write the opinion; no other justice had a medical background comparable to his. Uniquely equipped among the justices to understand the complicated issues that were involved, he also believed he could write an opinion that would build a solid majority, what he felt was needed in so important and controversial a case.

Blackmun also felt the weight and the responsibility of such a case. In his first term at the Court, he had proven to be the Court's slowest, most meticulous worker. In later interviews he would speak of the weight of the work, observing that while other justices seemed to thrive on being the court of last resort, he could not.

The rest of that winter and spring, Blackmun devoted most of his time to working on the opinion. He buried himself in the justices' library. He studied memos his clerks had prepared on key issues. He plodded through all the previous cases on privacy and birth control. Most helpful in terms of pure information were the numerous amici curiae briefs that had been submitted.

Practically everything that could be known about abortion to date was contained in the record submitted with the cases. There were no rows of books in the Library of Congress, no long lists of articles in ethical, philosophical, or even medical journals; all that would come later as the experts set about analyzing his opinion. Lader's book *Abortion* (published in 1966), which Blackmun read, broke down the taboo against discussing the subject, but only a handful of other books had been written about it since. Alfred Kinsey, director of the Indiana University Sex Institute, had been influenced to include abortion in his studies after attending an abortion conference in the mid-1950s, but his research was largely conducted with white, middle-class people, and one of the most pressing issues in abortion reform was whether the present laws discriminated against poor and minority women.

The pro-choice briefs were most impressive. Sponsored by respected organizations with whom Blackmun and the other justices were familiar, such as the American Bar Association, American Medical Association, American College of Obstetricians and Gynecologists, American Association of University Women, and Planned Parenthood, all of whom had hired expert legal minds to prepare their briefs, they were gold mines of information and statistical data on abortion. Having hired the best lawyers they could afford, they had then taken enormous care to obtain the most accurate, up-to-date

information. Margery Hames recalled rushing to obtain the most recent statistics on abortion deaths, which had been compiled by the
Center for Disease Control, so that she could make them available to
the Supreme Court.

In contrast, the amici curiae briefs for the opposition were
propagandistic as well as inaccurate. Two of the more flamboyant of
the opposition's amici curiae briefs were prepared by leaders of the
antiabortion movement, Dr. Jack Willke and Barbara Willke, who
taught sex education to church groups across the country, and Robert
L. Sassone, a lawyer and self-styled expert on population. The
Willkes' brief included a copy of their booklet *Handbook on Abortion*,
which would become the antiabortion movement's best-seller. Its
most salient feature was a series of color pictures of fetuses—photos of
developing fetuses and pictures of dismembered, bloodied, aborted
fetuses. There were no informative or dated labels on the photographs. The photos of developing fetuses were greatly magnified,
although no labels ever revealed this to the unobservant or uninformed reader. One photograph, which showed several battered
fetuses in a garbage can, was labeled "Products of a morning's work in
an abortion clinic."

The handbook was written in a seemingly factual question-
and-answer format, although the answers were usually masterpieces
of evasion. For example, in answer to the question "Isn't it true that
restrictive abortion laws are unfair to the poor?" the Willkes wrote, "It
is probably true that it is easier for a rich person to break almost any
law than for a poor person to do so. Perhaps the poor cannot afford all
the heroin they want." In answer to the next question, "But it's
unfair, isn't it?" they responded, in part, "We will not eliminate
poverty by killing people," thus implying that abortion was a form of
genocide of the poor.

Sassone devoted his brief to debunking what he considered to
be the myths of population control. Resources were only mismanaged,
not in short supply. All the world's people, some four billion at the
time, could fit comfortably in the United States. "Even India," he
wrote, "is so empty that they can keep all those useless cows and still
feed their people."

The state's brief was also more propagandistic than legal.
Almost half was given over to examination of the developing fetus,
which was often erroneously referred to as a "baby." This section

contained several misleadingly labeled and greatly enlarged photographs of developing fetuses and made numerous misleading statements, such as one indicating that after the eighth week until adulthood, "the changes of the body will be mainly in dimension and in gradual refinement of the working parts."

An analysis of fetal brain waves implied that a fetus was sentient as early as the twentieth day, when in fact biologists and physicians thought of sentience as occurring in stages that culminated sometime between the eighth and ninth month. Noting that a fetus's heart was fully functioning at twenty-eight days, the brief writers ignored (or were ignorant of) the fact that various other organs could not yet sustain life outside the womb. They wrote: "The new body not only exists, it also functions." It might have been helpful to know that a three-month-old fetus is less than two inches long. In another claim they asserted, "Every child shows a distinct individuality in his behavior by the end of the third month," and, "The child hears and recognizes his mother's voice," another contention most biologists say they simply cannot answer for sure.

Not until the end of the section did one find a reference to the fact that a fetus had no chance of surviving until "twenty to twenty-five weeks," but the authors of the brief quickly added: "The concept of an artificial placenta may be a reality in the near future and will push the date of viability back even further, and perhaps to the earliest stages of gestation," thereby implying that the day was not far off when women could be dispensed with entirely as child containers.

Such was the nature of the material from those opposed to abortion. Unbiased antiabortion experts seemed remarkably hard to come by. As the months went by, Justice Blackmun spent every spare hour buried in the Supreme Court library, while the abortion controversy swirled around outside the Court like a huge tornado funnel, gathering emotional and political debris in its path and growing more frantic and hysterical by the day.

In Washington, a southern city where spring comes early, winter turned into early spring and early spring into full-blown spring, and Justice Blackmun still had not produced an opinion. No one had read his draft. Nor had he discussed the case with anyone.

Not until mid-May did Blackmun begin to circulate a rough draft of the opinion. It was, to the relief of the Court's liberals, in favor of striking the abortion laws. But there were problems—many problems. It opened with a lengthy discourse on the history of abortion, tracing it through ancient and common law, English and American law, and describing the changing positions of the American Bar Association, the American Health Association, and the American Medical Association. Written almost entirely from the physician's point of view, it dealt with the doctor's right to give advice and make his best professional judgment. The only ground for striking the laws was vagueness, the traditional doctors' defense. Totally absent, to several justices' dismay, was any discussion of the woman's constitutional right to abortion, the argument that had been the crux of Weddington's defense.

The draft also contained a lengthy discussion of viability, the point at which a fetus could survive outside the womb, and tied to that was an idea that had not been presented in any of the arguments or briefs: the notion that as a woman's pregnancy lengthened, the state's interest in abortion grew stronger. Blackmun had decided that at some point as yet undetermined in the pregnancy, the state had a compelling interest in protecting the fetus.

For all this, Douglas was not unhappy with the draft. He was convinced that Blackmun was solidly in the pro-choice camp along with Marshall and Brennan, who joined Blackmun's opinion. Stewart soon joined the majority. But everyone agreed it was not as well written, nor as well thought out, as it needed to be.

Douglas even entertained the hope that he might be able to persuade Blackmun to expand this draft into a broader, more encompassing opinion, something along the lines of what he himself or Brennan would have written. On May 19, he sent Blackmun a memo urging him to address what Brennan had referred to in his ten-page letter as the "core issue"—the right of a woman to do what she liked with her body. The possibility of rearguing the cases must have arisen again because Douglas also expressed his feeling that there was no need to reargue the cases, especially *Doe* v. *Bolton*, which he noted had always seemed to be the easier case. On May 25, the day before the opinion was to be discussed at conference, Douglas sent Blackmun a note complimenting him on his work on the opinion, although he indicated that he still might write a separate concurring opinion.

Another problem was the speed with which Blackmun worked. Douglas wanted the opinion to come down that term, which meant Blackmun would have to rework the opinion by the end of June at the very latest.

At the Friday, May 26, conference, the first after circulation of the draft, White read aloud from a dissent he had prepared. He attacked the idea that the abortion laws were vague, stating instead that they were absolutely clear: an abortion could be done only to save a woman's life.

Blackmun was surprised at the heated tone of White's opinion. Angry and inflexible, it served to persuade him that his draft needed more work. That weekend he wrote a memo withdrawing his opinion; he asked that all copies of it be returned. Blackmun wanted to work on it over the summer, redrafting it and adding new research and ideas. He also seemed convinced that the case should be reargued before a nine-man court.

For the second time Douglas was furious over abortion. He felt that the "Minnesota twins" were at work again. He had heard rumors that on a recent Saturday in May, Burger had paid a call on Blackmun, who was known to work in his chambers on weekends. The two men had talked for some time behind closed doors, with no one else present, and it was after that that Blackmun had withdrawn his opinion. Court scuttlebutt held that a deal had been struck. In return for Blackmun's agreement to delay opinion in the abortion cases, Burger would provide (as he did in a few days) the deciding vote in another case that mattered a great deal to Blackmun, *Flood* v. *Kuhn*, a baseball antitrust suit.

It was not the first time that rumors of vote trading would echo through the Court, nor would it be the last. Clerks who seemed to understand the persuasion that went on under the auspices of the pen—that is, in written opinions—apparently found the same persuasion offensive when it occurred verbally. Besides, no one really knew whether a deal of sorts had been struck, but even if it had, what had been achieved? Blackmun had not agreed to change his vote in the abortion cases or even to back off from his opinion, which would only become broader with rewriting. He had merely agreed to withdraw an opinion he himself had come to feel was incomplete.

From the beginning, however, Douglas suspected that Burger wanted to stall the abortion decision for political reasons, primarily to avoid embarrassing President Nixon, who had aligned himself with the antiabortion forces. For a civil libertarian like Douglas, the fact that a president had sided with a major religious group as Nixon had would have been reason enough to bring down an opinion setting the matter straight once and for all. Brennan and Stewart were also upset over the delays.

Black's and Harlan's successors, Lewis Powell and William Rehnquist, had now been seated, and in a Friday conference in early June they joined in the vote to put the case over to the next term for reargument. Since only four votes were required to reargue a case, the matter would have been settled with Blackmun's and Burger's votes. But Brennan soon added his vote.

Douglas's frustration grew. Had he assigned this case to himself, as he should have, none of this would have happened. As the Court's fastest writer, the opinion would have been handed down months ago. Douglas would not have asked anyone else to write it. There was no one else, anyway. As the Court's only Catholic, Brennan could not fairly be expected to tackle it, and as the Court's only black, Marshall would also be subject to partisan criticism if he wrote the opinion.

Disgusted that he had not asserted his right to assign the case and also angry at Burger's usurpation of his powers, Douglas decided he could still do something about the situation. He labored over a memo outlining his problem with Burger regarding the misassignment and his belief that the Court was becoming politicized. Then he departed before the end of the term, as was his custom, for his summer home in Goose Prairie, Wisconsin, leaving behind the memo along with orders to his clerks to release it if the cases were put over.

Douglas was threatening to break one of the cardinal rules of the Court: Never air internal disagreements publicly. Some of the justices thought he was bluffing; others felt sure he would carry through with his threat. Blackmun and Burger offered to drop the call for reargument. After keeping the Court on edge for several days, tradition won out, and Douglas withdrew the dissenting memo. Blackmun reassured him that he would not back off from his original opinion over the summer, that indeed he was looking forward to time in which to rethink and rewrite the draft in order to make it stronger. Blackmun was even optimistic that the majority might be able to pick up another vote over the summer. Rehnquist was unlikely to join the majority, but Powell just might be with them. Douglas relented. In 1971 sixteen cases were put over for reargument; the Texas and Georgia abortion cases were among them.

A week after the decision to reargue the abortion cases was announced, *The Washington Post* and *The New York Times* published articles describing the controversy over the case, including Douglas's threatened dissent. The *Post* quoted from Douglas's memo. Douglas wrote several notes to Burger attempting to smooth over the situation and reassure the chief, who hated any publicity, that he had not leaked the memo to the press. In a note written on August 7, he asked Burger and his wife, Vera, to visit him and his wife, Kathy.

Holding over the cases dismayed most pro-choice reformers, mostly because it led to speculation that the Court was not going to strike the state abortion laws after all. Over the most recent term, the Court was thought to have displayed a decidedly conservative bent, especially regarding issues of criminal law. The new posture was that of renewed reluctance to interfere with states' criminal proceedings, such as the one in which Dr. Hallford was involved. The Court was cautious and increasingly reluctant to strike down state criminal laws. With the two new Nixon appointees on the Court, there were fears that this attitude might become even more prevalent.

When the case was put over for reargument, Weddington realized she would be spending her second consecutive summer working on *Roe* v. *Wade*. Usually when the Court decides to put over a case for reargument, it requests counsel to address specific issues the second time around, but no such request was made with the abortion cases. This further fueled speculation that Court politics rather than a theoretical struggle had prompted the decision to reargue the cases.

Despite the lack of specific guidance, Weddington decided to prepare a supplemental brief bringing the Court up to date on new developments and cases in abortion reform. She, Coffee, Bruner, and Merrill worked on the brief. Reacting to speculation that the Court would be reluctant to interfere with state criminal proceedings, they took care to note that Hallford had requested an injunction against future prosecutions only and not his own, which was under way. Wary of the growing strength of the opposition, the brief reviewed the common-law position that a child must be born alive in order to be subject to the crime of murder. A list of cases in which fetuses were found to have been denied legal rights prior to birth (although courts occasionally awarded some inheritance rights contingent on live birth) was appended to the brief.

Lucas's name was on the new materials, but by then he had little to do with either *Roe* or the reform movement, at least the East Coast network. He had moved the James Madison Law Institute to San Francisco shortly after the first oral arguments. Having been essentially drummed out of the East Coast abortion-reform movement, he felt there was no reason to stay in New York and had retreated to the West Coast, where he continued to build his practice counseling providers.

Lucas's last attempt to claim something from the movement occurred in summer 1972 as Coffee and Weddington were preparing to reargue the case. He wrote Weddington a five-page letter chastising her for the way she had handled the first argument and listing the reasons that she should let him handle the reargument. She had, he pointed out, completely bungled the first argument. Furthermore, it was only fair that he should argue the second time since she had had her chance to do so the first time. He reminded her that the James Madison Law Institute had provided her with the support and resources she had needed to build the case and was still funding the appendix she was preparing. How could he be expected to raise money for the case, Lucas asked, if someone else had argued it? Lucas believed that Weddington had turned the case over to him and had only gotten interested again when it was obvious that the Supreme Court would hear the case, but he also undoubtedly recognized that this might be his last chance for glory in the reform movement. More than anything else, Lucas wanted to be the lawyer who argued the case that legalized abortion in the United States.

The letter shocked Weddington and shook her confidence briefly. Had she given her case away, as Lucas charged? If so, it had not been intentional. She would always be horrified and deeply insulted at even the slightest suggestion of impropriety on her part. Soon, though, Weddington's shock turned to indignation. Apart from a small salary she had taken the summer she worked in New York (and her husband had contributed his time), she had never earned a cent on *Roe* v. *Wade*. She and Coffee would have filed the case *in pauperis* had Lucas not come along with his offer of help from the James Madison Law Institute, but she would never have given up on it. Weddington had a sense of déjà vu: she had been here before with Lucas. She reached the same conclusion she had the first time. She would reargue the case. It was hers now, anyway.

17

Reargument

The reargument of the abortion cases took place on October 10, 1972, two and one-half years after *Roe* v. *Wade* was filed in the lower court. The only new note of interest was provided by the arrival of two new justices, Lewis Powell and William Rehnquist, who had been seated at the end of the 1971 Term. Like Blackmun and Burger, both men were Nixon appointees. No one knew for sure how the two new justices stood on abortion.

Reformers were not optimistic about Rehnquist's support, with good reason. A former assistant attorney general under John Mitchell, he was known to be a strict constructionist and was on the record specifically as being opposed to the use of the Fourteenth Amendment to expand individual rights. Rehnquist had testified against the Civil Rights Act in 1964 and in favor of a limited school desegregation plan in 1967. He supported electronic surveillance, no-knock entry into people's homes, and mass arrests of demonstrators. In a break with a tradition of endorsing virtually all nominees, the American Civil Liberties Union had opposed his nomination, and the American Bar Association was reportedly planning not to give him a favorable rating until matters were smoothed over by Republican Senator James Eastland, chairman of the Judiciary Committee.

Even less was known about southerner Lewis Powell, although he was considered a political moderate. As chairman of the Richmond (Virginia) school board, Powell had kept the public schools open after the *Brown* v. *Board of Education* decision despite pressure to close them, and he had worked for legal services for the poor. His legal record was outstanding. Like Blackmun, reformers were optimistic that he might join the majority.

Regardless of speculation, no one knew how the two new justices felt about abortion—or how they would vote. Once they were on the bench, the picture of abortion reform might change. Both men were essentially unknown elements and would remain so until the decisions were handed down.

For the second argument, the courtroom was again filled with pro-choice activists and press, but there were fewer of both, and the atmosphere was decidedly anticlimactic.

Since counsel had not been asked to address any specific issues during the rearguments, Weddington planned to focus on new developments that strengthened her case, such as recent court decisions on birth control and abortion. With her at the table were Linda Coffee and Ron Weddington. Lucas, who now ran the James Madison Law Institute from San Francisco, was not present for the second argument.

The argument for the appellee—that is, the state of Texas— would be presented by Robert Flowers, assistant attorney general of Texas, who had taken over the argument from Jay Floyd. Flowers had no complaint with the way Floyd had handled the first argument, but he felt the honor of arguing before the Supreme Court should be passed around. With Flowers at the Texas counsel's table were Attorney General Crawford Martin and Jay Floyd.

Flowers was probably the only participant and possibly the only person in the courtroom who would not find these arguments anticlimactic. In part, this was because he was so unprepared for them. Flowers had not even written an outline of what he planned to discuss. Neither he nor Floyd had ever talked with Dorothy Beasley, who would be arguing in behalf of the state of Georgia in the companion case, *Doe* v. *Bolton*. With hindsight, Flowers would tell me he felt his lack of preparation was a mistake on his part, that he should have done more to prepare. He regretted not having gotten together with Professor Joseph Witherspoon to work out an outline or rehearse his arguments, but at the time none of that had seemed necessary.

During the three-judge court and even the first Supreme Court arguments, no one in the attorney general's office believed the Court would come to grips with the merits of the case. They thought *Roe* would be decided on procedural issues, such as standing and mootness or even on jurisdiction, and they were confident that they had the upper hand there. Only when the Supreme Court ordered the second argument did the attorney general's men realize that the Court was going to come to grips with the issues of merit. But they still did not believe they could lose this case. They thought the majority vote was with them.

Through their own grapevine and the press reports, the Texas state lawyers had learned that the justices had rendered a decision the first time and that the opinion had been withdrawn at the end of the 1971 term. They knew its withdrawal had angered Douglas. From this they calculated that Douglas, Brennan, and Marshall, the Court's known liberals, were probably the votes to strike down the Texas abortion law. They thought White was the fourth vote in favor of striking the Texas abortion law, but they believed he was a swing vote who could be converted to their side. Blackmun, they believed, was already on their side because of his stance on pornography. He was known to have said that the community should be the judge of its own morality, and from this the state's lawyers deduced he was a supporter of states' rights. The state thought all the other justices, including the two new Nixon appointees, would be votes in support of the Texas abortion law. They calculated the vote at four to three, their favor. They honestly believed they had nothing to worry about and therefore not much need to prepare.

In any event, Flowers had too many other things on his mind to spend much time preparing *Roe* v. *Wade* for the Supreme Court. In an upset, Attorney General Crawford Martin had not been reelected, and as a result Flowers and most of his staff were about to be unemployed. They were devoting as much time to job hunting as to the still heavy load of cases that sat on their desks. Although Flowers knew he would be leaving the department two months after the argument to work on the governor's staff, he was still too preoccupied to do much work on the abortion case.

Morale was low enough over the department's lame-duck status, but equally disturbing to Flowers was the fact that Martin, a boss he revered, was in poor health. Blind in one eye from an automobile accident and suffering from a cataract in the other, he had attempted to hide his poor vision during the campaign. The campaign, too, had taken its toll on him, or so it seemed to those close to him. The last thing Crawford Martin ever expected was to be voted out of office.

His eye problems were so serious that Flowers doubted that he could see any of the Court proceedings even though he was in the midst of them. He was present in the courtroom, in fact, only because he was en route to Johns Hopkins for cataract surgery. Flowers was proud and pleased, however, to have Crawford Martin seated at the counsel's table with him.

Like most lawyers arguing before the Supreme Court, Flowers had come to Washington, D.C., several days before the arguments were scheduled to be heard. When we talked years later, he would recall that just about everything went wrong after his arrival. He and Floyd stayed at a Holiday Inn that, in retrospect, seemed too far away from the hub of activity. His first shock, he reminisced, occurred "when we walked up those first big steps outside the Supreme Court. There was hardly a place to sit. All the people were there in support of Sarah. They had 'Down with Abortion Laws' signs. We had to walk through all of that."

Upon learning that *Roe* v. *Wade* was the second scheduled argument for that morning, Flowers and Floyd headed to a cafeteria in the court building for some breakfast. "Somehow we hadn't eaten," Flowers said. "We went down to a cafeteria and ordered up breakfast. I nearly choked to death trying to get one swallow down, I was so—not terrified, but excited. Jay, who had already been through it, was getting a big kick out of my discomfort. It was truly agony, it was, for a country boy. I believe I could handle it better now, after many years of being under extreme pressure. I was not prepared for it, for that part of it," he said, referring to the oral argument.

Flowers's mounting panic was not eased any when he entered the courtroom. It looked eerie, not as he had remembered it from an earlier visit several years ago when he had been presented at the Supreme Court bar. The courtroom was in the process of being remodeled; everything was draped with canvas. And then there was the remarkably small size of the room itself. "I thought the justices would be way remote," he recalled, "but they aren't. The bench is concave. The end men are here [gesturing to the sides of the room], and the chief justice just looms over you." The scene reminded him of a huge painting he had recently seen of the Last Supper. "They tell you to stand in a certain spot, and you are totally within the picture," Flowers recalled. "Well, that's the sense you have in the Supreme Court. It's not you and these great guys you've read about, way off somewhere. Man, you're right there in the fray with them."

Fortunately Weddington was to speak first, so Flowers had some time to collect himself before he would have to speak.

At 10:04 A.M. the second argument of *Roe* v. *Wade* began. Weddington stood up to talk. She began by tying up loose ends, trying to anticipate any questions the justices still might have about the case and assuage their doubts. She reminded the Court, for example, that Dr. Hallford had joined the case after it was filed as a way of emphasizing that her clients' interests took precedence over his. Using new research that had been released since the last hearing, she revealed how many Texas women were traveling to New York to obtain abortions, trying to show the Court that women would go to great lengths to obtain them. She spoke without interruption for a long time.

When she was interrupted, it was by Justice White, who set about trying to do the very thing Weddington had been warned about during the moot court rehearsals. White wanted to back her into a corner on the issue of fetal rights. If the fetus were found to be a person, he queried, would she lose her case?

Weddington hemmed. She cited the long history of state abortion laws and common law and pointed out that the fetus had never been found to be a person.

Did the Texas statute, White wanted to know, make any distinction between the first and the ninth month with regard to fetal life?

"Our statute does not," she replied.

"Do you?" he pressed.

Weddington replied that the appellants were asking the Court to declare the statute unconstitutional, to find, in effect, that the state had no compelling interest whatsoever in regulating abortion.

Pressed further, she acknowledged that some states, such as New York, had imposed limits, but she hastened to add that they permitted abortion when the woman's life was threatened and in cases of rape and incest.

White pursued his line of questioning. Was she not really talking about balancing rights?

Weddington reminded the Court that the fetus had never been considered a person under the Fourteenth Amendment. It was a poor answer. Sensing that Justice White wanted to find a way to balance rights in this case, she might better have responded with reasons not to do so or have made a strong argument in favor of the women's superior right.

White then asked: "Well, if it were established that an unborn fetus is a person . . . you would have almost an impossible case here, would you not?"

A more experienced constitutional lawyer would not have been intimidated, but Weddington was. "I would have a very difficult case," she replied, hoping no doubt that her answer would at least close out the argument so she could redirect the Court's attention to other issues. Later, constitutional lawyer Charles Allen Wright would tell her he thought she had erred by letting White back her into a corner like that. He said she could have argued that the fetus could be a person and still not be given rights equal to those of the mother. Corporations, he pointed out, are legal persons, but they are not entitled to all the rights and freedoms of individuals.

Blackmun asked so few questions at the second hearing that no one who did not know would have suspected he was writing the majority opinion. He did, however, avidly pursue any line of argument that involved physicians. Why had she not said more in the briefs about the Hippocratic oath? he wanted to know. What about the fact that it specifically forbade abortion? Would this pose a conflict for physicians if the Court found that abortion laws were unconstitutional?

Weddington dismissed the oath, saying the lawyers had written little about it because it was old.

Referring to a case the Supreme Court had decided only three months earlier on capital punishment, Blackmun asked if there would be "any inconsistency" in the Supreme Court supporting abortion at the same time that it struck down the death penalty.

Weddington replied there was none since the fetus was not considered a person within the meaning of the Constitution.

Her argument ended shortly thereafter. She had been asked so few questions that she still had time for a five-minute rebuttal to Flowers's arguments.

In our conversations, Weddington would later recall the argument as having been so uneventful that she had the feeling the justices were simply going through the motions of holding an oral argument. She thought that the justices had already made up their minds, although from what they said, she could not tell what they had decided.

Flowers stood to make the state of Texas's argument. He had regained some of his confidence, if only because he thought Weddington's argument had gone so poorly. She never had answered a question straight out, and seemed to turn the argument into whatever direction she wanted it to take rather than responding directly to the justices' questions. All the coaching he had heard she had undergone hadn't helped her much, as far as he could tell.

Flowers thought there were only two issues to be argued, and he intended to press them both. First, abortion properly belonged to the state; it was a legislative issue, not a judicial one. If any court would understand this argument, it was, Flowers felt, this one. Second, the fetus was a person from the moment of conception. With this Flowers felt all people except for a few radical reformers were in agreement.

White almost immediately began a similar line of questioning with Flowers as he had with Weddington, delving into whether the fetus was a person. He asked Flowers: "Is your case over if the fetus is not a person?"

Flowers answered: "Yes, sir, I would say so."

Prodding further, White asked if the state had no other interest in regulating abortion.

Unprepared to make any argument other than states' rights and the fetal right, Flowers had trouble coming up with an answer.

"Preventing promiscuity, maybe. . . ."

Flowers believed White's questions showed he was on the state's side, though, and when Justice Stewart asked if Texas had any statutes prohibiting mutilation, Flowers took this as a sign that Stewart was also on his side. He replied that he did not think Texas had any such statutes.

Stewart asked if abortion were the only surgery that the state set apart with such special restrictions. Flowers agreed that it was.

About ten minutes into his thirty-minute argument, Flowers's confidence seemed to ebb. His lack of preparation caught up with him. He had presented his two lines of argument, not even very effectively, and had little else to say. The Court wanted more information—facts and statistics—that he was unable to supply. He had never really seized control of the arguments, and now he surrendered it almost visibly to the Court. As sometimes happened when a counsellor was less well informed or skillful at arguing than he might be, the justices began to conduct the argument among themselves, using Flowers as a sounding board. Gradually his answers were reduced to cursory responses indicating agreement or disagreement with no chance to offer any further explanation. Responding only "Yes, sir" and "No, sir," he did not seem to understand the direction the arguments were taking. When he pressed his claim that the fetus was just like a baby, for example, the Court pressed him to cite some medical evidence that this was the case. He could not.

At one point Flowers attempted to recover by pointing out that he felt that abortion was properly a matter for the state legislature. The rejoinder, more sarcastic than kindly, came back that if the fetus were indeed a person, as Flowers argued, then the Court could not leave it to the state legislatures "to play fast and loose with that person." That was the point at which it became obvious, if it had not been before, that the Court was going to address the issue of fetal personhood. In closing, Flowers returned to his theme that the Court had no choice but to grant the status of personhood to fetuses. He said he thought abortion was murder.

Flowers sat down feeling confused and at a loss to explain what had happened to him. He felt chewed up, as if the Court had tried to "nail" him in a way they had not with Weddington. The justices seemed to have gone easy on her and been overly tough on him, but he could hardly believe they would do this. Flowers was especially troubled with the questions of Thurgood Marshall. "I got a sense that the rest of the Court was a little aggravated [with Marshall]," he said. "They wanted to get on with the questions, and he'd ask, How high is up? When does life begin? and they'd all look down at him and then go on to something else." Only Burger, he felt, had been sympathetic to his plight. "Burger must have seen my horror," Flowers recalled. "He said, There's a country boy. He was so kindly when I'd be mystified at something. He'd clarify things for me. I took it that he showed a great amount of pity—not pity, compassion—for me."

In her rebuttal Weddington managed to rally from her earlier lackluster performance, holding her ground against the justices and insisting that the restrictive Texas law infringed on a woman's basic liberty and was therefore unconstitutional. Nothing would do but for the Court to find that women had a constitutional right to abortion.

The reargument had gone poorly. If the second round had been the first, it would have spelled disaster for both sides. Court watchers liked to say that brilliant arguments sometimes won a case while poor ones never lost it, but the second arguments on abortion were so poor that they might well have proven to be the exception had they really counted. An experienced constitutional lawyer would have relished the opportunity to have a second chance with the Court and would have done virtually anything to control the course of the arguments, to press whatever points he or she thought relevant. Weddington and Flowers, however, had been too acquiescent and had pressed too few points. That they had not been in charge was obvious; what was less obvious was whether their problems were due to lack of skill or simply a function of the mood in the courtroom that day. Other people besides Weddington felt that the justices were merely going through the motions, that the case had already been settled in their minds. After two hours of argument (*Doe* v. *Bolton* was also reargued), it was unclear whether Powell and Rehnquist would change the vote of the Court. Pro-choicers could take heart, however, that the arguments had probably not lost them the case on at least one level. It was unlikely that the Court would decline to rule after hearing two rounds of oral argument.

Reformers' spirits were dampened a month later, though, when a referendum to repeal Michigan's 126-year-old abortion law was defeated. Using the same group as in Washington, the Voice for the Unborn, the Church waged the same kind of campaign against liberalized abortion laws. It retained the services of an advertising firm, Maywood & Hammer, which developed a series of dramatic radio-spot commercials featuring a simulated fetal heartbeat. The advertisement was heard everywhere. Professional actors were hired to do man-in-the-street interviews against abortion. Highway billboards showed a picture of Christ admonishing: "Stop abortion now. Don't take a life that I have given." Eight thousand canvassers went door to door pressing the antiabortion message.

Toward the end, the campaign became frightening. A prominent pro-choice doctor's life was threatened. A priest in clerical garb accosted a pro-choice legislator, called him a "foul murderer," and tried to push him down the steps of the Michigan Capitol. Dr. Jack

Stack, who led the pro-choice campaign in Michigan, recalled: "At first the fear was a creeping force. It got to be paranoia in some quarters until logic faded and scare tactics were screaming in our faces."

Three weeks before the election, polls showed that 56 percent of the people favored reform, while 36 percent opposed it, and 11 percent were undecided. On election day 61 percent voted against reform.

The Michigan defeat was all the more stunning for its unexpectedness. It left pro-choice reformers enervated and with little hope other than the Supreme Court decision. In a consolation note Whitehill sent to Dr. Stack, she wrote: "We are plugging away, but of course still holding out a ray of hope for the Supreme Court to come through."

The other ray of hope—in Texas, at least—was that Weddington won her election. From her seat in the Texas legislature, she would be able to continue the fight for abortion reform regardless of how the Supreme Court ruled.

18

The Supreme Court Decision

Blackmun spent the summer of 1972 working on abortion. He returned to Minnesota, where he worked in the Mayo Clinic library and in his office in Rochester. A clerk had agreed to work through the summer so that Blackmun could send revisions back to him to be incorporated into the original opinion.

Aware that even his colleagues who had joined his opinion did not think it was as concisely written or well thought out as it should be, Blackmun set about to clarify his thinking and writing on abortion. He knew that his views needed further shaping; in addition, there were subjects, such as the Hippocratic oath, that he wanted to explore further.

As he worked Blackmun still found himself thinking of abortion primarily as a medical problem. The footnotes clearly reflect this, sprinkled as they are with references to medical texts and treatises such as *A History of Medicine*, *The Genealogy of Gynaecology*, an article on the Hippocratic oath written in 1943, and a more recent article on medical abortion practices in the United States. He also read a lot about the ethical and philosophical aspects of abortion, including, most notably, a definitive article on the Roman Catholic view, "An Almost Absolute Value in History," by the respected birth control scholar John Noonan. Blackmun read original sources on the British common law.

Particularly helpful to him, to judge by the frequency with which they were cited, were the two articles written by New York Law School Professor Cyril Means, who had helped Weddington prepare for the arguments. Means had been involved with abortion reform from the start. A founding member of the Association for the Study of Abortion, he was active in NARAL, serving as its legal counsel for several years. In the late 1960s he had served on an eleven-member commission appointed by Governor Nelson Rockefeller to review New York's abortion laws. A specialist in religious and medieval law, Means's interest in abortion was scholarly, but as he became an activist, it became a personal crusade for him as well.

Means had obtained funding from ASA to do research on the legal history of abortion. Part of his research had consisted of reading original historical sources dating back to medieval times. Means's first article, "The Law of New York Concerning Abortion and the State of the Foetus, 1664–1968," was published in fall 1968. Weddington had discovered it when she met Means in New York through her ASA contacts and included it with the *Roe* record. A second article, "The Phoenix of Abortional Freedom," was on press at the time of the first oral arguments. In early December Means wrote Chief Justice Burger to ask whether he might not hand deliver prepublication copies to the Court. The Court, which welcomed additional material from a respected scholar, was pleased to grant him permission.

Means's research revealed that abortion prior to quickening had never been a crime or even a misdemeanor under the common law, and after quickening it had been only a misdemeanor. The fact that it had gradually become a misdemeanor prior to quickening, as revealed in the common-law texts of the 1600s, was the result, Means argued, of a politically and religiously motivated rewriting of the common law by Sir Edward Coke, seventeenth-century jurist and author of a common-law treatise that was widely used in law schools throughout the United States.

The importance of Means's discovery could hardly be underestimated. Many people assumed that abortion had always been illegal or at least had been illegal for hundreds of years. This argument was often advanced by those opposed to liberalized laws and was one that John Tolle had made, in fact, during the Dallas oral arguments.

Somewhat paradoxically, considering the nature of his research, Means did not believe the restrictive laws could be overturned on constitutional grounds. He felt it would be too awkward, since the laws had been on the books for 140 years, for justices suddenly to find them unconstitutional. Instead, Means believed the Supreme Court could find the statutes illegal on another ground, an old principle of law, *Cessante ratione legis cessat et ipsa*, which, roughly translated, meant that when a law was no longer rational or had no factual basis for existing, it ceased to exist.

Most lawyers working in abortion reform disagreed with Means and thought there were constitutional grounds for overturning the abortion laws, but his views were respected nonetheless, mostly because of the solid body of research that stood behind them.

Means devised what was, in retrospect, a rather convoluted rationale to support his theory. Convinced that the restrictive American laws passed in the mid-eighteenth century were intended to protect women's health in an era when any kind of surgery, including abortion, was life-threatening, Means reasoned that the abortion laws ceased to be meaningful as abortion became safer. He thought that was, roughly speaking, the historical moment at which abortion had become safer than childbirth.

He was able to test his ideas with another abortion scholar and fellow ASA member, Christopher Tietze, while sharing a plane ride between Washington, D.C., and New York. Tietze became excited about Means's theory and offered to help find supporting medical evidence to pinpoint the moment when abortion had become safer than childbirth.

Within a few days he called Means to report that his review of medical records revealed that after Lister had invented antiseptic surgery, the dangers associated with abortion had begun to decline. It had become increasingly less dangerous until some point shortly before 1950, when abortion became even safer than childbirth as a result of advanced surgical techniques. That, Means argued, was the point at which the abortion laws ceased to be rational.

Blackmun ultimately did not accept Means's theory that the laws should be overturned because they were defunct, but several threads of Means's work did make their way into the opinion. Blackmun was interested to learn, for example, that the abortion laws had originally been intended to protect the woman's health and not the fetus. He was impressed with the improving safety record of abortions in recent years. Finally, he accepted Means's idea, although the Court was undoubtedly leaning in this direction anyway, that the fetus had never throughout history been considered or granted the status of a legal person. Means had cited several medieval cases that were among the earliest precedents for this ancient principle.

Over the summer Blackmun settled on the degree to which the states could, if they chose to do so, limit the abortion right. He also established what he believed was the constitutional basis for the abortion right. It was to be considered a part of the privacy right.

Blackmun also decided he could not give up the long history section. He was aware that this would displease several of his colleagues, especially since it came on the heels of another case, *Flood v. Kuhn*, in which he had indulged in a similarly rambling (in others' eyes, not his) digression on the history of baseball. In that case he had written a paean to baseball; the historical section on abortion was hardly that, but both seemed to satisfy a need on Blackmun's part to provide his cases with a human as well as a legal context.

Like Douglas, Blackmun was also undoubtedly upset by the articles *The New York Times* and *The Washington Post* printed over the Fourth of July weekend. Blackmun was already angry over rumors that Burger had persuaded him to delay the decision. Too much notoriety was attaching itself to his first important case. His relationship with Burger, already strained by the charge that they were "Minnesota twins," would be strained even further—to the breaking point, some said—by the abortion cases.

The 1972 Term began as it always did on the first Monday in October. Within two weeks Blackmun was circulating a draft of his revised opinion. By all accounts it was more concise and well thought out than the first draft. Several of the justices and clerks were dismayed, as Blackmun had known they would be, to see that he had not cut the rambling section on the history of abortion and that it still contained so much medical material, but the basic idea—that women had a constitutional right to abortion—had finally emerged. Blackmun recognized the importance of obtaining a solid majority to stand behind the opinion, and he was willing to compromise to get it. Most of the debate that ensued centered on viability.

Brennan still found the opinion lacking in several respects. He felt it was too oriented to the physician's concerns and too little concerned with the woman's right to abortion. He was most concerned, though, to see that Blackmun had tied the state's interest in regulating abortion to viability. He thought that might eventually be the undoing of the opinion. What if science pushed back the point of viability? What about artificial support, which Blackmun had touched upon only in passing? Douglas was also concerned about using viability as a dividing line.

Brennan composed a lengthy memo—forty-eight pages, to be exact—of suggestions, which he sent to Blackmun's chambers. Blackmun liked them and agreed to incorporate most of them into the opinion. He would not, however, delete the material on viability, even after it was pointed out as a potential weakness. Perhaps he clung to viability as the dividing line because it was the point at which abortion began to trouble many physicians.

Stewart accepted the new draft with the proviso that Blackmun clarify that the fetus was not a person under the Fourteenth Amendment. This prompted Blackmun to add a detailed section listing all references in the Constitution to legal persons, coupled with a discussion on how none of these had ever been used to grant the fetus the status of legal personhood. Stewart also announced that he would write a separate concurrence, a rather unusual thing for him to do.

Burger read the draft and reportedly opposed the opinion, but Blackmun thought he knew how to win his support. He had devised a plan to divide pregnancy rather loosely into trimesters. These were guidelines for when and how the states could limit a woman's right to abortion. Now he offered to tighten these up, thinking that this would help obtain the chief's support.

It did, but this left Marshall upset about such specific cut-off points. What would they do to poor women who typically suffered from nutritional and health problems that frequently affected the course of their pregnancies and who often did not see physicians until late in their pregnancies?

Yet again Blackmun revised the opinion, this time changing the language to make the divisions more approximate. The " 'compelling' point," Blackmun wrote, "is at approximately the end of the first trimester." Another " 'compelling' point is at viability."

Upon returning to the Court in the fall, Powell had let it be known that he was a firm vote in favor of striking the abortion laws. His decision to join the majority was not surprising to those who knew him. His father-in-law and two brothers-in-law were obstetricians, and he had heard them talk about the problems and horrors of illegal abortion. Powell had also done some reading of his own on abortion over the summer. Unable to find any conclusive guidance in the Constitution or other sources, he had decided to vote his conscience.

Douglas, of course, was with the majority, which had now grown to six. White and Rehnquist had announced that they would dissent. The as-yet undecided vote was that of the chief. The abortion case would either come down with a six-to-three or a seven-to-two vote. Blackmun was pleased to have rounded up so solid a majority. He felt it was important for the Court to be as much of one mind as possible on so important an issue. Abortion had in the last year become a major—if not the major—issue in American life. Like desegregation and school prayer, it had taken on a wider meaning, one that was laden with political, religious, and sexual overtones. Abortion had become a code word, more than that, a *symbol*, of the struggle between the federal government and the states, Church and State, and men and women caught in the midst of dramatically changing roles.

Majority opinions are formed through a process of give and take. In a court where each justice is in a sense the ruler of his own independent fiefdom, these opinions are the one area where the justices, out of necessity, work together to create a compromise. Written by one person, they are never, in actual fact, the work of one person. Anthony Lewis, who has observed and written about this process many times, has noted: "Inevitably, in trying to please eight editors, the author of the majority opinion finds himself removing much of the personal flavor of his product. The dissenter, on the other hand, as Chief Justice Hughes said, can 'express his individuality.' He is not under the compulsion of speaking for the Court and thus of securing . . . a majority." It had happened with the *Roe* opinion. Blackmun had been amenable to the many suggestions that had been offered, and many of them had been incorporated into the opinion, at a cost to the opinion's individuality. In contrast the dissents would be remarkably more individual and personal documents.

In November Richard Nixon was reelected president. Abortion had continued to be an important issue throughout the 1972 campaign, filtering down through all levels of American politics. Political commentators now frequently pointed out how important single-issue politics had become; what they meant was how important the single issue of abortion had become. Droves of voters, part of the newly formed conservative majority and some members of the Right to Life party, voted for or against candidates solely on the basis of how they stood on abortion.

By early December the final draft of the opinion was ready. Blackmun, who had handed down no other opinion two months into the Court's term, was eager for the abortion opinions (he had written a separate one for *Doe* v. *Bolton*, the companion case) to come down. Stewart's concurrence was written, as were Rehnquist's and White's dissents. The Court was still waiting, however, for word from Chief Justice Burger. Nothing happened throughout December.

When the Court reconvened after the holiday break, the justices let it be known to the chief justice that they were eager to release the decision. Several of them believed Burger was delaying the abortion decision, at first until Nixon was reelected and now because he did not want to embarrass the president right before his inauguration. The opinion was going to be glaring proof that the Nixon High Court appointees had done little to redirect the liberal leanings of this Court. At the first conference of the new year, Justice Stewart issued something of an ultimatum, telling Burger he should vote immediately or let the decision come down with eight votes.

Partisanship such as Burger was displaying was frowned upon at the Court. Supreme Court justices did not campaign for their jobs, nor did they campaign for anyone else. This chief justice, however, a lifelong activist in the Republican party, had remained intensely attuned to politics even after he had come on the Court. Burger enjoyed the attention he got from the president, although he was fond of pointing out that he was chief justice of the United States, not merely the Supreme Court. He would not like to diminish the man he regarded as his only counterpart in American life. But Burger also liked to be in the majority, particularly on landmark decisions like this one, so he finally announced that he would join the majority opinion. Noting that he wanted to write his own concurrence, he promised to prepare it by the next conference.

At the January 19 conference, Burger still had nothing ready. Aware that the inauguration was scheduled for the following Tuesday, the justices decided to go ahead and set a date, Monday, January

22, several days after the inauguration, as the day they would hand down the abortion decisions. Burger committed to prepare a concurrence by Monday.

No one outside the Court is given advance notice of when an opinion is being released or what it contains, but this time both were known in advance. The current issue of *Time* magazine contained a story announcing that the Supreme Court would strike the state abortion laws, a virtually unprecedented leak. Burger, who held the press in such disdain that he would one day shove a reporter who said something he disliked, was reportedly furious over the leak. The news story was more pressure to release the opinion.

Mondays—opinion days—are often exciting, but the Supreme Court was truly abuzz on Monday, January 22. Only important opinions are read aloud, but the Supreme Court is one of the few remaining courts anywhere in the world that still issues any of its opinions orally. Court activity would slow to a standstill that morning as every Court employee who was able to do so filtered into the marble hall to hear the morning's activity. Having received an excellent tip, the press was there en masse, and there were rumors that Justice Blackmun's wife was present, too.

As the Court convened, reporters who had been given printed copies—eighty pages for the majority opinion and thirty pages of dissenting opinions—were already frantically filing their stories from the Court pressroom. In the courtroom Blackmun began reading an abbreviated version of the opinion, first noting that his reason for doing so was to provide immediate information to those state legislatures that were still in session and might want to begin revising or repealing their laws immediately.

In his quiet but steady voice, Blackmun read: "We forthwith acknowledge our awareness of the sensitive and emotional nature of the abortion controversy, of the vigorous opposing views, even among physicians, and of the deep and seemingly absolute convictions that the subject inspires. One's philosophy, one's experiences, one's exposure to the raw edges of human experience, one's religious training, one's attitudes toward life and family and their values, and the moral standards one establishes and seeks to observe, are all likely to influence and to color one's thinking and conclusions about abortion." In publicly confessing the difficulty of writing this opinion, Blackmun had gone against the advice given to him by Justice Hugo Black, who when Blackmun first came to the Court had warned him: "Never display agony. Never say that this is an agonizing, difficult decision. Always write as though it's crystal clear." But perhaps because Blackmun was incapable of feeling such dispassion over an opinion that was going to tear the country apart, he also saw no reason to hide his feelings.

As had happened in the lower federal court, the Supreme Court found that the Does had no standing to sue, ruling that since their case was speculative, it presented no real controversy. Because it was loath to interfere with a lower court criminal proceeding, the Supreme Court also threw out the case of Dr. Hallford—a decision that only Douglas opposed. Only Norma McCorvey remained as an appellant, and it was on her situation that the entire abortion decision was based.

Although the Court noted the state's plea that McCorvey's case was moot (on grounds that her pregnancy had ended) the justices took a more pragmatic view of the situation than did the state of Texas, observing that "the normal 266-day human gestation period is so short that the pregnancy will come to term before the usual appellate process is complete. If that termination makes a case moot, pregnancy litigation will seldom survive much beyond the trial stage, and appellate review will be effectively denied. Our law should not be that rigid. Pregnancy often comes more than once to the same woman, and in the general population, if man is to survive, it will always be with us. Pregnancy provides a classic justification for a conclusion of nonmootness."

That the opinion was heavily slanted toward the medical profession was obvious from the first few pages of the history section, in which Blackmun had traced the history of the Hippocratic oath, for example, arriving at the conclusion that its condemnation of abortion need not concern modern doctors because it had been written by a small radical sect, the Pythagorean Christians, and was representative of neither mainstream Christianity nor medicine at the time. He supported his view with numerous citations from professional associations, most of them medically oriented, which now favored more liberal abortion.

That Blackmun had also accepted much of Means's research was also apparent when he declared that it was "doubtful that abortion was ever firmly established as a common-law crime even with respect to the destruction of a quick fetus." In a Court that liked to stand by historical precedent, the importance of this observation could not be overestimated. It was an acknowledgment that the Court knew it had the weight of historical example behind it in striking the abortion laws.

Because of the *Time* magazine leak, the fact that the Court was going to strike the restrictive abortion laws was no mystery to most persons present in the courtoom that day or even to reformers across the country. What remained to be learned, and made people listen with bated breath, was what limits, if any, the Court would put on the woman's abortion right.

For those in the courtroom who were hearing the opinion for the first time, that answer could not come soon enough. The wait seemed interminable, but finally Justice Blackmun read: "This right of privacy . . . is broad enough to encompass a woman's decision whether or not to terminate her pregnancy." This privacy right to abortion, the opinion further noted, was grounded in either the "Fourteenth Amendment's concept of personal liberty . . . or . . . in the Ninth Amendment's reservation of rights to the people." A palpable sigh of relief went through the courtroom. That was the crux of the opinion—the victory for pro-choice forces, as it were. The Court had ruled that a woman's right to abortion was constitutionally protected.

But the opinion did not stop there. There were, as it turned out, to be some qualifications on the right. The Court wrote that the right to privacy was not absolute, that "the pregnant woman cannot be isolated in her privacy." The Court felt that three circumstances might warrant a state's intrusion on the abortion right. First, it might want to do so for moral reasons. Second, a state might want to restrict abortion in order to protect a woman's health. Third and finally, the state might have an interest in protecting what the Court called "potential life."

The first claim, that of protecting morals, the Court dismissed (undoubtedly with relief), saying that since the state of Texas had not raised this argument, it need not concern itself with it, either. The second claim, hardly surprising considering Blackmun's medical background, was self-explanatory. The third and most surprising claim—actually, it was astonishing—related to a concept of potential life that the Court appeared to be creating with this opinion. Blackmun read: "Logically, of course, a legitimate state interest in this area need not stand or fall on acceptance of the belief that life begins at conception or at some point prior to live birth. In assessing the state's interest, recognition may be given to the less rigid claim that as long as at least *potential* life is involved, the state may assert interests beyond the protection of the pregnant woman alone."

This concept of potential life appeared to be the Court's own creation. No one on either side of the debate had raised any claim about potential life. The Texas lawyers had argued that actual human life, as complete as any fully born person, existed from the moment of conception, while the appellants' lawyers had denied that this was possible. When the Court asserted that the states might protect potential human life, those present could not help but wonder whether this meant that the Court was going to grant the fetus some rights of personhood.

The answer came quickly, as Blackmun continued reading: "We need not resolve the difficult question of when life begins. When those trained in the respective disciplines of medicine, philosophy, and theology are unable to arrive at any consensus, the judiciary, at this point in the development of man's knowledge, is not in a position to speculate as to the answer."

He next began to spell out exactly how the states could, if they chose to do so, limit the woman's right. Introducing another idea that had not been raised in either the briefs or the oral arguments, Blackmun described how the abortion right changed at various states of pregnancy. In the first trimester, the state could not intervene in any way to regulate abortion. In the second trimester, it could intervene only to protect the woman's health. In the third trimester, or at the approximate point of viability, when the fetus "presumably has the capability of meaningful life outside the mother's womb," the state could intervene to protect it.

Having thus provided what constitutional scholar Norman Dorsen called the "framework" for the abortion right, Blackmun also read briefly from the second abortion opinion, *Doe* v. *Bolton*, in which the Court set forth some specific applications of the right—actions states could and could not take to limit women's access to abortion. For example, the Court struck down hospital licensing requirements, a residency requirement, and a requirement that two physicians certify a woman's need to undergo an abortion, which seemed designed only to limit women's access to abortion. Margery Hames recalled feeling that her case was what made *Roe* v. *Wade* comprehensive, that the *Doe* opinion eliminated years of waiting to see what the states would do with the *Roe* v. *Wade* ruling.

After Blackmun finished reading the abbreviated opinions, Justices White and Rehnquist read their dissents. A public dissent was rare and not the friendliest thing one justice could do to another, but years later Blackmun's reaction was to say, "I'd had it done to me before, and it would be done again."

In White's dissent, which applied to both cases, he berated his fellow justices for indulging in "an improvident and extravagant exercise of the power of judicial review," one that could only be interpreted as a return to substantive due process. White also revealed his mistrust of women's ability to act responsibly in terminating their pregnancies when he wrote: "At the heart of this controversy . . . are those recurring pregnancies that pose no danger whatsoever to the life or health of the mother, but are, nevertheless, unwanted for any one or more of a variety of reasons—inconvenience, family planning, economics, dislike of children, the embarrassment of illegitimacy, etc."

A scathing dissent from anyone's point of view, it both offended and concerned women, who rarely had abortions out of inconvenience and who thought illegitimacy entailed more than mere embarrassment—if not for themselves, then for the children who were condemned to be reared under its shadow. White's dissent was also surprising, coming as it did from a man who had voted with the majority in *Griswold* v. *Connecticut*, the birth control case that had established that a married couple's right to use contraceptives was protected under the privacy right. Rumor held that White's feelings about abortion were personal.

Rehnquist's dissents (he wrote two brief ones) were more even-handed but no less adamant about denouncing the majority view. He essentially took what would soon become familiar to Supreme Court watchers as his strict constructionist view of the Constitution. Rehnquist, more than any of the other justices of that time, would unflinchingly support the dogma of a literal, unchanging Constitution, for which he allowed few exceptions on humanitarian grounds.

Like White, he opposed *Roe* v. *Wade* on the ground that it was "judicial legislation," by which he was referring primarily to the trimester division of pregnancy. Although he did not specifically protest that the use of the Fourteenth Amendment was a return to substantive due process, he observed that when the amendment was added to the Constitution, thirty-six states had abortion laws, to him a sign that if the framers of the amendment had intended it to protect the abortion right, they would have made some specific mention of the fact. That his view ignored hundreds of years of American and British common-law precedent in favor of 150 years of legislative history seemed not to concern him, nor did he anywhere in his dissent probe the reasons for the laws' existence or contemplate the validity of those laws in light of present-day knowledge. Finally, Rehnquist agreed with the state of Texas's argument that *Roe* v. *Wade* was moot because McCorvey was almost certainly no longer pregnant at the time the appeals were filed.

Not read aloud that Monday morning were three concurrences, one written by Chief Justice Burger, another by Justice Douglas, and yet another by Justice Stewart. Burger's opinion, a scant three paragraphs long, seemed an attempt to distance himself from a majority he had not been too pleased about joining in the first place. Using a tactic he had employed in other concurrences, he appeared to be trying to impose his own limits on the decision when he wrote: "Plainly, the Court today rejects any claim that the Constitution requires abortions on demand." Douglas's concurrence, a rather rambling opinion for him, seemed to be an attempt to reinforce the views on privacy that he had put forth in *Griswold*.

Of the three concurrences, Stewart's was the most interesting, if only because it was so puzzling. Stewart had dissented in *Griswold* on grounds that the opinion marked a return to substantive due process, which according to his understanding the Court had agreed was not sound judicial policy. If the Court were returning now to substantive due process, he would go along with it. In fact, in his concurrence he wrote that he favored protecting the abortion right under privacy and cited several cases involving privacy—the right to send a child to a private school, the right to have one's child taught a foreign language, to name but two—that he found important but certainly less significant than a woman's right to privacy regarding abortion.

For all its seeming logic, however, Stewart's concurrence made little sense, particularly in light of his earlier *Griswold* dissent. If he had believed in the right to use birth control that was defined in *Griswold*, he could surely have found grounds other than substantive due process for supporting it. There was, for example, Supreme Court Justice Arthur Goldberg's eloquent and erudite concurrence on the use of the Ninth Amendment to define the privacy right. And now that he was supporting *Roe*, no need existed for him to disavow his former disavowance of the Fourteenth Amendment, because Blackmun had written that the privacy right resided in both the Fourteenth *and* the Ninth amendments.

In 1983, when Stewart spoke to a class at Columbia University, he was asked about his dissent in *Griswold* and his concurrence in *Roe*. Replying that he was a believer in *stare decisis*, a judicial principle by which previous precedent-setting cases were followed in subsequent cases, he said that once the right to privacy had been established, he intended to follow it. The body of Stewart's opinions, however, which seemed never to have been based on any clear-cut judicial philosophy, pointed to the fact that he had not always been such a great defender of *stare decisis*. Others believed there was another explanation for Stewart's about-face. A story made the rounds in Washington and among those who worked on *Roe* that his wife, long active in Planned Parenthood, had been appalled at his vote in *Griswold* and not given him a moment's peace on the subject in the intervening ten years. When *Roe* came along, it was said that Stewart seized the opportunity to repent of his past mistake—and made sure to put his repentance in writing.

Believing (albeit erroneously) that its work on abortion was finished, the Court turned its attention to its other business.

19

Reaction

News of the abortion decision was knocked off the front pages of most newspapers across the country when former president Lyndon Johnson died the same day the decision was handed down. Reformers worried that women would not learn of the monumental decision that would do so much to change their lives. The pro-choice reformers were ecstatic over it, but women who had had little or nothing to do with the reform effort felt that the victory was theirs as well.

The Supreme Court notifies counsel of decisions by telegram, but when a case is as important as *Roe* v. *Wade*, news of a decision usually arrives via the media. Weddington was home getting ready to go to the Capitol the morning of January 22 when her telephone rang. A friend who had heard about the decision on the morning news congratulated her. Weddington asked, "For what?" To which her friend replied, "You won your case." Coffee first heard the news on the radio as she was driving to work.

Upon reaching their offices, both women were deluged with called from the media asking for comment, but they could only respond cautiously that since they had not yet read the opinion, they could not comment on it. A written copy of the opinion would not reach them for several more days and possibly even weeks.

Two telegrams sent to Roy Lucas, the counsel of record, on January 22, informing him of the decision, were returned with the message that he had moved from Patchin Place and left no forwarding address. (Dorothy Beasley, who had argued *Doe* v. *Bolton* for the state of Georgia, was so infuriated by the decision that she refused to accept her telegram.)

Norma McCorvey burst into tears when she read about the decision in her local newspaper that night. A friend who was with her said: "Don't tell me you knew Lyndon Johnson?" "No," McCorvey replied, "I'm Roe." It was the first time she had told anyone of her role in the case. When Weddington called her several days later to ask how she felt knowing that she had changed so many women's lives, McCorvey replied, "It makes me feel like I'm on top of Mt. Everest."

People on both sides of the issue were astonished by the decision. Pro-choice forces could not believe they had won so much, and antiabortion forces, who had never dreamed they might lose at all, could not believe they had lost so much. For several months antiabortionists had believed the battle was turning in their favor.

It is no exaggeration to say that to reformers the opinion "came like a thunderbolt," as Lawrence Lader put it, and went "beyond what anyone had predicted" in guaranteeing free choice. Harriet Pilpel, who was so sure the Court would not approve abortion-on-request that she had counseled Weddington to argue for a more limited right, echoed the surprise of many other reformers when she said: "It scaled the whole mountain. We expected to get there, but not on the first trip."

NARAL executive director Lee Giddings wrote of the decision: "Reaching farther and deeper and approved by a more decisive vote than we ever expected, this landmark decision established what we have been fighting for long and tirelessly. . . . It was a staggering victory—the sweeter still because it came at a time when we were gearing up for what would surely have been the toughest battle in the history of the movement, with the 1970 New York law as the spoils."

The decision was supported by most of the country, or at least over half of it, according to the most recent polls, which showed that 64 percent of Americans believed that abortion should be a personal decision to be made by a woman and her physician. *The New York Times* heartily approved the decision and sought to console the opponents of abortion by writing: "Nothing in the Court's approach ought to give affront to persons who oppose all abortion for reasons of religion or individual conviction. They can stand as firmly as ever for those principles, provided they do not impede the freedom of those with an opposite view."

Predictably, the hierarchy of the Catholic church was outraged by the decision. John Cardinal Krol, president of the National Catholic Conference, accused the Court of opening the doors to the "greatest slaughter of innocent life in the history of mankind." Archbishop Francis J. Furey of Texas called the authors of the decision "fetal muggers." Two right-wing Catholic publications, *The Wanderer* and *Triumph*, called for the excommunication of Justice Brennan.

That there is no appeal from the Supreme Court is a fact that most Americans accept, and Supreme Court decisions generally unite the nation more than divide it. For example, although only a minority of people believed the public schools should be desegregated before the *Brown* v. *Board of Education* ruling, polls taken in the weeks after the Supreme Court decision ordering desegregation showed a shift in opinion that could only be attributed to a fairly widespread acceptance of the Court's ruling. *Roe* v. *Wade*, unfortunately, would prove to be the exception, a rare decision that did not unite the nation. Instead, it ignited a firestorm of controversy that still rages a decade and a half later, although ironically the majority of Americans who favored legalization before the decision did not waver in their support despite intensive campaigning on the part of antiabortion forces.

At the heart of the controversy over *Roe* v. *Wade* was one issue about which everyone, pro- or antilegalization, seemed to have an opinion. Was *Roe* a good or a bad ruling? Had the Supreme Court, in its wisdom, hammered out the best-possible decision? The answers did not line up predictably according to which side one supported. Those opposed to abortion, of course, unanimously rejected any notion that *Roe* was a fair or just decision, but many people who favored legalization also worried that the decision was flawed.

The biggest problem with the decision, at least in the eyes of academic critics (whose thinking, one scholar noted, seemed to echo public opinion), was the very one the Dallas judges had sought to circumvent by relying on the Ninth rather than the Fourteenth Amendment—a ruling that the Supreme Court had now reversed with its reliance on the Fourteenth Amendment. By grounding the abortion right in the Fourteenth, many critics claimed that the Court had resurrected substantive due process.

The most shocking criticism along this line—because it did not come from the enemy camp—was an article by respected constitutional scholar John Hart Ely, then professor of law at Yale and later dean of law at Stanford, who felt that *Roe* was a bad ruling on several counts. While acknowledging that he personally favored liberalized abortion ("Were I a legislator, I would vote for a statute very much like the one the Court ended up drafting," he wrote), Ely objected to the use of substantive due process and also to the Court's designation of the abortion right as fundamental and thus worthy of special protection. Ely thought the Court had erred in not permitting regulation of abortions in the first trimester.

In fact, Ely believed that *Roe* was even worse than the earlier substantive due process cases. In those, at least, the Court had found laws unconstitutional because they did not bear a rational relationship to an underlying constitutional value, a kind of ruling that Ely found acceptable. But in *Roe*, Ely thought the Court had simply announced that the government's goal of protecting women's health and life was not important enough to sustain the legislative restriction on abortion, a pronouncement that, as far as he was concerned, merely substituted one rational judgment—that of the Court—for another rational judgment—that of the legislature. Furthermore, in examining the extent to which the states could regulate abortion, the court had not applied the rational-relationship standard, but rather had ruled that the abortion right could not be infringed upon without a state showing a compelling reason to do so, a standard that was used only to protect the most important fundamental rights. While Ely agreed that a woman's right to abortion was probably grounded in the Fourteenth Amendment, he could find no reason for the elevation of the abortion right to a level equal, or even superior, to other fundamental, superprotected rights. He wrote that the protection afforded the abortion right was "so stringent that a desire to preserve the fetus's existence is unable to overcome it—a protection more stringent, I think it is fair to say, than that the present Court accords the freedom of the press, explicitly guaranteed by the First Amendment."

For all his academic clout, Ely was not without his biases. For one thing, he seemed unwilling to struggle with the Court's conclusion that fetal life was potential, not actual. Ely also tended to undervalue the effects of unwanted (or for that matter, wanted) childbearing on women's lives, implying, as had Justice White, that a woman's desire to undergo an abortion had more to do with a desire to make childbearing convenient than with other substantial difficulties it could present in terms of a woman's ability to provide emotional and economic sustenance for a child. In this vein Ely wrote: "Whether antiabortion legislation cramps the life-style of an unwilling mother more significantly than antihomosexuality legislation cramps the life-style of a homosexual is a close question."

The Fourteenth Amendment had its defenders, among them, it· must be noted, the Supreme Court justices themselves; while obviously aware of the controversy surrounding the amendment, the justices nonetheless had seen no reason not to rely on it. Perhaps the brethren had all along agreed with Justice Harlan's view that there was nothing intrinsically wrong with the Fourteenth Amendment, and that an unwillingness to use it was no guarantee that the Court would never err by deciding a case based on the justices' own opinions or views. Justice Brennan may well have had the Fourteenth Amendment in mind in a 1987 public television interview when he was asked if any part of the Constitution were more sacred than any other part. His answer was an emphatic no, that all the parts were equal. Debate might rage in academic circles about the role of the Fourteenth Amendment, but all the while the Court had continued to use it, most notably, to develop the string of family law and privacy cases of which *Roe* was but one more. This was perhaps the amendment's most meaningful defense.

Another debate revolved around the fact that the abortion right was grounded in the larger, more encompassing privacy right. Outraged antiabortionists charged that the Court had overstepped its bounds and created a new right—one, they felt, that had no reason to exist. Nowhere in the Constitution, they insisted, was there anything—neither a word nor a phrase—to suggest a right of privacy and by association the right to abortion.

In essence, this was yet another round in the battle between the strict and loose constructionists about the extent to which constitutional rights must be grounded in the Constitution. On one side were the loose constructionists, who believed the Constitution had to be subject to interpretation if it were to survive as a useful document in a democratic society. On the other side were the strict constructionists, who believed the Constitution could only be taken literally and was not to be subjected to what they regarded as mere changing fashion in moral values.

Needless to say, those on both sides of the issue were capable of using their points of view to rationalize whatever needed rationalizing. Ironically, the opinion itself could not be so deftly tucked into one category or another. Blackmun had, for example, loosely interpreted the right to privacy while strictly interpreting the fetus's lack of personhood.

Defenders of the privacy right were quick to point out that many rights, including some of which the conservatives supported, such as the right to school prayer, were also not explicitly described in the Constitution. Most liberals viewed the strict constructionist view as little more than a way for conservatives to use the Constitution to discriminate against minorities and other groups who were not represented at the Constitutional Convention. They liked to remind strict constructionists that for the nation's first one hundred years, the Constitution had not counted blacks as persons, and that women had been denied the right to vote until 1920, two situations that were remedied not because of what the Constitution said, but rather because of presumptions about the underlying values that the Founding Fathers were believed to have intended when they wrote the Constitution.

As for justification of the privacy right, advocates claimed that privacy, like liberty, ran throughout the Constitution rather than being located in any one place within it. The breakthrough in *Griswold* had not been that the decision had "created" a right of privacy, as critics carpingly claimed, but rather that it had given a cherished, respected value, privacy, a name. *Griswold* also freed the Court from having to ground privacy or any other fundamental right, often arbitrarily, in one specific amendment. The penumbral approach developed by Brennan in *Lamont* v. *Postmaster* and elaborated in *Griswold* by Douglas was but a means of acknowledging the basic values that ran throughout the Constitution.

In *Poe* v. *Ullman* Douglas had written that the right of privacy emanated "from the totality of the Constitutional scheme under which we live." It was this, according to Stanford law professor Thomas Grey, that accounted for Blackmun's "strikingly casual" reference in *Roe* to the constitutional grounds for privacy. Blackmun had allowed that the privacy right emanated from either the Ninth Amendment, as the Dallas judges had decided, or the Fourteenth, as the Supreme Court had decided. Because the privacy right was so basic to a

democratic system of government, its defenders insisted that Blackmun had seen no need to tie it or the abortion right to a specific
amendment.

Beaten back by the fact that most Americans wanted to believe
in a right to privacy, antiabortionists argued that abortion was still not
about privacy. What possible comparison could be made, they asked,
between the right to use contraceptives and the right to abortion? The
former involved highly intimate relations between two persons, while
the latter involved a third party beyond the woman and the fetus,
namely, the physician who was expected to perform the abortion. In
Griswold Douglas had pointed out that no way, short of the government barging into people's bedrooms, existed to enforce a ban on
contraceptives, but *Roe*'s critics contended that government snooping
was not required to enforce a ban on abortion.

In voicing this criticism, the antiabortion forces touched a raw
nerve. From the day of the decision, pro-choice forces had worried
that it could be undone, and now their opponents seemed to have
found a loophole. Perhaps the decision, after all, should not have been
based on privacy. The fact that a physician and possibly a hospital
and its staff were intimately involved did perhaps remove abortion
from the realm of privacy.

The role of third parties in abortion was truly a troubling
problem since Catholic medical personnel and hospitals would find it
repugnant, even immoral, to participate in abortions. Did the decision
mean that third parties could be forced to perform abortions regardless of their personal beliefs, in order to protect a woman's right to
abortion?

Norman Dorsen, who had argued *Vuitch* in the Supreme Court
and supervised the preparation of the *Roe* brief, thought not. In one of
our conversations, he pointed out that despite the ruling, no physician
could be forced to do an abortion any more than he or she could be
forced to remove tonsils or a kidney against his professional judgment.
Beyond that, he said, a physician who had a religious conviction
opposed to abortion could not be compelled to violate his or her
conscience in this way. This makes the physician an uninvolved party
to abortion if he chooses to be.

The *Roe* critics' charge that enforcement of a ban on abortion
required no government snooping would prove to be an erroneous
assumption, as two events in 1986 demonstrated. In the first instance,

a woman was charged with murdering her own child, or rather her own fetus, which she had allegedly neglected in utero, thus causing its death within days of birth. The mother, a drug user, also had a bleeding problem and as a result had been advised to forgo sexual intercourse, an order she had disobeyed. Although the woman was found innocent, the case demonstrated how intrusive the government could become when intent on protecting potential, or fetal, life, and it raised many questions about how the state would protect fetal life.

For example, could a court order be obtained commanding a pregnant woman to eat a certain diet or submit to certain medical tests or even, as in the case of the woman charged, to abstain from marital relations? Who would monitor such orders? And what could happen to women who disobeyed? Would they be removed from their homes and put into halfway houses for rebellious pregnant women? How would the state know which women were likely suspects? Would women have to register all pregnancies? At what stage of pregnancy? And with whom?

The other event was the announcement in France of a new contraceptive, RU-486, which since it was designed to prevent implantation functioned as an abortifacient. (The Pill and the intra-uterine device [IUD] may or may not be abortifacients; no one knows for certain how they work.) RU-486 is taken by a woman in the privacy of her own home, either at a certain point in her menstrual cycle or whenever she has had unprotected intercourse. It eliminates the need to be concerned about third parties to abortion. RU-486 is clearly an advance in abortion technology, one that removes it once and for all from the public realm and puts the decision entirely in the woman's hands. It would make early abortion virtually impossible to police, at least without considerable and excessive intrusion from the government. Like the case of the woman charged with murdering a fetus, RU-486 seems to reinforce the wisdom of grounding the abortion right in privacy.

Pro-choice reformers were troubled by the decision's medical orientation. Noting that the "state has a legitimate interest in seeing to it that abortion, like any other medical procedure, is performed under circumstances that ensure maximum safety for the patient," the Court had ruled that states could restrict the abortion right throughout the entire second and third trimesters in order to protect the woman's health.

The reformers, who had invested so much in the idea of repeal, felt that the Court had made the doctor and the woman co-partners in the abortion decision and in doing so had given women something less than total control. Aware of physicians' roles in creating and prolonging the restrictive abortion laws, most pro-choice women had hoped that doctors would play no role in the abortion decision.

Apart from its stated intention of protecting public safety, a function that might better be undertaken by state legislators whose job was to write laws, the Court offered no explanation of its decision to permit doctors a role in the abortion decision. What, then, was the doctor's responsibility, not in the medical aspects of the abortion decision, but in its moral aspects? Was he, as opponents of legalization would claim, a third party to the abortion decision? If so, most reformers felt this was an unnecessary encroachment on the abortion right, one that made the *Roe* decision look as if the Court were conferring the abortion right on women with one hand while removing it from them with the other.

The idea of a doctor as a third party to abortion created several problems, the most perplexing of which was how much weight to assign to the doctor's opinion. Did his opinion matter as much as that of the woman who sought an abortion? More? Less? Reformers tried to figure out why the Court had decided the doctor should be the third party. Was it, as they suspected, because women could not be trusted to make the abortion decision on their own? If this were true, then the Court's ostensible reason for creating a medical role, to protect public health, was little more than a smoke screen, and women had won a very fragile right.

The Supreme Court does not explain itself beyond what it writes in a decision, and few clues exist regarding this strange medical orientation to what is essentially a legal question. The Court's conservatives may have had a subconscious or conscious desire to limit women's power over abortion, but evidence indicates that Blackmun's motivation was much simpler. As a result of his Mayo years, he was known to have great respect for the medical profession, as do most people. In constructing the opinion, Blackmun simply may not have been able to imagine (as indeed many people could not) that a medical procedure would not need medical input in the decision-making stage.

People had not yet begun to take any responsibility for their own health decisions.

Pro-choice reformers also overlooked their own role in inviting *Roe*'s medical orientation. Although they were angry over the role doctors had played in perpetuating the restrictive laws, they had nonetheless courted the physicians' support, and the *Roe* briefs were full of medical testimony supporting the abortion right. In addition, as noted earlier, the pro-choice movement had largely been responsible for the exaggerated concern over the physical dangers of illegal abortion. It is hardly surprising, therefore, that the Court should have reflected this same concern, and Blackmun indicated as much in the opinion. He created the doctors' role, at least in part, out of a perceived need to protect women from maiming and death at the hands of unskilled abortionists.

Evidence exists that Blackmun may not have intended to create as large a role for physicians as some people read into the decision. In the years afterward, he would through public statements and actions reveal himself to be a strong supporter of women's rights. And in further decisions on abortion, the Court invariably declined to expand the physicians' role in abortion.

The most unsettling problem with *Roe* in feminists' eyes was ironically the problem that had most perplexed the justices: the use of viability as the point at which the states could, if they chose to do so, begin to protect potential, or fetal, life. Feminist lawyer Rhonda Copelan compared viability in the *Roe* decision to the phrase "with all deliberate speed" in *Brown* v. *the Board of Education*, the 1954 desegregation decision. Both were, she felt, tacit expressions of compromise, a way of giving something to each side.

Certainly, viability was a puzzling standard. It had not been raised in any of the briefs or oral arguments and was, in the words of one Texas reporter, a "judicial originality." (There was also some speculation on why Blackmun had divided pregnancy into trimesters, but this could be easily explained: physicians had divided pregnancy into trimesters for years.)

Considerably more speculation arose over why Blackmun chose viability over quickening, the point at which a woman first felt movement, at around the fifth month of pregnancy. For centuries it had been a natural and legal dividing line in many societies. The common law eventually decreed that abortion was a misdemeanor (and later held it to be a felony) after quickening. Most courts through the late nineteenth century declined to find abortion a crime prior to quickening, and juries were notoriously reluctant to convict anyone of aborting an unquickened fetus. Historically, women have proven to be reluctant to abort a quickened fetus, however unwanted it may be. Norma McCorvey, for example, told her lawyers that once she felt movement, she was no longer willing to undergo an abortion.

Several physicians suggested to me that Blackmun used viability, the point around the seventh month of pregnancy at which a fetus could survive outside the womb, because it was the more modern, scientific measure. But viability presents several difficulties. For one thing, it is not upon close examination the scientific measure that it at first appears to be. Viability, doctors agree, is at best only a projection of when a fetus will be able to survive outside the womb. Survival is highly variable, however, from one fetus to another. One may survive at twenty-six weeks, while another born at the same stage of development has no chance to live.

Nor is viability, as historian Rosalind Petchesky has pointed out, a guarantee of normality. Of fetuses born between twenty-four and twenty-six weeks, not even the bottom line for viability, only 50 percent survive. Thirty percent of those who survive will be blind, and 20 to 30 percent will have severe learning disabilities.

The use of viability rather than quickening also appeared to have opened the door to the whole issue of fetal rights, something Blackmun may have done only inadvertently since in his opinion he had firmly rejected the notion that fetuses had any of the legal rights of personhood. As a conciliatory gesture, viability seemed inconsistent with the rest of the opinion.

Feminists felt that the injection of viability raised the question of whether women had really been granted an abortion right. If the woman's abortion right existed, why did it not exist throughout her pregnancy? Why arbitrarily draw the line at the point of viability?

Also unanswered by the opinion was what the states' interest in protecting potential life might be. Feminist theorists wondered, for example, why a state would need or want to protect potential life. Did the states' interest in potential life lie in a desire to create more soldiers or engineers? More men than women? More whites than blacks? Were these valid reasons? they wondered. Were there any valid reasons for the states to protect fetal life? A woman seeking to protect fetal life was one issue, and a highly understandable one at that, but the decision had found that it was the state, not the woman, that had an interest in protecting potential life during the third trimester.

Another issue was how far the states could go in protecting potential life. Could it, as some rabid antiabortionists hoped, take on the task of removing all unwanted fetuses from women's wombs and rearing them in laboratories? It was an undertaking that most scientists agreed was impossible. Artificial wombs sound like science fiction, and they probably are; few scientists believe they will ever exist. But perhaps the states would undertake the care of these protected fetuses once they were born? Would the states, which do not adequately care for those now under their care, be prepared to cope with this enormous additional economic burden?

If so, then the emotional toll of removing fetuses and babies from their natural parents to rear them in institutional environments must also be tallied. Experience has shown that children do not do well in institutional settings. Would we as a society really want to sever the unique parental bond in favor of a sterile, regimented institutional environment? One seriously doubts that the Court or anyone else was suggesting such a drastic rearrangement of society, but feminists point out that such speculation, however absurd, also demonstrates the weakness of establishing a state's interest in potential life.

If a state's intention was to protect potential life, then feminists could only ask why the line had been drawn at the third trimester. Why is a fetus any more valuable at twenty-two or twenty-eight weeks than it is at two or twelve?

But the biggest problem with viability, as far as the abortion right was concerned, was that it was soon (as the justices had feared) in a state of flux. At the time of the *Roe* decision, viability was put at the twenty-sixth to the twenty-eighth week of pregnancy. Since then medical science has pushed it back to the twenty-first or twenty-second week, a fact that has been the basis of several court challenges attempting to put further restraints on the abortion right.

What did shifting viability do to the abortion right? Was the woman's right to abortion fixed at the time of the *Roe* decision? Most constitutional scholars felt otherwise. They thought shifting viability encroached on the woman's right, a belief that was echoed in a 1983 dissenting opinion in *Akron* v. *Akron Center for Reproductive Health* in which Supreme Court Justice Sandra Day O'Connor declared that the *Roe* v. *Wade* framework was on a collision course with itself.

Most doctors say that viability will not be pushed back any further than it is now, but based on past experiences with medical advances, this is questionable. The idea of heart transplants seemed farfetched up until the moment they occurred, and medical attention is still riveted, as it should be, on the treatment of fetuses. So the question remains, What happens to the abortion right if, against all medical odds, viability is pushed back even further, say, into the first trimester? Should a right that the Supreme Court has held to be so basic to individual liberty be subject to the vagaries of technology?

Feminists have been hopeful but basically frustrated over the possibility of getting an additional court ruling that would more firmly establish the woman's right to abortion. While the antiabortionists have not changed public opinion or made substantial inroads against the legal protection offered in *Roe*, they have grown more vehement and insistent over the years, and a feeling has emerged among those who must be sensitive to political constituencies that they cannot be ignored. Even many important movement lawyers and reformers do not believe women have an unequivocal right to abortion at any stage of pregnancy.

As a result, many feminist historians and theorists have proposed the use of quickening rather than viability as a dividing line. They believe that even though it would shorten the period when women were at complete liberty to obtain abortions, it would at least safeguard the abortion right from further fluctuation. The abortion decision would, in other words, be safe from technology and politics. Quickening would also be a measure with which many women are comfortable.

The Supreme Court decision on abortion took effect immediately, leaving Texas and thirty other states with restrictive laws without any laws on abortion. Even the four so-called repeal states—New York, Washington, Hawaii, and Alaska—were not in complete compliance with the Court's ruling. The New York law came closest, except that it cut off women's right to abortion at twenty-four weeks, and the Court allowed unrestricted abortion until viability, which most physicians at that time put at twenty-six to twenty-eight weeks. In the states with reform laws similar to Georgia, the parts of those laws that limited abortion in the first two trimesters were invalidated, and other provisions that restricted women's access to abortion were struck down.

In the states with restrictive laws, some state legislatures went to work declaring the laws unconstitutional. Some attorneys general issued opinions rendering the laws unconstitutional, and several governors issued declarations that the laws could simply be ignored. Some states also announced they would take immediate action to rewrite their abortion laws, and as a result, within a week of the ruling Representative Bella Abzug of New York announced that she would introduce a bill in the House of Representatives forbidding any state to make any laws regarding abortion. (The bill was not enacted.)

Roe v. *Wade* brought to a halt all court cases on abortion. In criminal proceedings, a simple motion to dismiss the case was all that was required. Test cases, abortion rights lawyers advised, could be disposed of summarily. All state and federal courts were bound by the decision.

Caught off guard by the decision, the opposition took some time to respond. They vowed to overturn *Roe*, but aware that this was unlikely, they instead set to work creating a strategy for undermining it. Within a few weeks the opposition was ready to mount its counterattack. Their strategy consisted of three main parts. First they would work for a constitutional amendment declaring that fetuses were legal persons. They also planned to pressure the state legislatures to pass laws restricting abortion. Finally, they would seek legislative change on a national level, primarily by cutting off access to abortion funding.

As abortion became widely available, antiabortion forces stepped up their campaign of harassment, which was aimed at providers of abortion services, hospitals, and women who sought abortions. Hospitals were picketed and economic and political pressure was applied to hospital administrations to hinder the provision of abortion services. Women entering and exiting abortion clinics were harassed.

Antiabortion forces opened their own counseling services, where they often lured women who sought abortions under the false promise that they would help them obtain one. Once the women showed up, high-pressure tactics were applied to keep them there long enough to present the antiabortion side of the issue. Women underwent counseling that typically included false information about the safety of abortion, misleading information about fetal development, and photographs and films showing mishandled abortions and dismembered fetuses. Occasional reports filtered to the press about women being held against their will for several hours.

Attempts were even made at censorship. One of the more notable ones occurred in October 1973, when antiabortion forces succeeded in censoring an episode of the television program *Maude* that dealt with abortion. Pro-choice forces responded by boycotting the sponsors, who in their eyes had crumbled under pressure.

Within a few years of the decision, a new tactic, violence, was added to the roster of antiabortion strategies. In the fifteen years after the *Roe* decision, almost three hundred separate incidents of abortion-related violence occurred in the United States. Most involved bombings, but one abortion clinic director was kidnapped and held at gunpoint for several days.

Although other religious groups acted, the Catholic church hierarchy, as usual, spearheaded the antiabortion fight. Abortion was the leading topic at the annual bishops' meeting in the spring of 1973. The bishops made four recommendations for action to the National Catholic Conference. First, the Church would organize strong groups at the state levels "so that the machinery will be there when the states are called upon to ratify a constitutional amendment." Second, the dioceses would be called upon to help fund the antiabortion effort within the Church and to provide financial support to other ecumenical antiabortion groups. Third, the National Catholic Conference would assist the National Right to Life Association in any way it could. Finally, one day a month would be set aside in Catholic churches across the country for prayer and fasting "in reparation for the killing of innocent life."

A mail campaign organized shortly after the decision flooded the Supreme Court with mail. Mail from unhappy constituents was and is extremely rare at the Court—most Americans simply do not think to write the Court to express their dissatisfaction with a decision—but it was still several months before the justices realized that the mail was part of an organized effort.

A massive mail campaign directed at Congress was organized on Good Friday 1973, followed by another on Easter Sunday. On the Monday and Tuesday after Easter, legislators were swamped with letters. Senator Carl Curtis of Nebraska reported receiving 3,500 to 4,000 letters, and Senator Roman Hruska, also of Nebraska, said that staff members spent an entire day opening thousands of letters in his office.

A Catholic-sponsored Committee of Ten Million conducted a national campaign for a human rights amendment. People were encouraged to sign petitions, which they were told would be provided by their local churches. Eyewitnesses reported on a mass held in Michigan City, Indiana, on May 13, 1973: "As the people walked out of the church afterward, the people working for Right to Life were stationed at their respective tables taking people by the arm and leading them over to the petitions—even small children (seven and nine years of age) were permitted to sign the petition."

When legislatures seemed unresponsive to antiabortion demands, the opposition turned to a new tactic—constitutional amendments were proposed in Congress. In June 1973 the National Right to Life Committee issued a press release announcing its support for a constitutional amendment that would protect life from the moment of fertilization and ban abortifacient devices and medication. The latter was a somewhat oblique reference to the birth control pill, the IUD, and menstrual extraction, all of which the sexually conservative New Right hoped to ban.

Other proposals for constitutional amendments were introduced in Congress. Only two amendments attempted to authorize the states to regulate abortion; the remainder were attempts to confer personhood on the fetus. One resolution, drafted along the lines of Rehnquist's *Roe* dissent, proposed that abortion be made illegal since nothing in the Constitution supported legalized abortion. Senator James Buckley proposed a constitutional amendment that would protect unborn children at every stage of their development. Senator Jesse Helms introduced another constitutional amendment that would protect life from the moment of conception.

A House resolution attempted to guarantee life to the "unborn, ill, aged, and incapacitated." Several of the resolutions even went beyond the coverage provided by the Fifth and Fourteenth amendments in their attempts to prevent the deprivation of life. Some of the resolutions permitted abortion to save the mother's life, but many did not.

Regardless of the considerable effort that went into these resolutions, there was little chance that one would succeed. Despite sixteen months of hearings on the proposed constitutional amendment to confer personhood on fetuses, no action was ever taken.

The opposition fared little better with the states. A constitutional amendment could originate among the states if two-thirds of them voted to call a constitutional convention. In the mid-1980s, of the thirty-four states that would have to agree to call a constitutional convention, right-to-life forces were reported to have support among a majority of legislators in only nineteen states.

Attempts to encourage the states to pass antiabortion laws were more successful. Within six months of the decision, 188 antiabortion bills had been introduced in forty-one states, and several states had enacted laws that were clearly in conflict with *Roe*.

In the years immediately after the decision, attempts to limit funding for abortions met with the most success. In October 1973 Senator Helms tacked an amendment onto a foreign aid bill that banned the use of American foreign aid funds for abortions and abortifacient devices or drugs. The bill passed the Senate by a vote of 54–42.

Between 1977 and 1980 Congress was involved in an annual skirmish over the scope of the Hyde Amendment, introduced by Henry Hyde of Illinois, which limited the use of public funds for abortion. In 1977, for example, the proposal under which funds were to be withheld was very restrictive, with no exceptions for rape or incest. In 1978 and 1979 it was slightly more lenient, permitting public monies to be used for abortion when severe and long-lasting damage to the woman would result. In 1980 public monies could be used to pay for abortion only to save the mother's life and in cases of rape and incest.

In 1981, when President Ronald Reagan took office, antiabortionists believed they had helped to put a sympathetic figure in the White House. And although they had, the president offered little in the way of concrete help during the first six years of his presidency. Not until mid-1987 was Reagan moved to action. Right-to-lifers were invited to the White House for the first time during Reagan's presidency, and in the course of speaking to them the president proposed a new set of initiatives, one of which included a cut-off of funds to family planning clinics that provided abortion counseling and referrals. (Clinics had long since been prevented from using federal money to fund abortions for indigent women.) Writing in *The New Republic*, Fred Barnes pointed out that the initiatives seemed to signal a new antiabortion approach—one directed at convincing the American public that abortion was immoral in much the same way that smoking was unhealthy.

A series of skirmishes in the Supreme Court tested *Roe*'s strength. The Court heard eight abortion cases between 1976 and 1983 and two in 1985. For the most part, it stood behind the *Roe* decision, although many people thought the Court was chipping away at the concept that abortion was a fundamental right. One constitutional scholar, Robert Burt, writing in the *Supreme Court Review*, pointed out that in their post-*Roe* rulings, the Court had managed to reproduce "a rough facsimile of the wealth and race discriminations that held prior to *Roe*. Middle-class women can now obtain abortions in every state with greater convenience and easier consciences than was possible before *Roe*," while "other women are hampered in seeking abortions in the same ways that they were disadvantaged by the pre-*Roe* statutory restrictions."

In *Planned Parenthood of Central Missouri* v. *Danforth*, the Court voided a state law requiring a woman to obtain her husband's consent before undergoing an abortion. The opinion stated: "[I]deally the decision to terminate a pregnancy should be one concurred in by both the wife and her husband. . . . But it is difficult to believe that the goal of fostering mutuality and trust in a marriage . . . will be achieved by giving the husband a veto power." The Court also overruled a Missouri law requiring a woman under eighteen to obtain parental consent before an abortion. The justices seemed to be taking an opportunity to clarify their earlier thinking in *Roe* when they wrote: "Inasmuch as it is the woman who physically bears the child and who is the more directly and immediately affected by the pregnancy, as between [her and any other party], the balance weighs in her favor."

By the time *Danforth* was issued, however, the *Roe* majority on the Supreme Court had dwindled to five, and White wrote a dissent in which he, if possible, sounded even more wounded than in his *Roe* dissent: "A father's interest in having a child—perhaps his only child—may be unmatched by any other interest in his life. [It] it truly surprising that the majority finds in the [Constitution] a rule that the state must assign a greater value to a mother's decision to cut off a potential human life by abortion than to a father's decision to let it mature into a child."

Pro-choice forces counted the *Danforth* decision more a victory than a loss. They were displeased when the Court reiterated its belief that viability included indefinite artificial support for the fetus but were pleased to see the Court rule out third parties as participants in the abortion decision. The *Roe* decision had referred to viability as including artificial support, and pro-choicers had hoped they might get the Court to back off from this; they were disappointed when they were not able to do so. Also counted as a minor victory, though, was the Court's refusal to fix the time of viability at a specific week; it declined on grounds that this was a medical determination.

The issue of viability was also dealt with in two other cases, *Colautti v. Franklin* in 1979 and *Planned Parenthood of Kansas City* v. *Ashcroft* in 1983. In the former, the Court rejected on grounds of vagueness a Pennsylvania statute that required a physician to predict viability prior to doing an abortion and in his judgment, if viability was probable, to do everything in his power to protect the fetus's life. In the latter case, the Court upheld a Missouri state law requiring that a second physician be present at all postviable abortions.

The Court took longer to settle the issue of minors' rights because it was more complicated than spousal rights. On the one hand, the idea that parents were entitled to exercise a certain degree of control over their minor children was an accepted part of the privacy right. On the other, a minor child who was pregnant might be even more in need of an abortion than other women; she was younger and, some argued, had even more to lose from an early, ill-timed pregnancy, particularly since physicians agreed that pregnancy threatened the health of young teens. Obviously the Court needed to tread carefully with this issue. It heard two more cases on minors' rights before arriving at a standard by which it would measure whether or not the abortion right had been infringed upon. In 1979 in *Bellotti* v. *Baird*, the Court established a standard, ruling that the state could require minors to get their parents' consent but that it must also provide an alternate method for consent. Four years later, in *Kansas City* v. *Ashcroft*, the Court upheld a Missouri consent requirement on grounds that it provided for an acceptable alternate method.

As the states and even the federal government sought to deny women abortions by restricting their access to public funding with which to obtain them, the Court began to rule on this issue, too. A six-to-three majority voted in 1977 in *Maher* v. *Roe* to uphold a Connecticut regulation granting Medicaid benefits for childbirth while denying them for nontherapeutic abortion. Vowing that this was not a retreat from *Roe* v. *Wade*, Justice Powell, who wrote the opinion, declared that "*Roe* did not declare an unqualified 'constitutional right to an abortion.' . . . Rather, the right protects the woman from unduly burdensome interference with her freedom to decide whether to terminate her pregnancy. It implies no limitation on the authority of the state to make a value judgment favoring childbirth over abortion, and to implement that judgment with the allocation of public funds."

Justices Brennan, Marshall, and Blackmun dissented. Brennan wrote: "None can take seriously the Court's assurance that its 'conclusion signals no retreat from *Roe*.' . . . today's decision seriously erodes the principles that *Roe* and *Doe* announced to guide the determination of what 'constitutes an unconstitutional infringement of the fundamental right' . . . to decide whether to have an abortion." He continued: "A continued insensitivity to the plight of impoverished women is inherent in the Court's analysis. The stark reality for too many, not just 'some,' indigent pregnant women is that indigency makes access to competent, licensed physicians not merely 'difficult' but 'impossible.' As a practical matter, many indigent women will feel they have no choice but to carry their pregnancies to term because the state will pay for the associated medical services, even though they would have chosen to have abortions if the state had also provided funds for that procedure, or indeed, if the state had provided funds for no procedure."

Statistics supported the wisdom of Brennan's words. In New York, after abortion was legalized and public monies were used to provide abortion services to indigent women, the birth rate for welfare recipients dropped by 30 percent, and a fifteen-year rise in illegitimate births dropped by 12 percent and was eventually reversed.

Pro-choice forces suffered a more important loss three years later in 1980 in *Harris* v. *McRae* when the Court, by a five-to-four vote, upheld the Hyde Amendment prohibiting the use of federal funds for abortions.

In 1985, when two cases, *Diamond v. Charles* and *Thornburgh* v. *American College of Obstetricians and Gynecologists*, both challenges to the constitutionality of state laws that impeded women's access to abortion, came before the Court, Charles Fried, acting solicitor general of the United States, filed an amicus curiae brief with the Supreme Court. The brief was extraordinary in that it was one of the few times in American history when the solicitor general asked the Supreme Court to reconsider one of its own decisions. It was indicative of the extent to which a conservative presidential administration was willing to go to gather support from antiabortion forces. And in turn, the antiabortionists, unable to muster support among the general public, had at least garnered the attention of the politicians.

The opposition's attempts to undo *Roe*, most notably the court challenges, for the most part failed. Whatever its flaws, most experts considered *Roe* v. *Wade* to be a solid decision, one that would stand the test of time. Furthermore, every time the opposition mounted another unsuccessful challenge, *Roe* was strengthened as the body of precedent-setting cases supporting it grew.

The most important reason that the antiabortion forces were unsuccessful in their attempts to undo *Roe*, though, was that public opinion was not behind them. No consensus existed among the general public that abortion should be totally outlawed.

Immediately after the decision ASA and NARAL recognized that the war had not been won, as they had hoped it would be when an abortion case had been handed down. In response to the vociferous opposition, they had no choice but to gear up for a renewed battle. ASA Executive Director Jimmye Kimmey recalled that the group, which had no desire to become involved in provider services or to "stay in the abortion business just because we had learned how to raise money," would have folded sooner, but the opposition "heated up so much that we had to stay and fight the brush fires." ASA believed it had accomplished its primary goal in the Supreme Court decision, and it eventually disbanded in January 1977.

Designed by its founder Lawrence Lader to be a more activist organization than ASA, NARAL had no intention of stopping before the victory was total. When *Roe* was handed down, Lader realized he was in the midst of an escalating war. Within days of the decision, he mailed NARAL members a warning letter: "The fight is not over; it has just begun. Before the decision, it was waged in some individual states. The battleground has now widened to include all fifty states and the Congress of the United States."

Within a month NARAL had mapped out plans for a counter-attack. The group distributed copies of the opinion and urged its members to copy and mail it to members of the health and medical establishment, the clergy, the media, and legislators to promote their understanding of the decision. Hospitals in particular were resisting the implementation of *Roe*, and to countermand this, NARAL suggested that its members meet with hospital administrators to discuss the need to carry out the decision and even arrange for a test case to see whether hospitals were really acting in compliance with the ruling.

Regarding the attempts to pass a constitutional amendment, Lader wrote the NARAL membership: "We may well be able to keep these proposals bottled up in committee, but if fifteen or twenty states pass a resolution memorializing Congress to propose a constitutional amendment, pressure will build up to release them. You may be convinced that a constitutional amendment will never pass; I would remind you that in New York we also never believed that the Roman Catholic Church could persuade the legislature to repeal the 1970 law!" NARAL provided its members with strategies for combatting the stepped-up harassment that occurred after the opinion was handed down. Local NARAL chapters were urged to continue the fight even in the midst of what most thought was an overwhelming victory.

* * *

More than fifteen years after the decision, and some would say in spite of it, abortion remains a great unresolved issue in American society. It is an issue for which there is no solution that will satisfy both sides. Pro-choice forces are more vehement than ever about protecting the abortion right and antiabortionist forces are equally vehement about dismantling it, with some groups insisting they will settle for nothing less than having full personhood conferred on the fetus. Most would be pleased, however, to let the states settle the issue.

Antiabortionists seem oblivious to the fact that conferring personhood on fetuses would not resolve the issue. Society would still be required to balance the fetus's rights against those of the woman, and most courts have found that the woman's life is superior to potential life, at least in some circumstances. And even if abortion became illegal once again, society would still be faced with the problem of illegal abortion. Millions of women, upon finding themselves pregnant when they did not want to be, would obtain abortions regardless of whether they were legal. They risked their lives to do so in the past and would do so again if the need arose.

If the abortion issue cannot be resolved, is it possible that it can at least be settled? It can be; it has been. Although everyone has been slow to recognize it, the *Roe* decision did in fact settle the issue of abortion to the extent that it can be settled. It permitted individual choice, the only course open, Douglas wrote in his dissenting opinion in *Vuitch*, when an issue is so volatile: "It is resolved by the moral code which an individual has." Lost somewhere in the struggle over abortion is the fact that, in their wisdom, the justices wrote nothing in the *Roe* decision that compels a woman to undergo an abortion if she does not wish to do so.

The justices also left birth as the moment that confers legal personhood. In doing so they followed thousands of years of legal, medical, and moral precedent not only in our society, but in most societies now and throughout time. Birth is a dividing line that has not only endured, but appeals to philosophers and ethicists as well. It is also a clearer dividing line than quickening or viability or any other stage of fetal development. Christian-feminist ethicist Beverly Wildung Harrison has described birth as a sort of watershed, an incontrovertible "emergence of human life" that philosophers can agree to, although she reminds us that this does not mean that "fetal life in the late stages of gestation is not worthy of respect." Harrison wrote of birth: "A newborn, although not yet a person in any developmental sense of the term, has 'joined' our human society, and from that moment onward the quality of moral relations sets constraints for the person the infant may become."

Drawing the line at birth also resolves many of the problems associated with the abortion right since the *Roe* decision. It protects the woman from unwarranted government intrusion. It avoids issues that cannot be controlled, such as how the government would go about policing a pregnant woman's uterus. It protects the lives of the retarded in a way that using brain waves as a standard does not. It is a clear measure, one that will not be changed by technology. It does not rely on intellectual standards—consciousness, reasoning, the ability to communicate—that a living person who is seriously ill or comatose may lack, nor does it permit infanticide because a newborn infant is deformed.

Also lost in the post-decision struggle is the fact that the decision did give something to both sides. Women have a virtually unrestricted right to abortion up to the final trimester of pregnancy, at which point the states may intervene to protect potential human life. Both feminists and antiabortionists may have wanted more, but this part of the decision satisfies most Americans, whose views toward abortion are firmly planted in the middle of the road. Most Americans do not agree with antiabortion forces who want women to have no access to abortion, but neither do they agree with the pro-choice movement's claim that women should have totally unbridled access to abortion. Most important, most Americans, including sizable numbers of Catholics, believe that abortion should be a matter of individual choice.

That the *Roe* decision has managed to raise the hackles of both conservatives and liberals is probably to its credit, proof that it is not in any sense a radical decision. Its greatest strength—and ours—is its own centrist position.

Epilogue

The Supreme Court reportedly has received more mail—45,000 letters at last count—on the abortion decision than any case it had ever handed down. In a *New York Times Magazine* interview with John Jenkins, Blackmun said, "Think of any name; I've been called it in those letters: Butcher of Dachau, murderer, Pontius Pilate, Adolf Hitler." Much of the mail is rumored to be in Blackmun's office. Also rumored to have ended in the wake of the abortion decision was any semblance of friendship between Blackmun and Burger.

For years after the decision, when he spoke in public Blackmun was booed and picketed by antiabortionists. Threats were made against his life. However, in private and public conversations, most recently in a 1987 public television interview, he has stated that he still stands behind the abortion decision and in fact considers it essential to protect women's equality.

A few years ago, while speaking at a small southern college, Blackmun was startled when a woman in the audience ran down an aisle and onto the stage, whereupon she swept up Justice Blackmun in a bear hug and said: "I can never thank you enough for what you have done for women." The woman was Mary Doe.

Norma McCorvey still lives in Dallas. She has held many different jobs and as of this writing works as an apartment house manager. McCorvey was ambivalent for many years about revealing her role as Jane Roe, sometimes giving interviews, at other times declining to do so. In recent years she has given several interviews to popular magazines and has permitted photographs of herself.

She declined to be interviewed for this book unless she was paid. On September 9, 1987, seventeen years after she became the plaintiff in *Roe* v. *Wade*, Norma McCorvey revealed in an interview with columnist Carl Rowan that she had not, in fact, been raped.

Mary and John Doe became lawyers. They have two children, and they live and work in a southern city.

Linda Coffee still lives in Dallas and practices corporate law at the same law firm she joined after she finished law school. Her fight to protect women's abortion right did not end with *Roe* v. *Wade*. Shortly after the Supreme Court decision, she filed a class-action suit against a large metropolitan Dallas hospital that was not providing abortion services to all women who needed them.

Sarah Weddington also got a lot of vilifying hate mail. Most of it she threw away, but the more imaginative letters she kept. A popular public speaker, she, too, was booed and picketed for several years when she spoke in public.

While serving her third term in the Texas state legislature, she was offered and accepted a job as general counsel to the Department of Agriculture. She moved to Washington, D.C., in late 1978. When Midge Constanza, special assistant to the president on women's issues, left in a flurry of controversy after she found President Carter less supportive than he had pledged to be on women's rights, Weddington was chosen as her successor. She accepted, even though President Carter opposed using public monies to fund abortions. Antiabortion, pro-choice, and feminist groups opposed her appointment.

At the White House her résumé no longer mentioned that she had argued *Roe* v. *Wade*. It said only she had successfully argued a Supreme Court case. In a magazine interview given at that time, she said that she and the president had agreed to disagree on abortion (Carter opposed the public funding of abortions), noting that he had told her she must abide by his decision when she took the job, and she had agreed to do so. When Carter lost his bid for reelection, Weddington took a job in Washington as a lobbyist for the state of Texas. She left that job in 1986 and returned to Austin to work in her own law practice. She plans to run for office again when the time is right.

Roy Lucas no longer practices law. He sold maritime art for a while and as of this writing is an art student. He was divorced from Uta Landy, his first wife, married two more times, and is presently single.

Ron Weddington, who was divorced from Sarah Weddington, remarried. He still lives and practices law in Austin.

James Clark received a lot of hate mail while he was serving in the legislature. It died out when he returned to private life. He still lives in Dallas with his second wife, the former Carolyn Tobian, whom he met when they were both working in the reform movement.

Jimmye Kimmey, the executive director of ASA who organized the amicus curiae briefs, became an Episcopalian priest. She lives in New York City.

Only one of the early movers and shakers in the abortion movement has changed his mind about abortion. New York obstetrician Bernard Nathanson, an active participant in NOW and director of one of New York's biggest clinics after the repeal law passed, became a spokesperson for the antiabortionists in the early 1980s. In 1986 he was instrumental in the release and publicity of an inflammatory and misleading antiabortion film entitled *The Silent Scream*.

Virginia Whitehill and her small band of reformers who did so much to change women's lives disbanded their group shortly after the decision. They had finally wearied of the hate mail and the angry, anonymous phone calls. The women continue to work in many areas to improve women's lives but still do not call themselves feminists.

Addendum: As I was finishing this book, I received word that after fifteen years with no law on abortion, Texas had passed a law banning late-term abortions except to save the mother's life or health or where a fetus was known to have a "severe and irreversible abnormality." No exceptions were permitted for rape or incest.

The restrictive law was hailed by antiabortion forces as a first step in reversing "bad public policy." It was opposed by feminists and civil libertarian groups. Gara LaMarche, executive director of the Texas Civil Liberties Union, voiced opposition to the bill but acknowledged it might be "the least intrusive measure in terms of a woman's right to choose abortion that could possibly have been passed.

"We would like to believe and hope that it is the end of the road on abortion," he continued. "But we know that the right-to-lifers and people who believe that abortion is murder will be back every session from now on trying to get what they couldn't get this time.

"And we'll also be back," he promised.

Notes

A note may cover one or more paragraphs up to several pages on which a particular theme or topic is discussed. Directly quoted material is listed separately.

The following abbreviations have been used:

NYT   *The New York Times*
DMN   *Dallas Morning News*
DTH   *Dallas Times Herald*

References to "Weddington" always mean Sarah Weddington.

CHAPTER 1: A MEETING

DESCRIPTION OF INITIAL MEETING: Interviews, Linda Coffee, Sarah Weddington; Milbauer, pp. 12–13; Friendly and Elliott, p. 203.

MCCORVEY'S PREGNANCY: Milbauer, pp. 10–11.

MCCORVEY FINDS COFFEE "NICE": Milbauer, p. 12.

MCCORVEY'S REACTION TO WEDDINGTON: Milbauer, p. 13.

MCCORVEY'S LIFE WITH CARNIVAL: Bell, pp. 148, 150.

MCCORVEY'S RAPE: For various versions of the rape, see Bell, p. 150; Milbauer, pp. 7–9; Friendly and Elliott, p. 202; interviews, Coffee, Weddington, Virginia Whitehill.

CAUTIOUS HELP ON ABORTION: Kass, 9/27/71, p. 2A.

CHAPTER 2: FINDING JANE ROE

CONSIDERATION OF TRO: Interviews, Coffee, Weddington.

MCCORVEY'S BACKGROUND: Bell, pp. 78, 79, 148; Milbauer, p. 10; Friendly and Elliott, pp. 202–203.

"like a pool cue": Bell, p. 148.

"It seemed like there wasn't anything to live for": Bell, p. 79.

COFFEE AND WEDDINGTON MULL OVER HOW TO HANDLE RAPE: Interviews, Coffee, Weddington.

MCCORVEY'S MOTIVATION: Interviews, Coffee, Weddington; Friendly and Elliott, pp. 202–203; Bell, pp. 150–151.

STATISTICS ON PREGNANCY: Lader, p. 17; Gebhard *et al.*, pp. 137, 147.

CHAPTER 3: TWO WOMEN IN SEARCH OF A CASE

Simone de Beauvoir: *The Second Sex*, p. 21.

ROLE OF CONSCIOUSNESS-RAISING GROUPS: Shreve, 7/6/86, p. 14; Luker, pp. 100–101. Shreve suggests that consciousness raising arose in the mid-1960s when a group of leftist women met in Tampa, Florida, for "self-criticism" sessions. Redstockings, a radical feminist group, incorporated the process into its manifesto, and by 1972 it had been adapted by NOW, which spread its use to large numbers of women throughout the 1960s and 1970s. When I asked women how they became interested in the abortion issue, I was told repeatedly, "Through discussions at consciousness-raising groups."

COFFEE'S EDUCATIONAL BACKGROUND AND EARLY CAREER: Interview, Coffee.

WEDDINGTON'S EDUCATIONAL BACKGROUND AND EARLY CAREER: Interviews, S. Weddington, R. Weddington, Whitehill; *DMN*,

10/2/83, 1983, p. E4; Ivans, pp. 4–5; Griffith, 12/2/71, p. 1; Smith, pp. 6–7; Dudley, pp. 24–31.

PREGNANCY COUNSELING SERVICE: Lader, *Abortion II*, pp. 42–44, 48.

PILPEL TESTIMONY: Committee on Health and Codes, New York State Assembly, A.I. 2568, S.I. 1562, testimony of Harriet Pilpel, 2/3/67.

COFFEE'S AND WEDDINGTON'S SEARCH FOR A PLAINTIFF: Interviews, Coffee, Weddington.

MARY AND JOHN DOE: Interviews, Coffee, Weddington, Whitehill; *DTH*, 3/15/70, p. E9; *Roe v. Wade*, record and briefs, p. 4.

UNITARIAN WOMEN: Interviews, Coffee, Weddington, Ellen Kalina (Lewis), Pat Cookson, Doris Middleton.

CHAPTER 4: AWAKENING A NATION'S CONSCIENCE

ABORTION POLLS: Blake, pp. 541–548; Luker, p. 236; *DMN*, 6/20/70, p. 4AA; *Washington Post*, 1/25/73, p. A5.

FINKBINE'S BACKGROUND: *NYT*, 8/5/62, p. 64.

FINKBINE'S PHYSICIAN TALKS TO PRESS: *NYT*, 7/27/62, p. 12.

FINKBINE'S LEGAL PROCEEDINGS: *NYT*, 7/26/62, p. 25; 7/27/62, 20; 7/30/62, p. 21; 7/31/62, p. 9.

JUDGE MCFATE RULES ON FINKBINE CASE: *NYT*, 7/31/62, p. 9.

BRITISH PARLIAMENT REFUSES TO ACT ON THALIDOMIDE BABIES: *NYT*, 7/25/62, p. 22.

AMERICANS AT RISK OVER THALIDOMIDE: *NYT*, 7/28/62, p. 20; 7/31/62, p. 9.

FIRST REPORTS OF THALIDOMIDE DEATHS: *NYT*, 7/26/62, p. 25.

RELIGION BECOMES AN ISSUE: *NYT*, 8/4/62, p. 20; Lader, *Abortion II*, p. 43.

SEVENTH-DAY ADVENTISTS REBUKE BOSTON BISHOP: *NYT*, 8/4/62, p. 20.

FINKBINES PLAN TO GO TO SWEDEN: *NYT*, 8/5/62, p. 65.

FINKBINE TELEVISION INTERVIEW: *NYT*, 8/5/62, p. 64.

REPORTS OF DANGERS OF PILL: *NYT*, 8/7/62, p. 15.

PRESIDENT KENNEDY'S PRESS CONFERENCE: *NYT*, 8/2/62, p. 8.

FINKBINE SUBJECT TO "PENETRATING INVESTIGATION": *NYT*, 8/7/62, p. 15.

FINKBINE OBTAINS ABORTION IN SWEDEN: *NYT*, 8/7/62, p. 15; 8/8/62, p. 19; 8/10/62, p. 6; 8/18/62, p. 7; 8/20/62, p. 9.

BELGIAN INFANTICIDE TRIAL: *NYT*, 8/8/62, p. 19; 11/6/62, p. 35; 11/7/62, p. 41; 11/8/62, p. 47; 11/9/62, p. 72.

HISTORY OF ABORTION PRACTICES: Devereux, p. 47; Degler, pp. 235–236.

HISTORY OF ABORTION LAWS: *Roe* v. *Wade*, record and briefs, appellant's brief, pp. 22–35; Means, "The Law of New York . . . ," pp. 411–515; Mohr, chaps. 2, 3, 4, 5, 6; Sarvis and Rodman, chap. 3; Luker, chaps. 2, 3, 4; Lader, *Abortion*, pp. 82, 85, chap. 9.

"PLASTICITY AND VARIABILITY" OF ABORTION BEHAVIOR: Devereux, p. 3.

PASSAGE OF RESTRICTIVE ABORTION LAWS IN U.S.: Mohr, chap. 8; Means, pp. 411–515.

THERAPEUTIC EXCEPTION: *Roe* v. *Wade*, brief, record and briefs, appellant's brief, pp. 35–38; Means, pp. 411–515; Mohr, pp. 27, 29–30, 38, 129, 186–87, 205–06, 211, 214.

MME. RESTELL: Mohr, pp. 48–50, 199.

E. P. CHRISTIAN ADDRESS: Mohr, p. 173.

GEORGE H. NAPHEY ON ABORTION: Mohr, p. 173.

COMMONWEALTH v. *BANGS*: 9 Massachusetts 387 (1812).

NEW YORK CASE: *People* v. *McGonegal* (1892).

MASSACHUSETTS CASE: *Commonwealth* v. *Taylor* (1882).

WOMEN LOSE IMMUNITY: Mohr, pp. 227–28.

PREGNANCY BECOMES SAFER: Luker, pp. 54–55.

GROWING TENSIONS BETWEEN PROTESTANT AND ROMAN CATHOLIC PHYSICIANS: Luker, pp. 44–45, 77–78.

THERAPEUTIC ABORTION COMMITTEES: Luker, pp. 56–57.

GERMAN MEASLES BIRTH DEFECTS: Lewis and Hellman, eds., *Williams' Obstetrics*, p. 786.

POLL ON FINKBINE APPROVAL: Luker, p. 82.

CALIFORNIA MEDICAL ASSOCIATION VOTES FOR REFORM: *San Francisco Chronicle*, 6/4/66, p. 11.

SAN FRANCISCO DOCTORS RAIDED: Lader, *Abortion II*, pp. 67–68; *San Francisco Chronicle*, 5/17/66, pp. 1, 17; 5/18/66, pp. 1, 11; 5/21/66, pp. 1, 12; 6/4/66, pp. 1, 11.

CALIFORNIA STATE MEDICAL BOARD ANNOUNCES CHARGES: *NYT*, 6/19/66, p. 20; *San Francisco Chronicle*, 5/17/66, pp. 1, 17; 5/18/66, pp. 1, 11.

DRS. SHIVELY AND SMITH DEFENDED BY COLLEAGUES: *NYT*, 6/19/66, p. 20; *San Francisco Chronicle*, 5/21/66, p. 12.

BEILENSON'S REFORM ACTIVITIES: Lader, *Abortion II*, pp. 68–70; Luker, pp. 70–72, 92–93.

CHAPTER 5: SUING THE STATE

"flophouses for hippies": Friendly and Elliott, p. 204.

HISTORY OF TEXAS ABORTION LAW: *Roe* v. *Wade*, record and briefs, jurisdictional statement, 4–5; Milbauer, pp. 14–15.

LEGAL RESEARCH: Interviews, Coffee, Norman Dorsen, Weddington.

WATSON v. *THE STATE OF TEXAS*: 9 Texas A 237 (1880); Milbauer, pp. 15–16.

BACKGROUND ON *GRISWOLD* v. *CONNECTICUT*: Interviews, Coffee, Dorsen, Lawrence Lader, Cyril Means, Harriet Pilpel, R. Weddington, S. Weddington; Friendly and Elliott, pp. 90–98; Emerson, pp. 219–34.

PRIVACY RIGHT: Interviews, Coffee, Dorsen, Robert Flowers, Roy Lucas, Means, Pilpel, John Tolle, R. Weddington, S. Weddington; *Poe* v. *Ulllman*, Douglas, dissenting, pp. 509–21; *Griswold* v. *Connecticut*, majority opinion, pp. 480–86; McKay, pp. 259–282; Sutherland, pp. 283–88.

GRISWOLD AS FORERUNNER TO *ROE*: Emerson, pp. 219–234.

BRANDEIS DISSENT: *Olmstead* v. *U.S.* 277 U.S. 438 (1928), p. 478; Schwartz, *Unpublished Opinions of the Warren Court*, pp. 227–230.

Brandeis first wrote about a privacy right in an article, "The Right to Privacy," 4 *Harvard Law Review*, 193 (1890). Pilpel and others recall that the use of the privacy right in connection with birth control and family law can be traced back to an American Civil Liberties brief written by Melvin Wulf for *Griswold*. In his *Griswold* dissent, Douglas obviously relied on the thinking enunciated in the brief.

CONSIDERING AN ARRAY OF GROUNDS: Lucas, pp. 730–778; *Griswold* v. *Connecticut*, majority opinion, pp. 482–86; *Griswold* v. *Connecticut*, Goldberg, concurring opinion, pp. 486–98; Sarvis and Rodman, p. 57; Emerson, pp. 221–23; Dixon, pp. 197–218; Kauper, pp. 235–58; interviews, Bruner, Coffee, Dorsen, Lader, Lucas, Means, Roy Merrill, Joseph Nellis, Pilpel, R. Weddington, S. Weddington.

BELOUS CASE: *People* v. *Belous*, 80 Ca. Rtr. 354, 458 2d 194, pp. 195–196; Lader, *Abortion II*, pp. 72–74, 109, 111; Luker, p. 134; *Los Angeles Times*, 9/27/68, p. 4; interviews, Bruner, Coffee, Dorsen, Flowers, Lucas, Means, Merrill, Pilpel, Tolle, R. Weddington, S. Weddington.

BELOUS DECISION (QUOTES): 80 Cal. Rtr., p. 203.

REACTION TO *BELOUS* DECISION: Interviews, Bruner, Coffee, Lader, Lucas, Means, Merrill, Pilpel, R. Weddington, S. Weddington.

VUITCH CASE: *U.S.* v. *Vuitch*, 402 US 61 (1971); 305 Fed. Supp. 1032 (D.D.C., 1969); Luker, p. 134; interviews, Bruner, Coffee, Dorsen, Lader, Lucas, Merrill, Nellis, Pilpel, Tolle, R. Weddington, S. Weddington.

"no clear standard": Lader, *Abortion II*, p. 15.

COFFEE'S AND WEDDINGTON'S ANALYSIS OF FETAL RIGHTS: Interviews, Coffee, Dorsen, Lucas, Means, Pilpel.

DISCRIMINATION AGAINST WOMEN: Interviews, Coffee, Weddington.

THREE-JUDGE COURTS: Stern and Gressman, pp. 72–73, 92–93; Peltason, p. 109.

FIFTH CIRCUIT: Peltason, p. 109; interviews, Bruner, Coffee, Lucas, Merrill, Weddington.

DALLAS TIMES HERALD BREAKS STORY OF CASE: interview, Coffee.

DALLAS TIMES HERALD EDITORIAL: 3/3/70, p. 8.

CHAPTER 6: THE STATE RESPONDS

General Note: The material on the legal proceedings was drawn from the record and briefs.

WADE BACKGROUND: West, pp. 108–112, 179, 1181–83; *DMN*, 12/30/86, pp. 1A, 5A; interviews, Bruner, Coffee, James Clark, Merrill, R. Weddington, S. Weddington, Whitehill.

ILLEGAL ABORTION DEATH RATE: Dunnigan, 11/15/70, p. 1C.

DISTRICT ATTORNEY'S REACTION TO SUIT: Interview, Tolle.

TOLLE'S STRATEGY AND PREPARATION: Interviews, Bruner, Coffee, Tolle.

HALLFORD'S BACKGROUND AND ROLE AS INTERVENOR: *Roe* v. *Wade*, record and briefs, jurisdictional statement, pp. 7–9, 22, 24; interviews, Coffee, Flowers, Merrill, Tolle, Weddington.

JANE DOE'S AFFIDAVIT: record and briefs, pp. 56–58; interviews, Coffee, Weddington.

REQUEST FOR JURY TRIAL: Interview, Tolle.

CHAPTER 7: REFORM, DALLAS STYLE

ABORTION REFORM IN TEXAS: Except where otherwise noted, the material in this chapter was obtained through interviews with the following persons: Virginia Whitehill, Doris Middleton, Ruth Bowers, Ellen Kalina (Lewis), Linda Coffee, Sarah Weddington, Carolyn Tobian (Clark), James Clark.

UNITARIANS ON ABORTION REFORM: Lader, *Abortion*, p. 100; *The Bridge*, December 1969, p. 12; *The Bridge*, Winter 1969, p. 69.

FEMINISTS' VS. BIRTH CONTROLLERS' VIEWS ON ABORTION: Gordon, pp. 341–42, 352, 391–92, 396; Planned Parenthood memo, 4/15/71, p. 1.

BETTY FRIEDAN'S BOOK: *The Feminine Mystique*.

DALLAS COMMITTEE TO STUDY ABORTION: The name of the Dallas abortion-reform group went through several incarnations, mostly based on the women's desire to portray themselves as a nonradical, educational group. Originally organized as the Dallas Committee to

Study Abortion, in May 1971 they became the Abortion Education Committee; in March 1972 this was changed to Texas Citizens for Abortion Education. Later (I was unable to pinpoint an exact date but estimate it was late 1972 or early 1973), after the opposition began to appropriate motherhood and other family values as their cause, the Dallas Committee renamed itself Texans for Motherhood by Choice. For simplicity's sake, I refer to the group as the Dallas Committee.

DALLAS COMMITTEE'S BUDGET: Treasurer's report. Dallas Abortion Education Committee, 1/5/70, Whitehill's personal papers.

EARLY LEGISLATIVE EFFORTS: *DMN*, 6/20/70, p. 4AA; 11/15/70, p. 29A; *Houston Post*, 9/30/70, p. 1A; 9/28/70, p. 3A; *Dallas Committee Newsletter*, 12/15/70, Whitehill's personal papers.

ALI LAW: *Model Penal Code*, American Law Institute, Philadelphia, 1962, pp. 189–90; Lader, *Abortion II*, p. 57; Dunnigan, 11/16/70, p. 12A; Luker, pp. 65, 68–69, 278 fn.; Sarvis and Rodman, pp. 40–41; *Dallas Committee Newsletter*, 12/5/70.

CLARK'S BACKGROUND: Clark biography, Clark's personal papers, undated but c. 1969; Kass, 9/28/70, p. 3A.

DOROTHY KENYON CRITICIZES ACLU: Letter, Dorothy Kenyon to American Civil Liberties Committee, 2/21/67, Dorsen's personal papers.

DISSENT AMONG REFORM GROUPS: Interviews, Lader, Lucas, Means, Pilpel, S. Weddington, Whitehill.

DALLAS COMMITTEE'S FIRST PUBLIC MEETING: DCSA Organization Report, 2/11/70, submitted by Pat White, Whitehill's personal papers.

POSTOPERATIVE COMPLICATIONS: Lader, *Abortion*, p. 21.

JAPAN AND EASTERN EUROPEAN COUNTRIES: Lader, *Abortion*, p. 73.

DALLAS COMMITTEE DEBATE ON REPEAL vs. REFORM: Newsletter, 12/15/70; interviews, Whitehill, Kalina (Lewis).

ABORTION IN REFORM STATES: Sarvis and Rodman, p. 40; *NYT*, 6/28/72, p. 21C; *DTH*, 4/22/70, p. C5; Kass, 9/29/70, p. 3A, 5; "A Suggested Abortion Law for Texas," Austin Women's Liberation Group, Whitehill's personal papers.

PRICE OF ILLEGAL ABORTIONS: "Suggested Abortion Law"; anonymous interviews with women who underwent illegal abortions in 1960s.

"rich ladies' laws": "Suggested Abortion Law."

GUARANTEE TO NEW YORK PHYSICIANS: Dallas Committee, "Abortion by Choice," undated flier, Whitehill's personal papers; Connor, p. 1.

CLARK'S SUPPORT OF REPEAL: *DMN*, 5/20/70, p. A3.

DALLAS COMMITTEE'S SUMMER READING LIST: Unpublished notes, Dallas Committee, summer 1970, Whitehill's personal papers.

DALLAS COMMITTEE'S FIRST FLIER: Letter to committee members, 5/4/70, Whitehill's personal papers.

CHAIN LETTER: Undated letter to committee members, Whitehill's personal papers.

DALLAS COMMITTEE'S EARLY PAMPHLETS AND FLIERS: "Abortion by Choice," "Motherhood by Choice," "Facts about Abortion," "History of Abortion Laws," undated fliers, Whitehill's personal papers.

PLANNED PARENTHOOD'S ACTIVITIES IN POPULATION CONTROL: In 1961 Planned Parenthood organized a new division called Planned Parenthood, World Population, whose goal was to take family planning to overpopulated, mostly Third World nations. The activities of this subgroup dominated the Planned Parenthood organization throughout much of the 1960s and 1970s. See Gordon, p. 397.

NEWSLETTER AND PACKET OF INFORMATION: Undated fliers, Whitehill's personal papers; "When Should Abortion Be Legal?" ASA Public Affairs pamphlet no. 429; "Abortion," reprint from *Scientific American*, January 1969.

ECUMENICAL DIALOGUE ON ABORTION: "Ecumenical Dialogue on Abortion" program, 5/19/70; *Highland Park Presbyterian Church Bulletin*, 6/5/70; *DMN*, 5/20/70, p. 3A.

REV. PAUL SCHOTT: Interview, Whitehill.

REV. CLAUDE EVANS: *DMN*, 11/17/70, p. 4A; *DTH*, 4/14/70, pp. A15, 17; interview, Whitehill.

CHAPTER 8: THE DALLAS HEARING

General Note: Material in this chapter, including direct quotations from the hearing, was drawn from the record and briefs, "Transcript of Oral Argument Before Statutory Three-Judge United States District Court for Northern District of Texas," filed 7/30/70, pp. 75–100; *DMN*, 5/23/70, p. 18A.

FIFTH CIRCUIT BACKGROUND: Read and McGough, pp. 24–26.

JUDGE WILLIAM TAYLOR: *DMN*, 6/19/85, pp. 1, 13, and 17A; interviews, Bruner, Coffee, Irving Goldberg, Merrill, Tolle, R. Weddington, S. Weddington.

JUDGE SARAH HUGHES: *DMN*, 4/25/85, pp. 1, 2, 20A; *Houston Post*, 4/25/85, p. 14A; interviews, Coffee, Louise Raggio, Whitehill.

JUDGE IRVING GOLDBERG: Interviews, Bruner, Coffee, Goldberg, Merrill, R. Weddington, S. Weddington; Read and McGough, pp. 180–81.

COFFEE DURING HEARING: Interviews, Bruner, Coffee, Flowers, Kalina (Lewis), R. Weddington, S. Weddington, Whitehill.

STANLEY v. *GEORGIA*: 394 U.S. 557 (1969).

WEDDINGTON DURING HEARING: Interviews, Bruner, Coffee, Kalina (Lewis), Merrill, R. Weddington, S. Weddington, Whitehill.

FRED BRUNER DURING HEARING: Interviews, Bruner, Coffee, Merrill.

BACKGROUND ON ATTORNEY GENERAL'S OFFICE: Interviews, Robert Flowers.

FLOYD DURING HEARING: Interviews, Coffee, Weddington, Whitehill.

JOHN TOLLE DURING HEARING: Interviews, Bruner, Coffee, Merrill, Tolle, S. Weddington, R. Weddington.

U.S. v. *LIVINGSTON* (both quotations): 179 F. Supp. 9, pp. 12–13.

FETUS NOT LEGALLY A PERSON IN TEXAS: *DTH*, 5/22/70, p. A2.

NO FETAL DEATH CERTIFICATE IN TEXAS: Kass, 9/30/70, p. 1A.

NO TORT RECOVERY FOR FETUS: *Roe* v. *Wade*, record and briefs, appellant's brief, pp. 120–121; *DTH*, 5/22/70, p. A1; Means, "Phoenix," pp. 337–340.

KEELER v. *SUPERIOR COURT*: 2 Cal. 3d 619, 470 2d 662, 87 Cal. Rtr. 481 (1970).

FETAL DEVELOPMENT: Collins, p. 217; Harrison, pp. 205–208, 213, 217; Levine, "Blinding Us . . . ," 7/16/85, p. 23; *Newsweek*, 1/14/85, p. 27; 3/25/85, p. 23.

"uneasy tenant": Levine, "Blinding Us . . . ," 7/16/85, p. 23.

ANALOGY OF FETUS TO BABY: Harrison, pp. 205–208; interview, Amy Fremion.

CHAPTER 9: THE DALLAS DECISION

General Note: Material in this chapter was drawn from *Roe* v. *Wade*, Opinion of the District Court, record and briefs, pp. 11–112.

RELEASE OF DECISION: Interview, Gilbert Ganasheau, Fifth Circuit Clerk, New Orleans.

"on the merits . . . Texas abortion law . . . declared unconstitutional": *Roe* v. *Wade*, opinion of the district court, p. 116.

"fundamental right of a woman": *People* v. *Belous*, 80 Cal. Rptr., p. 194.

RIGHT TO ABORTION NOT "UNFETTERED": *Roe* v. *Wade*, Opinion of the District Court, p. 120.

BAIRD v. *EISENSTADT*: 401 US 934 (1971).

ATTORNEY GENERAL'S VIEW OF DECISION: Interview, Flowers.

RUMORS REGARDING DECISION: Interviews, Bruner, Coffee, Flowers, Goldberg, Merrill, Tolle, Weddington.

JUDGES' DELIBERATIONS: Bruner, Coffee, Goldberg, Merrill, Weddington, *DMN*, 6/19/70, pp. A14, 20.

RELIANCE ON NINTH AMENDMENT: *DMN*, 6/19/70, p. A14, p. 20; Emerson, p. 227; Tribe, p. 99; Redlich, pp. 20–34; interview, Rhonda Copelan.

BABBITZ CASE: *Babbitz* v. *McCann*, 310 F. Supp. 293; 320 F. Supp. 219; *NYT*, 3/15/70, p. 69.

LUCAS ON NINTH AMENDMENT: Lucas, p. 755, fn 99.

HISTORY OF FOURTEENTH AMENDMENT: Dorsen, *Frontiers of Civil*

Liberties, pp. 291–92; Ely, pp. 926–945; Emerson, pp. 224–25; Gelinas, pp. 628–46; Grey, pp. 703–718; Law, pp. 981–1,041; Silverstein, pp. 37–40; interviews, Copelan, Dorsen, Sylvia Law, Means, Pilpel.

LOCHNER v. *NEW YORK*: 198 U.S. 45 (1905).

HOLMES'S *LOCHNER* DISSENT (QUOTE): *Ibid.*, p. 76.

"Out of the language": Tribe, p. 64.

SUPREME COURT DELIBERATIONS ON *GRISWOLD*: Schwartz, *Super Chief*, p. 577–78.

"uncommonly silly": *Griswold* v. *Connecticut*, 381 U.S. 479, Stewart dissent, p. 527.

"the protection of the Bill of Rights": Brennan, concurrence, *Lamont* v. *Postmaster General*, 381 U.S. 301 (1965), p. 308.

"Specific guarantee in the Bill of Rights": *Griswold*, p. 484; Dixon, pp. 197–218; Kauper, pp. 235–58.

"We do not sit as a superlegislature": *Griswold*, p. 482.

HARLAN'S CONCURRENCE IN *GRISWOLD*: Pp. 499–502.

GOLDBERG'S CONCURRENCE IN *GRISWOLD*: Pp. 486–99.

"The essence of the interest": *Roe* v. *Wade*, 410 U.S. 113 Opinion, p. 116.

"How likely must death be?": *Roe* v. *Wade*, 410 U.S. 113 Opinion, p. 121.

"the door is not open": *Porter* v. *Kimzey*, 309 F. Supp 993 (1970), p. 995.

CHAPTER 10: THE APPEALS

General Note: Material for this chapter was drawn from interviews with Bruner, Coffee, Flowers, Lucas, Tolle, Weddington, and the record and briefs.

"Apparently we're still free to try them": *DMN*, 6/19/70, pp. 2D, 14A.

DISTRICT ATTORNEY'S GUIDELINES ON ABORTION LAW ENFORCE-MENT: Record and briefs, appendix B, testimony of Paul C. Mac-Donald, p. B8–9.

DOES' NEWSPAPER INTERVIEW: *DTH*, 3/15/70, p. E9.

APPEALS PROCESS: Stern and Gressman, pp. 24, 93, 98, 504–7; Read and McGough, p. 185.

JAMES MADISON LAW INSTITUTE: Interviews, Copelan, Dorsen, Lucas, Means, Nellis.

LUCAS'S BACKGROUND: Interviews, Coffee, Copelan, Lader, Lucas, Jimmye Kimmey, Means, Nellis, Pilpel, R. Weddington, S. Weddington, Pat Windle; Clark, pp. 1–11.

"God, the Supreme Court of the United States": Friendly and Elliott, p. 204.

SUPREME COURT DECISION TO TAKE *ROE*: Interview, Dorsen; Stern and Gressman, pp. 25, 375, 382–83, 458, 504–9.

BLACKMUN'S BACKGROUND: Blackmun Senate hearings, pp. 12–15; Dorsen, "A Change in Judicial Philosophy," p. 1; Jenkins, pp. 20–24, 26, 28, 29, 57, 61, 66.

CHAPTER 11: THE OPPOSITION

CATHOLIC VIEWS ON ABORTION: Blake, pp. 541–57; Sarvis and Rodman, pp. 10–11; Sanders, p. 26; *NYT*, 10/27/71, p. 1.

KINSEY ON ABORTION: Sarvis and Rodman, p. 4.

CLARK ON FAILURE TO PASS REFORM BILL: *DMN*, 6/20/70, p. 4AA; Kass, 9/30/70, p. 1A.

HAWAIIAN ABORTION REFORM: *NYT*, 3/17/70, p. 18; "Profile," NARAL, p. 3.

NEW YORK REPEAL: Sanders, pp. 26–27.

TEXAS CATHOLIC CONFERENCE ON DECISION: *DMN*, 7/2/70, p. A3.

CATHOLIC WOMEN RESPOND TO DECISION: *DTH*, 6/18/70, p. A2.

AMERICAN COUNCIL OF MEDICAL AND SOCIAL EDUCATION: *DTH*, 8/31/70, p. A12.

SONS OF THUNDER: *DMN*, 6/8/70, p. 3A.

VATICAN II AND DECLINE OF CATHOLIC POWER: Miller, p. 8; Roddy, pp. 21–25; Dunnigan, p. 3C.

TYDINGS BILL: Miller, p. 8. The bill was introduced by Senator Joseph Tydings, who had served on the White House Commission on Population Growth and the American Future.

ROMAN CATHOLIC CAMPAIGN AGAINST ABORTION: Sanders, pp. 26–27; Lader, *Abortion II*, p. 72; *NYT*, 4/25/71, p. 32; Miller, p. 8.

RIGHT-TO-LIFE MEETING AT BARAT COLLEGE: "Profile," p. 1.

GENERAL TACTICS OF CATHOLIC CHURCH: "Profile," pp. 1–4; Sanders, p. 4; Lader, *Abortion II*, p. 74; King, pp. 37–38.

TARGETING PRO-CHOICE CANDIDATES: Miller, p. 8; "Profile," p. 1; Merton, pp. 63–66.

LOBBYING BY CATHOLIC CHURCH: "Profile," pp. 1–4; NARAL, "Report from the Iowa Association for Medical Control of Abortion," undated flier, c. 1971; Lader, *Abortion II*, p. 43; Sanders, p. 26.

CHURCH'S EFFORTS IN CALIFORNIA POLITICAL CAMPAIGN: King, p. 37.

WASHINGTON STATE CAMPAIGN: "Profile," p. 1; *NYT*, 3/17/72, p. 18; Lader, *Abortion II*, pp. 70–72, 161–66; *Seattle Post Intelligencer*, 12/2/70, p. 4; 12/11/70, p. 7; letters, Thomas A. Connolly, archbishop of Seattle, to diocesan priests, 3/30/70, 4/14/70.

RESENTMENT OF CATHOLIC CHURCH: *Argus* (Washington), 9/11/70, p. 3; *Tappenish Review* (Washington), 9/3/70, p. 2.

NARAL BULLETIN ON ORGANIZATION: "Profile," pp. 1–4.

CATHOLICS FOR ABORTION REPEAL: "Profile," p. 4; Lader, *Abortion II*, p. 190.

CATHOLICS FOR INDIVIDUAL RESPONSIBILITY CONCERNING ABORTION (QUOTE): "Profile," p. 4.

REACTION OF PROTESTANTS: Kass, pp. 1, 3; "Profile," p. 4.

PROFESSOR ROBERT BYRN'S SUIT: Interview, Copelan; Lader, *Abortion II*, p. 163; Merton, pp. 67–68.

CHAPTER 12: RENEWED VIGOR

FEMINIST INVOLVEMENT: Interviews, Whitehill, Copelan, Law, Lader; Sarvis and Rodman, p. 10; Clapp, pp. 1–4; Lader, *Abortion II*, pp. 80–81; *Abortion Rap*, pp. 96–100.

"We had to have support of mass feminist involvement": Lader, *Abortion II*, p. 80.

"a real southern belle": Interview, Kalina (Lewis). Other Dallas reformers also described Weddington as a "lady" or "ladylike," and they were not the only ones to see her in this light. Molly Ivans, writing in the *Texas Observer* (p. 4), described her as follows: "She is, to use an old-fashioned term frowned on by women's lib, a lady, a perfect lady. She is grave, graceful, and composed."

DALLAS REFORMERS MEET WEDDINGTON: Interviews, Kalina (Lewis), Whitehill.

DALLAS REFORMERS TAKE POSITION ON REPEAL: *DMN*, 10/8/70, p. 1C.

CONTACT WITH NARAL: Interviews, Whitehill, Lader; letter, 8/19/70, from Mary Anne Press, administrative assistant, NARAL, to Pat White, Whitehill's personal papers.

PROTESTANTS TAKE STAND ON ABORTION: *DTH*, 4/24/70, p. 1; 6/3/71, p. 1; 6/19/70, p. 3; *DMN*, 5/23/70, p. 5AA; 6/21/70, p. 3AA; 11/17/70, p. 1C; *Texas Baptist Convention Bulletin*, 11/6/69.

CLAUDE EVANS: Letter, 5/22/73, Whitehill to Bowers, Whitehill's personal papers; *The Daily Campus*, 5/1/70, p. 7; Dunnigan, p. 1C; Mann, p. A15; *DTH*, 4/24/70, p. A1; 8/10/70, p. A1.

"If my daughter found herself pregnant": *Daily Campus*, p. 7.

DALLAS COMMITTEE ENDORSEMENTS: *DMN*, 2/12/71, p. 3C; "Facts About Abortion."

TMA STUDY AND RECOMMENDATION ON ABORTION: Texas Medical Association Report of Special Committee on Abortion Laws in Texas, no date; *DMN*, 5/9/71, p. 1A.

CLARK LOBBIES DOCTORS: TMA report.

DALLAS COMMITTEE LOBBIES DOCTORS: Interviews, Whitehill, Kalina (Lewis), Middleton; letter, Dallas Committee to Dr. Hugh Savage, Whitehill's personal papers, 1/27/70.

DALLAS COMMITTEE LOBBIES TEXAS LEGISLATORS: Interviews, Whitehill, Weddington, Kalina (Lewis), Middleton; *DMN*, 3/11/71, p. 1A; *Daily Texan*, 1/13/71, p. 5; "Capitol Capsule," newsletter, Senator Tom Creighton, 3/19/71, p. 1.

MEETING WITH RUTH BOWERS: Interviews, Whitehill, Kalina (Lewis), Middleton.

BOWERS'S HELP: Interviews, Weddington, Whitehill, Coffee, Kalina (Lewis), Middleton.

DALLAS COMMITTEE REFORM ACTIVITIES, 1970–71: NARAL executive director's report, 6/6/73; Dallas Committee, minutes of 6/24/70 meeting; Dunnigan, p. 29A.

DALLAS COMMITTEE RELATIONS WITH TAC: Minutes, TAC Steering Committee meeting, 12/2/70, 12/12/70; report, Debbie Leonard to Dallas Committee, 12/18/70; report, Evelyn Sell to Dallas Committee, 12/19/70; TAC Steering Committee report, 12/19/70; letter, Miriam Kass to Whitehill, 12/24/70; minutes, TAC Steering Committee report, 12/19/70.

SCHISMS ON THE PERSONAL LEVEL: Letter, Linda Dunson to Whitehill, 1/15/71, Whitehill's personal papers.

"WOMEN'S LIBERATION: A SOCIALIST APPROACH": Campaign flyer, Austin, 1971.

REPEAL BILL INTRODUCED IN TEXAS LEGISLATURE: *DMN*, 3/11/71, p. 1A; 3/14/71, p. 32A; 4/14/71, p. 19A; 5/9/71, p. 21A.

DALLAS WOMEN ORCHESTRATE FLOOR HEARING: Interviews, Whitehill, Weddington, Kalina (Lewis), Tobian (Clark); Texas Legislature abortion hearing agenda, 3/29/71.

LAMM COUNSELS DALLAS WOMEN: Letter (undated), Lamm to Whitehill, c. March 1971.

CHAPTER 13: PREPARING FOR THE HIGH COURT

COST OF ROE: Budget, James Madison Law Institute, January 1971.

ASA SUPPORT OF *ROE*: Interviews, Kimmey, Means, Pilpel, Weddington.

LUCAS AND NARAL: Interviews, Lucas, Means, Lader, Margery Pitts Hames, Windle, Weddington; minutes, NARAL annual meeting, 10/3/71.

WEDDINGTON AT JAMES MADISON LAW INSTITUTE: Interviews, R. Weddington, S. Weddington, Pilpel, Lucas, Coffee.

"an excellent pinch hitter": Dudley, p. 27.

PREPARATION OF THE BRIEF: Interviews, R. Weddington, S. Weddington, Lucas, Means, Hames; Stern and Gressman, p. 717.

"The shaping of the facts": Lewis, p. 53.

LUCAS'S AND WEDDINGTON'S DEALINGS WITH THE SUPREME COURT: *Roe* v. *Wade* file, National Archives, letter, Court to Lucas, 5/4/71; letter, Lucas to Court, 7/20/71; letter, S. Weddington to Court, 9/30/71; letter, Lucas to Court, 10/7/71; letters, Court to Weddington, 7/20/71, 12/7/71; *Daily Texan*, 12/2/71, p. 1.

"The sheer volume": *Roe* v. *Wade* file, National Archives, letter, Lucas to Court, 7/20/71.

ASA ON AMICUS BRIEFS: Interview, Kimmey.

TEXAS PREPARATION FOR SUPREME COURT: Interview, Flowers; *Roe* v. *Wade* file, National Archives, letter, Floyd to Court, 8/23/71; letter, Floyd to Court, 9/10/71; letter, Court to Floyd, 9/14/71; letter, Floyd to Court, 11/30/71.

"Dear Joe, Of course I consent": Letter, Dorsen to Joseph Witherspoon, 8/14/71, Dorsen's personal papers.

CHAPTER 14: LADIES' DAY AT COURT

General Note: Material for this chapter was drawn from an interview with Sarah Weddington; a taped transcript of the oral argument, National Archives; and a written transcript of the oral arguments, Supreme Court Library.

LUCAS TRIES TO ARGUE *ROE*: Interviews, Coffee, Hames, Lucas, Kimmey, Means, R. Weddington, S. Weddington; *Roe* v. *Wade* file, National Archives, letter, Lucas to Court, 11/18/71; Coffee to Court, 11/24/71; letter, Weddington to Court, 11/29/71; Supreme Court memorandum, 11/29/71; letter, Court to Weddington, 11/30/71.

LUCAS AND *VUITCH* CASE: Interviews, Dorsen, Hames, Lucas, Means, Nellis.

MOOT COURTS: Interviews, Hames, Means, Nellis, Pilpel, Weddington.

"Of course, I remember the majesty": Sweeney, p. B9.

WHITEHILL AND BOWERS ATTEND ORAL ARGUMENT: Interviews, Whitehill, Bowers.

WEDDINGTON DESCRIBED AS SECRETARY: Interview, Whitehill.

"We all knew something important": Interview, Kimmey.

ORAL ARGUMENTS: *Washington Post*, 12/14/71, p. A2; *NYT*, 12/14/71, p. A21; Sweeney, p. B15; Woodward and Armstrong, pp. 165–67.

CHAPTER 15: WAITING

ABELE v. *MARKLE*: 452 F. 2d 1124.

"obstacles to the exercise of individual freedom": *NYT*, 3/17/72, pp. 1, 18.

"This calls for a strong voice": *NYT*, 4/14/72, p. 42.

NUMBERS OF NEW YORK ABORTIONS: *DMN*, 4/14/71, p. 23.

"They even advertise"; *Ibid*, p. 23.

"I'm concerned about diluting": *Ibid*, p. 23.

"From personal and religious beliefs": *NYT*, 4/14/71, p. 28.

DONOVON-CRAWFORD BILL: Lader, *Abortion II*, p. 198; *NYT*, 4/18/72, p. 43; 4/19/72, p. 94; 4/25/72, p. 40; *Village Voice*, 4/27/72, p. 27.

"box score of deaths": *Greenbush* (New Jersey) *Area News*, 4/13/72, in Lader, *Abortion II*, p. 196.

RIGHT-TO-LIFE SUNDAY: Lader, *Abortion II*, p. 198.

"The busloads unloaded": Lader, *Abortion II*, p. 200.

ANTIABORTION LANGUAGE: Interview, Kimmey; Sanders, pp. 26–28.

NIXON'S LETTER TO CARDINAL COOKE: Lader, *Abortion II*, p. 202; *NYT*, 5/5/72, p. 29.

RESPONSE TO LETTER: Lader, *Abortion II*, p. 203; *NYT*, 5/9/72, pp. 1, 26.

"President Nixon's dismaying interference": *NYT*, 5/8/72, p. 36.

"sloppy staff work": Lader, *Abortion II*, p. 203.

"I do not believe it is right": *NYT*, 5/13/72, p. 1.

WHITEHILL LETTER: Whitehill to Weddington and Bowers, 4/22/72.

"an awful lot of money": Letter, Whitehill to Bowers, 4/1/72.

KALINA'S DISMAY OVER REFORM MOVEMENT: Letter, Kalina (Lewis) to Whitehill, 4/13/72.

PAT WHITE DROPS OUT: Letter, White to Whitehill, 9/22/72.

WHITEHILL ON HER TRAVELS: Letter, Whitehill to Bowers and Weddington, 4/22/72.

"Things are rather slow": Letter, MORAL to Whitehill, 4/30/72, Whitehill's personal papers.

DIFFICULTY GETTING MAILINGS OUT: Letter, Whitehill to Bowers, 6/25/73, Whitehill's personal papers.

CHAPTER 16: DELIBERATIONS

MISASSIGNMENT OF ABORTION CASE: Urofsky, pp. 180–81; *Washington Post*, 7/4/72, p. 1; *NYT*, 7/5/71, p. 27; *Time*, 2/5/73, p. 51; Woodward and Armstrong, pp. 169, 170–75; *New York Times Magazine*, 2/20/83, pp. 26, 28.

BLACKMUN AND BURGER'S TIES: Jenkins, pp. 22, 28–29; Woodward and Armstrong, p. 87; Totenberg, pp. 1, 18.

BLACKMUN'S AND BURGER'S VOTING PATTERN: "The Supreme Court, 1970 Term," *Harvard Law Review*, p. 35.

BLACKMUN WORKS OF DRAFT OF OPINION: Woodward and Armstrong, pp. 180–83; Jenkins, 2/20/83, p. 20.

"Isn't it true that restrictive abortion laws": Merton, p. 74.

"Even India is so empty": Merton, p. 82.

"The changes in the body": *Roe* v. *Wade*, record and briefs, appellee's brief, p. 41.

"The new body not only exists": *Ibid.*, p. 38.

"Every child shows a distinct individuality": *Ibid.*, p. 44.

"The concept of an artificial placenta": *Ibid.*, p. 53.

FIRST DRAFT OF *ROE* OPINION: Urofsky, pp. 182–183; Woodward and Armstrong, pp. 183–85; *Time*, 2/5/73, p. 51.

JUSTICES VOTE TO HOLD OVER CASE: Urofsky, pp. 182–183; Woodward and Armstrong, pp. 186, 192; *Time*, 2/5/73, p. 51.

DOUGLAS THREATENS DISSENT OVER DELAY: Urofsky, pp. 184–186; Woodward and Armstrong, pp. 186–89; *Time*, 2/5/73, p. 51; *NYT*, 7/5/71, p. 27.

LUCAS'S LETTER ASKING TO ARGUE CASE: Interviews, Lucas, Weddington, Whitehill.

CHAPTER 17: REARGUMENT

POWELL AND REHNQUIST AS NEW JUSTICES: *NYT*, 12/14/71, p. 12; *New York Daily News*, 8/4/86, p. 4; *Time*, 6/30/86, pp. 27–28; Woodward and Armstrong, pp. 161–63, 231; interviews, Coffee, Hames, Weddington, Whitehill.

TEXAS ATTORNEY GENERAL AT REARGUMENT: Interview, Flowers.

WEDDINGTON AT REARGUMENT: *Washington Post*, 10/12/72, p. 2; interviews, Coffee, Hames, R. Weddington, S. Weddington.

FLOWERS AT REARGUMENT: *Ibid.*; interview, Flowers.

MICHIGAN ABORTION REFERENDUM: Sanders, p. 26.

"At first the fear was a creeping force": Sanders, p. 26.

CHAPTER 18: THE SUPREME COURT DECISION

MEANS'S INFLUENCE ON OPINION: Means, "Law of New York," pp. 411–515; "Phoenix," pp. 335–410; interview, Means.

PRESS RUMORS OVER DECISION: *Washington Post*, 7/4/72, p. 1; *NYT*, 7/5/72, p. 27.

JUSTICES READ DRAFT OF OPINION: Woodward and Armstrong, pp. 236–37.

POWELL JOINS OPINION: Woodward and Armstrong, p. 231.

"inevitably in trying to please eight editors": Lewis, p. 183.

DELAY OF DECISION: *Time*, 2/5/73, pp. 50–51.

"We forthwith acknowledge": *Roe* v. *Wade*, opinion, p. 116.

"Never display agony": Jenkins, p. 26.

"the normal 266-day period": *Roe* v. *Wade*, opinion, p. 125.

"doubtful that abortion was ever established": *Roe* v. *Wade*, opinion, p. 136.

"The right of privacy . . . is broad enough": *Roe* v. *Wade*, opinion, p. 153.

"The pregnant woman cannot be isolated": *Roe* v. *Wade*, opinion, p. 159.

"logically, of course, a legitimate state interest": *Roe* v. *Wade*, opinion, p. 150.

"We need not resolve": *Roe* v. *Wade*, opinion, p. 159.

"I'd had it done to me": Blackmun, television interview with Bill Moyers, PBS, 1987.

"an improvident and extravagant exercise": *Roe* v. *Wade*, opinion, White, dissenting, p. 222.

"Plainly, the Court today rejects": *Roe* v. *Wade*, opinion, Burger, concurring, p. 208.

STEWART EXPLAINS CONCURRENCE: Friendly and Elliott, p. 206, f.n.

CHAPTER 19: REACTION

WEDDINGTON AND COFFEE LEARN OF DECISION: Interviews, Weddington, Coffee.

MCCORVEY LEARNS OF DECISION: Friendly and Elliott, p. 207.

"came like a thunderbolt": Interview, Lader.

"It scaled the whole mountain": Interview, Pilpel.

"Reaching deeper and deeper": Lee Giddings, NARAL executive director's report, 2/5/73.

"Nothing in the Court's approach": *NYT*, 1/24/73, p. 40.

"greatest slaughter of innocent life": Sanders, p. 26.

"fetal muggers": *Ibid.*, p. 27.

"Were I a legislator": Ely, p. 926.

"So stringent that a desire": *Ibid.*, p. 935.

"whether antiabortion legislation cramps the style": *Ibid.*, p. 924.

"from the totality of the constitutional scheme": *Poe* v. *Ullman*, 367 U.S. 497, Douglas, dissenting, p. 521.

GREY'S CRITICISM: Grey, p. 709.

"state has a legitimate interest": *Roe* v. *Wade*, opinion, p. 50.

VIABILITY VS. QUICKENING AS A STANDARD: Interview, Copelan; Rosalind Petchesky, speech, Mid-Atlantic Women's Seminar on Abortion, University of Pennsylvania, December 1985.

AKRON v. *AKRON CENTER FOR REPRODUCTIVE HEALTH*: 462 U.S. 416 (1983).

NATIONAL CATHOLIC CONFERENCE RECOMMENDATIONS: NARAL, executive director's reports, 3/26/73, p. 2; 6/6/73, p. 4.

MAIL CAMPAIGNS: *Ibid.*, 6/6/73, p. 4.

"As the people walked out of the church": *Ibid.*, 6/6/73, p. 4.

REAGAN ADMINISTRATION GUIDELINES: Barnes, pp. 16–19.

"a rough facsimile": Burt, pp. 372–73.

"Ideally, the decision to terminate a pregnancy": *Planned Parenthood of Central Missouri* v. *Danforth*, 428 U.S. 52 (1976), p. 52.

"Inasmuch as it is the woman": *Ibid.*, p. 52.

"a father's interest in having a child": *Ibid.*, p. 93.

"*Roe* did not declare": *Maher* v. *Roe*, 432 U.S. 464 (1977), pp. 473–474.

"None can take seriously": *Ibid.*, Brennan, dissenting, p. 483.

HARRIS v. *MCRAE*: 448 U.S. 297 (1980).

"stay in the abortion business": Interview, Kimmey.

"The fight is not over": Lader, memo to NARAL members, 1/24/73.

"We may well be able": Lader, memo to NARAL members, 4/5/73.

"It is resolved by the moral code": *Vuitch*, Douglas, dissenting, p. 80.

"A newborn, although not yet a person": Harrison, p. 220.

EPILOGUE

MCCORVEY CONFESSES SHE WAS NOT RAPED: *NYT*, 9/9/87, p. 23; *Newsday*, 9/9/87, p. 7.

WEDDINGTON AT WHITE HOUSE: Weinraub, pp. 36–37; Sweeney, p. B8.

"We would like to believe": *DMN*, 5/31/87, pp. 41A, 42A.

Selected
Bibliography

Association for the Study of Abortion. "When Should Abortion Be Legal?"
Public Affairs Pamphlet No. 429, undated.

Association of American Law Schools Committee on Supreme Court
Decision. Report prepared by Professor Newton Pacht, Howard
University School of Law, 1971.

Austin Women's Liberation Group. "A Suggested Abortion Law for Texas,"
flier, 1970.

Barnes, Fred. "Reagan's Full-Court Press." *New Republic*. June 10, 1987.

Beauvoir, Simone de. *The Second Sex*. New York: Knopf, 1953.

Bell, Joseph. "A Landmark Decision." *Good Housekeeping* 176 (June 1973).

Blackmun Senate Hearings, 1970. Testimony of Richard Kliendienst, Deputy
Attorney General.

Blake, Judith. "Abortion and Public Opinion, The 1960–1970 Decade."
Science 171 (February 1971).

The Bridge. "Abortion Laws: A Progress Report." Winter 1969.

Burns, Robert E. "The Examined Life." *U.S. Catholic*, July 1972.

Burt, Robert. "The Constitution of the Family." *Supreme Court Review*, 1979.

Calderone, Mary S., ed. *Abortion in the United States*. New York: Paul B.
Hoeber, 1958.

Callahan, Daniel. *Abortion: Law, Choice, and Morality*. New York: Macmillan,
1970.

Cisler, Lucinda. "Unfinished Business: Birth Control and Women's Liberation," in *Sisterhood Is Powerful*, edited by Robin Morgan. New York:
Vintage, 1970.

Clapp, James. "Abortion Legislation in New York State: What Really
Happened, and What Can be Learned from It." New Yorkers for
Abortion Law Repeal, flier, 1970.

354

Clark, Tom C. "Religion, Morality, and Abortion: A Constitutional Appraisal," *Loyola University Law Review* 2 (1961).

Civil Liberties. "New Threats: Saving Abortion." September 1973.

Collins, Anne. *The Big Evasion: Abortion, the Issue That Won't Go Away.* Toronto: Lester & Orpen Dennys, 1985.

Committee on Health and Codes, New York State Assembly, A.I. 2568, S.I. 1562. *An Act to Amend the Public Health Law in Relation to Therapeutic Abortion.* Testimony of Harriet Pilpel. February 1967.

Connor, Michael. "Moonlighting Medics: Liberal Abortion Law Proves to Be a Bonanza for New York Doctors. *Wall Street Journal*, June 6, 1971.

Copelan, Rhonda. "Toward Rethinking *Roe* v. *Wade*." Unpublished paper, presented at the Mid-Atlantic Women's Seminar on Abortion, University of Pennsylvania, December 1985.

Dallas Committee Publications and Papers:
"Abortion by Choice," mimeographed flier, undated.
"Motherhood by Choice," mimeographed flier, undated.
Treasurer's Report, 1/5/70.
Organization Report, 2/11/70.
Newsletter, 12/15/70.
"Facts About Abortion," mimeographed flier, 1971.
"History of Abortion Laws," mimeographed flier, undated.
Texas Legislature Abortion Hearing Agenda, unpublished paper, March 1971.

Degler, Carl N. *At Odds: Women and the Family in America from the Revolution to the Present.* New York: Oxford University Press, 1980.

Devereux, George. *A Study of Abortion in Primitive Societies.* New York: International Universities Press, 1955.

Dixon, Robert G., Jr. "The Griswold Penumbra: Constitutional Charter for an Expanded Law of Privacy." *Michigan Law Review* 64 (December 1985).

Dorsen, Norman. "A Change in Judicial Philosophy?" *National Law Journal*, February 1985.

———. Introduction to *Frontiers of Civil Liberties*. New York: Pantheon, 1984.

Drinan, Robert F. "The State of the Abortion Question." *Commonweal*, April 17, 1970.

Dudley, Mary. "The Odyssey of Sarah Weddington." *Texas Woman* 1 (November 1979).

Dunnigan, Carolyn. "Abortion Dilemma." *Dallas Morning News*, November 11, 16, 17, 1970.

Eastman, Nicholson, and Louis Hellman, eds. *Williams' Obstetrics*, 12th ed. New York: Appleton-Century-Crofts, 1961.

Ely, John Hart. "The Wages of Crying Wolf: A Comment on *Roe* v. *Wade*." *Yale Law Journal* 82 (April–July 1973).

Emerson, Thomas M. "Nine Justices in Search of a Doctrine." *Michigan Law Review* 64 (December 1965).

Feldman, David M. *Marital Relations, Birth Control, and Abortion in Jewish Law*. New York: Schocken, 1968.

Friedan, Betty. *The Feminine Mystique*. New York: Norton, 1963.

———. *The Second Stage*. New York: Summit, 1981.

Friendly, Fred W., and Martha J. H. Elliott. *The Constitution: That Delicate Balance*. New York: Random House, 1984.

Gebhard, Paul et al. *Pregnancy, Birth, and Abortion*. New York: Harper & Row, 1958.

Gelinas, Alexis A. J. "*Roe* v. *Wade* and *Doe* v. *Bolton*: The Compelling State Interest in Substantive Due Process." *Washington and Lee Law Review* 30 (Fall 1983).

Gordon, Linda. *Woman's Body, Woman's Right: A Social History of Birth Control in America*. New York: Grossman, 1976.

Graham, Fred P. "The Court: Are the Justices Losing Their Cool?" *New York Times*, April 11, 1971.

Grey, Thomas. "Do We Have an Unwritten Constitution?" *Stanford Law Review* 27 (February 1975).

Griffith, Dotty. "Woman Lawyer Outspoken." *The Daily Texan*, December 12, 1971.

Guttmacher, Alan F., ed. *The Case for Legalized Abortion Now*. Berkeley, Ca.: Diablo, 1967.

Hall, Robert E., ed. *Abortion in a Changing World*. New York: Columbia University Press, 1970.

Harrison, Beverly Wildung. *Our Right to Choose: Toward a New Ethic of Abortion*. Boston: Beacon Press, 1983.

Harvard Law Review. "The Supreme Court, 1970 Term." November 1971.

Hentoff, Nat. "How Can the Left Be Against Life?" *Village Voice*, July 16, 1985.

Ivans, Molly. "This Right of Privacy." *The Texas Observer* 65 (February 16, 1973).

Jenkins, John A. "A Candid Talk with Justice Blackmun." *The New York Times Magazine*, February 20, 1983.

Kass, Miriam. "Abortion," Parts 1–6. *Houston Post*, September 27, 28, 29, 30, 1970; October 1, 2, 1970.

Kauper, Paul G. "Penumbras, Peripheries, Emanations, Things Fundamental and Things Forgotten: The Griswold Case." *Michigan Law Review* 64 (December 1965).

Kennedy, Florynce, and Diane Scudder. *Abortion Rap*. New York: McGraw-Hill, 1971.

King, Lawrence T. "GOP and God." *Commonweal*, October 9, 1970.

Lader, Lawrence. *Abortion*. Indianapolis: Bobbs-Merrill, 1966.

———. *Abortion II: Making the Revolution*. Boston: Beacon Press, 1973.

———. "The New Abortion Laws: A Discussion of the Ethical and Medical Considerations That Underlie." *Parents Magazine*, April 1968.

Lamm, Richard. "Abortion: A Case Study in Legislative Reform," in *The Patient Earth*. New Haven, Conn.: Yale University Press, 1975.

Lamm, Richard, and Steve Davison. "Abortion Reform." *Yale Review of Law and Social Action* 55 (1971).

Law, Sylvia. "Rethinking Sex and the Constitution." *University of Pennsylvania Law Review* 132 (1984).

Levine, Judith. "Abortion: Where We Are Now." *Village Voice*, July 16, 1985.

———. "Blinding Us with Science." *Village Voice*, July 16, 1985.

Lewis, Anthony. *Gideon's Trumpet*. New York: Random House, 1964.

Lucas, Roy. "Federal Constitutional Limitations on the Enforcement and Administration of State Abortion Laws." *North Carolina Law Review* 46 (June 1968).

Luker, Kristin. *Abortion & the Politics of Motherhood*. Berkeley, Ca.: University of California Press, 1984.

McDonnell, Kathleen. *Not an Easy Choice: A Feminist Re-examination of Abortion*. Boston: South End Press, 1984.

McKay, Robert B. "The Right of Privacy: Emanations and Intimations." *Michigan Law Review* 64 (December 1965).

Mann, Martha. "Face in the Crowd: Rev. Evans." *Dallas Times Herald*, April 14, 1970.

Means, Cyril. "The Law of New York Concerning Abortion and the State of the Foetus, 1664–1968: A Case of Cessation of Constitutionality." *New York Law Forum* 14 (Fall 1968).

———. "The Phoenix of Abortional Freedom: Is a Penumbral or Ninth Amendment Right About to Arise from the Nineteenth-Century Legislative Ashes of a Fourteenth-Century Common Law Liberty?" *New York Forum* 17 (Fall 1971).

Merton, Andrew. *Enemies of Choice: The Right-to-Life Movement and Its Threat to Abortion*. Boston: Beacon Press, 1981.

Milbauer, Barbara, in collaboration with Bert N. Obrentz. *The Law Giveth . . . . : Legal Aspects of Abortion*. New York: Atheneum, 1983.

Miller, Norman C. "Opposition to Birth Control Wanes." *Wall Street Journal*, August 14, 1970.

Mohr, James C. *Abortion in America: The Origins and Evolution of National Policy, 1800–1900*. New York: Oxford University Press, 1978.

National Abortion Repeal Action League (NARAL):
    Annual Meeting Minutes, October 3–4, 1971
    Executive Director's Reports
        October 20–21, 1973
        November 21–22, 1973
        February 5, 1973
        March 26, 1973
        June 6, 1973
    Memos to members
        January 24, 1973
        April 5, 1973
        July 23, 1973
        October 3, 1973
    Opinion and Summary re U.S. Supreme Court Decision, February 1973
    "Profile of the Opposition," undated flier, c. 1973.
    Report from the Iowa Association for Medical Control of Abortion, undated flier, c. 1971.

National Archives:
    Roe v. *Wade* file
    Roe v. *Wade* taped transcript of Supreme Court Oral Argument
    U.S. v. *Vuitch* taped transcript of Supreme Court Oral Argument

Newsweek
    "America's Abortion Dilemma," January 14, 1985.
    "The Medical Quandry," January 14, 1985.
    Report on abortion conference sponsored by Kennedy Foundation, September 18, 1967.

New York City Health Services Administration Report, February 20, 1972.

Noonan, John T. "An Almost Absolute Value in History," in *The Morality of Abortion*, ed. by John T. Noonan. Cambridge, Mass.: Harvard University Press, 1970.

O'Meara, Joseph. "Abortion: The Court Decides a Non-Case," in *The Supreme Court Review*. Chicago: University of Chicago Press, 1974.

Patterson, Bennett B. *The Forgotten Ninth Amendment: A Call for Legislative and Judicial Recognition of Rights under Social Conditions of Today*. Indianapolis: Bobbs-Merrill, 1955.

Peltason, Jack. *Fifty-Eight Lonely Men: Southern Federal Judges and School Desegregation*. New York: Harcourt Brace & World, 1965.

Petchesky, Rosalind. Speech, Mid-Atlantic Women's Seminar on Abortion, University of Pennsylvania, December 1985.

———. *Abortion and Woman's Choice: The State, Sexuality, and Reproductive Freedom*. Boston: Northeastern University Press, 1985.

Pilpel, Harriet. *The Abortion Crisis* 6 (1969).

———. "Abortion U.S.A.—1966–1967: The Legal Aspects," unpublished paper.

Planned Parenthood. Memo, Assistant Regional Director Richard Ferguson to membership, April 15, 1967.

Prosser, William Lloyd, and John W. Wade. *Cases and Materials on Torts*, 5th ed. Mineola, N.Y.: Foundation Press, 1971.

Read, Frank T., and Lucy S. McGough. *Let Them Be Judged: The Judicial Integration of the South*, Metuchen, N.J.: Scarecrow Press, 1978.

Rebone, Joseph W. "Personhood and the Contraceptive Right." *Indiana Law Journal* 57(4):1982.

Redlich, Norman D. "Are There 'Certain Rights' . . . Retained by the People?" *New York University Law Review* 787 (1962).

Report of the Commission on Population Growth and the American Future, 1972.

Roddy, Joseph. "The Power and the Glory Are Passing," *Look* 35 (October 1971).

Roemer, Ruth. "Abortion Law: The Approaches of Different Nations." *American Journal of Public Health* 57 (November 1967).

Sanders, Marion K. "Enemies of Abortion." *Harper's*, March 1974.

Sarvis, Betty, and Hyman Rodman. *The Abortion Controversy*, 2d ed. New York: Columbia University Press, 1974.

Schwartz, Bernard. *Super Chief: Earl Warren and His Supreme Court—A Judicial Biography*. New York: New York University Press, 1983.

———. *The Unpublished Opinions of the Warren Court*. New York: Oxford University Press, 1985.

Scialabba, George. "The Trouble with *Roe* v. *Wade*." *Village Voice*, July 16, 1985.

Shreve, Anita. "*The Group*, 12 Years Later." *The New York Times Magazine*, July 6, 1986.

Silverstein, Elliott. "From Comstockery through Population Control: The Inevitability of Balancing." *North Central Law Review* 6 (Fall 1974).

Smith, Jan. "Carter's Assistant Talks About Texas." *Townes Hall Notes: A Magazine for the Alumni of the University of Texas Law School*, Fall 1978.

Stern, Robert L., and Eugene Gressman. *Supreme Court Practice*, 5th ed. Washington, D.C.: Bureau of National Affairs, 1978.

Sutherland, Arthur E. "Privacy in Connecticut." *Michigan Law Review* 64 (December 1965).

Sweardon, Anne. "High Profile: Sarah Weddington." *Dallas Morning News*, October 2, 1983.

Sweeney, Louise. "Sarah Weddington: Spokeswoman at the White House." *The Christian Science Monitor*, May 4, 1979.

Texas Abortion Coalition:
> Minutes, Steering Committee Meeting, December 2, 1970.
> Minutes, Steering Committee Meeting, December 12, 1970.
> Report, Debbie Leonard to Dallas Committee, December 18, 1970.
> Report, Evelyn Sell to Dallas Committee, December 19, 1970.
> Steering Committee Report, December 19, 1970.

Time:
> "Legal Abortion: Who, Why, and Where," September 27, 1971.
> "A Stunning Approval for Abortion," February 5, 1973.
> "Reagan's Mr. Right," June 30, 1986.

Totenberg, Nina. "Judge Worries About Ties to Chief Justice." *National Observer*. April 20, 1971.

Tribe, Lawrence. *God Save This Honorable Court: How the Choice of Supreme Court Justices Shapes Our History*. New York: Random House, 1985.

Urofsky, Melvin I., ed. *The Douglas Letters*. Bethesda, Md.: Adler & Adler, 1987.

Weinraub, Judith. "Carter and His New Feminist Aide, Sarah Weddington, Agree to Disagree on Abortion." *People* 10 (September 18, 1978).

West, Richard. "The Chief." *D Magazine* 13 (May 1986).

Westoff, Charles, and Larry Bumpass. "The Revolution in Birth Control Practices of U.S. Roman Catholics." *Science* 174 (June 1973).

Williams, Glanville. *The Sanctity of Life and the Criminal Law*. New York: Knopf, 1957.

Willis, Ellen. "Putting Women Back Into the Abortion Debate." *Village Voice*, July 16, 1985.

Woodward, Bob, and Scott Armstrong. *The Brethren: Inside the Supreme Court*. New York: Simon & Schuster, 1979.

Index